# Democracy's News

# Democracy's News

A Primer on Journalism
for Citizens Who Care
about Democracy

G. MICHAEL KILLENBERG
AND ROB ANDERSON

University of Michigan Press
Ann Arbor

For questions or permissions, please contact um.press.perms@umich.edu

Published in the United States of America by the
University of Michigan Press
Manufactured in the United States of America
Printed on acid-free paper
First published January 2023

A CIP catalog record for this book is available from the British Library.

*Library of Congress Cataloging-in-Publication data has been applied for.*

ISBN 978-0-472-07584-3 (hardcover : alk. paper)
ISBN 978-0-472-05584-5 (paper : alk. paper)
ISBN 978-0-472-22107-3 (e-book)

Cover illustration courtesy Shutterstock.com / samui

*Dedicated to the memory of Robert Dardenne and John Pauly*

# Contents

*Dedication*                                                                              xi
*Acknowledgments*                                                                        xiii

INTRODUCTION: A FOUNDING INTERSECTION IN DISREPAIR                                          1

1  A DESCENDING DARKNESS                                                                   11
   The Shades of Darkness                                                   14
   Snapshots of Journalism Fading in the Distance                          17
   What Happens When We Grow Estranged?                                     25
   The First Amendment Shows Its Age                                        32
   The Dangerous Intersection of Trump, Journalism,
      and Public Discourse                                   35
   Where Do We Go from Here?                                                41

2  A BUDDING NATION FINDS ITS VOICE                                                        44
   An Immigrant Printer Confronts the King's Authority                      48
   A War of Words before a Volley of Muskets                                51
   After War and Missteps, a Meeting of Minds and Words                     55
   The Glory and Mythology of the Founding                                  63
   "Make No Law" Comes into Clearer Focus                                   65
   In Retrospect: Lessons from the Founding                                 71
     *Public Talk Then and Now / Appreciation of Journalism /*
     *Knowing Our Founding Documents*

3  THE YARD SIGN THAT SAID "NO" TO CENSORSHIP                                              78
   What a Forty-Five-Word Sentence Can Do                                    82
     *The First Amendment Projects and Protects Rights / The*
     *First Amendment Enables Community and Conversation /*
     *The First Amendment: Its Evolution and Exceptions*
   A Manuscript Comes to Life                                               93
   License Plates, T-shirts, and Middle Fingers                            104
   Shifting Ground, Slippery Footing                                       109
   The Constitution and the Court                                          112
   A Postscript for Troubled Times                                         115

4  AN EPIC BATTLE, THEN A VICTORY FOR PRESS FREEDOM    117
   "A Sacred Trust and Great Privilege"    122
   Jim Crow Meets the Press    125
   When the News Intrudes on Private Lives    130
   The Right to Know Put to the Test    133
   The Imperfect Alliance of the Press and Lawmakers    137
     *Open Meetings and Records / Shield Laws and Journalist's Privilege /*
     *Privacy Protection Act / Whistleblower Laws*
   Our Stake in the Press Freedom Clause    149

5  INSIDE THE NEWSROOM, BEHIND THE STORY    153
   The Essence of a Journalist    157
     *Civil and Patient / Deadline Motivated / Grounded in Local Reporting /*
     *Neither Apolitical nor Partisan / Altruistic by Inclination / Rarely*
     *Saints, Occasionally Sinners / Satisfied, though Seldom Fully /*
     *Increasingly Diverse, but Insufficiently So*
   The Mixed Meanings of "News"    162
   "Mainstream" and Other Models of News    168
     *Mainstream News / Digital News / Niche or Specialty News /*
     *Independent News / Hyperlocal News / Documentary News /*
     *"Wire" News*
   How Journalism Defines Its Roles    177
     *Monitorial Orientation / Anticipatory Orientation / Explanatory*
     *Orientation / Advocacy Orientation / Humane Orientation /*
     *Investigative Orientation / Engaged Orientation*
   How News Becomes Journalism    184
   What Keeps Journalism Strong    195
     *Professional Organizations / Journalism Education / Auxiliary*
     *Resources / Internal Controls*

6  UNTANGLING ACCUSATIONS OF JOURNALISM BIAS    198
   Accusations and Actualities    199
   Politicians Want to Win, Journalists Want to Report    202
   Misconceptions about Media Bias    207
     *Media Organizations and Sources Can Be Bias-Free / Perceptions of*
     *Media Bias Can Be Bias-Free / News Must Be "Balanced" to Be*
     *Considered Bias-Free / American News Content Is Rigged to Reward*
     *Political Liberals*

Journalism's Persistent Practical Biases 225
*Media Coverage Is Biased toward ... —the Truth, inasmuch as It Can*
*Be Verified / —Official Sources / —the Immediate / —Conflict /*
*—Tasty Pudding When Possible / —Keeping News Organizations*
*Financially Healthy / —Digging / —Compassion*
Old Ball Game, Played with New Rules 233

7 JOURNALISM, EVERYDAY TALK, AND THE FUTURE
FOR PUBLIC LIFE 236
A Republic of Conversation 240
Are You a Talker or a Doer? Yes 245
Journalism's Environment for Talk: Dialogue, Deliberation,
Divisiveness, Deception 254
How Journalism Succeeds, and How It Fails 261
Listening for the Next Journalism 265
*Authenticator / Sense Maker / Investigator / Witness Bearer /*
*Empowerer / Smart Aggregator / Forum Organizer / Role Model*

8 A CITIZENSHIP ETHIC FOR A TIME OF
DIMINISHED JOURNALISM 270
A Shaky Start for American Citizenship 272
Contemporary Models of Citizenship 276
*The Monitorial Citizen / The Informed Citizen / The Engaged Citizen /*
*The Reasonable Citizen / The Inclusive Citizen*
Finding an Ethic in the Citizenship-Journalism Relationship 289
Toxic Political Action:
Diminishing Both Journalism and Citizenship 291
Lies and Trust 294
Complicity and "Serious Reflection" 299
How Systematic Attacks on Journalism Damage Citizenship 304
An Ethic Tested: The (Current) Big Picture 308

9 ASSUMING RESPONSIBILITIES FOR THE REPUBLIC 311
A Reemerging Alliance of Citizens and Journalists 312
Journalism and Its Evolving Role in a Republic 315
*Journalism's Conversation with Citizens, Refreshed / The Promise of*
*Engagement / Journalism Arising from Conversation, not Conflict*
Journalism Reassesses Its Role, and Rightly So 323
*Reinforcing Sustainable Models / Merging Resources and Promoting*
*Historic Preservation / Implementing Innovative Methods / Stressing*
*Local Coverage / Laying Out Welcome Mats / Addressing Trust Issues /*
*Confessing Past Sins*

Citizens Taking on More Civic Responsibility                333
   *Relying Less on Social Media for News / Practicing Skepticism /*
   *Advocating for Truth / Supporting Local News / Tuning In,*
   *Turning Out / Expanding Sociocultural Awareness*
Our Hopeful Conclusion                                        340

Notes                                                         345
Index                                                         385
About the Authors                                             397

# Dedication

We dedicate *Democracy's News* to two friends and colleagues who are no longer with us. Although we are sure both would have appreciated our theme here, we are just as confident that they could have straightened us out on multiple oversights and misjudgments, and as a result you would be holding a better book in your hands now.

**ROBERT DARDENNE** was a versatile and immensely popular teacher-scholar-leader at the University of South Florida St. Petersburg. His work linking journalism and narrative was well known in the field; he also wrote *A Free and Responsible Student Press* and coauthored with us *The Conversation of Journalism: Communication, Community, and News*. Bob seemed to do most of his writing and class prep with his feet up on his desk and his door wide open, hoping for students to interrupt him, which they did. He rarely called his students by their first name: It was "Hey, Mattioli" or "Gogick, come on in here." They loved it, and they valued his advice, even when he would return a submitted research paper or news story with margins overflowing with scrawled comments. After his death in 2013, contributions from family, friends, and students underwrote the Robert W. Dardenne Award for Humanistic Journalism given to an outstanding student each year.

Bob was a fount of homespun wisdom. He kicked around wonderful ideas in the company of others and, occasionally, when holding a cigar and glass of bourbon. His contemplations contributed to the birth of the USF Department of Journalism and Digital Communication and to our philosophy of news, found throughout the following pages. Bob's widow, Barbara O'Reilley, and his son, Rob, need not be told how much we miss Bob, but we say it nonetheless.

**JOHN PAULY,** for almost a decade the chair of Saint Louis University's Department of Communication and one of the intellectual lights of the entire campus, rode to work most days in a St. Louis MetroBus. He had assigned himself a kind of informal mission: he did not want to lose track of the city itself and its kaleidoscopic array of citizens going different directions for different reasons. Listening fascinated him, a good impulse in a journalist. But at lunch with John, you wanted to carry a pencil and notepad to remember later his offhand impressions of newspapers, basketball, Louis Prima's jazz, or pompous administrators. His interests were sharp, but his way, his demeanor, was soft. Students, at first intimidated by the intellect, grew to love him. Of course, they did—they had his full attention. He eventually left St. Louis for Marquette, in Milwaukee, and some years ago left Marquette, too—well, he just moved on, but he is with us in *Democracy's News*. John's widow, Lindsey, and their two children, Kevin and Melanie, will find John's intellectual presence herein.

# Acknowledgments

The seed that becomes a book owes its origins to a complex mixture of thought, luck, and, most of all, the generosity of others. If authors acquire a sufficient understanding of subjects worth writing about, it is often because along the way colleagues, relatives, and, at times, strangers knowingly or indirectly shared their knowledge, values, and even thoughtful disagreement. In our case, the indebtedness would fill a thick ledger.

Our spouses, Penny and Dona, kept us grounded and sensitive to the truly important parts of a good life. Careers that require hours of researching, brainstorming, writing, advising, preparing for classes, grading, and attending faculty meetings are sometimes only possible alongside more sacrifices than any family ought to make. But in our households, they did make them. Penny and Dona were teachers, too, and understood why we often cloistered ourselves and forgot to take out the trash. What word could possibly express something far enough beyond "grateful"? We would not, and could not, have done it without their love and support.

As professors who enjoyed more than forty years apiece in the classroom, we thank the students who helped us crisscross disciplinary boundaries to explore, in theory and practice, the overlaps. Over the years, we learned as much from them as they did from us, and while we often told them so, they probably never realized how much they made a difference. Students who genuinely care about learning should be celebrated as teachers, too. Moreover, those who hope to be experts need to be reminded of the value of what Zen philosophy calls the wisdom of the "beginner's mind."

If the term "influencer" holds a meaning beyond the Instagram world, we admit to having soaked up others' ideas, all over the place. Incisive minds fired our imaginations and revealed trails of thought we might not have discovered otherwise. We have been fortunate enough to know some of these influencers personally, but others we have met only through their writing, their skills as formal and informal educators, and their lives of public service. Instead of providing a long and inevitably incomplete list, we credit those who use wide-angle lenses to depict how journalism, citizenship, and political talk are interrelated. These shake-us-up thinkers include James

Carey, Eve Pearlman, Jeff Jarvis, Danielle Allen, David Mathews, Barnett Pearce, Eric Liu, Parker Palmer, Kwame Anthony Appiah, Hannah Arendt, Masha Gessen, Cass Sunstein, James Fishkin, and many others.

As our book took shape, our thoughts returned to some of the most extraordinary "ordinary citizens," including journalists, whose commitment to community and justice resists recent partisan lies big and small, unevidenced attacks on general interest media, and the degradation of the not so old-fashioned ideals of evidence, truth, and civic dialogue.

Some of these volunteers for democracy march unafraid into contested public spaces even when their calls for social justice go unheeded and they get blamed, even arrested, for protesting those very conditions. Scores of other volunteers work hard to keep the conversation going despite bellowing opponents who try to silence them with insults, threats, and lies. Everywhere, underpaid and underappreciated local journalists, although puzzled by why so many Americans consider them the enemy, continue to report about civic conditions so citizens know what is going on in their divided communities and might acquire the means to do something together. Then there are countless unsung citizens found wherever people call home, like the local bookstore owners who just want to make sure that small-town folks have something they want to read and a free space to talk about books. (Special thanks to Liz Welter and John Maggitti, owners of Novel Bay Booksellers, for good conversation and generous friendship.) Our community inspired us to write with a hopeful theme when so many other books suggest pessimism about democracy.

Finally, we owe thanks to Elizabeth Demers, editorial director at the University of Michigan Press, who found our proposal worth a look when so many manuscripts about threats to democracy vie for attention. She and her staff, particularly production editor Kevin M. Rennells and senior designer Paula Newcomb, excelled in reviewing, editing, and designing *Democracy's News* and positioning it in the national conversation about the health of the republic.

# A Founding Intersection in Disrepair

No bronze plaque, granite monument, or oil portrait commemorates the historic moment essential to the birth of American democracy. Democracy happened, but not on a particular date, at a specific place, or in the presence of distinguished witnesses. In crafting the Declaration of Independence, the Constitution, and the Bill of Rights, the Founders staked the future of the newborn nation on three mutually supportive and interdependent ideals—a vigorous, provocative press; a knowledgeable, engaged citizenry; and a free-flowing and politically viable exchange of ideas, protected by the First Amendment. They never articulated that tricornered vision in a single, sweeping declaration. It developed over time, an amalgam of political philosophy and practical experience set down in various speeches, newspaper commentary, pamphlets, public letters, diaries, and legislative annals.

In *Democracy's News*, we reimagine that founding civic core as an *intersection* where journalism vital to self-governance interacts with receptive citizens to facilitate open, truthful, and rational discourse that, if all goes well, results in deliberative outcomes—such as immigration reform, domestic aid programs, economic initiatives, and public works projects. Democracy itself succeeds and struggles depending on conditions at the intersection. But of late, it resembles a multicar pileup, clogged with angry citizens figuratively honking at one another. Instead of helping to untangle traffic, certain politicians, media outlets, and extremist groups further impede productive public talk. Journalists assigned to the intersection face resistance and mistrust, as if entering enemy territory.

Enough tax dollars can restore our aging highways, bridges, and schools, but if the infrastructure of democracy collapses, repairs may be too late. Regardless of party politics, religious beliefs, race, or other differences, citizens ought to know that the intersection exists, that it dates to the founding, and that if it is allowed to deteriorate, the very existence of the republic is in jeopardy.

Nearly all Americans care about the condition of our democracy, but talk of its demise for a while seemed hypothetical when more immediate, tangible problems beset the country—the ongoing pandemic, social upheaval over racial injustices, and the precarious state of the economy, among others. Many voters who stood in long lines on November 3, 2020, hoped that the election of a new president would bring a healing reconciliation and, from there, progress in addressing a host of national and local challenges. It did not.

Even after losing by more than seven million votes, President Donald J. Trump refused to accept the outcome. With only days left in office, he summoned his most ardent followers to Washington, DC, for a rally on January 6, 2021. From a temporary stage just south of the White House, Trump and other handpicked speakers addressed an agitated assembly of thousands, many of whom wore MAGA hats, chanted "Fight for Trump," and waved American and Confederate flags. Trump immediately reasserted the disproven claim of massive voter fraud:

> All of us here today do not want to see our election victory stolen by emboldened radical-left Democrats, which is what they're doing. And stolen by the fake news media. That's what they've done and what they're doing. We will never give up. We will never concede. It doesn't happen. You don't concede when there's theft involved.

He attacked journalism repeatedly, saying at one point: "Our media is not free, it's not fair. It suppresses thought, it suppresses speech and it's become the enemy of the people. . . . It's the biggest problem we have in this country." At the end of his rambling, hour-long harangue, he called for action:

> And we fight. We fight like hell. And if you don't fight like hell, you're not going to have a country anymore. . . . The Democrats are hopeless—they never vote for anything. Not even one vote. But we're going to try and give Republicans, the weak ones because the strong ones don't need any of our help. We're going to try and give them the kind of pride and boldness that they need to take back our country. So, let's walk down Pennsylvania Avenue.[1]

Hundreds did what Trump asked, moving toward the iconic rotunda where Congress had convened for its pro forma responsibility of certifying the election of Joseph R. Biden. En route, the rally transformed into a mob, and a once seemingly abstract threat to democracy became reality as Trump supporters violently forced their way inside the U.S. Capitol; senators, representatives, and staffers barricaded themselves behind office doors, fearing for their lives. The Secret Service whisked to safety Vice President Michael R. Pence, on hand to preside over the certification vote count.

Trump never joined his supporters as he indicated he would. He ordered his Secret Service agents to drive him to the Capitol, but they refused, insisting that the situation was turning too dangerous to ensure his safety. The president reluctantly returned to the White House, where he, along with staff and advisers, watched live television coverage. Based on insider accounts, *Washington Post* investigative reporter Carol Leonnig reconstructed the scene: "He is in the dining room, off the Oval Office, watching it and almost giddy."[2]

At a little after 2:00 p.m., the first rioters breached the Capitol. In short order, they routed police, smashed windows, and chanted "Hang Mike Pence," presumably because the vice president rejected Trump's demands to block the certification of the election results.

Stunned by the news video of the brutality, the president's family members, aides, and leaders in Congress urged him to issue a tweet calling for the attacks to cease.[3] He chose not to. He also never communicated with the National Guard or law enforcement units about protecting the Capitol, although Pence did ask for military reinforcements. At 2:24 p.m., the president posted: "Mike Pence didn't have the courage to do what should have been done to protect our Country and our Constitution, giving States a chance to certify a corrected set of facts, not the fraudulent or inaccurate ones which they were asked to previously certify. USA demands the truth!"[4] Using a bullhorn, a follower read Trump's inflammatory message to the mob. Trump knew the vice president was still in the building.

The mayhem went on for hours before Trump finally made a sixty-second video statement released on Twitter and carried at 4:17 p.m. by major networks in which he said:

> I know your pain. I know you're hurt. We had an election that was stolen from us. It was a landslide election and everyone knows it, especially the other side. But you have to go home now. We have to have peace. We have to have law and order. We have to respect our great people in law and order. We don't want anybody hurt. . . . So go home. We love you. You're very special.[5]

A Capitol police officer suffered two strokes and died the day after an assailant had saturated him with an irritant believed to have been bear repellent. Four other officers who fought off the mob later committed suicide. Four protestors also died during the assault and 140 law enforcement officers were injured, dozens severely. By December 2021, prosecutors had charged more than seven hundred participants with crimes that included pummeling victims with baseball bats, fire extinguishers, and scaffolding pipes.

The shock of the Capitol insurrection momentarily quieted the furor encouraged during the Trump presidency. But it quickly reignited. Throughout 2021 and into 2022, verbal and physical clashes broke out over voting rights, critical race theory, abortion, gun control, and vaccinations. Health measures previously considered commonplace became flashpoints of partisanship. The mere prospect of a congressional inquiry into the January 6 riot sparked outrage among Republican leaders who tried to block an investigation. But House Democrats, joined by two Republicans who broke ranks, mustered enough votes to create an independent commission with subpoena power. It quickly went to work. Beginning in the summer of 2021, the committee conducted interviews, amassed documents, released reports, and later held public hearings that solidified a case against Trump in planning and inciting the Capitol attack.

Of particular impact was the live televised testimony of twenty-six-year-old Cassidy Hutchinson, top aide to President Trump's chief of staff, Mark Meadows. Her dramatic account under oath on June 28, 2022, included details of an exchange between Meadows and White House counsel Pat Cipollone, who implored Meadows to confront Trump, end the rioting, and protect Pence from harm. According to Hutchinson, Meadows reacted by saying, "You heard him, Pat. He thinks Mike deserves it. He doesn't think they're doing anything wrong."[6]

Her testimony—and the select committee's work in general—served democracy by sharing with citizens evidence of an unlawful plot to overturn the 2020 presidential election. Still, in interviews and commentary carried prominently by right-wing media, detractors persistently challenged the committee's constitutional legitimacy, its findings, and its political motives. Trump lashed out at Hutchinson in a series of posts on his social media site, Truth Social, calling her a phony and third-rate social climber. Citizens squared off over the hearings, among them Trump advocates who said they never watched a minute of testimony. Once again, the United States found itself a living irony of disunification.

We decided to write Democracy's News well before January 6, 2021, after we saw sustained, widespread assaults on democratic norms. New books attempted to explain if not solve an array of troubling conditions—

the demise of newspapers, the disappearance of local news, another resurgence of white nationalism, a culture of lies and disinformation, a toxic social media system, the state of the presidency, and the corrosiveness of civic talk. But unlike other contemporary prescriptions for one or more of these ailments, we chose to focus on the endangered historic intersection. By considering journalism, citizenship, and civic dialogue *together*, not as separate issues, we follow the lead of the Founders, whose communication-based assumptions created a republic in which citizens are expected to speak, listen, argue, and participate across conflicts so that they might self-govern. The Declaration of Independence and the Constitution set the stage for a nation of active *communicators*, not *combatants*.

As "We the People" respond to contentious political conflicts, our civic environment must honor facts, reasoned talk, and direct engagement with each other's ideas. Journalism encourages us to act as citizens who, in turn, encourage better journalism. Yet millions of citizens readily disqualify the best efforts of the news media. They fail to appreciate an institution that pursues truth, stimulates conversation, and clarifies the issues fragmenting us.

Let us be both realistic and blunt about our political climate.

Where we *now* stand: A nation of angry citizens talking past each other, if they talk at all. A nation needing facts but too often fed conspiracy theories and official lies. Cable talk shows filled with half-baked solutions, rampant speculation, and ugly name-calling. Social media platforms trading on the darkest impulses of often anonymous users. Local journalism vanishing in communities when and where most needed. A First Amendment misunderstood and compromised by hate speech and personalized attacks. Uncertainty about what everyday citizens can accomplish in such a hostile, volatile environment.

Where we *could* go from here: A nation with renewed respect for a journalism long unfairly maligned by political strategies. A republic of citizens willing to consider facts and base social decisions on them, working for the common good. A communication network through which we better comprehend our lives and those of diverse others—where we discover shared problems and the common ground from which to address them.

No single cause explains the decline of democratic engagement. Foreign agents manipulate opinions of online audiences with messages that sound authentically American but might be bots or speak Farsi between tweets and web postings. Mainstream news institutions struggle to stay alive and retain credibility. Once vibrant local newspapers die off by the thousands, with too few mourning their passing. Elected leaders use hateful, threatening words to villainize colleagues. Ordinary people, perhaps you, your neighbors, or your family, shun bona fide journalism, replacing it with Facebook, Twitter, Instagram, Snapchat, and TikTok—or with nothing at all. In doing so, they often turn to less reliable and far more partisan sources of information and blithely ignore or, worse, discredit scientific research, investigative evidence, and plausible reasoning.

When the Founders laid the national foundation, a majority of Americans shared a set of accepted truths about governance, civility, civic virtues, and deliberative decision-making. Today, the United States suffers from a critical shortage of what journalist-scholar Jonathan Rauch refers to as "reality-based" citizens who, while differing in party affiliation and stances on government policy, accept a common democratic knowledge—knowledge grounded in facts provided by dedicated "reality builders," among them journalists.[7]

Distressingly, a contingent of political actors that includes a past president, members of Congress, and high-ranking state officials seems comfortable with a nation of tribes reduced to the status of intractable foes, not potential partners in a republic. Citizens become pawns or a candidate's "base" mobilized for anger on demand. The politicians and opinion shapers accuse opponents of "fake news" or a "leftist agenda" in nearly every political disagreement, hobbling political compromise and denigrating journalism's role of connecting citizens with a shared reality of accurate news. A shared reality of news does not mean agreement will always be the result—it is enough that agreement will be a possibility.

Rebuilding the historical intersection—and keeping it secure—depends on caring citizens and conscientious journalists who understand *what* is at stake and *how* they can defend democracy. They need little motivation. But a much larger population fits into problematic categories such as these:

- Citizens who lack enough knowledge of institutional journalism to separate what is and is not true about its practices and ethics. The profession becomes a too inviting and lightly defended target—a traditional ally of the people propagandized as the enemy.
- Younger citizens who wrongly assume that public life has always been this divisive and cutthroat and that large-scale lying and hatred will forever dominate public life. That assumption is too glib, is too cynical, and, ultimately, offers too convenient an excuse to disengage from civic life.
- Voters who assume their responsibilities are limited to expressing their personal preferences—sometimes based on simplistic political messages—rather than also becoming conversant with issues, espe-

cially as others see them. Such behavior undercuts the notion of a republic.

- Journalists who need to enact their responsibilities as public listeners, enabling thoughtful democratic dialogues in which citizens are treated as public actors with their own sense of agency and community.
- Elected officials who put personal ambition ahead of the public good. They need a remedial course on how the nation was founded and why so many Americans have defended it.

Our mention of "primer" in the book's subtitle suggests our desire to describe public life in an accessible, commonsensical manner to citizens who share our concern about the nation's civic well-being. *Democracy's News* relies on plain language and examples from everyday life to raise key questions and offer realistic answers: Why do so many citizens favor dismissiveness over talking things through with fellow citizens? Why have so many politicians spurred citizens to erect roadblocks to deliberation rather than to clear spaces for it to occur? Why have citizens allowed themselves to be so manipulated? Why are political attacks on traditional journalism now so acceptable, and expectations for truthful communication, evidence, and science so suspect? In confronting these and other questions, we rely on traditions of constitutional law, media studies, history, public dialogue, deliberative democracy, pragmatism, social justice, ethics, and community building.

Our integrated approach focuses on the following elements:

- *An account of the Founders' experience and faith in communication as they established a republic.* We offer a booster shot of civic awareness while stressing what is often absent in today's political discourse.
- *An emphasis on hometown journalism, entrusted to keep communities connected, informed, and in good health.* Local news is an endangered species. People lose parts of their lives when newspapers wither or die and strain to recover a sense of community.
- *An explanation of the First Amendment in terms that ordinary citizens can appreciate.* People know phrases like "freedom of speech" and "freedom of the press," but too few have more than a rudimentary sense of how and why expressive rights are protected. We open chapters 3 and 4 with narratives of important Supreme Court decisions, examine how the First Amendment has been formed by judicial, statutory, and philosophical influences, and stress how the rights it protects amount to a fuller conception of citizenship.

- *A view of news from the inside out, starting with newsrooms.* We explain how news professionals see their roles and what motivates them. Our perspective helps citizens understand journalism beyond stereotypes.
- *An analysis of accusations about liberal media bias.* If one attack tars all journalism, it is the complaint that the news is slanted to serve political or cultural motives. Media bias exists, but not in ways citizens and critics usually claim. Our discussion provides new evidence that can dispel misconceptions.
- *A case for the democratic centrality of citizens' interpersonal conversations and deliberations.* In a time of political estrangement, even within families, getting together to consider community or nationwide issues sometimes seems hopeless. There are, however, effective ways to encourage better dialogue to replace sparring from separate corners.
- *A blueprint for a reconsidered "citizenship ethic"—ways of modeling practical choices people can make to participate with others for self-governance.* A key feature of the citizenship ethic is recognizing the dangers of complicity and dismissiveness in a climate of political lies and misrepresentations.
- *An extended argument that journalism serves democracy beyond reporting the news.* In disseminating factual information alone, no matter how well written or researched, the profession falls short of the Founders' expectations. Journalists must address audiences as citizens engaged in ongoing conversations about their own futures.
- *An abiding optimism for the future of journalism and citizenship.* If citizens can rally around campaigns like "Save the Manatees," when properly informed and motivated they can mobilize to support local journalism and community advancement.

Our backgrounds in teaching, research, and writing brought us together, and together we developed a mutual perspective for journalism and public dialogue that we believe remains relevant. In our 1994 book, written with Robert W. Dardenne (1946-2013), *The Conversation of Journalism: Communication, Community, and News*, we wrote:

We see no other institutions that are as qualified and as prepared as journalism to help people talk about the political, social, environmental, and personal choices they face in an increasingly technological world. What is deficient is not the information needed by the public to vote, make plans for civic improvements, or decide on the merits of school referenda. . . . What we need is more motivation and opportunity for readers to become more of a public—that is, for citizens to converse, discuss, argue and engage each other in a dialogue of comparisons and futures.[8]

We made that claim more than a quarter of a century ago, before advertisers largely abandoned print for the Internet and newspaper circulation plummeted. Even then, though, we knew that preexisting conditions left newspapers vulnerable to new technology and shifting economic pressures. However, we anticipated neither the speed nor the extent of the freefall. It motivated us to revive our premise about journalism as the stimulant and agent for public dialogue.

The old business model of journalism, particularly in local communities, lost its viability years ago. We hope to see new models of defining and communicating news. The health of communities requires, as well, an infusion of human and financial capital to sustain journalism where it languishes and resurrect it in places where it has disappeared. Our republic fundamentally needs journalism. What we do not need is a wave of politically targeted criticism dismissing mainstream journalism completely without understanding its historic mission and its everyday contributions.

In *Democracy's News*, we extend a long writing and research partnership. As coauthors, we hope to achieve a creative harmony of the type singer-composer David Byrne discusses in his 2012 best-selling book *How Music Works*. Byrne frequently has teamed with artists from genres and orientations different from his own. "I'll risk disaster," he says, "because the creative rewards of successful collaboration are great. I've been doing it all my life." Even when creative partners do not initially share a vision, similar interests, or even skills, Byrne has learned that their differences can be liberating and their individual approaches invite playing to each other's strengths. "You don't try to reverse the river or get it to jump over a mountain," he says, "you harness its flow and energy to gently urge that it join up with other tributaries." He finds that "music written by teams makes the authorship of a piece indistinct."[9]

When we first began to collaborate, each of us was surprised by how little we knew about the other's taken-for-granted beliefs. Now in our fourth book together, we have the advantage of agreeing about the role of valid journalism in service to democracy. Long ago we decided to make a case for bridging different versions of communication study: professional journalists and media researchers were congregating in one camp and interpersonal and rhetorical communication researchers were in another, with relatively few crossovers or mergers. We value the importance of our different perspectives, but beyond differences, we recognize how seemingly separate orientations often overlap, connect, and produce fresh insights. Each of us listens for disagreements that tell us when and what to reconsider. In this latest project, we continue to think it important to make our coauthorship voice somewhat *indistinct*, as Byrne would put it, while trying to remain *distinctively* focused on problems of democracy's news.

No book, no movement, and no groundswell of reform will solve all problems. Not everyone will listen or care, often for excusable reasons, burdened as we all are by the exigencies of everyday life—holding jobs, supporting family life, paying medical bills. Others will hold rigid in their general distrust of journalists. They may never be interested in news that explores multiple interpretations and experiences. The disrupters of the world will continue a campaign to divide citizens into good "us" and evil "them." The damage to the republic is severe and ongoing. It may not stop until enough citizens realize what already has been lost and what lies ahead if they do nothing about it. We contribute in that spirit, hoping to spark additional conversations vital to journalism and civic life.

# CHAPTER 1

# A Descending Darkness

On June 1, 2020, within sight of the White House, a battle-clad phalanx swept through peaceful protesters to clear a zone around St. John's Episcopal Church, the modest sanctuary where presidents have come to worship. In scenes captured on live cable and network broadcasts, lines of soldiers and police—some dressed like Robocop, some on horseback—swiftly advanced on multiple fronts. They wielded riot shields like scythes and randomly fired flash-bang canisters, rubber bullets, and pepper spray. The military-style operation enabled President Trump and his entourage to walk unimpeded from the White House to St. John's, where, for a few awkward minutes, he posed outside for photos, holding aloft a borrowed Bible.[1]

The police killing of George Floyd in Minneapolis a few days earlier brought a nationwide campaign for racial justice to the president's doorstep. Demonstrators took to the streets of the Capital, setting the president on edge and stiffening his resolve to reestablish control, to show who was boss. By nearly all accounts, the participants were emotionally charged, confrontational, and occasionally belligerent. They yelled, chanted, carried hand-drawn placards, dropped f-bombs, and raised middle fingers. A few tossed "projectiles" into police lines, objects later determined to be water bottles and eggs, not bricks or fire bombs, as several police accounts initially claimed.[2] Unruly? At times. Provocative? Probably. Enemy combatants? Certainly not. For a nation born of protest against oppression, the coordinated attack on citizens exercising their First Amendment rights mocked a heritage of free speech. Journalists reported what happened on June 1 while under assault themselves. They exposed a darkly authoritarian show of force, underscoring *darkness* as a fitting metaphor for a country whose founding ideals seemed no longer as bright.

For four years, the forty-fifth president had subjected the American psyche to despair and anger; his term ended with a shocking attack he instigated on the Capitol while Congress met to count electoral ballots and certify the election of the new president. Trump's subsequent banishment from Twitter felt at first "like the hush of an overnight snowfall," in the words of *Washington Post* columnist Ruth Marcus.[3] "Exhale," she said.

Still, anxiety lingered—a polarized citizenry, a vilified journalism, a civic discourse corroded by hateful speech, and a population of millions who had embraced falsehoods and rejected truth. Just days after Biden defeated Trump, media analyst Zeynep Tufekci, a native of Turkey, predicted:

> Make no mistake: The attempt to harness Trumpism—without Trump, but with calculated, refined, and smarter political talent—is coming. And it won't be easy to make the next Trumpist a one-term president. He will not be so clumsy or vulnerable. . . . And they have at their disposal certain features that can be mobilized: The Electoral College and especially the Senate are anti-majoritarian institutions, and they can be combined with other efforts to subvert majority rule.[4]

Trump never faded away. He retreated to Mar-a-Lago, where he played ringmaster for a cast of partisan performers who variously perpetuated the Big Lie of Democrats "stealing" elections; demanded audits or recounts of already certified vote totals; passed in Republican-held state legislatures election laws designed to impede Democrats and minorities from voting; employed filibusters and dilatory tactics to thwart passage of bipartisan legislation; posted menacing online threats against political foes; acquiesced to acts of vigilantism; whipped up hostility over mask and vaccine mandates; and precipitated paranoia over bogus allegations that critical race theory is taught in public schools. Whatever Trump decides about 2024, the rough-hewed ideology that bears his name appears destined to endure, indicative of where the country might be headed—one mired in polarization manufactured by false, dangerous narratives meant to deter civic engagement and problem-solving.

Instead of slinking off in disgrace after the January 6 debacle, Republican leaders fortified their allegiance to the former president, seeing their political fortunes inevitably tied to his. Indeed, several political observers believe that aggressively advancing a Trump-linked agenda might be the only way for the GOP to survive.[5] That prospect led one hundred scholars to issue a statement in June 2021 declaring that "our entire democracy is at risk" by the mobilization of extremist groups known for violent protests, a deeply financed network of conservative political action committees, and a roster of candidates for elected office committed to Trumpism.[6]

Matthew MacWilliams, author of *On Fascism: 12 Lessons from American History*, adds a worrisome perspective. Nearly 20 percent of Americans, his research found, are highly disposed to authoritarianism, based on answers to four simple survey questions used by social scientists to measure ideological tendencies. "A further 23 percent or so are just one step below them on the authoritarian scale," MacWilliams said. "This roughly 40 percent of Americans tend to favor authority, obedience and uniformity over freedom, independence and diversity."[7] They form much of the Trump base. A total of seventy-four million Americans voted to reelect Trump, an indicator that in 2024 either he or a doppelgänger could be back in the White House, joined by followers who win office in Congress, statehouses, and county governments. These prognostications do not go unnoticed, but as Americans look for a degree of everyday normality, many prefer not to worry excessively about a possible dystopian future.

Citizens of our imperfect but durable democracy should not grow politically complacent, assuming that authoritarianism cannot take hold here, that election outcomes will be determined fairly by candidates with the most votes, that the press will remain resolute in holding the government and the powerful accountable, and that democracy will prevail. June 1, 2020, was a preview of what America without democracy might look like. Six months later, the unthinkable happened. Evidence surfaced that a top Trump legal adviser had devised a six-step scheme by which Vice President Mike Pence could overturn the election results. "In practical terms," wrote Matt Ford in the *New Republic*, "it describes a plan for carrying out a coup d'état—one in which Pence would single-handedly throw out legitimate votes for Biden until Trump had enough to win."[8] Under intense pressure from President Trump to do otherwise, Pence eventually followed the law and the Constitution.

The inauguration of President Biden occurred as twenty thousand National Guard troops stood on watch around the District of Columbia. With the traditional parade cancelled and so few attending the ceremony, the day passed somberly and quietly. Afterward, work crews resumed repairing damage to the Capitol caused by the rioters. A far greater effort will be necessary to reassemble the broken pieces of democracy and keep them intact.

While serious issues divide us, none of them appear extreme enough to precipitate outright warfare or the death of democracy. Yet, violent skirmishes continue to erupt, fueled by unrelenting demagogic rhetoric designed to provoke violence and dangerous behavior. A Black man in Georgia goes jogging and neighborhood vigilantes chase him down, slaying him with a shotgun blast. A member of Congress who tweets a doctored animated video that depicts him killing Rep. Alexandria Ocasio-Cortez and swinging two swords at President Biden goes unsanctioned. Tucker Carlson falsely calls Dr. Anthony Fauci, the president's chief medical adviser, "the guy who created Covid," and millions of Fox News viewers absorb what he says.

We intend the phrase "a descending darkness" as a warning, not a foregone conclusion. In the following pages, we take stock of what has happened to wedge citizens apart and attack our democratic structures. We pay particular attention to the weakening of journalism and why citizens across the political spectrum need trustworthy, civic-minded news. As journalism struggles, everyone else struggles to get along in any setting where politics or, for that matter, public decision-making comes up. We describe how outside forces contribute to social anger and division. Through scholarly studies, opinion surveys, practical examples, and historical narrative, we highlight threats both ugly and bleak—but not hopeless or beyond our ability to counteract. After all, ordinary Americans embody "We the People," the words enshrined in the preamble to our Constitution. They ultimately set the nation's course.

## The Shades of Darkness

In 2017, the *Washington Post* unveiled a slogan on its digital front page, "Democracy Dies in Darkness." Amazon founder Jeffrey P. Bezos, who bought the *Post* in 2013 for $250 million, used the phrase at a technology forum in May 2016, before Donald Trump won the GOP presidential nomination. "I think a lot of us believe this, that democracy dies in darkness, that certain institutions have a very important role in making sure that there is light," he said.[9] Bezos echoed the sentiments of other supporters of open government who see sunlight as a disinfectant. In the 1960s, a wave of federal and state statutes, known as "Sunshine Laws," opened previously closed meetings and records to the public. Since 2005, news organizations throughout the United States have celebrated "Sunshine Week," held every March. The darkness Bezos referred to in 2016 seemed downright benign to journalists several years later. Citizens seldom appreciate just how difficult and important it is for journalists to overcome political obstacles meant to thwart news coverage and deny access to information that belongs to the public.

Today, journalism finds its mission impaired by two forms of darkness. The first envelops a political system dominated by lies and distortions meant to obscure the truth and dupe the public. Members of that camp brand mainstream news media as "the enemy of the people." They pass legislation to vacate long-established voting rights, and they block attempts to enact laws that would protect the integrity of elections for *all* Americans. They support candidates willing to espouse authoritarian methods, spread conspiracy theories, and condemn fact-based information.

The second darkness prevents citizens from clearly seeing the consequences of journalism's loss of institutional and economic vitality. In thousands of communities, perhaps where you live, hometown news—entrusted to keep communities connected, informed, and in good civic health—inches closer to extinction. The *Charleston Gazette-Mail* won the Pulitzer Prize in 2017 for investigative coverage of the opioid crisis in small-town West Virginia, reported by Eric Eyre, one of our former students. Days later, the newspaper filed for bankruptcy.[10] While financially shaky, the *Gazette-Mail*, under new ownership since 2018, hopes to rebuild by boosting e-edition subscribers, telling visitors to its web page that "Local journalism makes a difference. Your support makes that possible—subscribe today for 99 cents." Despite its reputation for excellence, the *Gazette-Mail* found itself marketing journalism at a cut-rate price.[11]

### Marginalia

Ask any shoppers at Target about the "Pulitzer Prize." A few could probably vaguely recall the name but not much more. Prizes in journalism buttress professional standards and promote aspirational reporting; they honor and bring glory to recipients. There are numerous international, national, regional, local, and specialized awards in journalism, but the gold standard is the Pulitzer, named for its benefactor, Joseph Pulitzer, a German-speaking immigrant who bought and built newspapers while amassing a fortune during the circulation wars of the 1880s through the turn of the twentieth century. Perhaps motivated by guilt for his role in spreading sensationalized journalism, Pulitzer burnished his image by donating funds to New York's Columbia University. "My idea," he said at the time, "is to recognize that journalism is, or ought to be, one of the great and intellectual professions; to encourage, elevate, and educate in a practical way the present and, still more, future members of that profession, exactly as if it were the profession of law or medicine."[12] Joseph Pulitzer bequeathed an icon of journalism excellence to a profession with a tattered reputation that ironically he helped to create.

Nearly all aspects of journalism have had to adapt to a highly competitive and economically challenging media marketplace. A few national news outlets thrived. Others held on by slashing operating costs. But a shocking number succumbed. Weekly and small-market daily newspapers, in particular, found themselves in literal darkness, with lights permanently switched off in newsrooms from Temecula, California, to McKeesport, Pennsylvania. Between 2004 and 2016, according to a University of North Carolina study, more than 1,900 print publications folded.[13] The *New York Times* covers these closures like obituaries: "The Last Edition: Dying Gasp of One Local Newspaper."[14] Nearly all surviving publications show signs of atrophy, with many abandoning regular coverage of important news beats. Some are outsourcing copyediting as far as India, as if journalism were another call center.

Then came 2020. More daily and weekly newspapers closed; veteran journalists lost good-paying jobs and collected unemployment. In China, news trickled out about a mystery virus that supposedly originated in the city of Wuhan. Within months, Covid-19, its scientific name, mutated into a deadly global pandemic that necessitated stay-at-home orders, mandatory face masks, and something distinctly un-American, social distancing. Under government orders, whole communities quarantined indoors. For a while, nearly every place where people previously gathered had closed—schools, churches, libraries, bars, museums, playgrounds. Covid-19 caused staggering hardship and grief even when victims survived. Journalists faced the suffering and risks head-on, interviewing ER staffs, funeral directors, survivors, families who lost loved ones, and health-care providers begging for masks, medicines, and ventilators. They carried on, driven by their own essential worker roles, to provide fact-based and, at times, comforting news about those who recovered and the medical people who cared for them. The virus's devastating spread underscored the need for comprehensive reporting, especially close to home. Unfortunately, in hundreds of communities, no local journalists remained to answer the public's need for credible and, arguably, life-saving information from health departments, scientists, and doctors.

As the coronavirus devasted communities, CNN, the *New York Times*, the *Wall Street Journal*, and other major news media covered the big story from national and global perspectives. It fell to weeklies, dailies, and local broadcast news to inform people with updates on coronavirus rates, how and where to get tested, which stores and restaurants did or did not require masks, and how the pandemic impacted the economic and mental health of the community. Perhaps the greatest contribution of local news was to bolster morale by telling stories of people helping one another and sacrificing their own welfare in the process. *San Francisco Chronicle* editor in chief Audrey Cooper commented, "If any good can come from this, it will be that people will shell out that $10 to keep their local paper in business."[15] In many communities, though, not enough residents have been willing or able to ante up.

**Quotables**

"The *institution* of a good newspaper is the beating heart of a community, and it embodies something living that goes beyond black type on compressed wood pulp. As I think back on the newspaper I have known longest—the *Greeneville Sun*—I remember an engagement with the town that all newspapers, including that one, should seek to recover and renew."[16]

—Alex S. Jones, *Losing the News*

## Snapshots of Journalism Fading in the Distance

We know firsthand how the demise of local journalism feels. In August 2019, as the tourism season peaked in our Wisconsin community, workers stripped away the facade of a 126-year-old institution—the *Door County Advocate*. Barely anyone paid attention. Once a thriving twice-weekly with a circulation of 12,000, the *Advocate* covered the whole county and brimmed with stories of public interest. The printed edition of the newspaper stills circulates twice a week, printed in Green Bay, where its owner, Gannett Company, Inc., publishes a daily. But the *Advocate* is a newspaper in name only. After renovation, the *Advocate* building now houses apartments and an art gallery.

The gutting of the *Advocate* building coincided with the announcement that New Media Investment Group, a holding company in control of GateHouse Media, was buying Gannett, the owner of *USA Today* and more than 100 other publications nationwide. According to business industry reports, a private equity firm, Apollo Global Management, financed the deal with a five-year secured loan of $1.8 billion. The purchase created a media behemoth of 260 daily newspapers and 300 weeklies.[17] The new company operates under the Gannett name, honoring founder Frank E. Gannett (1876-1957).

J. Jeffry Louis, chairman of Gannett, said he expected that the merger would result in savings of up to $300 million annually. How could he make such a claim with so many newspapers dying or slashing budgets? The savings, he said, would come primarily from "sharing of best practices, leveraging existing infrastructure, facility rationalization and other judicious cost reductions."[18] In plain English, he meant consolidating operations, such as copyediting, in central hubs (sharing of best practices); selling buildings, parking lots, and printing equipment (leveraging existing infrastructure); reducing office space and standardizing operating costs (facility rationalization); and assigning reporters multiple duties, recycling stories from one publication for use by other publications, and, of course, laying off staff or eliminating positions (judicious cost reductions).

In 2019, a study by the nonpartisan Pew Research Center—an important source of newspaper audience studies—reported that nearly three of every four survey respondents believed that local news outlets remained in good financial shape.[19] Actually, some do yield a profit, as corporate executives put the bottom line, not the news, first. They seldom view a newspaper acquisition as a long-term investment, preferring to trade, buy, and sell properties for quick returns. "What they're there to do is to strip mine these properties and get as much profit from them as they can in the short term," said media columnist Margaret Sullivan. "And that is very bad for journalism."[20] And bad for communities journalism serves.

Describing today's for-profit newspaper business requires terminology from the investment marketplace: holding companies, hedge funds, and private equity firms. Until the mid-1980s, a majority of America's newspapers were founded, owned, and led by men and women with printer's ink in their blood—the families of Chandler (*Los Angeles Times*), Medill-McCormick (*Chicago Tribune*), Bingham (*Louisville Courier-Journal*), and Meyer-Graham (*Washington Post*). As the bloodlines thinned, second- and third-generation heirs, less interested in carrying on family tradition, cashed out. Legacy newspapers such as the *St. Louis Post-Dispatch*, acquired by Joseph Pulitzer in 1887, slipped into the hands of business people and investors who saw their acquisitions as streams of revenue but not opportunities for public service. The contemporary ownership structure seldom duplicates the stewardship of family-owned newspapers edited by committed, competent journalists.

Our little Door County newspaper retains an address—a P.O. box eighty miles away in Appleton, Wisconsin—but in the county it supposedly serves, no place remains for reporters and editors to collaborate, for phones to ring, and for residents to stop by to chat, offer a story tip, or grouse about coverage. A meager array of chamber of commerce announcements, local sports, and paid obituaries now passes for news, with considerable content imported from the *Green Bay Press-Gazette*, fifty miles distant, or other Gannett-owned publications in Wisconsin. A recent front-page headline in bold type announced the imminent arrival of a TJ Maxx store. For months in 2019, the *Advocate* functioned without a full-time, locally based reporter until the hiring of a fresh journalism graduate from the University of Wisconsin-Madison, who was given the impossible task of serving the needs of twenty-eight thousand residents and the hundreds of thousands of vacationers and seasonal residents who flood the Door County peninsula annually. As of 2022, the *Advocate's* local coverage remains sparse, at best.

Door County otherwise subsists on a lean local diet of piecemeal radio news and the online and print output of the *Peninsula Pulse*, a weekly whose tourist-themed articles typically outnumber public affairs news stories. With the threat of Covid-19 and social upheaval over the George Floyd killing, an energized *Pulse* stepped up hard news coverage. We wonder how many of our neighbors noticed. If people hereabouts and elsewhere seem blasé about the health of local journalism, perhaps it is because newspapers often slip slowly and quietly into critical condition—itself a consequence in part of waning citizen interest and support. Inattention to civic problems often results in vicious cycles. Local journalism can recover, but without grassroots community support for the profession's mission and economic well-being, the long-term prognosis is poor.

Surviving print and local news operations steadfastly cover their communities even if abandoned by subscribers or taken for granted. Most residents rarely reflect on how much they need local news or what they would miss without it. It is too easy to overlook the selfless work done by local newspeople. In July 2020, the *New York Times* profiled Evan Brandt, age fifty-five, the one-man staff of *The Mercury* in Pottstown, Pennsylvania, a town of twenty-three thousand about forty miles northwest of Philadelphia. It read: "Nearly all of his colleagues who didn't quit have been laid off or bought out, effectively making him the last reporter covering Pottstown. His newspaper's distinctive building was abruptly emptied and later sold, so he works in his attic, surrounded by a display of thirty-six journalism awards, many for public service."[21] The awards, Brandt said, remind him that journalism is important.

The energetic Brandt is the norm, not an outlier. Why does he persevere? "I think of it as a calling, the same way that some people are called to the priesthood," he said. Brandt earns $46,000 a year and worries he will be jobless before long. Weighed down by a responsibility he bears alone, Brandt still ferrets out local news by day and on several nights a week leaves home to cover government meetings. He asks questions, presses for answers, and conveys what he learns to the public, including those who no longer subscribe to his newspaper but still read discarded copies at the barbershop or McDonald's.

Point to any small, rural community on a U.S. map and the odds are good that you will land on a news desert where no thorough local news coverage exists. Or, your finger might pause over a ghost town, slang for a place where the local newspaper is a ghost of its former self, holding on with a handful of editors and reporters, perhaps just one, as in the experience of Evan Brandt and of the lone reporter assigned to the *Door County Advocate*.[22]

The outlook is bleak, too, in metropolitan areas. In 2019, for example, the *Chicago Tribune*, founded in 1847, came under control of Alden Global Capital, a hedge fund notorious for stripping assets of the newspapers it acquires, including the *Denver Post* and the *Mercury News* in San Jose. In August 2020, another hedge fund acquired the McClatchy Company, a newspaper chain owned by the same family since 1857 whose holdings included the *Sacramento Bee*, the *Miami Herald*, and more than two dozen other media outlets in fourteen states.[23] Everywhere, journalism is in a state of distress for reasons that include lost advertising and audiences to "free news" online, changing readership habits, and a politicized distrust of "mainstream media." As a media analyst colorfully described the journalism crisis: "If 2019 signaled a change, it was the realization that not only is the ship sinking, but that there aren't any lifeboats."[24]

A major study in 2019 reported a startling statistic, even to those of us who closely monitor journalism: Between 2008 and 2019 the number of newspaper jobs for editors, reporters, photojournalists, and graphic designers dropped from 71,000 to just under 35,000, a loss of more than half the workforce. But it was no mystery why the positions disappeared.[25] From the 1960s through the early 1990s, the total weekday national circulation of U.S. daily newspapers remained stable and profitable, reaching a pinnacle of 63.5 million in 1984. From that point on, readers increasingly dropped newspaper subscriptions. In 2018, daily weekday circulation was 28.5 million. Meanwhile, the U.S. population grew from 250 million in 1990 to an estimated 330 million in 2020, and newsworthy events, if anything, increased in importance.

A growing portion of the audience turned to social media platforms preferred by younger Americans and increasingly popular across the demographic spectrum. Many of them, of course, emphasized entertainment and personal connections. More than one in five people surveyed by the Pew Research Center between October 2019 and June 2020 reported getting news from social media, and those numbers included older citizens. For 30 percent of survey respondents, network and local TV was their primary news source. Only 3 percent listed print journalism as a preference. Pew also revealed another point of concern: social media users pay less attention to mainstream news, which, the report said, "goes hand in hand with lower levels of knowledge about major current events and politics."[26]

Why the hand-wringing over the decline of newspapers, a legacy medium from the age of the rotary printing press? Indeed, each new media platform—radio, TV, cable, satellite, online—quickly surpassed print in delivery of breaking news about earthquakes, military operations, mass shootings, high-profile trials, and live coverage of congressional hearings. Loyal longtime newspaper subscribers began to ask, "Why pay to get the *Daily Observer* when I can access a near bottomless reservoir of news and information by pressing a remote control or touching a screen?" Readers stopped renewing subscriptions, and younger generations never acquired the newspaper habit. The information spread through social media may present itself as truthful and important, yet much of it is neither. Novelist-critic Greg Jackson warns about the dangerous subtext of heavy consumption of "newsy" material:

> When you think you are doing something serious but you are doing something trivial and fun, you grow to believe that serious things are effortless and enjoyable. You are experiencing a *format*, while believing you are experiencing a *content*. The content suggests you are learning about truth, when you are really learning how to *feel*. You are learning how you should feel in the presence of certain information. These feelings go on to determine your expectations and worldview.[27]

Jackson is not sounding a "code blue" to resuscitate the good old days of print journalism empires, many of which, frankly, were more old than good. Rather, he reminds us that not all news is of equal value. Online and digital journalism can be every bit as good as print publications, but it seldom matches what a local newspaper with adequate resources provides.

As print news withers or disappears, a community loses the professional expertise of a cadre of dedicated journalists and the stories they write; it loses, as well, their behind-the-scenes local knowledge. Journalists typically build weblike relationships from which they acquire tips and alerts, often the bases of news stories. With so many newspeople missing, the community stumbles around in its own form of darkness. In towns and small cities reduced to news deserts, researchers report that governmental bodies grow lax, residents disengage from politics, citizens are tempted to forego voting, public officials operate unburdened by public scrutiny, and misconduct by local businesses breeds.[28] At thousands of city halls—a beat once covered routinely by nearly all print outlets—the mayor, city council, zoning board, public works department, and a host of other offices go unmonitored and thus to a degree unaccountable. Without journalists, a community becomes less aware of and more vulnerable to creeping indifference. In an interview with the *New York Times*, David Cohea, a resident of newspaper-less Mount Dora, Florida, said: "After years without a strong local voice, our community does not know itself and has no idea of important local issues or how the area is changing and challenged by growth and the impact of climate change."[29] Remnants of "news" leak out, usually traveling by word of mouth in a process that ensures the circulation of a fair share of rumor and misinformation.

## Quotables

"When people lament the decline of small newspapers, they tend to emphasize the most important stories that will go uncovered: political corruption, school-board scandals, zoning-board hearings, police misconduct. They are right to worry about that. But often overlooked are the more quotidian stories, the ones that disappear first when a paper loses resources: stories about the annual Teddy Bear Picnic at Crapo Park, the town-hall meeting about the new swimming-pool design, and the tractor games during the Denmark Heritage Days.

These stories are the connective tissue of a community; they introduce people to their neighbors, and they encourage readers to listen to and empathize with one another. When that tissue disintegrates, something vital rots away. We don't often stop to ponder the way that a newspaper's collapse makes people feel: less connected, more alone. As local news crumbles, so does our tether to one another."[30]

—Elaine Godfrey, writer for *The Atlantic*, talking about her hometown newspaper, the *Hawk Eye*, of Burlington, Iowa

Without local newspeople, whose job is it to illuminate the events most crucial to our civic and personal lives? Who investigates those sirens in the middle of the night: Was it a fender bender or a chemical spill at the nearby refinery? Without exaggeration, reporters are precious resources;

they can be our eyes, our ears, our voice, and, at times, our soul. Maine native Phil Di Vece, another of our former students, shared his feelings about hometown journalism with the readers of the online *Penobscot Bay Pilot*. "No matter where I happen to be, I always look for a local newspaper. There's no better way to learn something about a place than reading what's in the local newspaper," he said, adding what disturbs him most about the closings of small-town weeklies and daily newspapers: "Something very important is being lost that added relevance and clarity to the communities they served."[31] The loss of local news is felt most keenly in poorer communities that seldom attract attention from national media—where citizens may especially need public service journalism.

Layoffs and closures forced a generation of journalists out of cherished careers. As the ranks of reporters and editors thin, observers worry that succeeding generations will struggle to find employment. They were counted on to bring much-needed enthusiasm and perspective to the profession from personal experiences, for example, of growing up in families of immigrants or as children going homeless and hungry. For a while, online reporting and editing jobs at places like BuzzFeed News and Vice absorbed print journalists left jobless. But revenues for digital news outlets began to dry up long before Covid-19 struck. The late Barbara Ehrenreich could relate. For her book *Nickel and Dimed: On (Not) Getting By in America*, she worked as a waitress, hotel maid, cleaning woman, nursing home aide, and Walmart sales clerk while living in trailer parks and low-rent residential motels.[32] She wanted to document firsthand the physically and emotionally exhausting conditions of millions of workers trying to make a basic living. Ehrenreich also saw a gloomy future for the dreamers anticipating journalism careers:

> They want to write—or do photography or make documentaries. They have a lot to say, but it's beginning to make more sense to apply for work as a cashier or a fry cook. This is the real face of journalism today: not million-dollar-a-year anchorpersons, but low-wage workers and downwardly spiraling professionals who can't muster up expenses to even start on the articles, photo essays, and videos they want to do, much less find an outlet to cover the costs of doing them. This impoverishment of journalists impoverishes journalism.[33]

Less anticipated consequences surfaced as well. A 2021 study concluded that the decline of local newspapers, coupled with the popularity of TV, cable, and Internet sources, had contributed substantially to political polarization and straight-ticket voting. Civic talk suffered, too. Residents of small and mid-sized cities—either by choice or without local alternatives—have come increasingly to view politics through a national prism.[34] Hometown disagreements once settled without name-calling confrontations now exhibit the raw hostility of congressional politics and hateful language of the type directed at Nancy Pelosi and Mitch McConnell. Moreover, small-town candidates once judged by their standing on local issues find themselves lumped with national lightning rods such as Republican Matt Gaetz or Democrat Adam Schiff.

Not all is bad. A few online news operations, such as Slate, Vox, ProPublica, and the Daily Beast, manage to produce hard news and investigative journalism with diminished resources. The development of community-supported nonprofit news venues looks promising but, so far, cannot begin to replace the loss of several thousand hometown newspapers. National Public Radio continues as a source of high-quality national and local journalism, but its network of nonprofit stations includes many that depend on an unpredictable mix of listener contributions, trusts, federal funding, and support from colleges or universities also trying to make ends meet. Even financially sound NPR stations and digital-only local news operations cannot begin to provide the depth of new awareness once available. There are simply not enough reporters on duty when and where news happens.

### Marginalia

The term *paywall* became journalism vernacular as print newspapers and magazines decided to require that online users pay for access to news either by subscription or through à la carte charges. Consumers accustomed to visiting the local newspaper website found their way inside the electronic edition blocked. Print newspapers often combine access to online content with delivery of weekday and Sunday print editions for an attractive price. And during the coronavirus outbreak, many news organizations temporarily removed their paywalls to Covid-19 stories as a public service. Nonetheless, confronted by a paywall, users of tablets and smart phones, in particular, may turn to less reliable information from free sources. News, though, is not free and never has been. Indeed, the public assumption of "free news" adds to the decline of paid circulation publications. Only a few, notably the *Washington Post*, the *Wall Street Journal*, and the *New York Times*, can attract a large enough online audience to make a profit and underwrite the substantial costs of high-quality national journalism.

A handful of national newspapers, as we noted, now profit from a dramatic increase in online readership. Broadcast and cable news outlets remain solvent, garnering advertising drawn by steady viewership. Local broadcast news appears sound, too. Several venerable print magazines stay in circulation through the devotion of print and online readers, among them the *New Yorker* and *Harper's*, and they contribute in-depth stories, profiles, and news analysis pieces. A few fortunate news commentary magazines—*The Atlantic*, *Time*, and *Fortune*—avoided funerals when they were purchased by billionaires interested in sustaining legacy publications.

Reliable news of substance can still be found by those able and willing to pay and search for it. However, in economically distressed towns and small cities underserved by news media, local news deserts stretch for miles. Week by week in more and more communities, the well of hometown news goes dry.

## What Happens When We Grow Estranged?

As darkness descends on local journalism, citizens everywhere face the challenge of reconciling how to self-govern within a political environment overcome by noxious disinformation. "What happens to a democracy when people stop talking to one another about what matters to them and the country?" asked David Winston, an adviser to Republican members of Congress. "What happens? That's when democracy dies."[35] The deterioration of civic life predates the Trump presidency, but he and foreign agents have disrupted public discourse to the point where citizens struggle to find common ground, show empathy, or tolerate those who differ from "us." People from all walks of life seem unwilling to discuss social issues without anger and rigidity. We come to dread a family gathering lest an argument explodes and ruins the day. Climate change: off-limits. Vaccinations: do not dare. Gun control: no way. Presidential behavior: bite your tongue. Black Lives Matter: blue (police) lives matter, too. Divisions personified by family estrangement did not materialize mysteriously from the ether. There is a backstory.

Beginning in 2014, Russia mounted an invasion of undercover agents who used advertising on Facebook, Instagram accounts, online commentary, and face-to-face contacts to legitimize Russia's annexation of Crimea and its support for separatists in eastern Ukraine. Its disinformation campaign evolved into a large-scale social media project sowing distrust and discord among unsuspecting Americans. The vanguard comprised hundreds of young, media-savvy Russians at work for the benignly named Internet Research Agency (IRA) in St. Petersburg. Funded by Russian oligarch Yevgeniy Prigozhin, the IRA acted as a mercenary army to do the dirty work of the Russian government.[36] Russia also deployed automated computer "bots"—short for robot—to spread disinformation on social media faster and with tireless stamina that humans, who need coffee breaks and a good night's sleep, cannot match.

In time, U.S. intelligence agencies concluded that Russian-linked organizations used hacks and information stolen from the Democratic campaign to promote Trump's candidacy and damage that of Hillary Rodham Clinton. Russian disinformation took advantage of a reduced faith among many Americans in genuine journalism.

Pressure mounted for an independent investigation, and in May 2017, Deputy Attorney General Rod Rosenstein appointed former FBI director Robert S. Mueller III as special counsel to head a probe that culminated with the release in 2019 of a two-volume study popularly known as the Mueller Report. It detailed how Russian operatives in "sweeping and systematic fashion" violated U.S. criminal law to sway the election. Twelve of them were indicted in absentia.[37] President Trump and his political allies denounced the report as a corrupt attempt by Democrats to smear the president, but in August 2020, after a three-year investigation, the Republican-controlled Senate Intelligence Committee substantiated the Mueller findings. In its own report of nearly one thousand pages, the Senate committee concluded that the Russian government used its propaganda apparatus to benefit Trump; its intelligence agencies easily manipulated the Trump campaign; and several Trump advisers welcomed Russian-acquired information damaging to the Clinton campaign.[38]

In the private sector, as well, clandestine actors worked to manipulate voters. Cambridge Analytica, a consulting firm hired by the Trump campaign, mined personal data, provided freely by social media users on Facebook and elsewhere, to target those most likely to allow loaded messages like "Crooked Hillary" to sway their vote. When exposed, largely by reporters from the British daily *The Guardian* and the *New York Times*, the scandal ruined Cambridge Analytica and sent Facebook stock tumbling.[39] Russian intelligence agencies certainly knew of Cambridge Analytica's activities and likely added its tactics to their repertoire. Other individuals, organizations, and nations motivated by mischief or ill intent also watched and learned. They learned how news had become more easily compromised in the new journalistic landscape.

A particularly insidious example of foreign sabotage surfaced in May 2017 outside a Houston Islamic center as protesters bearing Confederate flags and "White Lives Matter" banners faced off with fifty counterprotesters answering an online call to "Save Islamic Knowledge." The two sides exchanged angry words, but police officers kept them apart and prevented violence. When reporters on the scene asked participants why they had turned out, members of each contingent said they were provoked by Facebook posts from two social media groups—Heart of Texas and United Muslims of America. Eventually investigators from the office of the special counsel established that both organizations were fictions manufactured by Kremlin operatives. They penetrated American social media platforms at will. Crossing digital borders requires no passport, no visual recognition scanning, or no questioning from customs officials.[40]

Digital invaders posing as newsmakers, influencers, and news providers now occupy all corners of global politics. The *Washington Post*, for instance, reported a tweet from Alicia Hernan, whose Twitter account described her as a wife, mother, and lover of peace, in which she railed at President Trump: "That stupid moron doesn't get that by creating bad guys, spewing hate filled words and creating fear of 'others,' his message is spreading to fanatics around the world. Or maybe he does." The account, "@AliciaHernan3," turned out to be what disinformation experts call a "sock puppet," that is, a fictitious online persona invented to inflame and deepen our divisions. "Alicia," by the way, was not a Russian sock puppet; her tweet, accompanied by a photo of a blond woman wearing large, round-framed glasses and a turtleneck sweater, originated in Iran.[41] Outsiders try to exploit the reputation of Americans as trusting souls who accept the legitimacy of online information. As Russians and other foreign agents get caught and exposed, more cyber espionage continues. In a 2021 congressional hearing, security expert Dr. Herb Lin of the Hoover Institution told lawmakers:

> The information warfare threat to the United States is different from past threats, and it has the potential to destroy reason and reality as a basis for societal discourse, replacing them with rage and fantasy. Perpetual civil war, political extremism, waged in the information sphere and egged on by our adversaries is every bit as much of an existential threat to American civilization and democracy as any military threat imaginable.[42]

To be clear, the United States is far from an innocent victim. Our intelligence operations engage in cyber warfare and reportedly hack foreign governments and strategic infrastructure, but with a major qualifier: Vigilant American journalists and domestic watchdog groups expose questionable spying and counterespionage when uncovered.

While a majority of foreign and domestic actors operate covertly, the occupant of the Oval Office inflicted damage openly with daily tweets and retweets that functioned as "news" for followers—eleven thousand by the thirty-third month of Trump's presidency, according to a 2019 *New York Times* study.[43] As of July 2020, another indicator, the *Washington Post*'s Fact Checker team, estimated that Trump to that point had made 20,000 false or misleading claims as president, largely through tweets to eighty-seven million followers.[44] From July to January 2021, he accelerated the pace, with a final total tally of 30,573, according to the *Post*.[45] The president had become a *faux journalist*, disseminating "news" with an air of certainty and disdain for factual accuracy—news packaged primarily for political fans already committed to a divisive agenda.

The ultimate impact of his campaign of deception defies calculation. Rabid supporters parroted him, labeling journalism objectionable to Trump as "fake news" and official investigations into his administration as "witch hunts." Trump retweeted messages from suspicious sources, among them a September 2017 tweet from Tennessee@10_gop, "We love you, Mr. President," to which Trump said, "So nice, thank you!" The Mueller investigation tracked @10_gop to Russian intelligence, and Twitter later banned the account.[46] As Trump created or amplified disruptive, bogus messages, ironically, he fell prey to them himself. He appeared especially susceptible to flattering online comments.

Apologists excused Trump's words and told us not to take them seriously; they were meant to entertain, and parsing them for meaning was pointless. Not so, said S. V. Dáte, senior White House correspondent for the online publication HuffPost, who warned: "Unfortunately, the nation and the world *do* parse Trump's words, because while they are often absurd and even more often false, he himself usually intends them seriously, and the powers at his fingertips are so vast that he cannot be safely ignored." Dáte speaks from experience:

> I've been a journalist for 33 years. I've covered Congress. NASA and the military space program. City and county halls. The Florida statehouse. Criminal courts, including armed robbers and serial killers. In all of that time, I have never encountered a public official, a candidate for office, a bureaucrat, a defense lawyer or, frankly, an actual criminal who is as regularly and aggressively dishonest as the current president of the United States. And that includes a dozen years covering the Florida legislature.

He described the frustration of covering a White House of lies that enter our lives as if normal and harmless. Dáte literally sighed: "It is simply where we are today."[47]

The *Washington Post* created its fact-checking column in 2007 to track political advertising and candidate statements during the 2008 presidential race. It became a permanent feature early in 2011. During his campaign and early in his presidency, Donald Trump sorely tested the ability of "The Fact Checker" to investigate false or misleading claims that poured from his mouth and through his fingertips. As the late diplomat and U.S. senator Daniel Patrick Moynihan (1927-2003) once famously observed: "Everyone is entitled to his own opinion, but not to his own facts."[48] Other organizations dedicated to disclosing falsehoods include PolitiFact, operated by Poynter Institute, a journalism school funded by the *Tampa Bay Times*; FactCheck.org, a nonpartisan, nonprofit project of the Annenberg Public Policy Center at the University of Pennsylvania; and Snopes, known for combating urban legends and fake social media posts. Even with Trump out of office, the fact-checkers continue to be busy and much needed. In an age of diminished authentic journalism, lies and disinformation pack more motivational punch for committed followers of Trump and his acolytes.

Psychotherapists, including Trump's niece Mary Trump, argue that his incessant use of falsehoods, deception, and spurious accusations may be symptoms of a mental disorder.[49] Other observers, such as Amanda Carpenter, believe they represent a crafty media strategy. Carpenter, author of *Gaslighting America*, explains how a verbal illusionist cleverly combines denials and misdirection to convince his audience to doubt its own experiences and reject known facts and evidence. The term comes from the 1938 play *Gaslight*, later a popular movie, in which a husband tries to convince his wife she is going insane while his perceptions are utterly dependable. In one scene, he manipulates the gaslights in the house to flicker. When his wife notices, he tells her it never happened—that she imagined it all. Repetition is a prime strategy for gaslighting others. When Trump repeatedly reminded TV audiences of how vigorously he defended America in the early days of Covid-19, he hoped the image would take root, like a hypnotic suggestion, among followers. Judging by attendees at anti-mask rallies, it did. Trump regularly gaslighted his audience, Carpenter contends, and his aides and spokespersons followed his lead.[50]

After the pandemic seized our lives, the falsehoods attributed to the president morphed from exasperating to dangerous, as he assured the nation that the virus was under "total control," touted unproven "cures," blamed others for a slow response to testing, and played politics with requests for ICU ventilators and virus test kits. Now we know, based on sixteen recorded interviews with legendary investigative reporter Bob Woodward, that the president privately had acknowledged as early as February 2019 that Covid-19 was a deadly, highly infectious airborne disease and that he admitted downplaying its dangers intentionally to avoid "panic."[51] In so doing, he also encouraged citizens to avoid preparedness, contributing to what the World Health Organization described as an "infodemic" of pseudoscience and conspiracy theories.[52] He continued to manipulate the truth after contracting the virus himself.

Ideological opportunists latched onto Trump rhetorical devices to advance their own agendas, including the Proud Boys, an organization of mostly white males known for its racist, xenophobic, and misogynistic beliefs. The Proud Boys stood alongside other hate groups at extremist gatherings, including a deadly 2017 protest in Charlottesville, Virginia. They doctored photographs, posted hateful memes, and manufactured false news reports to further their aims. Like-minded groups followed suit. During the George Floyd murder protests, social media outlets circulated reports about vandalism done to military cemeteries and the stockpiling of bricks and Molotov cocktails by protesters. A photograph posted in mid-2020 enraged Twitter users by showing a swath cut through a field of white crosses and American flags. Messages attached to reposts of the photo cited it as evidence of vandalism committed by Black Lives Matter activists. When fact-checked, the photo turned out to be dated to May 2016 when a drunk driver plowed through a Memorial Day display in Henderson, Kentucky.[53] The public knows truthful details of such events primarily because of reporting *from* traditional news media.

Those who deliberately produce *dis*information act with malice because they engage in deliberate deception. Those, though, who innocently spread *mis*information usually do so because they mistakenly trust what they see or read online, especially when it reinforces their particular worldview. Citizens whom disinformation purveyors hope to exploit, especially heavy users of social media, enter dark, virtual alleys where they invite a mugging, posing a problem for citizen responsibility.

Can citizens become more discerning in evaluating online content and reduce their chances of being misled, victimized, and unwittingly recruited by information twisters? Perhaps, especially if people close to them calmly discuss fact-based counterarguments while listening carefully to others' replies. Still, as Nobel Prize-winning columnist Paul Krugman observes in his book *Arguing with Zombies*, a growing segment of Americans prefers to believe that experts are somehow conspiring against them.[54] "Ideas that should have been killed by contrary evidence," he writes, "instead keep shambling along, eating people's brains." To expand on Krugman's thesis, there are those who refuse to read or discuss anything contrary to what they learn from like-minded partisans, a rhetorical gambit we later discuss as *dismissiveness*. They embrace the puzzling notion of "alternative facts" coined by Trump adviser Kellyanne Conway. In their minds, data, science, and history (always necessary for valid journalistic context) are not to be trusted. Perhaps they will never trust expert information. Conscientious citizens maneuver around dismissive arguers by fact-checking, as journalists do, and by continuing to seek out productive opportunities for engaging disbelievers in evidence-based conversation and deliberation.

When citizens choose to denigrate the viewpoints of others rather than acknowledge them, they circumvent an essential component of the democratic experience. In their book *How Democracies Die*, Steven Levitsky and Daniel Ziblatt stress the consequences of such behavior. "The weakening of our democratic norms is rooted in extreme partisan polarization—one that extends beyond policy differences into an existential conflict over race and culture," they write. "If one thing is clear from studying breakdowns throughout history, it's that extreme polarization can kill democracies."[55]

Leading up to the 2020 elections, foreign intelligence stoked partisan discord through a renewed campaign of bogus news and repurposed video posts, such as one of a woman telling the operator of a taco truck parked on her street, "Let's go baby girl. Vámonos. I'll call ICE [Immigration and Customs Enforcement]." Russian agents retweeted the video with the goal of turning America against itself, possibly sparking real-life violence. Being forewarned does not necessarily mean we are forearmed. Agents of digital espionage, with China a growing player, continue to zero in on soft targets. Victims of disinformation insist, "It's true. I actually *saw* it online," when what they believe to be "true" is wrenched out of context, patently unreliable, or, worse, fabricated by propagandists, planting messages like digital IEDs designed to enrage.[56]

In his final days in office, President Trump—reinforced by a handful of passionate surrogates—repeatedly questioned the legitimacy of the election results.[57] Zealots listened, believed, and rallied to "stop the steal." Extremists spread the word online and joined Trump in urging a show of force on January 6, 2021. We witnessed the results on live TV. In the Kremlin and in China's seat of power, Zhongnanhai, we can envision a robust round of high fives.

Politicized "truths" can render citizens incapable of recognizing values and beliefs they might hold in common. In the extreme, some people see the same set of facts in diametrically different ways. The result? A dysfunctional, split-screen approach to *real* problems in our lives. When you hear critics accuse local and state officials of "overreach" for mandating face masks in public or closing restaurants, juxtapose those stances against demands for *more* government involvement in the form of crackdowns on public demonstrations. Citizens pay a price for failure to scrutinize and question what they hear or read. The price inflates when citizens, left and right, become political extremists, unwilling to distinguish between each other's legitimate and illegitimate views.

The First Amendment, meant to ensure the dissemination of truthful information as the basis for public dialogue, now harbors dissemblers and saboteurs, allowing them often to escape consequences. We have never needed an active, alert journalism more—and a citizenry that pays attention.

## The First Amendment Shows Its Age

Traditional news organizations fight to hold on while communities grow further apart, and the catalyst expected to empower both journalism and public life, the Constitution's First Amendment, is becoming increasingly impotent. Designed to deter government censorship and promote the free flow of diverse, reason-based perspectives and information, it has not, thus far, counteracted many new threats posed by manipulative politicians, powerful corporate interests, and foreign intelligence interlopers. Google, Amazon, Apple, and Facebook deserve credit for the bounty of information available at our fingertips. But they also opened floodgates without sufficient concern for the toxic sludge that poured in.

At the nation's birth, no one thought to call the press "the enemy of the people." It was printer's ink, not gunpowder, that produced a wave of resistance to British rule and articulated colonists' desire for independence. By no means, though, was that loose collection of weekly newspapers and pamphleteers widely admired and respected. George Washington, while a champion of freedom of speech, still resented attacks on his administration, saying they came from "infamous scribblers."[58] He and other Founders, however, tolerated the flaws and failings, believing the new republic required an outspoken, unfettered press to empower its people.

The First Amendment was adopted in 1791, elevating press freedom to a constitutionally protected right: "Congress shall make no law . . . abridging freedom . . . of the press." Despite ambiguity and perpetual disagreement over the so-called original intent of the Founders, they meant for the First Amendment generally to protect the sovereignty of "the people" rather than to immunize the press from legal accountability. The press served citizens, a point stressed by Thomas Jefferson when he said, "No experiment can be more interesting than that we are now trying, and which we trust will end in establishing the fact, that man may be governed by reason and truth. Our first object should therefore be, to leave open to him all the avenues to truth. The most effectual hitherto found, is the freedom of the press."[59]

The Founders expected that the First Amendment would serve broader purposes. If the people were to self-govern wisely, they required solid information, widely available to all, that stimulated thought, conversation, and deliberation and that would "leave open . . . all avenues to truth." Access to truth, for Jefferson, was a criterion by which to judge a free press in a democracy. For James Madison, the pursuit of truth encompassed voter education: "The value and efficacy of this right depends on the knowledge of the comparative merits and demerits of the candidates for public trust, and on the equal freedom, consequently, of examining and discussing these merits and demerits of the candidates respectively."[60] The First Amendment, then, steeped in the Founders' respect for the power of communication, opened the door toward fully actualized citizenship. Implicitly, it assured informed citizens that they could speak critically of public officials, search unfettered for the truth, demand accountability, and seek social reform through their *talk*. It stood as an invitation and an incentive for Americans to decide their own fate. This emphasis on communication, even in difficult times, is a concern to which we return often in subsequent chapters.

As the nation expanded and the press matured, the republic held firm, surviving a bloody civil war, two world wars, the agonizing assassinations of four presidents, the buffeting social revolutions of the 1960s, the constitutional clash between President Richard M. Nixon and the rule of law, the 9/11 terror attacks, and, now, the Covid-19 pandemic, protests of the Black Lives Matter movement, and a deadly mass assault on the Capitol building. Institutional journalism, although far from perfect, helped inform and stabilize the nation. The First Amendment evolved as well, adjusting to crises that threatened to destroy the nation and acquiring substance and definition from landmark decisions and opinions by justices of the Supreme Court.

If a time capsule transported the Founders to the present day, they would encounter a wounded republic susceptible to attacks on its basic principles made purposely wobbly. Jefferson and Madison would lament structural fractures in the nation's foundational pillars. If they sampled what passes for news and opinion online, they might find the marketplace of ideas theory of John Milton's 1644 essay *Areopagitica* hopelessly naive: "Let her and Falsehood grapple; who ever knew Truth put to the worse in a free and open encounter?"[61] Truth? It can be pretty thin when political leaders continually deny verifiable facts to credulous followers. Yale historian Timothy Snyder, an expert on twentieth-century totalitarianism, cautions: "To abandon facts is to abandon freedom. If nothing is true, then no one can criticize power, because there is no basis on which to do so. . . . Post-truth is pre-fascism."[62]

The post-truth world shelters fringe groups that find truth an impediment to their goals. Among them: QAnon, an amorphous collection of conspiracy theorists who contest facts by planting outrageous lies on social media. They have persuaded thousands that liberals are Satan-worshipping pedophiles who permeate government, media, and corporations. Increasingly, people in "Q" T-shirts holding banners gather at pro-Trump rallies and protests against Black Lives Matter. The Founders might be aghast to learn that QAnon beliefs are now represented by elected members of Congress. Kevin Roose, a *New York Times* technology writer who tracks QAnon's infiltration of online platforms, labeled it a "misinformation super-spreader."[63] In October 2020, Facebook said it would ban any groups, pages, or Instagram accounts that "represent" QAnon.[64]

The major contributor to a post-truth world has been the Internet, ironically foreseen in the late 1990s as the great liberator of individuals' speech. It is still a positive force in many ways. In the 1997 Supreme Court case *Reno v. American Civil Liberties Union*, Justice John Paul Stevens enthusiastically hyped the Internet for its ability to make "any person with a phone line . . . a town crier with a voice that resonates farther than it could from any soapbox."[65] Today we know that the Internet has produced a web of contradictions. At its best, the Internet empowers us to learn, question, and comment on every subject known to humankind. The Internet aids immensely in the pursuit of truth by debunking myths and exposing charlatans; conversely, it facilitates the viral spread of lies, hoaxes, and propaganda. Its critics contend that overexposure to the Internet numbs us intellectually with unprecedented information overload, pacifies us as a habitual diversion, encourages cyberbullying, enables identity theft, and weakens our ability to think and act independently. People cannot resist going online for trivial information, diversion, and, most alarming, avoiding real news.

Efforts to quell false messages or deter their spread implicate First Amendment fundamentals, among them the marketplace of ideas concept. Facebook and other social media employ thousands of "content moderators" who scour video and text in the near impossible task of screening for ill-defined "objectionable" material. They are private gatekeepers, not government censors. So, for better or worse and often in arbitrary fashion, the content moderators control public access to an ocean of information, generally focusing on filtration of falsehoods or verbal attacks deemed a threat to public order and safety. Chapter 3, particularly, discusses the sticky constitutional dilemma raised when freedom of expression includes protection for fringe and false claims aimed at endangering democracy.

## The Dangerous Intersection of Trump, Journalism, and Public Discourse

The forty-fifth president arguably has done lasting damage to the institution of journalism by discrediting honest reporting and dissembling or retweeting flagrant dishonesty online. Relentless misrepresentations of the profession penetrate deep into the national consciousness, conditioning many citizens to distrust the entire mainstream news system and, ultimately, to wall themselves off from ideas they are ill-equipped to discuss. The fake news refrain weakens the civic and democratic fabric dating to the nation's birth at a time when journalists and other citizens need each other's support more than ever. Masha Gessen, an expert on totalitarianism, believes that journalism can unite us in a shared reality. "Without this shared reality, a public sphere—the term philosopher Jürgen Habermas uses to describe the space where public opinion takes shape— cannot exist."[66] Gessen describes the nexus of a democratic republic that we explain more thoroughly in chapters 7 and 8.

Relying on a "fake news" excuse makes it easier for people to deflect damaging but accurate reporting about an administration, or its policies, business dealings, and family behavior. The mantra relies on a political base that accepts automatically the view of journalists as radical leftists out to destroy government and trash American "values." According to figures compiled by the *New York Times*, President Trump tweeted the term "fake news" to demean journalists more than six hundred times between December 2016 and November 2019.[67] Dozens of officials around the world, including leaders of other democracies, have mimicked the "fake news" ploy since Trump put it in play. The *Times* report did not count the president's use of the term at rallies, impromptu news conferences, and White House meetings. David E. McCraw knows from his experience as an attorney for the *New York Times* the impact of constant repetition of the term: "It is asking people to skip over the analytical step of weighing what is true and what is not and instead prodding them to simply dismiss what they don't like hearing."[68] It is an all-purpose get-out-of-answering-free card, with accountability and citizens' trust of journalism the losers.

The attacks on journalism here and abroad do more than undermine the legitimacy of mainstream media; they endanger the women and men who bring us news. The Committee to Protect Journalists, especially sensitive to threats to journalists in foreign countries, offered a "safety kit" for American reporters covering rallies and political events during the 2020 presidential campaign. The kit advised wearing clothes without media logos and avoiding eye contact with aggressive individuals in the crowd. When the president or other political leaders damn journalists, they encourage broader acts of repression and retaliation. The publisher of the *New York Times*, A. G. Sulzberger, explained:

> The phrase "enemy of the people" has a particularly brutal history. It was used to justify mass executions during the French Revolution and the Third Reich. And it was used by Lenin and Stalin to justify the systematic murder of Soviet dissidents. The treason charge is perhaps the most serious a commander in chief can make. By threatening to prosecute journalists for invented crimes against their country, President Trump gives repressive leaders implicit license to do the same.[69]

A nonpartisan organization called U.S. Press Freedom Tracker collects data from multiple press freedom groups to document and publicize threats against journalists just doing their jobs. In 2020, it reported 431 physical assaults on reporters and nearly 1,500 incidents of arrests, detentions, and seized or damaged equipment.[70]

**FYI**

---

Journalists Maria Ressa and Dmitry Muratov daily put their lives in danger to defend freedom of speech and the press. In 2021 they shared the Nobel Peace Prize. "The fight against the media is not a fight against the media," Muratov said in an interview. "It is a fight against the people."[71]

Muratov is founder and editor in chief of the newspaper *Novaja Gazeta*, known for exposing abuses of power in Russia. Ressa is a former CNN Southeast Asia correspondent who cofounded Rappler, a digital media company that focuses on investigative reporting in the Philippines.

In announcing the awards, the Norwegian Nobel Committee asserted that "freedom of expression and freedom of information help to ensure an informed public. These rights are crucial prerequisites for democracy and protect against war and conflict."

Ressa exposed President Rodrigo Duterte for massive corruption and his murderous antidrug campaign. Nineteen Filipino journalists have been killed under his regime. Six of Muratov's colleagues at *Novaja Gazeta* have been murdered since 1993 as the newspaper pushed back against the reign of Vladimir Putin, although some pro-democracy groups in Russia contend it has not pushed hard enough.

Ressa and Muratov know how effectively their governments use social media to spread disinformation, harass opponents, and manipulate public discourse. "The collapse of democracy starts with the breakdown of facts," Ressa said. "And if you don't have facts you don't have the shared reality to find the right path. This is a global problem."[72]

Hostility toward journalists is not a recent development, but the current intensity is new and disturbing. Journalists serve our Constitution, our institutions, our way of life, and our common welfare. Whether or not you believe the news media—particularly national outlets—are unfairly biased against Trump and unabashedly pro-liberal, they are *not* in the business of turning events into fictions. Award-winning general interest journalism can be found at the *Washington Post, The Week*, the *New York Times*, CNN, the *Christian Science Monitor, Mother Jones*, MSNBC, *The Hill*, the *New Yorker*, Axios, Politico, NPR, the *National Review*, Reuters, and the *Wall Street Journal* and from reliable, dedicated print, cable, and Internet journalists on duty throughout the country. Do not confuse daily news reporting with the role of those who write columns and editorials or appear as pundits on talk shows. They may or may not be helpful sources of interpretation and context. But within traditional newspapers, the news department and the editorial department occupy separate spaces and hold separate meetings. When accusations of media bias and fake news arise, it is often due to a general misunderstanding about the line separating the two functions, news and commentary. Later, in chapter 6, we focus on media bias and clarify how the term can be weaponized as an accusation rather than a description of an inevitable truism. But for now, we note that on the whole, articles and columns marked as "news analysis" or found on op-ed or editorial pages usually offer points of view grounded in verifiable facts.

Any discussion of the state of journalism must include controversial Fox News, whose daily prime-time audience reached nearly four million viewers in mid-2020, leading all other network or cable programs in the 8:00-11:00 p.m. (Eastern Time) time slot. Fox News perpetuates the news values of its founder, Roger Ailes, hired in 1996 by newspaper and entertainment magnate Rupert Murdoch to create a conservative alternative to CNN. Ailes gained experience in the use of news to influence public opinion early on as a media consultant to Richard M. Nixon in 1968, Ronald Reagan in 1984, and George H. W. Bush in 1988. Under Ailes, Fox News attracted a substantial, loyal audience of mostly older, white, male, conservative-leaning viewers who considered CNN and the big three news networks too liberal. Ailes dominated Fox News for two decades until multiple accusations of workplace sexual harassment forced him to resign. He died in 2017, leaving a legacy—the prime-time power lineup of Sean Hannity, Tucker Carlson, and Laura Ingraham and many conservatives' favorite morning program, *Fox & Friends.*

Contrary to the network's original "fair and balanced" promise, each of these popular programs, according to nearly all fact-checking organizations, presents news with a decidedly rightist slant. Fox News stands credibly accused, too, of ignoring news reports inconvenient to its agenda of amplifying Trump's attacks on journalism, promoting anti-immigrant rhetoric, advancing refuted conspiracy theories, spreading misinformation about Covid-19 and vaccines, and uncritically promoting the Trump agenda on air.[73]

The network's cozy relationship with Trump's White House can hardly be doubted. During the January 6 attack on the Capitol, three prominent Fox News hosts independently texted chief of staff Mark Meadows to offer advice on the insurrection *in progress.* Laura Ingraham, for example, said, "Mark, the president needs to tell people in the Capitol to go home. This is hurting all of us. He is destroying his legacy." Note the clear reference to "all of us" being hurt. Who, we might ask, is the "us" being referenced? The text messages were released by the House select committee investigating January 6.

The revelation prompted Ann Marie Lipinski, curator of the Nieman Foundation for Journalism at Harvard, to comment: "For there to be an ongoing, live violent riot playing out at the Capitol during which anchors are communicating their preferences about what the president should do with the president's staff is inappropriate in the least, and highly unethical by my lights."[74] Fox News's most popular personalities crossed a near inviolable line respected by nearly all journalists. Instead of *reporting* the news, they attempted to *influence* it, a practice with which they had experience.

Fox News skirts ethical norms in other ways. Its programs deal heavily in opinion provided by hosts and paid analysts, as do its rivals MSNBC and CNN. But no matter the political bent, opinion presented under the name of "journalism" or "news," whether on cable news, on broadcast news, or in print publications, should never be knowingly false or based on unsubstantiated information. No such practice is taught in college journalism programs or condoned by demanding editors within newsrooms. Responsible news organizations are expected to challenge and, if possible, correct misinformation, inaccuracies, or questionable claims. Not all do. On September 12, 2020, Jeanine Pirro of Fox News sat across from the president on the south portico of the White House for an exclusive interview that eventually led to a discussion of the upcoming presidential debates. Here is a verbatim exchange from the program transcript:[75]

> TRUMP: Debates have worked out well for me. I don't know what's going to show up with Biden. I mean, I see different guys, I see a Biden that really tied Bernie. You know, everyone thought he was going to be killed by Bernie and it was tie. It was nothing—it wasn't Winston Churchill but it was fine. But I've also seen him in some of the other debates where he wasn't even coherent.
>
> PIRRO: How do you think he goes from incoherent to coherent?
>
> TRUMP: I think there's probably—possibly drugs involved. That's what I hear. I mean, there's possibly drugs. I don't know how you can go from being so bad where you can't even get out a sentence—I mean, you saw some of those debates with the large number of people on the stage. He was—I mean, I used to say how is it possible that he can even go forward?
>
> PIRRO: All right.

The interview ended with no follow-up questions or request for proof of Trump's "probably—possibly" claim. Opinion programs such as *Justice with Judge Jeanine* generate huge profits for Fox News and its conservative cable rivals, Newsmax and One America News Network. But citizens who believe they are receiving objective *news* should be aware that they are digesting *commentary* not necessarily backed by factual analysis or tested by tough questioning. The warning, of course, also applies to liberal commentary, such as the political satire of *Saturday Night Live* and *Last Week Tonight with John Oliver.*

To best appreciate journalism, pay attention to the front lines of local news. The grunt work falls to women and men whose beats are city hall, the courthouse, and police headquarters. They are bound by the traditional tenets of news reporting, such as fairness, objectivity, verification, and truth telling. When readers or listeners get irked over what they misconstrue as "news," they might wrongly assume that all journalists are alike. People might also be surprised to learn that most bona fide journalists, like Evan Brandt, consider journalism a *calling* to public service, not just a paycheck. Reporters put their own worries aside for the benefit of the community. When a tornado knocks out power and destroys their own homes, they step through debris and downed power lines to tell the story. They overcome their own grief and report on a gunman who entered the newsroom and killed five colleagues. They often forsake lucrative careers for one with a median hourly pay of under twenty dollars.[76]

Complicating their already demanding jobs, journalists confront systematic propaganda operations not only headquartered in the White House but now adopted increasingly on a smaller scale by other political figures or groups espousing various political positions. Whirlwinds of lies and accusations confound journalists who, by professional training, try hard to report from a position of impartiality. Recently we have learned that no matter how outlandish the lie or how bizarre its defense, it will make news and potentially deflect public attention from factual accounts. Trump senior adviser and son-in-law Jared Kushner marveled: "You send out a press release and it goes into the ether and nobody cares," he told Bob Woodward. "He [President Trump] puts out a tweet and it's on CNN one and a half minutes later."[77] Traditional journalism finds itself trying to combat lies—lies the profession, by adhering to its norms, has treated as newsworthy.

A debate now grips journalism over whether "both sides" objectivity should be replaced by the concept of "moral clarity"—an imperative for news organizations to call out racists and liars unequivocally. A veteran public radio news director raises an underlying problem inherent in both models: "In replacing their decidedly strawman version of the 'objectivity' ideal with a more courageous 'moral clarity,'" said Liam Moriarty, "journalists are trading the unattainable for the unknowable, and consciously elevating narrative 'truths' over verified facts."[78] The debate, however, highlights a vital question about the role of journalism as the supposed guardian of mainstream discourse. Writing for Vox, senior correspondent Zack Beauchamp observed: "Does every idea that's popular in power, no matter how poorly considered, deserve some kind of respectful airing in mainstream publications? Or are there boundaries, both of quality of argument and moral decency, where editors need to draw the line—especially in the Trump era?"[79] We continue the discussion when we deal with newsroom standards in chapter 5 and follow up in chapter 6 with an analysis of media bias.

## Where Do We Go from Here?

The mutual disintegration of journalism, citizenship, and civic discourse leaves the republic vulnerable—but not without resources for self-repair. In the opening pages of this chapter, we said that citizens who care about democracy need better education, particularly about how journalism stimulates self-governance, protects vital individual and societal rights, and informs citizens of facts impacting us locally, nationally, and globally. Good journalism exists across the political spectrum; sample widely but stay alert for bogus information.

Understanding, supporting, and, indeed, criticizing journalism should be expected of citizens. Still, some denounce reporters without knowing who they are, what they do, and, especially, why they work *for* not *against* the people. They form judgments on snippets of information and superficial analyses prevalent on social media instead of engaging in deep reading and reflection. They put too much faith in what they encounter online and carelessly repost unverified material on personal Facebook pages or spread it via text or email to friends, without knowing its validity or source. Even those who abhor gossip and hearsay routinely retransmit scandalous details, gleaned from online posts from who knows who, that falsely accuse public figures of immorality, sexual abuse, or corruption. People from every walk of life fall victim to online exploitation they often absorb unconditionally. When asked to provide facts and specifics about information acquired online, people may choose to become megaphones for talking points designed by strangers nursing hidden agendas. Genuine journalism gives us tools to do more than that.

Citizenship is not a spectator sport. It requires an effort that can be noticed or measured, like giving blood or volunteering at a food pantry. What if you look in the mirror and ask, "How do I stack up as a citizen?" You might think, well, I keep up with community issues, obey the law, pay my taxes, respect the flag, and, of course, vote faithfully. Take a closer look: Do I follow issues outside my immediate community? Do I accept legislation and political decisions uncritically if they come from politicians I support? Do I know how my tax money is spent? Do I understand why some citizens would burn the American flag and others would attack them for doing so? Most fundamental of all: Do I vote without doing my civic homework, filling out the ballot based on blind party loyalty, slick political ads, or dubious online commentary? Responsible citizenship requires something more. Astra Taylor, author of *Democracy May Not Exist, but We'll Miss It When It's Gone*, puts a fine point on the subject: "The promise of democracy is not the one made and betrayed by the powerful; it is a promise that can be kept only by regular people through vigilance, invention, and struggle."[80]

It is especially troubling to witness citizens who reject one another, refusing to listen, acting like combatants, and arguing about the Constitution and its Bill of Rights without ever having read them. As a nation committed to informed self-rule, too many of us of every political orientation lack even an informal understanding of history, law, journalism, citizenship, and democratic processes. When talk turns to contentious issues, many resort to language and imagery that *enrage*, not *engage*, forsaking dialogue. When we air grievances, we must be prepared to listen for opposing points of view. To be fair, this preparation is too rare. Let us all accept a fair share of blame for our troubled times.

The state of the nation is not good, and most Americans apparently agree. Yet, for befuddling reasons, millions of citizens seem unable or unwilling to address matters tearing at us. Civic inertia puts our national fate in jeopardy to those who would like nothing better than to see the United States self-destruct. A much-quoted line from *Pogo*, a satirical cartoon strip popular in the mid-twentieth century, seems to apply today: "We have met the enemy, and he is us." The ultimate danger to our democracy comes from a national failure to respect and support journalism and truth, behave as responsible citizens, deliberate with open minds, and defend ourselves from antidemocratic forces that gnaw away at the republic from the inside.

The massive turnout in 2020 elections suggests heightened civic awareness. But higher vote totals do not translate necessarily into a more responsible citizenry or better days ahead. Self-governance cannot occur unless citizens proactively encourage communication about diverse ideas that focus on the common good. The process requires a determined effort, as do other aspects of citizenship. Part of the answer may rest on one of the most mundane of everyday activities, conversation: a willingness to continue talking across differences, listening for how others define the differences, seeking out evidence, and comparing possible futures.

Clearly, we are worried about a diminished republic. The chapters to follow are intended to help journalists and citizens reconnect in the founding spirit of a deliberative democracy. We need journalism that exposes injustice, encourages civic engagement, and enables a restoration of public discourse. We need conscientious, self-starting citizens who contribute to democracy's news. Admirable examples lie ahead.

## CHAPTER 2

# A Budding Nation Finds Its Voice

The seeds of the republic germinated from spirited discourse, some of it punctuated by the clang of tankards. The irrepressible American urge to speak one's mind emerged as many citizens completed the consuming burdens of settling the land, erecting shelters, tilling crops, and establishing livelihoods. Eking out an existence had left little time, energy, or compulsion to engage in intellectual pursuits or political discussions. By the early 1700s, conditions were ripe for civic talk to flourish.

Colonial America raised its voice in churches, taverns, and meeting halls. One particular space especially promoted civic togetherness— the public square, sometimes called the "common" or "commons" in the North or a "green" in the southern and middle states. As people clustered in towns and villages for security, commerce, and companionship, they set aside shared ground around which they built homes and opened shops. These town squares served multiple purposes—grazing livestock; conducting militia drills; selling, buying, and bartering goods; and congregating for public events, including political speech making. Local leaders with something to say shared their ideas alongside farmers selling potatoes. Here, the community assembled and interacted in social and political encounters. In colonial and prerevolution days, the public square often was unkempt and pitted with tree stumps, not at all like the tranquil, picturesque green spaces that now draw tourists. Ramshackle as most were, the town common served as the amphitheater for a republic soon to bud.

### Marginalia

Some urban planners and landscape architects now encourage the restoration of public squares to create and sustain a sense of community. People from different neighborhoods find a common bond through attending art shows, concerts, green markets, and nonviolent protests. Traditions of block parties in large cities like Chicago can serve similar purposes.

Community conversation flourished indoors as well. People gathered for hours in coffeehouses to sip and exchange gossip and news, often from weeks-old newspapers and correspondence carried across the Atlantic by schooner. They craved human contact and did not hide behind books or newspapers as latte lovers with tablets now tend to do at Starbucks. In the evening, discussions broke out in candlelit taverns and public houses— inns where travelers lodged, dined, and conversed while warmed by a fireplace. Taverns and inns provided newspapers and assorted reading material to lure customers clamoring for the latest information. These venues excluded Blacks, American Indians, and, with few exceptions, women. Otherwise, entry did not require tailored clothing or refined manners. Farmers mingled with carpenters, blacksmiths, and lawyers. In the process, diverse issues, experiences, and personalities encountered one another in vigorous civic discourse necessary for a successful republic.[1]

Not all approved of liquor as an elixir of democracy, for it clashed with prevalent Puritan values of sobriety and industriousness, although Puritans were not necessarily prohibitionists. Nevertheless, the presence of fermented spirits reeked of sin. Preachers of various denominations condemned "demon rum." Upright citizens shunned places where the idle and intemperate commingled. But by 1720, taverns had evolved as places where civic complaints circulated and democratic ideals were professed. Ale and hard liquor contributed to nation building. In his book *In Public Houses*, David W. Conroy said, "Taverns became a public stage upon which colonists resisted, initiated, and addressed changes in their society. Indeed, in these houses men gradually redefined their relationships with figures of authority."[2] By the mid-1760s, talk of revolution resounded in drinking establishments that served as informal forums for citizens seeking self-rule. Brawls broke out on occasion, but a semblance of decorum often kept the peace. For the most part, prerevolutionary taverns remained institutions where "the rising political tension could be released but be constructively engaged," according to Conroy.[3]

In less inclusive settings, well-connected men of means joined private political clubs. Meeting in chambers smoky with pipe tobacco, they set policy and selected candidates for local offices, away from the prying eyes of the middling class, the ordinary people. The greater community knew what they were up to.

New England contributed the town hall meeting to the rhetorical mix. The town form of government provided a platform to nearly anyone who wanted to be heard, although generally only property-owning, adult whites males could vote. From colony to colony and from one community to another, the rules and membership of the town meeting varied. In places with a strong church presence, ministers and churchgoing elite tended to control town meeting business. At its best, though, the town meeting was an introduction to participatory democracy. For a country moving toward nationhood, the town hall meeting provided practical experience at speaking up, arguing points of view, and hammering out agreements, all elements of citizenship.

Church services also brought communities together, side by side in rows of pews, to pray and afterward, outside, to socialize. Before the birth of colonial newspapers, the sermon "stood alone . . . as the only regular medium of public communication . . . that combined religious, educational, and journalistic functions," according to historian Harry Stout. Churchgoing, in fact, was "the only event in public assembly that regularly brought the entire community together."[4] The sermons rankled some parishioners and inspired others. The congregants nodded or voiced approval without always heeding the good word. Religious services, however, encouraged people to gather, listen, and reflect in a communal way.

**FYI**

Contemporary American clergy are bound by the 1954 Johnson Amendment (named for its key sponsor, then U.S. Senator Lyndon B. Johnson [D-Texas]), which limits political speech of churches and other nonprofit organizations under penalty of losing their IRS tax-exempt status. Under the law, clergy cannot endorse or oppose candidates for elected office—a restriction applicable to sermons, although apparently ignored in many churches. It remained relatively uncontroversial for half a century, but after his inauguration in 2017, President Trump vowed at the National Prayer Breakfast to "totally destroy" the Johnson Amendment. Only Congress has that power and has chosen, so far, to keep the law in place.[5]

Anywhere people gathered in colonial America offered occasions for civic talk, particularly as folks went about their daily life, shopping for a new Sunday dress, buying stew meat, or picking up a tincture from the apothecary. They walked most places and encountered friends and strangers en route or inside cramped shops and businesses. Information—the newer the better—became a commodity to be traded and exchanged. Townspeople depended on customers, neighbors, and passersby for news. With business and political information in short supply, residents perked up especially upon hearing descriptions of developments in distant communities. A story or rumor traveled via word of mouth through settlements until it often boomeranged back to its original source. As spoken communication passed hither and yon, recipients enlarged the conversation by blending news of their own into the mix. Fleeting and factually suspect, oral news nonetheless found its way into the public sphere and, as it did, amplified ordinary voices that elites eventually heard.

The sermonizing, liquor-induced arguments and face-to-face exchanges of information only went so far, literally. Words on paper carried conversation to a broader audience across longer distances. A practice increasingly uncommon in the age of texting, letter writing produced a body of political communication that ranged from the eloquent and reasoned to the stilted and pompous. Thomas Jefferson and other prominent figures wrote about private matters, of course, but as public men, they also reached ordinary citizens through open letters intended as political essays. Their readers found the political musings as entertaining and informative as twenty-first-century citizens find our favorite newspaper columnists and cable commentators. The published letters of political leaders typically touched the country's psyche as deeply as oratory before a legislative assembly or a stump speech delivered in the town square. Colonial editors relied on letters, including those from abroad, to fill pages and sell newspapers and pamphlets.

Literate people of lower status wrote, too, about the mundane, certainly, but they put to paper an array of ideas, grievances, and requests—such as a servant arguing for emancipation from her master. Even personal letters circulated through communities and became topics of conversation. The addressees willingly passed around correspondence because nearly everyone enjoyed reading or hearing about worlds outside their own. Letters, in that sense, approximated personal postings on Facebook and Instagram. They contained fact-based accounts of births and deaths, crop failures, land disputes, smallpox outbreaks, and violent crimes, resembling an early form of citizen journalism found today in news reports posted online by nonprofessionals.

Aside from disseminating content, letter writing in itself served a liberating and participatory function—an exercise in autonomy. Women, children, and those without status or power drew strength and resolve from letter writing. Historian Konstantin Dierks believes correspondence in early America not only prompted social, economic, and political change; it also helped to create the middle class with its own agenda.[6] Unsigned letters and pseudonyms enabled thousands of disenfranchised citizens to contribute to civic dialogue when otherwise they would be ignored or silenced. In general, eighteenth-century lay correspondents crafted important accounts of a nation taking shape.

Events abroad further influenced public discourse. The expiration of the Licensing Act in 1695 unleashed a long-shackled British press. Until then, printers bowed under a strict censorship law that required the licensing of nearly all printing presses and the vetting of publications by a de facto censorship board with the benign name of "Stationers' Company." Once censorship laws were relaxed, England's newspapers provided editorials and commentary the colonial press gratefully appropriated once they finally crossed the Atlantic.

Widely circulated pamphlets and essays from freethinking British writers heightened demands for freedom and liberty in the colonies. Two British journalists, John Trenchard and Thomas Gordon, attracted receptive audiences through a series of essays, first published in the *London Journal* in the fall of 1720. Under the pseudonym "Cato," the pair produced 138 essays—or letters, as they were called—over three years. Colonial newspapers frequently quoted from the Cato letters and reprinted them entirely. In Cato Letter 15, Trenchard and Gordon wrote, "Where a man cannot call his tongue his own, he can scarce call anything else his own. Whoever would overthrow the liberty of the nation, must begin by subduing the freedom of speech; a thing terrible to publick traitors."[7] Rightly, historians credit Cato for championing freedom of expression in early America.

In the 1730s, the colonial press amounted to fewer than a dozen newspapers, all small weeklies. Their impact, though, was disproportionate to their circulation. Copies rarely landed in the gutter. Wrinkled and smudged, they were read and reread, passed along throughout the community and carried on foot or horseback to outlying areas. Newspapers gained respect as advocates for a people yearning for freedom. Several bold publications directly challenged the Crown's oppression.

## An Immigrant Printer Confronts the King's Authority

From the first newspaper published on American soil in 1690 until the adoption of the First Amendment in 1791, scores of publishers—more tradesmen than journalists—promoted freedom of the press and nourished the need for citizens to be informed and heard. They did so at great personal risk. One of these early heroes was the immigrant John Peter Zenger.[8]

Zenger learned the printing trade as a thirteen-year-old apprentice newly arrived from Germany. He was taught to set type, one letter at a time, and slowly assemble columns that would be locked in a page-sized frame. He then sponged the type with ink, laid a piece of coarse paper over the page, and, using a strong forearm, cranked a heavy metal plate downward to imprint the paper. He hung each sheet to dry, repeating the process hundreds of times. Once dry, the other side of the paper was printed. The work was tedious, tiring, and dirty. One edition of a two-to four-page newspaper took dozens of hours to produce.

After eight years of indentured servitude, Zenger became a freeman and by his mid-30s owned a print shop in the city of New York. As he earned a modest income, Zenger probably had little inkling that a political storm was about to engulf him. King George II's recently appointed governor, William Cosby, so alienated the colony's leaders that a group of them asked Zenger to publish an anti-Cosby newspaper, the *New-York Weekly Journal*. Zenger would set the type and run the press; his partners would provide the content. Starting with its inaugural edition on November 5, 1733, the newspaper unceasingly attacked Cosby's character and actions, often by means of anonymous accusations and veiled insults. If he had any qualms about what we now call journalistic bias, he evidently overcame them after considering the more dangerous threat of George II to democratic freedom in the colonies.

Zenger did the bidding of others, but he was no pawn, knowing he bore legal responsibility for the newspaper; other colonial governors had punished printers for publications far less critical of the king's rule. Cosby's ultimate weapon against Zenger was the charge of seditious libel, a remnant of English common law imported to the colonies. Unlike the civil offense of libel—an individual suing to protect his or her good name, standing, or livelihood—seditious libel constituted a serious crime, at one time punishable in England by death. Seditious libel applied to speech, images, or printed words that brought public officials or institutions into "hatred or contempt", and thereby threatened insurrection against the government. In colonial America, punishment for seditious libel amounted to fines and jail sentences. The mere existence of seditious libel laws deterred the publication of words remotely seen as an affront to public officials.

Knowing the risks, Zenger's newspaper nonetheless kept taunting Cosby, including a published assertion that the governor improperly permitted a French navy vessel to reconnoiter the city's harbor defenses. It hinted of treason on Cosby's part. The governor retaliated by ordering copies of the *Weekly Journal* burned outside city hall, within view of a pillory. Cosby also unsuccessfully sought indictments against Zenger from grand juries composed of ordinary citizens sympathetic to Zenger's cause. Exasperated, Cosby ordered the sheriff to arrest Zenger. Unable to raise funds for bail, Zenger stayed locked in the attic of city hall until his trial date in August 1735. During his nine-month confinement, Zenger's friends and family kept publishing the newspaper, and its editorial attacks on Cosby continued.

On August 4, as the sheriff led Zenger into the dock, a murmur arose in the crowded courtroom. Addressing the court, Zenger's attorney, Andrew Hamilton (no, not related to Alexander Hamilton), adopted a bold strategy. He admitted to the court that Zenger printed libelous accusations, but he urged the jurors to accept truth and lack of malice as defenses. Hamilton told the jury that the prosecution had the burden of proving the falsity of Zenger's publications. In his powerful summation, he said:

> The question before the Court and you, Gentlemen of the jury, is not of small or private concern. It is not the cause of one poor printer, nor of New York alone, which you are now trying. No! It may in its consequence affect every free man that lives under a British government on the main of America. It is the best cause. It is the cause of liberty.

The jurors, defying the judge's instructions to convict, took ten minutes to acquit Zenger. Cheers erupted in the crowded courtroom, and the celebration spilled into the streets.

The Zenger case was a symbolic victory for freedom of the press in the colonies. The Declaration of Independence was still forty-one years away, but clearly the king's rule was ebbing, and an American-forged identity was forming, to culminate in the Constitution and the Bill of Rights. The fledgling press imitated rhetorical styles from British newspapers, particularly satire, which the *Weekly Journal* used liberally to ridicule authorities. James Alexander, the newspaper's unofficial editor, referred to Cosby,

## Marginalia

The pillory, a medieval instrument of torture, was used sparingly in colonial America. It shamed its victims while inflicting physical discomfort in full view of the community. An offender, usually a petty criminal, stood upright, held in place by hinged cross boards that locked head and hands. Passersby pelted the victims with insults and rotten vegetables. This public display was intended as a deterrent for objectionable behavior, including the production of publications by pesky newspaper editors.

though not by name, as a mischievous monkey that its master (the king) needed to recall home. Satire stung public officials more sharply than dry news accounts of misdeeds.[9]

## A War of Words before a Volley of Muskets

The Zenger verdict did not lead to a ban on seditious libel prosecutions. Nor did it free editors from the specter of censorship or embolden them to challenge government power at will. The ordeal left Zenger shaken; he had a business to maintain and a family to support. Still, the *Weekly Journal* sustained its campaign against Cosby, who died a year later, cursing Zenger to the end, according to Eric Burns in *Infamous Scribblers*.[10]

While heartened by the trial's outcome, some of his fellow publisher-editors, knowing the ordeal he went through, avoided controversy as best they could. Freedom of the press was far from established. Constitutional scholar Leonard W. Levy said the image that colonial Americans overall cherished freedom of expression "is a hallucination of sentiment that ignores history."[11] Intolerance for unorthodox, heretical, and scandalous speech was widespread, particularly when aimed at public officials and colonial assemblies that in Zenger's time were generally loyal to the king. Using contempt power inherited from the British House of Commons, the state assemblies tried to quash political speech that allegedly defamed its members or condemned their actions. Retribution could be swift, with sergeants at arms dispatched to haul offenders into chambers for chastisement, fines, or physical punishment like the pillory. Levy, though, later admitted that he understated the independence of those editors and firebrands who defied government orders to cease and desist.[12]

The Zenger case earned a hearty hurrah from common folks who considered seditious libel an anathema to democracy. The case fortified an evolving philosophy within the colonies that the people should govern, not the appointed rulers sent to America from abroad. Aggressive newspapers spoke for the people and set an example for homebrewed dissent.

Despite some reticence, colonial newspapers, ministers, lawyers, and merchants circulated hundreds of pamphlets, adding spice to the political stew. These mainly anonymous publications allowed authors to spout off without the degree of legal liability faced by editors. Ranging from five to forty-eight pages, the pamphlets often included subjects less inflammatory than revolution, such as advice on planting crops or leading a moral life. By far, though, the best-selling tracts criticized oppressive laws and policies. Such dissent included broadsides—single sheets of densely packed type brimming with political vitriol—tacked to trees and tavern doors. Pamphlets and broadsides stepped into the breach when newspapers exercised self-restraint.

The rudimentary channels of communication in colonial times grew more political as relationships between the Crown and its colonial subjects, in turn, grew more strained. At times the Crown's representatives practiced laissez-faire rule, but by the 1760s, George III, who had succeeded his grandfather, George II, and Parliament imposed more taxes. They also demanded compensation for British troops quartered on American soil and cracked down on public protests.

Political militancy escalated in the years leading to the Declaration of Independence. Activists, including many newspaper publishers, increasingly resented attempts by the British to suppress colonial dissent through petty laws and nuisance taxes, notably the Stamp Act imposed by Parliament in 1765. The law required that a wide range of documents produced in the colonies—commercial contracts, newspapers, wills, marriage licenses, diplomas, pamphlets, and even playing cards—carry a tax stamp. The Stamp Act and other unpopular actions by the Crown politicized printers to evolve "into a new species of journalist, the writer or editor . . . whose goal is not just to keep his press busy but to change the world," according to Christopher Daly in his 2012 history of American journalism.[13] The transition included taking clear sides and clashing with opposing points of view. To an extent, what some colonists and editors meant by freedom of the press, Daly said, "was freedom for the press they agreed with." Patriots who sought to break free from British rule still lived alongside loyal subjects of George III, and arguments were common. Occasionally, both revolutionary and loyalist newspapers suffered boycotts, threats, and mob violence from angry opponents.

The stamp tax heightened resistance and led to frequent clashes with British authorities in Boston and elsewhere in the colonies. Two volatile forces moved to the forefront: Samuel Adams, second cousin to John Adams, who later became the second U.S. president, and a collection of societies known popularly as the Sons of Liberty. Samuel Adams denounced the Stamp Act in essays in the *Boston Gazette* and by name accused local stamp tax collectors of disloyalty. Historical records show Adams was in league with the Boston Sons of Liberty, who welcomed both gentlemen and ruffians. Egged on by Adams, its members threatened public officials, burned government offices, hanged tax collectors in effigy outside of their homes, and, reportedly, in a cruel and potentially fatal practice of the day, tarred and feathered a few opponents.[14] The revolutionary fervor boiled over at times; divisive confrontations were part of our American DNA from the beginning.

Adams reluctantly turned to mob action, which he knew often succeeded when words alone failed. The tactics put the king under intense pressure, and Parliament repealed the Stamp Act in March 1766. But Adams and the Sons of Liberty were far from finished. Driven by an unabating hatred of British rule, they pressed forward on other grievances.

The barrage of verbal attacks spurred additional demonstrations. A few turned violent, including one in 1770 known as the Boston Massacre. It erupted when adults joined children to throw snowballs and hunks of ice at a contingent of armed British "redcoats" who occupied the city and enforced Crown authority. Such encounters were common, and in the face of persistent harassment, the redcoats grew increasingly skittish. The inevitable happened on March 5. British soldiers fired into the crowd, killing three at the scene and wounding two others who died later.

Three years later, Adams and the Sons of Liberty pulled off a brazen act of defiance known to generations of American schoolchildren as the Boston Tea Party. Once again, the opposition to taxation was the stimulus, and the popular story of patriots posing as renegades who boarded cargo ships and dumped bundles of tea into the harbor oversimplifies what happened. Historian Benjamin Carp, author of *Defiance of the Patriots: The Boston Tea Party and the Making of America*, said the British Tea Act of 1773 was a gambit to bail out the financially strapped British East India Company by unloading 544,000 pounds of old tea on the colonies at a bargain price.[15] So why protest? Carp said the Sons of Liberty considered the Tea Act a ploy for justifying other tax measures. The escapade ended up as a public relations victory without injury, looting, or damage to property—other than the stale tea. Outraged by Boston's resistance and the destruction of Crown property, Parliament passed a series of punitive laws known in Boston as the Intolerable Acts and in England as the Coercive Acts. Rather than breaking rebel resolve in Massachusetts, the laws provoked further acts of resistance and strengthened patriotic bonds among the colonies.

The Boston Harbor vandalism prompted cheers in some colonial quarters and fears in others. The people were not of a singular mind; times were tense. John Adams heard folks in Maine describe the tea party as "mischief and wickedness." Adams showed his ambivalence in a letter published later in which he justified destructive acts so long as they were carried out for the public good against intolerable policies. Maine historian J. Dennis Robinson summed up the dilemma Adams faced: "The real question,

Adams knew, was—how can we tell the difference and who decides?"[16] The question is particularly relevant today as we watch police cars burn or crowds violating curfew orders and recall that is how our nation took hold.

If domestic activists and writers dominated the conversation of independence early on, it took an English transplant, Thomas Paine, to energize the masses and frame the rhetorical role of the press in a republic. Paine met Benjamin Franklin on a visit to London, and with the great man's blessings, Paine sailed to America and in short order began writing for the *Pennsylvania Magazine*. Paine developed a colloquial style, easily read and understood in its language of freedom and revolt. He reached unsurpassed popularity after publishing his pamphlet *Common Sense* in January 1776. It became America's first best seller, with more than 120,000 copies bought in its first three months. Possibly half a million were sold in its first year in a country with a population of under three million, which included about 700,000 slaves, according to media critic Jon Katz.[17] Newspapers scrambled to reprint it; people quoted it to one another. *Common Sense*, a cry to arms, moved the country closer to the Declaration of Independence later in 1776, on July 4. According to Katz:

> If any father has been forsaken by his children it is Thomas Paine. Statues of the man should greet incoming journalism students; his words should be chiseled above newsroom doors and taped to laptops, guiding the communications media through their many travails, controversies, and challenges. . . . The modern-day press has forgotten this brilliant, lonely, socially awkward progenitor, who pioneered the concept of the uncensored flow of ideas . . . in the service of the then-radical proposition that people should control their own lives.[18]

Paine believed that journalists needed to be bold and courageous in expressing support for independence, and, indeed, there were heroes among them.

When fighting broke out in 1775, revolutionary writers and editors joined the ranks, armed mainly with quills, ink, and galleys of type, although a handful actually drew swords and went into battle. Editorials and commentary rallied the people and boosted morale as the war ebbed and flowed. With the British defeat, the press turned its attention to the challenges of creating a national government that would survive and prosper. By the time the Constitution was ratified, about one hundred newspapers served the whole of the nation. Some of them had fewer than two hundred subscribers, but their influence on public opinion was decisive for the ratification of the Constitution and the Bill of Rights.

**Marginalia**

As much as the first citizens came to depend on their newspapers, they surely struggled to consume their content, usually set in long gray columns of minuscule type without large headlines, photographs, or graphics. Reports and commentary were often bogged down in stilted prose. Reading a newspaper required both mental concentration and a strong set of spectacles.

## After War and Missteps, a Meeting of Minds and Words

Imagine an infant nation, one still recovering from a brutal eight-year struggle for independence, obviously challenged to create a new government in a postwar period of dissent and disillusionment. The challenge included a revolt by debt-strapped farmers in Massachusetts and the failed first attempt at nationhood. America needed both structure and order to stave off chaos. An assembly of distinguished lawyers, diplomats, merchants, and planters representing their respective states answered the call and embarked on a journey with an uncertain destination.[19]

In May 1787, fifty-five out of seventy-four state-appointed delegates to the Constitutional Convention gathered in Philadelphia to reengineer, most thought, the unworkable Articles of Confederation, a constitution-like document drafted in 1777 and ratified by the thirteen original colonies in 1781. Among its shortcomings, the Articles of Confederation left the government powerless to raise operating revenue. The articles needed to be strengthened or replaced. An account from the National Archives sets the scene: "Freshly spread dirt covered the cobblestone street in front of the Pennsylvania State House, protecting the men inside from the sound of passing carriages and carts. Guards stood at the entrances to ensure that the curious were kept at a distance."[20] To acclaimed historian Forrest McDonald, the quality of the delegates was unparalleled: "It would be impossible in America today to assemble a group of people with anything near the combined experience, learning and wisdom that the 55 authors of the Constitution took with them to Philadelphia in the summer of 1787."[21] Perhaps McDonald overstates, but, no doubt, it was an extraordinary group.

The Constitutional Convention convened with hope for its success outweighing confidence. The delegates were relieved when the commander of the Continental Army, General George Washington, agreed to preside as the convention's president. Washington almost stayed at home to manage his Mount Vernon estate and avoid taking on the weighty responsibility of nation building. He finally set aside his reservations and, at age fifty-five, journeyed by carriage to Philadelphia, arriving to cheers and a thirteen-gun salute. Washington chose the role of moderator. He let others, especially James Madison, lead deliberations. But his presence in military uniform lent an air of gravitas and resolve no one else in the country could provide.

Historians credit Madison as the "Father of the Constitution." He downplayed his accomplishments, saying they were "the work of many heads and many hands." Nonetheless, he assumed a leading role from the outset. Madison hoped to create a new federal government, not merely revise the existing one. He prepared for the convention by immersing himself in political literature for guidance. While waiting for tardy delegates to arrive, he drafted the Virginia Plan, which became the Constitution's blueprint. In it he proposed a bicameral legislature and a separation of powers divided among the executive, legislative, and judicial branches. Once the convention opened, Madison persuaded others of the merits of his proposals and reasoned with those in opposition. His ability to communicate in writing and in person helped shepherd the nation into existence. Madison belonged to a political-intellectual collective of Founders about whom Harvard political philosopher Danielle Allen concluded: "These men knew how to get things done with words. That was a crucial source of their power, so much so that we could stretch the point about as far as it will go and say: *this country was born of talk.*"[22]

No matter his interpersonal prowess, Madison anticipated a contentious, difficult process. The would-be nation lacked a unifying vision to ensure an uncomplicated birth. The delegates confronted a number of potentially explosive issues, greatest among them slavery, which went unresolved, and deep disagreements over states' rights, presidential powers, and the allotment of seats in Congress. Participants knew the fate of the nation was entrusted to them; failure was not an option. By experience and inclination, they worked together, tested new approaches, cajoled, argued, negotiated, and compromised. Madison took copious notes, released in 1840, four years after his death. In 1787, there were no contemporaneous news accounts. Sequestered behind locked doors and sealed windows, the delegates imposed an information blackout, almost unthinkable in the media-saturated environment of the twenty-first century. Had the convention occurred two hundred years later, a small army of journalists would have camped at the scene, resembling the spectacle of the 1995 O. J. Simpson trial. As it was, the Framers deliberated free of outside distractions, able to speak frankly and modify political positions to build consensus. The absence of the press and public in the gallery likely saved the convention from disintegrating into political theater.

Any number of sticking points arose as the delegates hammered out an agreement. One in particular stood out—how to choose the president and vice president. It was no simple matter. Not all delegates trusted ordinary citizens with a direct national vote, assuming they lacked the requisite civic knowledge and fearing that a populist president might lead the gullible astray; they preferred that Congress handle that important duty. Other delegates worried that a president, generally expected to be both independent and a check on Congress, would be neither and instead beholden to whichever faction held congressional power. A third contingent, mainly from slaveholding states, worried that the North's clear population advantage in a popular election would forever deny a southerner the presidency.

The delegates settled on a cumbersome mechanism that called for "electors" from each state to officially "elect" the president and vice president. The plan became Article II, Section 1, of the proposed Constitution. Neither citizens nor Congress would decide, at least directly. The job would go to intermediaries. After state election officials hand-counted citizen ballots, a slate of electors loyal to each ticket of candidates would travel to the state capital and formally verify which candidates garnered the highest number of popular votes. The number of electors amounted to the total of senators (two) and representatives (apportioned at a ratio of one for every thirty thousand residents) allotted to each state. The South gained politically with a concession that slaves would count in elections as three-fifths a free person. Article II, Section 1, was sorely bereft on details, leaving it up to each state to determine who would be electors and how they would function. Its inclusion, however, allowed the delegates to circumvent a potentially disastrous stalemate.

**FYI**

The flaws inherent in Article II, Section 1, quickly surfaced in the 1800 presidential election. Thomas Jefferson defeated incumbent president John Adams, but when the electors, pursuant to Article II, met to officially name the new president, the unexpected occurred. Representatives of each state cast an equal number of votes for Jefferson *and* his vice presidential running mate, Aaron Burr. Why? The Constitution initially failed to provide for separate votes for "President" and "Vice-President." The result: Each candidate received seventy-three votes.

As Article II additionally stated, a tie required the House of Representatives to decide who would be president. Then another unanticipated complication: The House was controlled by Federalists, whose candidate, John Adams, lost the popular vote. It took five days and thirty-six ballots before Adams's vice president, Alexander Hamilton, broke the logjam by deeming Jefferson a safer choice than Burr. (Burr later killed Hamilton in a duel.) Ratification of the Twelfth Amendment in 1804 essentially cleaned up the original confusion over how electors cast votes and established procedures for what came to be called the Electoral College.

The Electoral College did not work well then, and it certainly presents problems today, when a candidate loses the national vote yet wins enough electoral votes to become president, as happened when Trump defeated Clinton in 2016 and four other times: 1824, 1876, 1888, and 2000 (George W. Bush over Al Gore). Under the Electoral College system, victory goes to the candidate who amasses 270 of the 538 total electoral votes. Although electors are apportioned according to the population of each state, even the least populous states are constitutionally guaranteed a minimum of three electors (one representative and two senators), potentially giving a preponderance of small states decisive weight over a lesser number of highly populated states.

Proposals to abolish the Electoral College and elect by popular vote require a constitutional amendment, a decidedly uphill battle, but the subject still comes up in national conversation.[23]

A related barrier to achieving truly democratic representation is gerrymandering, that is, the act of redrawing boundaries of legislative districts, both state and congressional, to benefit one political party over another, but mainly Republicans over Democrats. In many states, the rural state representatives outnumber those from urban areas. That enables the minority party to control the legislature and influence the outcome of elections to the U.S. House of Representatives. In Wisconsin, for example, the popular vote for Republicans in 2018 was 44.7 percent; but Republicans controlled 64.6 percent of the seats in the statehouse. Democrats have legally challenged the fairness of partisan redistricting but without much success. As a result, majoritarian rule at times yields to minoritarian stratagem.

While there was keen interest in the proceedings, the nation as a whole waited patiently, trusting Washington and the other leaders to get the job done. After more than four months of debate and several rejected drafts, the Constitution was ready for approval. It was a remarkable accomplishment. The convention had opened eleven days past its appointed starting date and included recesses for the delegates to travel home and back. Like a community barn raising, the Framers, in their work, cut beams, raised them into place, secured the connecting joints, and erected a roof. By mid-September, they stood back to assess the product of their labors, not knowing whether it would survive ratification, much less endure the nation's inevitable growing pains.

What did they behold? A newly constituted United States of America that should be a "republic," a Latin-based term suggesting a *structure* of government and a *philosophy* that sovereignty—supreme power—rested with the people. Most of the Framers believed in government of, by, and for people, not rule by a monarch, the noble class, Congress, the clergy, or the military. The people would exercise sovereignty through the ballot box. Those they elected to federal office would act on their behalf in enacting legislation, setting policy, and making a host of minor and major decisions.

Historians later called the creation of the Constitution a grand experiment that tested an uncertain hypothesis: Could a once-subjugated populace, after turning rebellious, peacefully transition into unfamiliar roles of deliberative and dutiful citizens? Could a newly united nation succeed if melded from thirteen separate and competing political systems? To Pulitzer Prize-winning historian Gordon S. Wood, such a formidable task depended less on political processes than on the fortitude and commitment of the people. "Republics," he wrote, "had to hold themselves together from the bottom up, ultimately, from their citizens' willingness to take up arms to defend their country and to sacrifice their private desires for the sake of the public good."[24] Did the Founders trust common people too much? The question uneasily hung over the Constitutional Convention in its final days.

When the delegates gathered to vote on September 17, 1787, the Constitution's passage was far from a sure thing. Jill Lepore's riveting history of the United States describes how the elder statesman of the convention, Benjamin Franklin, seemed lukewarm in his support. On the convention's last day, Franklin, then eighty-one and wracked with gout, asked a younger colleague to read aloud a statement addressed to George Washington, the presiding officer. "Mr. President," he wrote, "I confess that there are several parts of this constitution which I do not at present approve, but I am not sure I shall never approve them." Age, Franklin explained, caused him to doubt his own judgment more frequently and listen more thoughtfully to the opinion of others. He closed with a measured endorsement: "Thus

I consent, Sir, to this Constitution because I expect no better, and because I am not sure, that it is not the best."[25] Later that day, the delegates, excepting a handful of holdouts, signed the four-page parchment document. Newspapers reprinted the entire proposed Constitution, and copies quickly spread from hand to hand, household to household, town to town, and across oceans to reach foreign lands.

American editors generally marked the event with effusive prose, such as an account published on September 24, 1787, in New York's *Daily Advertiser:*

> We have now offered to us a Constitution, which, if happily received, will disappoint our enemies, render us safe and happy at home, and respected abroad. Heaven, in mercy to us, has furnished this auspicious event, in order to snatch us from impending ruin, and to re-establish this favored land on the substantial basis of liberty, honor and virtue. The means of wiping opprobrium from our country are now in our power; let us neither reject nor forego them. It will be the duty of all honest, well-disposed men, friends to peace and good government, as well in this State as throughout the Union, to cultivate and diffuse, as far as their walk may extend, a spirit of submission to the counsels of this great patriot band; who have sought to procure, and have been anxious in their endeavors to establish, our liberty, and aggrandize our fame.[26]

As everyday people pondered the proposed Constitution, they surely fixed on its three-word opening, highlighted as it was in bold script:

> *We the People* of the United States, in Order to form a more perfect Union, establish Justice, insure domestic Tranquility, provide for the common defence, promote the general Welfare, and secure the Blessings of Liberty to ourselves and our Posterity, do ordain and establish this Constitution for the United States of America.[27]

People rejoiced from Concord, Massachusetts, where volleys of deadly gunfire in 1775 had opened the War of Independence, to Savannah, Georgia, where British troops in 1782 pulled their colors and withdrew to England. The signing of the Treaty of Paris on September 3, 1783, officially ended the war.

Despite celebrations, an inescapable question remained. What happens next? The time had come for war veterans, shopkeepers, and farmers to weigh in. No other issue loomed as large. On unsteady legs, the nation toddled toward a decision on ratification. People who were scattered about in cities, towns, and farmsteads understood the gravity of the moment. Would the Constitution fail? If rejected by the states, would the nation muster the resolve to undergo another constitutional convention? Would the states, instead, reinstate a confederation to address issues expediently and settle for a loosely formed *united states*, lowercase, without a strong central government and a president?

In hindsight, the newest citizens acquitted themselves well. In his massive 2021 examination of the Constitution's creation, *The Words That Made Us*, Akhil Reed Amar commended "common folk" for their involvement. "Americans high and low participated not just by voting," he wrote, "but by speaking and listening, writing and reading—by *conversing* with each other pro and con, up and down the continent, in newspapers and elsewhere."[28] Amar's reference to "conversation" implies that people read, assessed, and discussed the proposed Constitution as it applied to themselves and their communities. Another recent analysis cited the document's relative brevity, its widespread dissemination in print, and the 80 percent literacy rate among adult white American males to explain its popular reception. The author, Linda Colley, pointed to a critical linguistic revision to a draft of the Constitution contributed by twenty-five-year-old New York delegate Gouverneur Morris, who altered the opening sentence from "We the people of the states of New Hampshire, Massachusetts, Rhode Island," listing all thirteen, to read "We, the People of the United States." According to Colley, "Instead of drawing attention to the separate, all-too discordant states, this word change presumed a united American nation which in reality did not as yet exist."[29] Perhaps the aspirational promise of a unified nation helped overcome objections raised by individual states.

The Founders hoped to avoid the destructive power of what they called "factions." Ironically, they themselves eventually succumbed at times to petty party politics. But surely Jefferson, Adams, and Madison never anticipated today's extreme partisanship and how it precludes compromise even when the health of the nation is at stake. Here the lessons of the past stand in stark contrast to the present. The founding generation accomplished the biggest job of all—they created a nation in four months. They committed to conversations (and arguments) that would achieve common ground.

As state legislatures considered ratification, debate intensified between two competing parties—the Republicans, or Antifederalists, and Federalists. The Republicans argued that the Constitution gave too much power to the federal government at the expense of state and local governments. Thomas Jefferson, although then still serving as America's ambassador to France, influenced and supported the Constitution, but demanded specific, written protections of individual liberties hard won on the battlefield, among them freedom of speech and trial by jury. "A Bill of Rights is what the people are entitled to against every government, and what no just government should refuse, or rest on inference," Jefferson wrote in December 1787 in a letter to James Madison.[30]

The Federalists had a strategic journalistic advantage in helping public opinion emerge—a collection of eighty-five essays written by Madison, Alexander Hamilton, and John Jay, all signees to the Constitution. Published under the pseudonym "Publius," the essays appeared serially between October 1787 and April 1788 primarily in New York newspapers. People clamored to hear or read them. Newspapers outside the city carried excerpts. Some historians believe the publication of these essays, later called the *Federalist Papers*, carried the day for ratification. On the two hundredth anniversary of the Constitution in 1987, historian Robert Allen Rutland stressed the importance of journalists in the ratification process:

> Imagine the difficulties the Federalists would have faced had the circumstances been reversed, and instead of having the support of some seventy-five newspapers they had faced their hostility. Even the name of Washington would have been difficult to invoke as the final argument in favor of the Constitution. Moreover, without this newspaper battle, the debate of a bill of rights would have been muted and probably would have led to nothing in the First Congress.[31]

Madison came to appreciate why so many citizens wanted legally binding guarantees to prevent the federal government from overstepping its bounds. He and his allies promised to add a bill of rights during the first Congress—if Republicans supported ratification of the Constitution.

After a two-thirds majority of nine states approved ratification in 1788, newly elected members of Congress slowly assembled in New York City, the first capital. There was no apparent sense of urgency. Stragglers delayed the scheduled March 4 opening for nearly a month. But once the gavel sounded, Congress showed no signs of lethargy. In quick succession, its members took oaths of office; adopted procedural rules; chose General Washington as president and John Adams as vice president; introduced bills to set tariffs and raise revenues; and established the departments of war and foreign affairs, the latter subsequently renamed the U.S. Department of State.

Madison again proved a formidable figure, belying his indistinct speaking voice and slight physical stature. He concentrated on fulfilling his pledge to add a list of individual liberties to the Constitution. He proposed twenty amendments that the House of Representatives reduced to seventeen. In the Senate, revisions and debate whittled five more proposed amendments. On September 25, 1789, twelve amendments went to the state assemblies for ratification. The original First and Second Amendments fell short of approval; number three moved to the top of the list. That happenstance resulted in the First Amendment protections heading the Bill of Rights, a stature that seemed appropriate to Madison.

Madison failed, though, to achieve all he sought. He had hoped to convince Congress to include the provision that "no state shall violate the equal rights of conscience, or of the freedom of the press." It passed the House but failed in the Senate. (It was not until 1925 that the Supreme Court declared that the First Amendment applied to state governments as well as to the federal government.) On December 15, 1791, with Virginia voting approval, the Bill of Rights became law. It proved decisive in the formation of the republic, although in 1791 no one knew how incredibly important those ten untested amendments would be in shaping the nation's future.

## The Glory and Mythology of the Founding

We tend to view the history of America's origins through a romanticized lens. The familiar slogans we learned as schoolchildren—"United we stand, divided we fall" and "Give me liberty or give me death"—gloss over the struggles of blending the privileged class with the common person, as each pressed for a say in government and their fair share of the good life. Politics more or less remained the sport of gentlemen. In speeches, essays, and correspondence, the Founders applauded the grit and wisdom of "the people." In private, though, many among the wealthy doubted the judgment of the masses and preferred to limit the public's civic role to voting, not active participation in discussing or resolving the issues of the day. They underestimated the determination of the people, partly because they knew the "public" only superficially, seldom meeting ordinary people outside those who served them meals, stabled their horses, or cobbled their boots. But as neophyte citizens grew more assertive and visible, the privileged class accepted a more inclusive view of public life.

When we refer to the "Framers," "Founders," or "Founding Fathers," we apply these terms generically to a collection of men, maybe 150 or so. This elite group included those who signed the Declaration of Independence, led the Revolutionary War, enacted the Articles of Confederation, created the Constitution, and bestowed on us the Bill of Rights. Citizens of today rightly appreciate the Founders' contributions, but best-selling biographies that portray Washington, Jefferson, Madison, and Hamilton as superstars glorify as much as they edify. Less renowned figures also contributed greatly to the birth of the nation, and most of them either knew, influenced, or collaborated with the so-called Founders. They include Gouverneur Morris, mentioned earlier, for his deft editing of the proposed Constitution; Roger Sherman of Connecticut, a self-taught career public servant who championed support for the Constitution and Bill of Rights; and John Dickinson, whose "Letters from a Farmer in Pennsylvania to the Inhabitants of the British Colonies" earned him the moniker "Penman of the Revolution." Neither George Washington nor any of his colleagues heard themselves called the "Founding Fathers." In fact, use of the phrase only became popular in the early twentieth century after Warren G. Harding introduced it at the Republican National Convention in 1916.[32]

By whatever label, the Founders exerted power over the lives of citizens of lower status and lesser means. A distinguished body of white, landed males, a majority of whom bought and sold Black slaves, also blocked the potential contributions of Indigenous people, women, young adults, and other human beings they treated as less-than-full persons. Had they been included in the nation building, the story of America and its founding might read far differently.

In a recent critique of the Constitution, Harvard's Danielle Allen called it a morally flawed work of practical genius. The great-great-granddaughter of a slave who counted as three-fifths of a free person, Allen argued that we must look for the diamond under the muck of the Constitution's origins. "Those who wrote the version ratified centuries ago do not own the version we live by today. We do. It's ours, an adaptable instrument used to define self-government among free and equal citizens—and to secure our ongoing moral education about that most important human endeavor. We are all responsible for our Constitution, and that fact is empowering."[33] Our later discussion of citizenship builds on the same idea of a flawed foundation, but one that continues to support enormously successful changes.

This abridged introduction to the founding barely scrapes the surface of early U.S. history, but it can refresh public memory and remind us of gaps in contemporary understanding. Citizens need an occasional booster shot of civic awareness. In the 2020s, while we comfortably recite the Pledge of Allegiance, if someone asked us to explain the difference between "republic" and "democracy," words might fail: "Well, a republic . . . well, you know, it's . . ." The Founders used both words to describe the country, and they did not always distinguish "representative" democracy from a "pure" or "direct" democracy, an unrealistic system the Founders never seriously considered. So, is it a republic? A democracy? The generally accepted answer: a little of both and not simply one or the other. But it is important for us to know the difference. We value a democracy and the ideals of freedom and equality, even if not fully realized by all Americans over the life of the nation. By understanding what is meant by a *republic*, we acknowledge that the Founders entrusted *citizens* with the ultimate civic responsibility, while knowing not everyone would accept it.

## *"Make No Law" Comes into Clearer Focus*

The historical record leaves little doubt about the Founders' solid commitment to a free press as fundamental to a free nation. Jefferson, for one, eloquently and persistently supported freedom of the press. From personal experience, he knew the press at times served to advance purely political agendas, falsehoods, rumors, and other unfounded information. During his second term in 1806 an irked President Jefferson wrote to a colleague in Massachusetts: "I recollect nothing new & true worthy communicating to you. As for what is not true you will always find abundance in the newspapers."[34] He expected far better behavior from an institution he so championed. But Jefferson resisted the urge to silence his foes in the press, standing firm in the belief that even an imperfect press nourished and sustained democracy. His defense of journalism was measured yet unmistakable:

> It is so difficult to draw a clear line of separation between the abuse and the wholesome use of the press, that as yet we have found it better to trust the public judgment, rather than the magistrate, with the discrimination between truth and falsehood. And hitherto the public judgment has performed that office with wonderful correctness.[35]

He restated the rationale of the marketplace of ideas theory of John Milton's 1644 essay *Areopagitica*—permit ideas and information to reach the public sphere and the people will discern truth from deception. At least that was the hope.

Adopting the First Amendment in 1791 did not guarantee freedom of expression for succeeding generations. It could not, in part because the Founders said little about how these untested freedoms would play out in daily life. A single sentence of forty-five words, strung together by two semicolons and three commas, encapsulated America's commitment: "Congress shall make no law respecting an establishment of religion, or prohibiting the free exercise thereof; or abridging the freedom of speech, or of the press; or the right of the people peaceably to assemble, and to petition the government for a redress of grievances." It did not elaborate on, for example, what constituted "abridgement" of speech or "peaceable" assembly.

The Founders generally regarded freedom of the press as freedom to *publish*. The free press clause, according to Michael Schudson in *The Good Citizen*, protected journalism as long as it corresponded with the goals of the central government.[36] The country no longer needed a revolutionary press to stir up dissent. Subsequent generations reconsidered the Founders' intent and more broadly defined freedom of the press, which we detail in chapter 4. For many Founders, though, a free press meant one expected to act responsibly and patriotically.

Freedom for journalists to report, cover newsworthy events, and investigate public corruption developed in the nineteenth century, as newspapers, by then attracting advertisers in search of mass audiences, transitioned from organs of partisan politics to businesses seeking sizable profits. But to the Founders, the freedom of press clause was mainly an appendage to the freedom of speech clause. Freedom of the press enabled the people to project their points of view and acquire information through the printed word.

Few American leaders in 1791 took the "make no law" provision as an absolute. Jefferson, for example, wrote in 1788 in an exchange of letters with James Madison, "A declaration that the Federal Government will never restrain the presses from printing anything they please will not take away the liability of the printers for false facts printed."[37] Jefferson echoed the legal consensus of his day that government, principally Congress, could not abridge freedom of the press by prior restraint, that is, laws or actions that prevent publication or pre-censor content. The Founders believed the First Amendment ought to yield on special occasions to accomplish *legitimate functions* of government and protect the *public good*, yet both are rather vague concepts.

The Jefferson-Madison correspondence referred as well to press *liability* under a legal theory known as "subsequent punishment." The leading proponent of subsequent punishment was William Blackstone (1723-80). His influential treatise, *Commentaries on the Laws of England*, published prior to the Declaration of Independence, explained the extent of freedom of the press as he saw it: "Every freeman has an undoubted right to lay what sentiments he pleases before the public: to forbid this, is to destroy the freedom of the press: but if he publishes what is improper, mischievous, or illegal, he must take the consequence of his own temerity."[38] Blackstone's theory, then, would permit publication without licensing and prepublication review, but it held writers and publishers responsible for any legal consequences of their speech or printed words—consequences that included possible prosecution for seditious libel. Subsequent punishment became known for its *chilling effect* on expression, meaning that the prospect of punishment, litigation, or sanctions was so immediate that it discourages speech. In a contemporary comparison: Prior restraint *kills* speech; subsequent punishment *chills* speech.

Blackstone, a British citizen, provided the raw material used to construct the Constitution and Bill of Rights. Other public men from that time also influenced the Founders. The Enlightenment, a philosophical movement that captured the attention of eighteenth-century European intellectuals, argued for a society guided by intellect, reason, personal rights, and public discourse rather than dogma and the divine right of monarchs. French philosopher Voltaire (1694-1778) campaigned relentlessly for freedom of speech and inquiry, drawing a following on both sides of the Atlantic. If you google Voltaire, a familiar but perhaps inaccurately attributed quote appears: "I may not agree with what you have to say, but I will defend to the death your right to say it."[39] If not actually Voltaire's words, the idea captures Enlightenment sentiments that resonated with the Framers. Voltaire, who died before the First Amendment became law, helped intellectually to align the ability to reason with free expression.

Ratification of the First Amendment did not inspire a free speech free-for-all. Few thought of the First Amendment as a shield; perhaps fewer still considered it a sword. The First Amendment did not prevent a rival whom you verbally insulted from challenging you to a duel. If someone burned an effigy of a public official in the town square, it likely would result in an arrest for disturbing the peace. The First Amendment applied only to the federal government, not to state or local officials who still could enforce laws against speech they arbitrarily judged harmful or offensive. Did the First Amendment boldly push the nation into far-ranging, serious debate and accelerate the resolution of important issues? It certainly gave encouragement, but major topics were dangerously divisive—for example, slavery, women's rights, and radical political thought. Editors, writers, and speakers frequently exercised self-restraint. Clearly, the protections of the First Amendment were limited; it offered no protection whatsoever for the nation's large population of slaves. Although slavery was debated openly, few dared question its morality outside the confines of a legislative body. Abolitionists who protested risked mob violence, certainly in southern states, and few in Congress defended their free speech rights. Another inescapable inequity was the Founders' decision to deny women the right to vote, relegating them to the shadows of citizenship. For women—single, married, divorced, or widowed—the First Amendment guaranteed nothing in terms of a voice in political and cultural deliberations.

The Founders clearly meant for the First Amendment to buttress the sovereignty of "the people" and promote access to "all the avenues to truth."[40] Thomas Jefferson particularly endorsed freedom of the press as an instrument to inform the people, give them a voice in self-government, and hold elected officials accountable. The Founders spoke glowingly of expressive freedoms. But in the moment, as they prepared to vote on the Bill of Rights, the First Amendment was far more important for its symbolic message than for its practical sense. It represented the nation's commitment to political discourse and other wellsprings of knowledge, such as art, science, medicine, history, philosophy, and literature. But who would define its scope? What expression would it specifically protect? The Founders endorsed the *ideal* of the First Amendment, but they left it to others to translate it into real-life application.

In the late nineteenth century, scholars began in earnest to scour historical records for clues about the First Amendment. The Founders and other public figures left attics full of correspondence, papers, and diaries. Additionally, the debates of legislative bodies before and after the American Revolution provided raw material for study. From those building blocks, contemporary theorists began to interpret and assign clearer meaning to the First Amendment. No one interpretation of the First Amendment stands definitively above the others, nor are they mutually exclusive. The body of First Amendment theory continues in flux, as scholars and commentators add new contributions, typically in lengthy law journal articles augmented with in-depth footnotes and comments. Each new interpretation of the First Amendment invites additional critical analysis that can find its way into the nation's laws, judicial opinions, and popular culture.

Ex post facto analysis of the Founders' intent has contributed significantly to how we view the First Amendment today. Zechariah Chafee Jr. (1885-1957) is most often credited as the founder of modern First Amendment theory. As an inquisitive young law professor, Chafee found a void of First Amendment theory and an absence of judicial precedent. He tried to fill the void: "After all, if freedom of speech means anything," Chafee said in a Voltaire-like moment, "it means a willingness to stand and let people say things with which we disagree, and which do weary us considerably."[41] Chafee was sure the First Amendment existed to protect unorthodox, even radical speech. From a contemporary perspective, this view seems commonsensical, but in Chafee's day, critics damned his theory for giving political legitimacy to enemies of the state. Chafee drew a line, however, that still holds firm in First Amendment law. He would tolerate speech until it presented a "clear and present danger" to the nation that necessitated government intervention.

Alexander Meiklejohn (1872-1964), a Chafee contemporary, urged utmost protection for political speech, that is, expression essential for a well-informed citizenry. His definition of political speech included academic research, classroom discussion, and debates over public issues circulated by mass media. The First Amendment, Meiklejohn insisted, existed to advance the collective good rather than individual rights, famously saying, "What is essential is not that everyone should speak but that everything worth saying shall be said."[42] In counterpoint, present-day legal scholar Rodney Smolla argues that Meiklejohn left ajar a door of opportunity for the state "to dictate what is 'worth saying' and when 'everything worth saying' has been said."[43] Individual speech is frequently how a community comes to arrive at the collective good.

In 1970, Thomas Emerson (1907-91) proposed a more expansive theory of the First Amendment to include goals beyond that of democratic self-governance. Published after the deaths of Chafee and Meiklejohn, *The System of Freedom of Expression* argued that the First Amendment was also meant to aid the advancement of knowledge and the discovery of truth, facilitate decision-making by all members of society, and ensure a stable community capable of adapting to challenges.[44]

Another twentieth-century scholar, Frederick Schauer, noted that the First Amendment now covers far more human activity than anything the Founders considered speech.[45] Today, it protects commercial advertising, campaign contributions, speech by public employees during working hours, nude dancing, tattoo artists, and motorists who flash their headlights to warn oncoming drivers of a speed trap. These activities fall outside the Founders' intent to protect speech essential to self-governance and democratic deliberation, but Schauer anticipates that the boundaries of the First Amendment will continue to expand if advocates, for example anti-mask proponents, succeed in redefining the meaning of free speech and gain acceptance within the law and the public arena.

Inspired by the feminist and human rights movements, legal theorists of the late twentieth and early twenty-first centuries found the First Amendment wanting in terms of speech equality. A leading proponent, Catharine A. MacKinnon, argues that traditional applications of the First Amendment rely on a type of false equivalency whereby all speakers and expressive acts merit equal protection. MacKinnon prefers a proactive First Amendment that recognizes the power differential between speakers. When the First Amendment protects racial taunts, pornography, and hate speech, for instance, it disempowers, injures, and silences their targets. Beyond just safeguarding speech, an equality-based theory would require government intervention by statute and judicial action to level the playing field.[46] In the 1980s, she and fellow activists campaigned for municipal ordinances to combat anti-pornography laws they found lacking in civil rights protections for women against the effects of sexually violent depictions in videos and, now, online. Although largely unsuccessful in passing legislation, her efforts helped expand conversation about unconventional interpretations of the First Amendment.

The work of MacKinnon and like-minded scholars encouraged the spread of controversial speech codes in universities, workplaces, public organizations, and other places where minority citizens find themselves in vulnerable situations difficult to avoid. Most codes attempt to limit expression that hurts listeners through sustained insults, threats, and harassment, such as enduring sexist jokes, seeing a Confederate flag daily displayed in a dorm room window, or encountering in the office email offensive claims that the Holocaust never occurred. Speech codes are unpopular with Americans who assume free speech should be synonymous with saying what you want to, whatever the effects on others, a situation that raises complex legal and moral questions in a country where hate speech is generally protected.

"Speech" is a process of both speaking *and* listening. Legal scholars who advocate "critical race theory," for example, extend equality-based reasoning when they assert that a listener threatened by "assaultive speech" deserves protection as well.[47] Free speech, they argue, is never absolute for the speaker. Courts have held that victims' and listeners' rights clearly matter in defamation law and in "fighting words" contexts. Organizations and courts, these scholars contend, ought to consider the victim's story before someone is forced to quit a job or forfeit an education when her race, gender, or sexual orientation are demeaned and most assuredly when personal safety is threatened. The newest battles over speech rights underscore Frederick Schauer's contention that the First Amendment will not remain static.

Our compact review of First Amendment theories offers a crosssection of past and present thinking. The First Amendment continues to draw critical commentary, and, accordingly, we discover additional ways to understand the First Amendment and question what we, as citizens, expect from it. In hindsight, the Framers' ambiguity left the First Amendment flexible enough to adjust to an ever-changing world, although not to everyone's satisfaction.

## In Retrospect: Lessons from the Founding

Each year thousands of visitors, many in jeans and T-shirts, make a pilgrimage to the National Archives Museum on Constitution Avenue in Washington, DC, to view the Declaration of Independence, the Constitution, and the Bill of Rights. Our forefathers left us a tangible inheritance— three documents encased in humidity-controlled glass displays filled with inert helium. But even the most earnest of present-day pilgrims are likely to pass through the archives oblivious to the extraordinary effort that brought each document to life. The Founders, and all others who sacrificed and fought to build the new nation, bequeathed generations of citizens a set of values that continue to inspire and define us—or should. These democratic values were not free-floating in the atmosphere of revolution, ready for the Founders to grab and apply as if they were consumer products. The values were constituted by words, probably millions of them, hashed out in closed rooms and knotty conversations, over arguments about meanings and acceptance of practical compromises. The documents preserve the final agreements about *wording*, but we should not overlook the complementary values of listening, probing, testing, and a willingness to hear the other side—processes that gave us the specific words of our cherished founding documents.

We have examined the early history of America with a critical eye that acknowledges the Founders' strengths and obvious weaknesses. In the effort to unite a postrevolutionary country with thirteen separate, potentially competing governments, they chose to discard an opportunity to overturn slavery in the southern states, a decision that led to a horrific

## Quotables

"There is also the territory of historical self-righteousness: If *we* had lived south of the Ohio in 1830, *we* would not have owned slaves; if *we* had lived on the frontier, *we* would have killed no Indians, violated no treaties, stolen no land. The probability is overwhelming that if we had belonged to the generations we deplore, we too would have behaved deplorably. The probability is overwhelming that we *belong* to a generation that will be found by its successors to have behaved deplorably. Not to know that is . . . to be in error and to neglect essential work. . . . How can we imagine our situation or our history if we think we are superior to it?"[48]

**Wendell Berry, poet, novelist, and environmental activist**

civil war that nearly destroyed the nation before it reached its centennial. They consciously denied citizenship based on one's gender, race, ethnicity, and landowner status. A few thousand entitled white males, in possession of diplomas, estates, and human chattel, spoke grandly about equality, but in truth, they, like lords of old, arbitrarily determined the fate of others less blessed.

Despite their failings, our forebears demonstrated how people, after decades of oppressive British rule, found the will and means to build and embrace a new nation. They taught us lessons in how to put democratic ideals into action. They were, as we say, products of their day. On occasion they contradicted their own worthy ideals for government, legislation, and citizenship by their instances of antidemocratic behavior. Those failings, however, did not stifle the spirit of ordinary citizens, even those denied suffrage and equal opportunity. A majority invested in the Founders' aspirations of justice for all, the pursuit of happiness, protection for individual rights, and, in particular, a chance for self-determination. Jefferson, Madison, and Hamilton were the grand architects; hundreds of thousands of their countrymen imagined how they, too, might draft at least modest plans for their own futures as citizens.

The first generation of citizens generally demonstrated civic virtues that seem in short supply these days. Those virtues included a sufficient amount of self-restraint, goodwill, and moderation. Forty-five years ago, public intellectual Irving Kristol described what the Founders expected of a responsible citizenry:

It means curbing one's passions and moderating one's opinions in order to achieve a large consensus that will ensure domestic tranquility. We think of public-spiritedness as a form of self-expression, an exercise in self-righteousness. The Founders thought of it as a form of self-control, an exercise in self-government.[49]

Kristol, said legal scholar Adam White, believed that in a "republic there is such a thing as the public interest apart from—and perhaps at odds with—one's own personal interests, and thus it requires citizens to restrain themselves in the slow, deliberative workings of constitutional and civic institutions, and even in their interactions with one another."[50] The original citizens managed to establish and maintain the republic—no small feat.

Madison and his brethren expected growing pains but certainly nothing like the unsettling conditions in the 2020s as the nation drifts toward an iceberg that political scientist Kevin C. O'Leary calls "soft authoritarianism"—or worse. O'Leary, author of *Madison's Sorrow: Today's War on the Founders and America's Liberal Ideal*, blames the Republican Party for its efforts "to fracture the liberal-conservative consensus and force an interruption of Madisonian government." The Founders, not always harmonious, did broadly endorse a liberal society under which "average people—unshackled by the traditions of privilege, hierarchy, class, and irrevocable inequality—could create a new civilization."[51] The Founders, he says, wanted a future America better than their own.

In *The Good Citizen*, Michael Schudson said the past can inspire us, but "we cannot import it." He added, "We require a citizenship fit for our own day. The use of history should not be to condemn the present from some purportedly high standard of the past, but to know where we stand in time."[52] Following his advice, we offer our observations on several points of comparison.

## Public Talk Then and Now

Early citizens were, by and large, hungry for news, ideas, and controversies that they enjoyed squabbling over. The literate read by candlelight from treasured books and periodicals that passed into their hands. They pressed the flesh and introduced themselves to strangers. Ratification of the First Amendment and the Bill of Rights came during a time when most everyday communication was face-to-face—when stating a fact or belief meant looking someone in the eye, saying your piece, and awaiting an often strong reply. It was difficult and dangerous to lie day in and day out with people you knew well and relied upon to maintain your job, business, or social connections. Interpersonal communication linked them, gave them a foundation for talk, and exposed them to ideas, foreign and domestic, from which they could choose and on which they could build.

Eligible voters gathered at courthouses and cast their votes out loud, for all to hear. A few hunkered down in what we now call "silos" of beliefs, but people in cities and towns lived too close to one another to ignore other points of view; there were too many occasions for chance encounters. In truth, they valued and depended on interactions of all sorts to maintain their personal lives and those of their communities. By knowing one another and living side by side or within a carriage ride, they had both good reason and ample opportunity to confront the common good, a critical ingredient of a republic such as ours.

Townspeople in colonial and prerevolution days took full advantage of places and events designated for public talk. They also displayed an aptitude now in short supply, according to historian and political scientist Adam Garfinkle. They participated with a deeper understanding of social issues and more soundly based opinions. Today's citizens enjoy "greater levels of at least superficial participation in political discourse, if not politics itself, thanks in part to social-media technologies," but he worries that social media have rendered people less discerning and quite willing to express half-baked opinions: "Vast numbers of people contribute scantily supported opinions about things they don't really understand, validating the old saw that a little bit of knowledge can be a dangerous thing."[53]

Whether Garfinkle is right is an apt question that will arise again in later chapters. Are we deluding ourselves that an abundance of information translates to a smarter, more discerning citizenry? Do we suffer from an information overload that swamps our abilities to grasp and discover helpful context for the news? Can we separate reliable and fair information from the defective products and points of view peddled by scammers? Have digital media, whatever their other consequences, broadened an awareness of possible viewpoints and made our awareness of them more solid? At a minimum, we need to recognize what we gain and what we lose within our digital-dominated lives.

**Quotables**

"I've wanted to believe that the country that started with dispossession of native peoples, slavery, and a dedication to white supremacy could live up to the more idealistic aspirations of its founding—the statements about equality and the pursuit of happiness, and the desire to create a representative democracy in which the people were sovereign. That vision of the future has been challenged of late. But, as in years past, the many people who share this vision have mobilized in support of it. I suppose that is the most that can be hoped for, because that kind of struggle is the only way better futures can be made."[54]

—Annette Gordon-Reed, "Hopes for the American Experiment"

Political speech, too, differs vastly from the past. The object of political speech from the 1730s to the advent of televised political ads had been to win voters by persuasion, by policy proposals, by ideas freely and vigorously discussed. Of course, political discourse in the eighteenth century could be as crude and scurrilous as it sometimes is these days. But, looking back, its overall quality of wholehearted participation by citizens sets a good example for us. Perhaps we should demand serious political speech and by our in-person participation encourage more civil dialogue.

## Appreciation of Journalism

Journalism mattered, although its essence was far different in the lives of our earliest citizens. The press was unapologetically partisan, far more so than anything we now label "biased" or "politicized." Journalism then included newspapers, magazines, books, pamphlets, and miscellaneous printed communication. While the press then spoke forcefully and courageously, it was frequently impolite, unfair, or inaccurate. Mainstream professional standards and social responsibility came much later in the history of American journalism. In the Founders' time, the press knowingly exacerbated political division. To this extent, it failed its responsibility to the public and conspired with favored politicians. Yet it prodded citizens, got them thinking, and encouraged political activism in some ways perhaps necessarily characteristic for the times. You could say its main bias was to support the democratic republic.

The circulation of news moved at the pace of a walker's stride or a horse-drawn cart. An event in Philadelphia might be news for residents of

Charleston weeks later, which tended to blunt its impact. A message like "Lock her up" likely would never reach a homestead a hundred miles from the site of its origin. The delay allowed for slower digestion of news and commentary and a respite before the arrival of subsequent installments. People could mull over ideas and arguments without succumbing to pressures that contemporary researchers call "high-arousal emotions," particularly anger, triggered by exposure to viral, negative Internet content.[55]

Journalism certainly is more prevalent in our lives, but the nation's original citizens seemed to appreciate its presence far more than some do now. How many present-day citizens defend the news media, tangibly support hometown journalism, or devote the time needed to absorb the information that journalists provide? By the sharp tone of criticism, some people find the *New York Times* best used to start a campfire or line a birdcage. Colonial newspapers made enemies, too, but they were read, got passed around, and sparked conversations that in themselves prompted round after round of oral and written communication about civic problems.

## Knowing Our Founding Documents

Strong disagreements broke out over each stage of our quest for nationhood. The first citizens were not united in declaring independence from England and certainly not about going to war. After the fighting ended, states resisted a government structure that would deprive them of local autonomy. Nonetheless, from 1776 to 1791, the Founders forged consensus and created three of the most momentous documents in U.S. history—the Declaration of Independence, the Constitution, and the Bill of Rights. Each remains influential today, for which we owe thanks to the Founders. After ratification, the country moved on, adjusting to the needs of the central government and the role of the president. Authoring our founding documents was not the occasion for bitter debate or outrage over whose rights prevail.

During 2020's public protests to reopen businesses closed by the pandemic, armed men carrying shotguns and assault weapons in city streets and outside state capitols challenged stay-at-home orders, saying they were unconstitutional infringements on *their* liberties. The same protestors said they were exercising *their* constitutional rights to assemble, bear arms, and shout epithets. Americans of all political orientations at times invoke the Constitution and the Bill of Rights without knowing much about either. Being unfamiliar with constitutional rights is one thing, but misinterpreting or misapplying them is a greater problem for society. The coronavirus crisis offers another example. In early May 2020, the Wisconsin Supreme Court, by a 4-3 vote, invalidated the state government's stay-at-home orders. One could argue with the court's opinion, but what many citizens found most objectionable was the position of Justice Rebecca Bradley, who said in oral argument: "Isn't it the very definition of tyranny for one person to order people to be imprisoned for going to work, among other ordinarily lawful activities?"[56] Bradley then compared an emergency public health order for controlling a highly infectious disease to the forced removal and incarceration of more than 120,000 Japanese American citizens and their families during World War II, an action originally upheld by the Supreme Court. The public deserves a high level of constitutional knowledge and perspective from public officials, fellow citizens, and, certainly, its judges. Rather than invoke sacred script haphazardly in political debate, we might focus more on the Founders' less tangible but more hopeful legacy—the importance of an informed citizenry with knowledge of history, a keen interest in civic discourse, receptivity to new ideas, an inclination to reason, and a willingness to find common ground.

That heritage may be what holds America together as each new president and generation face a future filled with anxiety, uncertainty, and deep divisions. In the revolutionary period, America needed a bare-knuckles press and bold citizens who pressed the cause of freedom through protest and civil disobedience. Citizens today engage in methods similar to early Americans, but no longer do we fight against a foreign oppressor; we vilify each other. The intensity of present-day political dissent and the backlash it generates puts the assumption of freedom and justice in jeopardy. Chapters 3 through 8 serve as an informal user's manual for the republic. We start with applications of the First Amendment, an expression of the Founders' faith in the collaboration of citizens and journalists to stimulate dialogue that leads to deliberation and political decision-making.

## CHAPTER 3

# The Yard Sign That Said "No" to Censorship

When neighbors plant yard signs each election year or when homeowners display messages on a host of contentious community issues—"Vote YES for Education," "Save the Manatees," "Black Lives Matter," "Say NO to Commercial Rezoning"—they engage in protected speech that an unassuming woman named Margaret Gilleo helped make possible. Someone with Gilleo's dogged sense of justice might live at the end of your block or in the town next to yours. Gilleo happens to reside in Ladue, Missouri, a suburb of St. Louis, where her story begins.

On December 8, 1990, as other residents attached holiday wreaths to their front doors, Gilleo placed a 24-by-36-inch sign on her lawn that in neat typeface read: "Say No to War in the Persian Gulf, Call Congress Now." Thousands of miles away, commanders of a massive multinational military force were finalizing plans to oust occupying Iraqi troops from Kuwait. Gilleo feared the nation was marching too eagerly into battle, and she felt compelled to speak out in what she assumed would be modest protest. Gilleo did expect some of her affluent neighbors, who included baseball legend Stan Musial, beer magnate August A. Busch III, and U.S. Senator John Danforth, to find her sign off-putting. She never expected what happened next.

Someone quickly snatched her first placard; its replacement ended up tossed away nearby. When she reported the incidents, Ladue police told her a city ordinance banned all residential signs, with a handful of exceptions. A real estate for-sale sign was okay. Hers was illegal, she found out to her surprise. (No violation, apparently, had been committed by those who took her signs.) Undeterred, she petitioned the city council for a variance, which its members duly denied by a 7-0 vote. With the backing of the American Civil Liberties Union (ACLU), Gilleo went to court to argue that the ordinance violated her First Amendment rights. The federal district court, with jurisdiction over cases involving the United States Constitution, issued a preliminary injunction blocking enforcement of the law. Feeling vindicated, Gilleo placed an 8.5-by-11-inch sign in a second-story window of her house that read: "For Peace in the Gulf." Ladue reacted by replacing its contested ordinance with one more stringent that banned all window signs. Two more federal court rulings supported Gilleo, but Ladue pressed ahead. Gilleo found herself dragged into a legal briar patch of appeals, depositions, briefs, and hearings.

In February 1994, three years after the forty-two-day Gulf War had ended, attorneys for the City of Ladue and those representing Gilleo took turns before a lectern to argue their positions and answer questions by justices of the United States Supreme Court in a public proceeding known as "oral arguments." Afterward, Margaret Gilleo faced a scrum of print and broadcast reporters gathered beneath the Supreme Court portico. She answered a barrage of questions calmly and directly. "Why is this so important to you?" a reporter asked. Gilleo turned toward him and said: "I really value as an American my right to free speech." Another reporter asked Gilleo if she believed the city acted because of the content of her message. "Yes," she said, pointing out that no one objected to her earlier front-yard sign, "Save Our Rivers." When asked what she feared if she lost in court, Gilleo replied: "If you restrict speech at a local level, I think it can happen at a much larger level."[1]

In legal briefs and public statements, the city's attorney referred repeatedly to Ladue's "unique aesthetic ambiance" and argued Ladue's right to protect its residents from the "visual blight," safety hazards, and deterioration of property values caused by the proliferation of signs. Indeed, Ladue, like all communities, can enforce local laws—until they collide with a higher authority, in this instance, the First Amendment.

On June 13, 1994, the Supreme Court announced its decision. Justice John Paul Stevens wrote the unanimous opinion, which emphasized the importance of the First Amendment to civic dialogue that involves specific listeners and goals:

> Ladue has almost completely foreclosed a venerable means of communication that is both unique and important. It has totally foreclosed that medium to political, religious, or personal messages. Signs that react to a local happening or express a view on a controversial issue both reflect and animate change in the life of a community. . . . Displaying a sign from one's own residence often carries a message quite distinct from placing the same sign someplace else, or conveying the same text or picture by other means. Furthermore, a person who puts up a sign at her residence often intends

to reach *neighbors*, an audience that could not be reached nearly as well by other means.[2]

The impact of *City of Ladue v. Gilleo* extends beyond the narrow parameters of a citizen fighting city hall. First Amendment cases rarely involve classic censorship to arrest a speaker or confiscate newspapers. More often the threat to free expression comes from arbitrary bureaucratic decisions that mushroom out of control. To the mayor and city council of Ladue, Gilleo challenged the community's well-manicured reputation. Her message, too, rankled for its pacifist tone. Thanks to her determination, though, Gilleo helped reinforce the First Amendment's crucial role to protect political dissent. She also ensured that no community or government authority can ban political signs, even if they are politically unpopular with neighbors.

Margaret Gilleo might have given up when the city council first rebuked her. But she had a formidable ally. Since the 1920s, the ACLU has championed civil liberties causes, helping groups and individuals ranging across the political spectrum, from extreme left to extreme right. In 1977, the ACLU drew condemnation for defending a neo-Nazi group that wanted to march through the Chicago suburb of Skokie, home of thousands of Holocaust survivors. Aided by the ACLU, the neo-Nazis won their First Amendment case, allowing the Skokie demonstration, even though they had already decided instead to hold a rally at Federal Plaza in downtown Chicago. To this day, the ACLU continues its robust defense of free speech. In a post on ACLU.com, executive director Anthony D. Romero wrote: "We fundamentally believe that our democracy will be better and stronger for engaging and hearing divergent views. Racism and bigotry will not be eradicated if we merely force them underground. Equality and justice will only be achieved if society looks such bigotry squarely in the eyes and renounces it."[3]

The Skokie case and *City of Ladue v. Gilleo* joined an ever-expanding body of First Amendment law built upon the convictions of an array of speakers, ranging from Jehovah's Witnesses who ring strangers' doorbells to preach the Bible politely, to white-hooded Klansmen who hold a rally that culminates with a cross burning. Their actions—admirable or despicable—demonstrate the power of ordinary citizens to test their beliefs before a court of law even when opposed by public opinion. In doing so, their voices join the unending conversation on the state of the nation. These First Amendment advocates challenge the rest of us to self-test our commitment to freedom of expression.

The battle to preserve free speech is ongoing. Shortly after the killing of George Floyd, police in a number of cities—including New York, Chicago, Los Angeles, and Minneapolis, where Floyd died—erected barriers and formed lines, shoulder to shoulder, to block Black Lives Matter (BLM) protesters from gathering. When the crowds pressed forward, police used force to disperse them or make arrests. There had been looting, damage to property, and attacks on police, but law enforcement responses often involved suppression of both lawbreakers and law-abiding citizens. Contrast the response to how state police reacted to anti-lockdown demonstrations at which protestors armed with assault weapons stood outside state capitols and walked on public roadways without official interference. Free speech advocate Nora Benavidez underscored the difference: "The First Amendment is no good if it is used to protect one side of the political spectrum but disregarded for the other."[4] The American experience provides vivid examples of preferential application of free speech rights, as evidenced by how adult white hecklers tormented the Black children who were among the first to integrate, under court order and federal protection, previously segregated schools. During the same era, Black marchers for civil rights were attacked by police dogs, beaten bloody by billy clubs, and knocked off their feet by water cannons.

While BLM protestors met police resistance, counterdemonstrations occurred on waterways around Florida, including Jacksonville, where an estimated one thousand recreational boaters cruised the St. John River to mark President Trump's birthday. They waved flags, blasted patriotic songs from sound systems, sang "God Bless America," and obstructed other boaters.[5] The Coast Guard did not break up the pro-Trump flotillas. "This First Amendment inconsistency comes straight from the top," according to Benavidez, evidenced by contrasting Trump tweets in which he described Minneapolis protesters as "thugs" and said the gun-toting opponents of stay-at-home orders were "very good people."

The Supreme Court opinions established that the First Amendment protects expression that challenges the political status quo and cultural orthodoxy. Freedom of expression cannot be based on whoever holds power at a given moment. Who would choose to live where your speech "rights" depended, for example, on whether the "political" slogan on your T-shirt passed the litmus test of the prevailing government establishment? Would you want authorities to roust one group of protestors arbitrarily and permit the protestations of rival group? First Amendment protections, formidable on paper, crumble at times to the whims and machinations of imperfect humans.

## *What a Forty-Five-Word Sentence Can Do*

A single forty-five-word sentence encompasses six expressive freedoms:

> Congress shall make no law respecting an establishment of religion, or pro-hibiting the free exercise thereof; or abridging the freedom of speech, or of the press; or the right of the people peaceably to assemble, and to petition the government for a redress of grievances.

Those words—the entire content of the First Amendment—came with no instructional manual from the Framers. Each word, each phrase, and each clause acquired definition, meaning, and substance over time, but not by the Founders and the courts of the day. They said little about the First Amendment. Over time, the Supreme Court and various jurists, attorneys, scholars, philosophers, and lawmakers all had a hand in developing and expanding the sizable body of law and literature encompassing today's First Amendment.

The First Amendment is best understood through its distinguishing characteristics rather than by a case-by-case examination of Supreme Court opinions. We derived our perspective from a distillation of political philosophy, legal commentary, landmark judicial opinions, and American history. We focus on how the First Amendment accompanies and serves us even as we go about the routines of everyday life.

## The First Amendment Projects and Protects Rights

The Framers did not lump all six clauses of the First Amendment into one basket by happenstance. They expected rights under the First Amendment to both align and crisscross, facilitating communication of values, beliefs, and aspirations in a variety of forums that, in turn, other citizens could hear and consider in pursuit of the common good. Exercising First Amend-ment rights in particular settings bolsters the expressive rights of others, across time, contexts, and circumstances. Somali Americans demonstrat-ing in 2018 against harsh working conditions at an Amazon warehouse tread a path established by coal miners of the 1930s who expressed their grievances in the face of violent resistance by mine owners and union-busting gangs condoned by police. Religious groups, labor unions, and civil rights activists all drew upon interconnections of the First Amendment to bequeath freedoms to succeeding generations. The First Amendment can be likened to a bouillabaisse of ingredients that, when combined, add richness to our tradition of free speech. Each generation contributes to the recipe.

Our available freedoms under the First Amendment enable most of us to develop as individuals with unique personalities and choice of vocations, lifestyles, and pursuits. We can read as broadly as we wish from an immense digital and print library of nearly unlimited options. We can develop unorthodox ideas and swim against the mainstream to realize them. We can converse in voices that can be overheard by others without worrying that the FBI will knock on the door to question us later. We can debate every important condition affecting our well-being, faith, community, and government, confident that no one in power will stop us. The First Amendment does all these things, and we benefit without giving our freedom of speech more than a passing thought. The ability to express beliefs and dissent when they collide with the beliefs of others seems part of our DNA as citizens. The First Amendment is woven into our lives because of battles fought and won 230 years ago. John Adams, our second president, once said, "You will never know how much it has cost my generation to preserve your freedom. I hope you will make a good use of it."[6] You will find his quote emblazoned on coffee mugs for sale online. Adams would be pleased that his words survive, even in pop culture.

Supreme Court decisions have vastly expanded conventional notions of speech. "Speech" now encompasses nonverbal expression, including the highly volatile acts of burning crosses and desecrating the American flag if done in the name of political expression. Speech deemed "political," that is, related to discussion of government decisions and policies, historically enjoys the greatest degree of protection. Two general rules apply. First, the lower the value to self-governance, the less protection a form of speech warrants. Product advertising faces government restrictions, particularly if it is intentionally misleading or inaccurate. The same standard, though, does not apply to candidate advertising because of its elevated status as political speech. It largely goes untouched no matter how untrue or manipulative it might be. Second, speech mainly in the form of conduct warrants less protection. For example, demonstrators expressing themselves by blocking an interstate off-ramp during rush hour are likely to be more quickly dispersed than a midday QAnon gathering in a public park. As social media and communication technology evolve, new questions arise over the level of protection afforded to memes, face-swapping apps, and artificial intelligence systems that generate facsimiles of human speech.

## Quotables

"In some instances, instrumentalities of the state will try to stifle free and open debate, and the First Amendment is the tried-and-true mechanism that stops or prevents such abuses of state power. In other instances, however, the state may have to act to further the robustness of public debate in circumstances where powers outside the state are stifling speech. It may have to allocate public resources—hand out megaphones—to those whose voices would not otherwise be heard in the public square. It may even have to silence the voices of some in order to hear the voices of others."[7]

—Owen M. Fiss, professor of law, *The Irony of Free Speech*

Often the difference between permissible and regulated speech boils down to consideration of time, place, and manner, a standard introduced by the Supreme Court.[8] Can right-to-life advocates with handheld loudspeakers hold a rally at midnight on sidewalks outside a private clinic that performs abortions? The logical answer would be "no." The Supreme Court has addressed similar situations and seems prepared to recognize the right to speak while expecting protestors to adjust their methods. Instead of loudspeakers they can carry placards. They can distribute leaflets but must allow staff and clients to enter and leave the clinic unhindered. Even inside a public building, the First Amendment has its limits. In June 2017, police arrested forty-three people, some in wheelchairs, who lined up outside Senator Mitch McConnell's office chanting, "No cuts to Medicaid, save our liberties."[9] Police merely would have observed the same behavior if it had occurred on the sidewalks outside the Senate office building. In this instance, though, the citizens clogging the hallway disrupted the flow of other citizens doing business with government officials. Under the First Amendment, circumstances matter, and our rights hinge on the ability to balance them reasonably in consideration of others' rights. At times, though, the law does allow for an enhanced ability to "reach" relevant, specific listeners in special circumstances, as our analysis of *Gilleo* illustrates.

The First Amendment is not absolute. The Founders purposely limited the scope of its protections to encroachments by government, and, then, only the federal government. The citizens of that day never seriously considered speech restrictions by a business proprietor or political club a violation of their rights. If a tavern owner booted out a Tory for defending the Crown, so be it. In 2016, San Francisco 49ers quarterback Colin Kaepernick knelt in silent protest during the national anthem. The 49ers cut him from its roster, and every other National Football League (NFL) owner as of late 2022 declined to hire him. He had engaged in symbolic speech. "I am not going to stand up to show pride in a flag for a country that oppresses black people and people of color," he explained.[10] Kaepernick paid a stiff price with no prospect of the First Amendment shielding him from repercussions from his employer, corporate sponsors, or NFL officials. In almost all private settings and events, the First Amendment is immaterial because its authority applies only to government action.

Censorship occurs in gated communities, at private schools, within shopping malls—almost anywhere outside direct government control. A counterintuitive example would be a newspaper, so dependent on the First Amendment, that acts to suppress the speech of its own employees. The First Amendment, for example, cannot force an editor to print a particular story, even one about the arrest of the publisher's son on sexual assault charges. Owners and managers of private enterprises control the extent of freedom of expression within their businesses, with a handful of exceptions, such as federal law protecting the right of workers to organize in unions. The First Amendment guards broadly against rules, laws, policies, and behavior springing from government at all levels; its jurisdiction usually ends at the boundaries of private property and private disputes. Where the private-public demarcation line lies can cause confusion. In the private sphere, online gatekeepers such as Twitter and Facebook occasionally block political speech, often in the name of protecting the rights of other online speakers. What social media do to moderate content remains private business despite how undemocratic their actions may appear. Social media might someday come under government regulation; however, it will probably require a carefully crafted statute or Supreme Court ruling designed to be compatible with First Amendment precedent that has prohibited interference with private speech.

## The First Amendment Enables Community and Conversation

Citizens govern by voting but also by everyday talk as they address issues of political importance. Consider, for example, a community, perhaps like yours, facing a difficult decision to fund a much-needed new high school by raising the property tax through a referendum. The school board holds public meetings to explain why the new school is needed and what it will cost. Taxpayers are allotted time to respond, argue, and even get testy. A conversation starts and spreads, fed by news accounts, informational mailings, yard signs, and door-to-door advocacy. It is a process backed and encouraged by the First Amendment. Across America, comparable deliberations play out under fresco ceilings in statehouses or inside nondescript concrete block buildings. Each of these deliberative processes, "collective self-determination" in the words of President Woodrow Wilson,[11] depends on a free flow of information and opportunities for citizens to express diverse points of view in civic settings. When everything works well, the decisions made and actions taken constitute a collective effort by citizens to sort through opposing arguments, weigh evidence, and consider alternatives beforehand. Not everyone will be satisfied, but when citizens know they participated in a fair, equitable process, they will be more likely to accept the outcome. Under a democracy, the object of civic decision-making is to serve the common good, not to defeat the opposing side.

The Founders expected their fellow citizens to put the First Amendment to work through the means of expression of their day, such as writing letters to elected officials, filling the galleries of meeting halls, holding coffeehouse rump sessions, and speaking up for themselves and the rights of neighbors. Many generations of citizens have been motivated by the First Amendment. Nowadays, though, evidence points to a decline in civic participation. Some people avoid the political arena because of its rabid partisanship. Many reside on the sidelines, content to observe. Still others withdraw altogether, assuming the system is not worth saving. That said, responsible citizenship means much more than voting or attending, on rare occasion, a meeting of the city council. The First Amendment cannot compel us to engage, but its array of protections extends to places and situations not all citizens may be aware of. Going to church, attending a play, inspecting property tax records, complaining about police service, speaking up a public meeting, reading a socialist magazine, donating to the National Association for the Advancement of Colored People (NAACP)— the First Amendment makes our participation in each of these activities possible and meaningful. Civic lethargy weakens the First Amendment. It is, after all, the insurance policy for a democratic public life. As its beneficiaries, it makes sense that we never let the policy lapse.

The First Amendment clearly protects a speaker's right to self-expression. Less established are the complementary rights to *hear* speakers and acquire information in the first place. A freedom to speak implies access to an audience of listeners. We spend far more time as listeners, broadly defined, than we do as speakers. Outright censorship seldom disrupts our rights to hear. Most often, a gatekeeper behind the scenes restricts our opportunity to hear in the first place. For example, organizers of a college lecture series might pass on inviting media personality Ann Coulter for fear of public backlash over her views on feminism and immigration or because they doubt the educational value of her message compared to messages of other available speakers. When an administrator denies an investigative reporter access to patients at a Veterans Affairs hospital, no story gets written and hence we hear nothing. When the Secret Service sequesters protestors in euphemistically named "free speech zones," their voices never come within earshot. In each instance, someone else, not by official edict but by administrative decision-making, negates our ability to hear and, moreover, our right to *choose* what to hear.

That freedom of choice is essential to citizenship. As a general rule, the greater our exposure to speech, the greater the opportunity to acquire understanding about the world around us. We think about what we have heard, and we communicate our thoughts to others, who, in turn, go through a similar sequence of thought and speech. Justice Thurgood Marshall, in *Kleindienst v. Mandel* (1972), explained the process: "The freedom to speak and the freedom to hear are inseparable; they are two sides of the same coin. But the coin itself is the process of thought and discussion. The activity of speakers becoming listeners and listeners becoming speakers in the vital interchange of thought is the 'means indispensable to the discovery and spread of political truth.'"[12]

Simply being present when someone speaks falls short of civic listening, which requires both attentiveness and a receptive attitude. Listening can be difficult, especially if we find a speaker's message abhorrent, disagreeable, obtuse, or inarticulate. Citizens, though, who do not listen proactively with an open mind fail to expose themselves to the possibility of learning something new or modifying a long-held opinion. Listening encourages more speech, and often better speech. Darren Walker, president of the Ford Foundation, believes listening strengthens democracy. "Listening gives meaning to speech, gives purpose to voice, and gives dignity to people," Walker advises. "Only when we listen can we find common ground. Only when we listen can we forge compromise and a common future. And only when we listen across differences can we begin to heal the divides throughout this country, and build the bridges that our democracy today so desperately needs."[13] Our expressive freedom includes the right to turn a deaf ear. With channels of communication dwindling or going silent, the willingness of citizens to listen becomes more critical to democracy, requiring closer attention to voices of discord, intolerance, and falsity so we can know them and answer them.

There was a time not long ago when nearly every community above ten thousand people had a weekly or daily newspaper. Very little of community importance escaped notice. If police, without a warrant, searched high school lockers looking for drugs, the community would likely learn about it from a teacher's tip to a local reporter. If a business folded and workers received pink slips, a spouse would call an editor to ensure the paper was looking into the economic impact on the community. Journalism's role goes beyond acting as a counterweight to government authority— beyond providing information. It monitors events and scrutinizes public records. It stimulates conversations in every setting—home, church, city hall, and bowling alley. Was the police search justified? Did workers' wage demands unfairly put the local business community in jeopardy? When local voices rise to a noticeable pitch, the press listens and amplifies those voices. When no one else listens to the voiceless, reporters often will, such as by investigating reports of abuse at a local nursing home. We count on journalists to let us know what is happening. To that end, "freedom of the press" means journalists can have access to public records, protect anonymous sources, and, uncommonly and regrettably, even commit mistakes in reporting the news. As primary beneficiaries of First Amendment protections, journalists typically come to the rescue when expressive rights face suppression in other settings. They know that if the rights of nonjournalists are in danger, so are theirs.

## The First Amendment: Its Evolution and Exceptions

When the Supreme Court has dealt with complex First Amendment cases, it has returned to less than settled issues to explain itself and, on occasion, change its mind. Does the First Amendment protect "hate speech"? "Yes, but . . . ," the Court has said in several controversial decisions. The Ku Klux Klan and white nationalist groups continue use of hang nooses and cross burnings in public protests ostensibly to express their political views. Such hurtful, offensive practices received First Amendment protection in several state and federal courts, including in a 1969 Supreme Court decision, *Brandenburg v. Ohio*. In their decision, the Court reversed the conviction of a Klan leader charged with advocating racial violence at a rally that featured white hoods, inflammatory speeches, and a cross burning, deciding to permit hate speech *unless* it directly incited violence.[14] It was not until 2003 in *Virginia v. Black* that the Court held that states could ban cross burning undertaken with the "intent to intimidate," often the apparent objective of people or groups promoting hate.[15]

As hate speech surfaces in other contexts, the courts struggle to balance the rights of the speaker against those of the intended targets. In hem-and-haw fashion, the Court has yet to settle on a unified approach to hate speech, such as online campaigns to vilify members of Congress, celebrities, and less prominent figures. The challenge of balancing competing rights occurs in other areas of First Amendment jurisprudence, such as whether campaign donations count as political expression. The First Amendment is best understood as a distinctly American *attitude* of independence—that we can freely speak and decide our own fates. We learn that there are limits to what we can say and do. We learn, as well, that we can push those limits. As it guides, the First Amendment sets the baseline of our rights, not the ceiling. Its boundaries continue to shift, expand, and, at times, contract. What keeps the First Amendment relatively stable are the ideals on which it rests. We embrace those ideals even when not fully aware of their historic and legal significance. It is our responsibility as citizens to understand the First Amendment and, by raising our voices, defend its ideals.

Figuring out what to do about obscenity has been especially vexing for lawmakers, courts, and citizens. In creating the First Amendment, the Framers appeared unconcerned about how or if the First Amendment pertained to sexually explicit speech. In the eighteenth century, bookstores in the American colonies carried what legal scholar Geoffrey R. Stone described as "an extraordinary array of erotica" that included books titled *The Politick Whore* and *Letters of an Italian Nun and an English Gentleman*. No law, Stone said, forbade obscenity during the colonial era. "It was simply not thought to be any of the state's business," he said.[16] That permissive attitude changed dramatically between 1815 and 1915, as official and unofficial censors crusaded for legal controls over beer and hard spirts, Sunday shopping, and "lustful, immoral" literature to the point of criminalizing its production, distribution, and possession. During this era, even a single phrase, passage, or image involving sex was sufficient to warrant a criminal conviction. Courts judged speech on its mere "tendency" to corrupt children and impressionable adults. By the 1920s, artists, writers, and civil rights activists advocated a contemporary standard for sexually explicit speech. After considerable trial and error in the lower courts, the Supreme Court majority in *Miller v. California* (1973) offered what it hoped to be a workable definition of obscenity, for use nationwide.[17] Before *Miller*, inconsistent rulings failed, for example, to distinguish sexually explicit works of art from amateur videos shot in a trailer park. Post-*Miller* confusion, though, continued as prosecutors struggled to discern the meaning of the Court's new terminology—"prurient interest," "contemporary community standards," and "patently offensive." Instead of bringing clarity to the question of obscenity, the Supreme Court found its docket filled with appeals based on the misapplication of *Miller*. Justice Potter Stewart once said in exasperation about obscenity: "I know it when I see it."

Cases of child pornography rarely generate judicial indecision. Federal and state laws make sexual depictions of children a serious crime punishable by long prison sentences premised on how child pornography can exploit and endanger minors who cannot protect themselves. Child pornography includes sexually themed depictions of children, including computer-generated images. No one can legally produce, possess, or distribute child pornography. But the Internet practically rendered moot the enforcement of state and federal anti-obscenity laws. Websites offer private viewing and downloads of every sort of sexual conduct with few legal consequences, although prosecutors and police fight hardest to combat child pornography. In Geoffrey Stone's words, "The law has simply been overwhelmed by technology and by changing social mores. The challenge for the future is no longer how to *ban* such material, but how to deal with its existence."[18]

Other factors impact how the law develops, and they are distinctly human. The women and men who analyze the First Amendment, including the nine justices of the Supreme Court, cannot fully insulate themselves from outside influences. Family, colleagues, socialization, education, and life experience all shape our opinions. Judges pledge by oath of office to be fair and impartial, at least as much as humanly possible. They cannot, as humans, remain invariably neutral. Despite the best of efforts, judicial opinions include a reflection of actual lives and individually developed criteria for judgment. Critics accuse members of the Supreme Court of ideological or political bias. The neutrality implicit in the First Amendment asks jurists to resist prejudging speech on its political message, its literary quality, its moral tone, or any other subjective factor. The First Amendment is intended to maximize our exposure to all types of speech. Theoretically, it protects both the bad and the good, allowing citizens to decide which is which. At the same time, the First Amendment protects us from coerced acceptance of speech contrary to our beliefs.

Citizens cannot rely solely on the law to ensure their rights. A stop sign commands us to obey; it cannot guarantee compliance. It falls to citizens to know how to fight back against a policy or official action they believe to be contrary to the First Amendment. Most people never get involved. Litigation is costly, time-consuming, and emotionally draining. Citizens often support the First Amendment in spirit. They seldom come face-to-face with an issue worth challenging. But speech violations happen almost routinely and will continue to occur unless an aggrieved party speaks up. If a school board bans a young adult book because a few outraged parents find it offensive and no one objects, do not be surprised if other forms of de facto censorship pop up. When it comes to student-related speech, the Supreme Court's opinions have been mixed. It appears, though not conclusively, that public schools can control speech to meet reasonable educational goals, and those include decisions to preclude material that is poorly written, inadequately researched, biased or prejudiced, vulgar or profane, or "unsuitable for immature audiences." No school district or any other public institution should be allowed to curb access to speech by civic default. Citizens should expect both explanation and justification from officials when they encounter a troublesome free speech issue.

Covid-19 became another lesson on the limits of the First Amendment when elected officials and ordinary citizens argued about the right to go without protective masks. Vice President Mike Pence spoke for the maskless contingent when he justified to reporters the absence of masks and social distancing at a June 17, 2020, Trump campaign rally in Tulsa: "I want to remind you again, freedom of speech and the right to peaceably assemble is in the Constitution of the U.S. Even in a health crisis, the American people don't forfeit our constitutional rights."[19] On balance, judicial opinions put the health, safety, and welfare of the community ahead of individual liberties.

Most of us enjoy a bounty of benefits inherent in the First Amendment. Freedom of speech, however, has little meaning to the homeless, the jobless, and the institutionalized preoccupied with daily survival. Their voices rarely enter into or seem to matter in the public sphere. Inequality exists in two other areas of speech. One arena of special inequality is political speech, now dominated by massive amounts of paid commentary from corporations and special interest organizations that advocate for the wealthy. Ordinary speakers cannot hope to compete, nor can candidates for political office likely succeed without cash from wealthy donors. The second type of inequality occurs, ironically, because the First Amendment principles shelter vicious verbal attacks by racists, misogynists, and other assorted haters. The targets of their threatening, hurtful words must often choose silence rather than confrontation. To date, judicial rulings stop short of addressing the very conditions responsible for speech inequality. Researchers in anthropology and interpersonal communication have studied for years the problems of members of "muted groups" whose voices have been constrained and undervalued by those in culturally and economically privileged groups.[20] Extending speech equality, it seems, is yet another task for responsible citizens, not the Constitution.

Finally, the First Amendment appears ill-prepared to balance fact-based truth with outright falsehoods. The 2016 elections featured a strategic tactic of documented lying that spread to become a normal part of political discourse. But lying falls under the First Amendment. Its legitimization came in 2012, when the Supreme Court ruled for the first time that intentional falsehoods are protected expression, provided they do no serious harm or break no existing laws—for example, lying under oath in court. The precedent-setting case involved Xavier Alvarez, a minor official on the Claremont, California, water board, who described himself at a public meeting as "retired Marine of twenty-five years. I retired in the year 2001. Back in 1987, I was awarded the Congressional Medal of Honor. I got wounded many times by the same guy." Nothing he said was true. Federal officials charged Alvarez with violating the Stolen Valor Act, a law passed in 2006 by Congress that made it a crime to lie about receiving military medals. A federal judge hearing the case said he feared that if the law were sustained, "there would be no constitutional bar to criminalizing lying about one's height, weight, age, or financial status on Match.com or Facebook, or falsely representing to one's mother that one does not smoke, drink alcoholic beverages, is a virgin, or has not exceeded the speed limit while driving on the freeway." Later, on appeal, the Supreme Court found the Stolen Valor Act an unconstitutional restriction by government on free speech.[21] As a result, under current U.S. jurisprudence most falsehoods in political speech—even deliberate lies—enter into public discourse freely. That is true despite a 1974 opinion by Justice Lewis F. Powell Jr. in which he said: "There is no constitutional value in false statements of fact."[22]

Valuable or not, falsehoods in political speech enjoy broad protection. So does unintentional false speech in the form of careless mistakes, rumors, forgetfulness, and unintentional mistruths, including those made by journalists. Citizens may assume that any lie or falsehood that circulates through the public arena ought to be corrected and expunged. The cure might be far worse than the disease. Indeed, policing lies and falsehoods through the legal system would likely entrap the courts in an unwelcome role of judicial fact-checking. By and large, the First Amendment is ill-equipped to block the creation or spread of lies.

If you want the truth these days, a vigilant watchdog press, a broadly educated public, and astute professional fact-checkers might be the best alternatives. Another option to curb lies is defamation law, under which deliberate falsehoods that damage reputations can result in a court judgment awarding monetary compensation to victims. In chapter 8, we return to journalism and responses to the problems of lying by public officials and public figures.

Our inventory of First Amendment characteristics invites you to pause and consider the First Amendment as you see it. How does your understanding of expressive freedoms fit ours? Perhaps your perspective includes firsthand experience with officially silenced voices or fear of speaking out socially or at work. The First Amendment holds personal meaning for many citizens. For others it amounts to little more than words on paper. But the fine print often does matter, like knowing what your credit card contract says about excessive fees for missed payments.

## A Manuscript Comes to Life

Until the start of World War I, the First Amendment, as if a sacred manuscript locked under glass, was more an artifact than an instrument in service to democracy. Even when Congress in 1798 passed the repressive Alien and Sedition Acts, the laws escaped judicial review despite a clear aim to censor speech. The Sedition Act imposed fines and imprisonment on anyone who dared to "write, print, utter, or publish . . . any false, scandalous and malicious writing" against the president, Congress, or the U.S. government. The punishment was reminiscent of seditious libel prosecutions by colonial governors that culminated in 1737 with a jury acquitting editor John Peter Zenger (see chap. 2).

The Alien and Sedition Acts, far from quelling dissent, fueled its spread. Proponents and opponents widely stressed the Constitution and the First Amendment in pressing their cases in Congress, state legislatures, and, of course, the press. No court intervened. The issue became moot in 1800 when Jefferson narrowly defeated Adams and the Sedition Act, set to expire in April 1801, slipped ignominiously into history. However, its arguments about criticism of and by government officials echoed recently as a president claimed that the rhetoric of political foes, among them BLM leaders, constituted acts of treason.

As the nation passed from one crisis to another, including President Lincoln's use of executive power to censor anti-Union newspapers during the Civil War, First Amendment cases seldom drew the attention of federal courts. Moreover, from 1801 to World War I, Congress passed few laws impacting speech or publication. Freedom of expression cases arising from state law—statutes, judicial rulings, executive orders, and local ordinances—were considered outside the purview of federal courts until 1925.

The Great War brought freedom of speech rights back to the foreground. While U.S. troops crossed the Atlantic in 1917 to join allies in fighting Germany, back home Congress passed the Espionage Act, which criminalized speech intended to interfere with conscription, undermine the war effort, or promote the causes of the nation's enemies. A year later, Congress passed a new Sedition Act, outlawing any speech that the authorities deemed "disloyal" or "scurrilous." Thousands of Americans, mainly socialists, pacifists, and Communists, were prosecuted under the two laws and faced prison sentences of up to twenty years.

With the world at war and revolution occurring across the globe, tolerance for anti-government speech was at a low ebb. The Supreme Court seemed swept up by the prevailing mood. Aggressive enforcement of the two acts resulted in a series of appeals heard between 1917 and 1920 that challenged the law's constitutionality under the First Amendment. In most of these, the Court decided unanimously that speech considered a threat to national security fell outside First Amendment protection, measuring such speech by its *tendency* to cause harm. Even the distinguished justice Oliver Wendell Holmes upheld a number of convictions: "The most stringent protection of free speech would not protect a man falsely shouting fire in a theatre and causing a panic. . . . The question in every case is whether the words used are used in such circumstances and are of such a nature as to create a clear and present danger that they will bring about the substantive evils that Congress has a right to prevent."[23] Those words created the *clear and present danger standard*, the legal yardstick used to judge whether speech seen as a threat to national security is punishable or protected. The dividing line between protected and unlawful expression remained fuzzy as Holmes and his colleagues on the Court gave insufficient consideration to the content, circumstances, intent, or impact of the speech in question.

By 1919, Holmes experienced a change of heart, prompted by advice from friends and colleagues who themselves faced attacks for their "radical" political expression. Joined by Justice Louis D. Brandeis, Holmes reconstituted the "clear and present danger" test by adding these memorable sentiments: "I think that we should be eternally vigilant against attempts to check the expression of opinions that we loathe and believe to be fraught with death, unless they so imminently threaten immediate interference with the lawful and pressing purposes of the law that an immediate check is required to save the country."[24] No longer did he and Brandeis calculate a perceived threat by its "tendency" to cause harm. The test, they argued, required concrete evidence of immediate, substantial harm that required government intervention.

Holmes advanced his revised clear and present danger test in the case of *Gitlow v. New York* (1925). Benjamin Gitlow, a socialist leader, was convicted and sentenced to prison under the New York state criminal anarchy statute for publishing 16,000 copies of an essay that advocated "the proletariat revolution and the Communist reconstruction of society" through strikes and "revolutionary mass action." New York and other states enacted such laws in response to threats and actual acts of violence by so-called anarchists who advocated the overthrow of government if justified by dire conditions. Over the dissents of Holmes and Brandeis, the Court upheld Gitlow's conviction.[25] Nonetheless, the case became a legal landmark for another reason. Midway through the majority opinion, Justice Edward T. Sanford paused for what seemed like an afterthought: "For present purposes, we may and do assume that freedom of speech and of the press which are protected by the First Amendment from abridgment by Congress are among the fundamental personal rights and liberties protected by the due process clause of the Fourteenth Amendment from impairment by the States." The Fourteenth Amendment, ratified in 1867, attempted to ensure that freed slaves would receive fair treatment. It proclaimed:

> All persons born or naturalized in the United States, and subject to the jurisdiction thereof, are citizens of the United States and of the state wherein they reside. No state shall make or enforce any law which shall abridge the privileges or immunities of citizens of the United States; nor shall any state deprive any person of life, liberty, or property, without due process of law; nor deny to any person within its jurisdiction the equal protection of the laws.

Several freedom of speech cases from the states came before the Supreme Court prior to World War I, but they were not measured against the First Amendment. Now, for the first time, the Supreme Court stated, almost casually, that protections of the First Amendment were the responsibility of all public officials and government entities, such as police chiefs, city councils, state assemblies, and public school boards. As of that day, the due process clause required state and federal governments to be held to national standards in regulating speech.

After *Gitlow*, the First Amendment quickly took on substance and character. New dimensions of "speech"—a word the Founders left undefined in the First Amendment—vied for inclusion, among them the right to express opinions through such actions as picketing on public land outside auto assembly plants, coal mines, and retail businesses. In the 1930s and 1940s, some state laws prohibited picketing broadly and made the activity punishable by fine or jail. Anti-picketing regulations historically served to protect the interests of the *targets* of picketing and minimized the rights of the protestors to press their arguments. Under prior judicial rulings, the acts of carrying signs, chanting slogans, and marching as a group were not considered First Amendment issues. Labor and social issues boiled over as police hauled away picketers. It took a while before the Supreme Court finally recognized that government restrictions on peaceful, law-abiding picketing violated not only the rights of free speech but also those of assembly and petition of grievances.

In 1943, with the nation again at war, the Supreme Court confronted whether the government could legally compel speech. Across the country, mandatory policies required students to begin the school day by saluting the U.S. flag and reciting the Pledge of Allegiance. In West Virginia, children of Jehovah's Witnesses refused to comply on religious grounds. School officials expelled students and threatened parents with the prospect of reform school for their children unless the resistance ended. State officials argued that the mandatory policy supported the important interest of national unity in wartime. The Court did not agree. Speaking for the majority, Justice Robert Jackson wrote: "If there is any fixed star in our constitutional constellation, it is that no official, high or petty, can prescribe what shall be orthodox in politics, nationalism, religion, or other matters of opinion."[26] Compelled speech, the Court reasoned, threatened the First Amendment as surely as gagging a speaker. Until a parent invoked the First Amendment, the practice of punishing children for being "unpatriotic" had prevailed.

Between the end of the Korean War and the volatile decade of the 1960s, a shift in judicial orientation transformed the Supreme Court. It began with the 1953 confirmation of Earl Warren as chief justice. The Warren Court, as it came to be known, confronted an astonishing range of constitutional disputes and societal issues such as interracial marriage, school busing, capital punishment, and abortion. Under Warren's leadership, the Court ended public school segregation based on the now discredited "separate but equal" rationale, and it gave us the *Miranda* warning, repeated in thousands of TV crime dramas—"You have the right to remain silent . . . ." Opponents launched an unsuccessful campaign to impeach Warren for his "liberal agenda," while some Court watchers must have wondered why protecting rights stated in the Bill of Rights had become a liberal issue and not a conservative one, too. The backdrop for the Court, as for all of America, was a series of major social movements—to fight racially suppressive Jim Crow laws, to pass the Equal Rights Amendment, to unionize farmworkers, and to end the war in Vietnam, among others. At times, violence begat violence in the form of Klan bombings, riots in major cities, and confrontations between campus police and students. Chaotic events captured by broadcast and newspaper reporters entered living rooms, requiring the nation to examine and reexamine its values, attitudes, and behavior. Dozens of free speech cases reached the Supreme Court in those years, solidifying America's legacy of freedom of expression under the direst of societal conditions.

In the early days of the civil rights movement, the Court extended protections under the freedom of assembly clause. It blocked Alabama officials from forcing the New York-based NAACP to identify its state members by name and address.[27] Top state officials allegedly hoped legal sanctions would drive the NAACP out of Alabama. The Supreme Court saw through the ploy. The Court weighed its decision against brutality directed toward Blacks, particularly in the South, that included beatings, cross burnings, and lynching. "Effective advocacy of both public and private points of view, particularly controversial ones, is undeniably enhanced by group association, as this Court has more than once recognized," said Justice John Marshall Harlan II for a unanimous court.

The ruling linked the rights of assembly and association used so effectively, for example, by followers of feminist leader Gloria Steinem and supporters of labor organizer Cesar Chavez, who cofounded the National Farm Workers Association, later renamed the United Farm Workers Union.

A few years later, the Court recognized a right of anonymous speech to buttress freedom of association. Police arrested Manuel Talley for distributing handbills urging the boycott of businesses that refused to hire minorities.[28] A California municipal court ruled that Talley violated a statute prohibiting distribution of anonymous leaflets and fined him ten dollars. A right of anonymity, the Supreme Court reasoned, shielded vulnerable speakers from harassment, retaliation, and physical abuse. Talley, founder of the Los Angeles chapter of the Congress of Racial Equality, fought not for his own anonymity. He fought for powerless people who otherwise would find public exposure too great a risk.

The Warren Court spent considerable time charting the boundaries of symbolic speech for anti-war protestors. In an incident widely covered by network news, a young man, David O'Brien, burned his draft card before an agitated crowd in Boston, intentionally contesting a 1965 federal law that criminalized mutilation of draft cards. O'Brien argued the law stifled a potent act of dissent—one he believed the First Amendment protected. Uncharacteristically, the Warren Court upheld O'Brien's conviction and his six-year sentence in a federal prison. The case, a setback for symbolic speech, resulted in a four-part test used in subsequent cases: Is the law within the constitutional power of the government? Does the law further a substantial or important government interest? Is the interest unrelated to the suppression of free expression? Is this regulation the *least restrictive means* with regard to free speech? The Court found that the draft card regulation passed all parts of the test, although O'Brien and free speech activists questioned in particular how the government met the third and fourth parts.[29]

The *O'Brien* test later helped support speech. In 1971, the Supreme Court reversed the conviction of Paul Robert Cohen, who was arrested for wearing a jacket bearing the words "Fuck the Draft" inside a California courthouse. As precedent, the Court cited *United States v. O'Brien*. Public officials, the Court said, should not use law enforcement powers as "a convenient guise" to ban unpopular, crudely expressed views. The enduring importance of *Cohen* is found in the words of Justice Harlan II when he said citizens, not public officials, are the ultimate judges of the value of speech:

> The constitutional right of free expression is powerful medicine in a society as diverse and populous as ours. It is designed and intended to remove governmental restraints from the arena of public discussion, putting the decision as to what views shall be voiced largely into the hands of each of us, in the hope that use of such freedom will ultimately produce a more capable citizenry and more perfect polity and in the belief that no other approach would comport with the premise of individual dignity and choice upon which our political system rests. . . . That the air may at times seem filled with verbal cacophony is, in this sense, not a sign of weakness but of strength.[30]

Written in an earlier era of civic turmoil, the words of Harlan resonate today against a backdrop of speech that frequently is raw, ugly, and tinged with threats of violence.

In another war-related case, this one from 1969, the Court chastised school officials in *Tinker v. Des Moines Independent Community School District* for denying students the right to wear black armbands to support a national moratorium day to end the Vietnam War. The Court rejected the common law principle that children should be seen but not heard. "It can hardly be argued that either students or teachers shed their constitutional rights to freedom of speech or expression at the schoolhouse gate," the Court said.[31] The *O'Brien* precedent again influenced the Court's position when, in another pair of cases, it established flag burning as freedom of expression in *Texas v. Johnson* (1989) and then struck down the Flag Protection Act, a law quickly passed by Congress to negate the *Johnson* decision, in *United States v. Eichman* (1990). In both instances, the Court majority concluded that governmental interest in preserving respect for a revered symbol did not outweigh a citizen's right to employ the flag as part of symbolic expression.[32]

The Court's inclusion of symbolic speech, picketing, and anonymous speech under the First Amendment umbrella protected collective expression used effectively by activists to draw attention to their causes and spur action. Groups marching outside drug makers' headquarters or assembled on Election Day at busy intersections can influence public opinion every bit as persuasively as testimony at a congressional hearing or a research report from the American Association of Retired Persons.

In the midst of deciding other momentous cases, the Supreme Court docket included the tricky business of whether—or how—to regulate broadcasting. The explosive growth of radio in the 1920s led to a succession of congressional laws that required station owners to obtain federally issued licenses and operate in the "public interest." In the 1930s, Congress revamped the existing broadcast regulatory structure and created the Federal Communications Commission (FCC) to oversee broadcast technology and ensure compliance with a set of content-based rules. In developing its meaning of "public interest," the FCC between the mid-1930s through the early 1970s required broadcast licensees to provide candidates for office "equal air time," ensure "fairness" in network and local programming that dealt with "controversial issues of public importance," and screen music lyrics for drug references.

What about First Amendment protection for broadcasters? At first, the industry welcomed government intervention, but station owners and professional groups came to resist regulations that encroached on freedom of speech and press. The Supreme Court justified federal regulation by deciding that radio and TV licensees were "trustees" of a "limited national resource," by which it meant the finite number of telecommunications frequencies available for transmitting radio and TV signals. In several key decisions, the Court majority placed the First Amendment rights of the audience above those of broadcasters. The justices affirmed the Founders' position that *the primary goal* of the First Amendment is "producing an informed public capable of conducting its own affairs,"[33] not just a factor to be balanced against a supposed right of broadcasters to say what they want.

In the 1970s, television came under intense scrutiny for its perceived power to peddle products, glorify violence, mold public opinion, and incite antisocial behavior. Congress held hearings, social scientists published studies, and, in general, groups fearful of harmful effects lobbied for greater regulatory control. The Court managed to bend the First Amendment to accommodate the competing free speech interests of broadcasters and those asserted by some audiences. For example, while the FCC did not ban advertising during children's programs, it did limit the number of minutes of ads per show. With justification, the FCC could impose rules over content.

By stark contrast, no regulatory rule or government agency oversees print content or ever has. In fact, the Supreme Court ruled in favor of the *Miami Herald* when a candidate for state legislature invoked Florida's "right of reply" law to force the newspaper to publish his response to editorials. The Court unanimously found the Florida law unconstitutional because it usurped an editor's right to decide what to publish or not to publish.[34] Until the rules were abolished in 2000, the FCC required broadcasters to provide airtime for candidates and others whose integrity was attacked on the airwaves.

Regulation of over-the-air broadcasting diminished as the public gained access to a multitude of platforms through cable TV and the Internet, reducing concern about monopolies of thought when broadcasters assigned airtime based on favoritism or put profits ahead of the best interests of the public. First Amendment observers eventually came to worry about an *overabundance* of speech that might crowd out serious ideas and discussion in favor of pablum.

The advent of the Internet in the 1990s opened a new frontier for wide-open, multilateral, multinational communication, as America Online and other Internet service providers (ISP) expanded access to content well beyond the limited media reach of print and broadcast. The Internet's emerging power came under First Amendment scrutiny, particular with regard to whether the federal government could impose regulatory rules. In the 1997 landmark case of *Reno v. ACLU*, the Supreme Court invalidated a portion of the Communications Decency Act, intended by

## Quotables

"What Orwell feared were those who would ban books. What Huxley feared was that there would be no reason to ban a book, for there would be no one who wanted to read one. Orwell feared those who would deprive us of information. Huxley feared those who would give us so much that we would be reduced to passivity and egoism. Orwell feared that the truth would be concealed from us. Huxley feared the truth would drown in a sea of irrelevance."[35]

—Neil Postman, *Amusing Ourselves to Death*

Congress to shield children from sexually themed online content. More significantly, the Court endowed the Internet with the highest degree of First Amendment protection, cutting off the possibility of FCC control through validating a provision of the law—Section 230—that said: "No provider or user of an interactive computer service shall be treated as the publisher or speaker of any information provided by another information content provider."[36] In other words, the burgeoning Internet's search engines and ISPs would not be held legally liable for questionable material put into online circulation by users, including pornographers. The Court concluded that ISPs were not publishers or editors, merely conveyors of online information. The decision seemed right at the time, but the new frontier devolved into the Wild, Wild West.

In a related 1997 case, *Zeran v. America Online*, the Fourth Circuit Court of Appeals said the First Amendment immunized ISPs from liability for material that passed through their portals. Without immunity, the court reasoned, ISPs would likely restrict content that, for instance, exposed them to defamation lawsuits and criminal charges of distributing obscene material. In turn, the court said, the public's right to receive a diversity of information and thought would be severely restricted as well.[37]

The two cases from 1997 unintentionally created a safe haven for online speakers who had little regard for the truth and were driven by motives ranging from racism to espionage. The development of search engines, led by the pioneering Google, encouraged people to search with abandon for information. They dredged up treasures, trivia, and trash. Google and Safari uncorked a genie that indiscriminately did the bidding of its users. It became clear that a First Amendment meant to facilitate information needed for self-governance actually stood relatively helpless to prevent a polluted flow of antidemocratic speech.

With the Supreme Court's stance in *Reno* and *Zeran*, responsibility for control over Internet content and access fell to the digital giant Google, joined by the social media might of Facebook and Twitter. Internet entrepreneurs profited greatly from explosive growth, while they shied away from the sticky management of advertising, blogs, websites, and tweets because the Supreme Court said they could avoid that responsibility. The public welcomed free and abundant online information available at a keystroke. Search engines siphoned off political speech, news, and advertising from traditional news outlets into the realm of profit-driven media conglomerates, unconstrained by professional news standards or communication ethics.

Recent antitrust investigations by the U.S. Department of Justice and several states may eventually offer remedies or force Internet powers to act more responsibly. Information powerhouses Twitter, Facebook, and YouTube are already moving in that direction by blocking or labeling content as false or objectionable. As private entities, they can do that without running afoul of the First Amendment. Section 230 might be abolished, too, but then what would be the consequences of an Internet policed by government? We should expect complaints by some citizens about *reduced* access along with demands by others for *stricter* controls.

As the Supreme Court shaped the terrain of freedom of speech, it gradually staked out new spaces for expression by businesses. It first protected paid advertising by reversing its own 1942 opinion, *Valentine v. Chrestensen*, in which it held that commercial speech fell outside the First Amendment.[38] Realistically, that precedent could never hold. The advent of in-home television after World War II opened the door to broadcast advertising for refrigerators, automobiles, and many other consumer products, such as TV dinners that families enjoyed while watching their favorite prime-time programs. If that sounds like a Trivial Pursuit moment, at the time, it was not. Paid advertising was fast becoming a dominant part of American lives, and its persuasive power expanded from selling goods and services to selling ideas, public policies, and political candidates.

Citizens became better aware of the methods and potency of political advertising when a book by a young reporter named Joe McGinnis climbed the best-seller charts with its behind-the-scenes account of the successful marketing of Richard M. Nixon, running for president after his poor showing in a series of televised debates with John F. Kennedy contributed to his defeat. He titled his book *The Selling of the President 1968*.[39] Quickly, political advertising grew into spendfests to win office, from county commissioners to the commander in chief. Before too long, accumulated evidence revealed that candidates were not only being sold, they were being bought, among them President Nixon, who accepted campaign contributions meant to win White House support for special favors.

The expansion of the First Amendment from individuals to massive multinational corporations and deep-pocketed special interests groups dramatizes how the rights that the Framers intended to encourage citizens to self-govern have been subsumed. Corporations did not exist in 1787; electioneering amounted to handbills, stump speeches, and face-to-face campaigning. We are a long way from those bucolic days. Certainly since the 1970s, Big Money with its powerful and often anonymous puppeteers has pulled the strings to accomplish political, ideological, and financial goals. For a while, laws passed at the federal and state levels attempted to maintain a somewhat fair playing field by limiting and monitoring campaign spending and campaign contributions. But those protective shields eroded under an onslaught of cash, some of it called "dark money" because it originated from intentionally hidden sources.

Then in 2010, the Supreme Court seemed to throw out the rulebook. The conservative majority decided in *Citizens United v. Federal Election Commission* that the free speech clause applied to political communications by *corporations, nonprofit organizations, labor unions,* and other associations, among them those representing foreign interests. In the lengthy, complex majority opinion, Justice Anthony M. Kennedy argued that the First Amendment does not permit political speech restrictions based on a speaker's corporate identity. "By suppressing the speech of manifold corporations, both for-profit and nonprofit, the Government prevents their voices and viewpoints from reaching the public and advising voters on which persons or entities are hostile to their interests."[40] Kennedy said he saw little constitutional difference between corporate speech and media speech. But in a powerful dissent, equally lengthy, Justice John Paul Stevens disagreed:

> Although they make enormous contributions to our society, corporations are not actually members of it. They cannot vote or run for office. Because they may be managed and controlled by nonresidents, their interests may conflict in fundamental respects with the interests of eligible voters. The financial resources, legal structure, and instrumental orientation of corporations raise legitimate concerns about their role in the electoral process.[41]

Post-*Citizens United*, little deters megadonors and monied corporate actors from using their checkbooks to support favored candidates and influence desired legislation and causes. The benefactors of *Citizens United* include Americans for Prosperity, a political advocacy organization founded by the Koch family of Kansas and funded through its massive business empire reportedly worth more than $100 billion. The Koch-funded operations hundreds of millions of dollars in 2014 Senate races and the 2016 presidential election.[42] Presumably, liberal corporate donors are trying to keep up. That kind of clout threatens to eclipse the voices of ordinary citizens, underfunded civic organizations, and, indeed, the news media.

The Founders might have shuddered at the prospect of freedom of expression so broadly conceived and so inconsistent with their beliefs. In his dissent, Justice Stevens observed: "While American democracy is imperfect, few outside the majority of this Court would have thought its flaws included a dearth of corporate money in politics."[43] In our experience, corporations and political entities rarely duplicate the moral conscience and personal responsibility of individual citizens and a committed free press, which the Framers singled out in the First Amendment for its role in the defense of democracy. Keeping a wary eye on campaign financing, particularly close to home, is decidedly in the best interests of all citizens who fear democracy is going to the highest bidder.

Two decades into the twenty-first century, we can look back and see for ourselves how the First Amendment evolved through periods of war, partisan strife, and cultural upheaval. Expressive rights ebbed and flowed, as the Supreme Court adjusted to cope with social and political change. The Supreme Court generally applied the First Amendment in ways consistent with the underlying principle that freedom of speech enables citizens to self-govern and decide matters of importance to themselves and the larger community. Americans can, should, and will argue about what the First Amendment means—or ought to mean. The Founders gave us values and principles to protect, not a set of commandments to obey.

## *License Plates, T-shirts, and Middle Fingers*

The First Amendment impacts our lives far more extensively than we might realize. Speech is woven into nearly every human activity. Most of our ordinary speech is inconsequential, like text chatter and social tweets. The closer speech comes to governance or our rights as citizens, the stronger its protection under the First Amendment. The right to post an antiwar sign in your front yard is clearly protected—unless you live in a private community managed outside municipal law and governed by restrictive covenant, that is, rules to ensure property values and maintain social order. As a patriotic resident you might want, for example, to raise a large American flag on your own backyard pole, but by agreeing to the terms of the covenant, it probably will not fly—too tacky, too obtrusive. Conformity usually quashes individuality. Often there is a steep payback for so-called freedom from government oversight, such as relinquishing freedom of expression in a gated community. Recall that Margaret Gilleo lived within the *city* of Ladue, which acted improperly as a *government* censor.

Sometimes we pass by occasions for freedom of speech without knowing the First Amendment is involved. What about camping overnight in a city park as part of a protest on homelessness? Can a Walmart shopper get away with wearing a T-shirt that reads, "Rope. Tree. Journalist. SOME ASSEMBLY REQUIRED"? When the answers are not clear-cut, disagreements over First Amendment rights might end up in a courtroom for resolution. When that happens, variables such as a judge's instructions to the jury or a defense attorney's competence could produce unpredictable outcomes. This much we can say: Without the First Amendment, staging a sit-in in a public space to advocate gender rights, shouting strong words that might offend others, or flipping off the president would likely be prohibited or punished.

Take such a mundane presence as automobile license plates. As you drive around town, check out the messages on specialty or, vanity, plates. Then look for state-issued plates carrying slogans ("Land of Lincoln"), promoting causes ("Support Education"), or recognizing organizations (Vietnam Veterans). These forms of expression fall under the First Amendment, as do more portentous concerns. License plates became a First Amendment issue forty years ago, when a New Hampshire couple, members of Jehovah's Witnesses, covered up the embossed state motto on their license plate, "Live Free or Die." The case made it to the United States Supreme Court, where Chief Justice Warren Burger said government cannot compel individuals to endorse an ideology.[44] Recently, the First Amendment debate reemerged over state attempts to regulate messages on vanity plates. States, at first, welcomed vanity plates as revenue generating and harmless. Then people took advantage and pressed the limits of acceptability with plates like AYRAN-1, SEXFIEND, and, if you remember the 1995 episode of *Seinfeld*, ASSMAN.

A few license plate cases have gone to court, and a federal court ruled that Vermont officials could deny a request for a vanity plate bearing the letters "SHTHPNS." The court determined that, in general, license plates are not a traditional public forum for speech and the regulation in question merely banned a person's use of the word "shit," not a political viewpoint. You might think that the First Amendment ought to safeguard more important interests. On the other hand, when government officials try to control mundane forms of speech, might they later impose more restrictive standards on the rest of us?

### Marginalia

The questions about everyday speech do pile up at times. What about hand gestures? People use them often enough in crude yet elemental fashion. Take the case of Juli Briskman, who lost her job after giving the middle finger to President Trump's motorcade after he had finished a round of golf at his course in Potomac Falls, Virginia. As the motorcade passed, Briskman, from the seat of her bicycle, kept her finger raised and repeated the gesture when she caught up to the presidential SUV in traffic. She avoided arrest, and rightly so, and her act of defiance served her well in the long run. A viral photo of Briskman spurred her election to the county board of supervisors in the Virginia county that includes the Trump National Golf Club. Briskman also sued for wrongful termination from her job as a government contractor, which she lost, although she successfully sued for severance.[45] One note of caution: One-fingered gestures can provoke a violent response, and police, even when they suspect it is a losing proposition, can detain you or press charges.

Throughout a typical day, citizens participate in speech activities most would never consider protected by the Constitution. These include situations that might annoy or inconvenience us, such as a civic group passing out leaflets outside a supermarket or street people asking for donations along a highway off-ramp. Are leaflets protected? Usually, unless the content promotes unlawful activity. Time, place, or manner regulation could apply, too. What about panhandling? Is it protected by the First Amendment? It appears so. A federal judge in New Orleans cited as precedent a U.S. Supreme Court ruling that charitable groups have a free speech right to ask for money. The judge said the Court's ruling extended to panhandling: "That holding compels the conclusion that the First Amendment also protects an individual's right to ask for charity," the judge said.[46] So, in his jurisdiction, panhandling is protected unless it becomes a traffic hazard. Yet anti-panhandling ordinances remain in force around the country.

Someday, the Supreme Court might have to settle such a matter so commonplace in cities with large homeless populations. Is begging for food, work, or a donation at the core of First Amendment theory that focuses on self-fulfillment? Is speech to *survive* the ultimate form of self-expression?

Speech activities that millions of us perform daily, particularly tweets and Facebook posts, seem safe because of the First Amendment. Still, its array of protections may buckle in the face of a lawsuit for defamation, breach of contract, or invasion of privacy. Here is where a few of us learn the hard way that the right to free speech does not belong to us alone. One's right to speak must be weighed against its impact on others. Say you encounter lousy service at In-Out Diner and dash off on your Facebook page an informal review in which you describe the owner as a "crook" or a "pervert" who "serves crap for food." Your innocent intent—just having a little fun—will probably strike the owner differently. You might prevail based on your rights of free speech or innocent intent—but perhaps not. Defamation law may apply, and while the First Amendment is meant to encourage pointed commentary, it most clearly applies to criticism against public figures and officials. By the way, dozens of law firms around the country specialize in seeking out potential online speech cases to file.

Another form of lawsuit aimed at ordinary people shuts down civic dialogue by means of intimidation and legal leverage. That category of lawsuit earned the acronym SLAPP—"strategic lawsuits against public participation." SLAPP cases arise in a variety of situations but usually when people go online to criticize, for instance, a local artistic performance, the conduct of an official during a public meeting, or the return policy of a neighborhood business. Such lawsuits punish or tend to deter altogether routine speech about public matters. A New York trial judge handling a SLAPP lawsuit colorfully described how he saw such cases: "Short of a gun to the head, a greater threat to First Amendment expression can scarcely be imagined."[47] And he came to that conclusion *before* online speech accelerated the use of SLAPP litigation. As of 2019, twenty-nine states offer a degree of relief through anti-SLAPP statutes that require expedited court action for lawsuits seen as retaliatory and allow for the defendant to recover legal costs.[48]

The First Amendment protects citizens against overt government censorship. Yet, the First Amendment gets bandied about when private parties face off over conflicting positions on freedom of speech. You can probably find an example quite readily. An illustrative brouhaha arose in late 2019 when a division of the American Library Association (ALA) voted to strip Laura Ingalls Wilder's name from a major children's literature award.

Why? Members of the ALA raised concerns about how Wilder referred to Native Americans and Blacks in her books, among them the *Little House* series, based on her own life on the Great Plains in the nineteenth century. In her defense, the Laura Ingalls Wilder Legacy and Research Association released a statement saying that while her writing included "the perspectives of racism that were representative of her time and place," it also made positive contributions to children's literature.[49] The First Amendment is ill-equipped to settle such disputes. Here, a long-standing subject of contention—political correctness—implicates the interconnected interests of freely deciding what to write and freely objecting to speech deemed insensitive, insulting, or injurious. Both sides invoke the First Amendment, at least rhetorically, if not in a legal sense.

Confusion over whose First Amendment rights are paramount includes the so-called cancel culture. The term commonly refers to online backlash that occurs over the allegedly offensive speech or behavior of prominent public persons. A well-covered example occurred in 2019 when *Saturday Night Live* hired and then quickly fired comedian Shane Gillis after a video that surfaced of an allegedly anti-Asian skit he performed the year before went viral.[50] In cancel culture episodes, free speech, again, cuts two ways. Those who "cancel" someone use First Amendment rights to punish or silence the expressive freedom of other speakers.

Critics contend that cancel culture amounts to unfair, indiscriminate mob retribution. From the other side of the argument, consider this reaction by essayist Sarah Hagi published in *Time* magazine:

> [Cancel culture has] turned into a catch-all for when people in power face consequences for their actions or receive any type of criticism, something that they're not used to. I'm a black, Muslim woman, and because of social media, marginalized people like myself can express ourselves in a way that was not possible before. That means racist, sexist, and bigoted behavior or remarks don't fly like they used to. This applies to not only wealthy people or industry leaders but anyone whose privilege has historically shielded them from public scrutiny. Because they can't handle this cultural shift, they rely on phrases like "cancel culture" to delegitimize the criticism.[51]

A related category is "wokeness," usually defined as highly sensitive awareness and reaction to social justice issues. Some conservatives use the word "woke" to mock liberals who call out racist or sexist behavior and speech, such as reactions at the University of Michigan when a music professor, a survivor of China's Cultural Revolution, played a clip in class from the 1965 movie *Othello*, in which Sir Laurence Olivier darkened his skin for the title role. A fellow faculty member called the professor's choice of film "a racist act" while students demanded his firing for failing to create "a safe environment." The professor apologized and kept his job, but school officials barred him from ever teaching the class again.[52] Wokeness critics publicized the episode for its alleged absurdity.

While cancel culture and wokeness clearly center on speech issues, the private clashes that ensue usually exclude the First Amendment. Here the bountiful avenues for freedom of expression—many of them digital platforms—help level the playing field. Reasonable citizens with grievances against public figures or situations can speak up, and their targets can respond. Banishing speakers on any side of an issue deters dialogue usually when it is most needed.

## Shifting Ground, Slippery Footing

Speech disputes come and go from one generation to the next, often over grievances deeply rooted in our history. In the wake of the George Floyd killing, protests and violence occurred in dozens of cities. A grand jury in Louisville, Kentucky, chose not to indict the three police officers who killed Breonna Taylor, a Black ER medical technician, after breaking down the door of her apartment at midnight and following up with a hail of gunfire in the mistaken belief a fugitive was with her. The struggle for racial justice has been at the heart of protests, from the abolitionists of the mid-1800s to the student sit-ins at segregated lunch counters in the 1960s to the 1992 riots in Los Angeles after the acquittal of the police officers who beat a Black man, Rodney King. The BLM movement arose in 2012 after the killing of a Black teenager, Trayvon Martin, in Sanford, Florida.

Oppression and injustice do not sit well with Americans, judging by visceral protests leading to the Revolutionary War and a succession of movements, marches, and acts of civil disobedience in opposition to a slew of perceived social injustices—gender equality, voting rights, and protection of the environment. Over time, attitudes shift and reactions fluctuate, but when conditions become unbearable, emotions boil over and occasionally result in a reckoning that cannot be easily ignored. Freedom of speech issues flare up over perceived denial of "rights," as defined by different groups in different eras.

Generally, freedom of speech protects marches conducted as peaceful, nonviolent means to bring attention and resolution to fractious issues.

When BLM protestors encountered forces they viewed as arbitrary or authoritarian, they revved up resistance. In response, authorities pursued aggressive means—rarely negotiations—to establish "law and order" through stricter policies, tactical strategies, and legislation. Throughout 2020, confrontations between police and demonstrators brought renewed attention to anti-protest laws now in force in more than a dozen states and prompted calls for stricter control of public demonstrations. At present, the anti-protest laws primarily cover infrastructure sites, such as power plants, refineries, and cell phone towers. The laws gained legislative support in various states after thousands of protestors occupied makeshift encampments to block construction of a controversial oil pipeline connecting North Dakota with Illinois, within a mile of the Standing Rock Sioux Reservation and its environmentally vulnerable water supply.[53]

How government authorities handled the pipeline protests previewed responses to BLM demonstrations in 2020. The Standing Rock occupation began in April 2016 and continued for more than a year, boiling over in police-protester confrontations that involved freedom of speech, the right to assemble and petition, and the sacred rights of Indigenous people. Both sides engaged in violent acts, but the police, backed by state troopers and the National Guard, held the upper hand, employing water cannons, tear gas, police dogs, and armored personal carriers to oust protestors. Hundreds were arrested for crimes ranging from trespassing to incitement, including journalists doing their jobs.

On February 22, 2017, the last occupants of the nearly abandoned central encampment left under police orders, and tribal officials decided to step up legal action and deemphasize physical resistance. Both sides hunkered down for years of litigious trench warfare. In July 2020, a federal court temporarily closed the pipeline and ordered a new environmental impact study.[54] In July, a federal appellate court reversed the finding, reopening the pipeline but upholding the order for an impact review. The courts, it now appears, will settle the dispute and, in the process, probably provide new guidelines for protest rights in a variety of circumstances.

## Quotables

"The one thing speech isn't is free. There are costs to those who produce it and costs to those who are subjected to it. . . . It does not protect you in private life, where speaking out carries with it the risk of censorship and penalty. Freedom of speech, despite ritual celebrations of it, is not all it is cracked up to be, and it is difficult even to say what it is."[55]

—Stanley Fish, legal scholar

Throughout the summer of 2020 and particularly in the weeks before the presidential election, law-and-order themes resounded from the White House and echoed across the country, especially in Republican strongholds. In Florida, Republican governor Ron DeSantis urged passage of a new law that would impose felony charges on protesters who are arrested for blocking traffic without a parade permit, who participate in gatherings of seven or more people that result in injuries or property damage, or who come from outside the state for demonstrations that later turn violent.[56] The law would absolve motorists who run down protesters if they were "fleeing for safety from a mob," with no specific definition of a mob. The legislature voted approval, and DeSantis signed the "anti-riot" bill into law in early 2021 in a largely redundant political gesture. Existing laws already punish nearly all the illegal acts the law covers. Nonetheless, the law poses a serious threat to nonviolent protestors who, by no fault of their own, get swept up in a net of arrests over the behavior of a few lawbreakers.

The tough talk by DeSantis and officials in other states attempts to reframe peaceful protests and petitioning of the government about grievances as disorderly and dangerous conduct. It appears that a comparable protest deterrent is emerging in civil courts. A negligence lawsuit brought by a Baton Rouge police officer seriously injured by a "rock-like object" thrown during a BLM protest targeted the organizer, DeRay McKesson, when the actual assailant could not be found. The case, *John Doe v. McKesson*, reached the Supreme Court, but the justices sidestepped the issue of McKesson's First Amendment rights by remanding the case to the Louisiana Supreme Court over a question of federal versus state jurisdiction.[57] In other states, expect cases similar to *Doe v. McKesson* to surface.

The Floyd fallout also saw the reemergence of old questions about people's legal rights to video and audio record police officers in the performance of their duties. With smart phones so prevalent, little that happens in public view escapes attention. In the recent past, police in various jurisdictions forced bystanders to stop recording and seized cameras, sometimes destroying recordings. Police less often have suppressed coverage by professional journalists more likely to respond with legal action. In federal jurisdictions and thirty-eight states, it now appears clear that the First Amendment protects the right to record police actions in public under corollary rights to gather, disseminate, and receive information.[58] Of the remaining states, several operate under statutes that require consent by all parties before someone can legally video or audio record a conversation. Called eavesdropping laws, they can be stretched to encompass recordings of police on the job. While the First Amendment widely protects the right of bystanders to record law enforcement officials, across the country individuals continue to face reprisals when they aim cameras to capture an arrest or use of force. If ordered by police to cease recording, the First Amendment is no guarantee that a citizen operating within the law will not be arrested or taken into custody.

From our overview, freedom of speech includes a rich variety of expressive activities. But interpretations of what is meant by "speech" vary. What one community considers permissible—say, fair housing advocates camping overnight in city hall—a nearby community considers trespassing. Regardless of personal politics, citizens of a republic should value the First Amendment as a vehicle that serves *all* people by protecting *all* lawful forms of expression, particularly speech outside the mainstream. It is too dangerous to stand by as speech we dislike or even hate is silenced or punished. To fully appreciate the First Amendment requires an understanding of why it exists, why people have fought so mightily to speak out, and why learned men and women try to convince us not to fear words that challenge our beliefs. The more we know about past threats to freedom of speech, the greater the odds that we can combat a resurgence of them.

The First Amendment remains in constant flux as lawyers and litigants latch onto ingenious ways to argue that rights are being denied. Court victories won in one generation will not preclude revisiting those cases decades later. Margaret Gilleo's antiwar protest goes back nearly thirty years. New slates of legislators, new laws, and repackaged legal arguments can pop up anywhere at any time.

## The Constitution and the Court

Margaret Gilleo's right to display an antiwar protest sign on her own property does not exist explicitly anywhere in the Constitution or Bill of Rights. The justices who decided in Gilleo's favor in 1994 found justification not by close reading of original documents but by reasonable interpretation of what the Framers *intended*—for those documents to be adaptable to changing times. "The Framers selected language flexible enough to anticipate social, economic, and political crises," said legal historian Kermit L. Hall, "leaving to courts and judges the task of giving precise meaning to these majestic generalities."[59]

This chapter's excursion through Supreme Court decisions supports Hall's contention that the Framers never expected the customs and traditions of the past to dictate the nation's future constitutional rights. Madison and his brethren wisely left room for an expansion of civil liberties meant to empower rather than constrain citizens.

For all the Supreme Court's present-day influence, its early contributions seemed comparatively irrelevant, largely because the Framers never specified its role other than to declare, "The judicial Power of the United States, shall be vested in one supreme Court, and in such inferior Courts as the Congress may from time to time ordain and establish." They prescribed nothing about its structure, authority, or procedural rules. In its first few years, the Court heard no cases of note, until *Marbury v. Madison* in 1803, when Chief Justice John Marshall seized an opportunity to establish both the Court's relevance and power. The decision established the principle of judicial review that gave the Supreme Court and other federal courts the authority to rule on the constitutionality of legislation and executive acts, including those of Congress and the president. The Supreme Court grew into its role, largely on its own.

*Marbury v. Madison* eventually established that all state and federal courts were bound by the decisions of the Supreme Court. In time, the Court's opinions came to influence judges, lawyers, and lawmakers from every jurisdiction, all of whom mine the Supreme Court record for guidance, precedent, and wisdom to help in their own decision-making. Once the Supreme Court issues an opinion, all other branches and levels of government are expected to defer. The Supreme Court has addressed some of the nation's most contested social and constitutional issues.

Its opinions typically are long, well footnoted, and analytically detailed. The writing style ranges from pedantic to engaging. Nearly all opinions, though, resonate through the American legal system, and a few achieve lasting significance. One of those was the concurring opinion of Justice Louis D. Brandeis in *Whitney v. California* (1927). Fears about the spread of Communism in the United States led to criminal prosecutions of party members and other citizens when Brandeis wrote:

> Those who won our independence . . . believed that freedom to think as you will and to speak as you think are means indispensable to the discovery and spread of political truth; that, without free speech and assembly, discussion would be futile; that, with them, discussion affords ordinarily adequate protection against the dissemination of noxious doctrine; that the greatest menace to freedom is an inert people; that public discussion is a political duty, and that this should be a fundamental principle of the American government.[60]

Legal scholar Vincent Blasi credits Brandeis with formulating a First Amendment-based "ideal of courage" that exhorts citizens to open themselves willingly to the potential for political and social change.[61] Blasi helps us understand why the influence of the Supreme Court extends beyond the confines of a particular case to encompass the bigger picture—our responsibilities as citizens to act with resolve.

Over its history, the Court has shifted from liberal to conservative orientations, back and forth, often dependent on which political party holds confirmation power when a Court opening occurs. Two judicial approaches especially have influenced how the justices review the constitutionality of laws or government actions—judicial restraint and judicial activism. They are neither mutually exclusive nor precisely defined. Conservatives can be activists and liberals can be restrained. Under a principle of restraint, judges generally defer to federal and state lawmakers, assuming the legislative branch makes law, not judges by their rulings. Judicial activists, however, by and large believe that constitutional issues should be decided within the context of values, needs, and conditions in contemporary society at the time a case is heard. The nine Supreme Court justices—no matter their particular legal philosophy—can faithfully honor the core meaning of the nation's original documents *and* recognize that the Framers counted on an evolving democracy.

The cardinal rule applicable across the judiciary is that judges should never let personal preferences, biases, or political aims influence their decisions. Unfortunately, contemporary debates over judicial philosophy usually devolve into "liberal" versus "conservative" warfare, with citizens considering the Court as either ally or foe. In such a climate, the relative merits of major Supreme Court opinions seldom go through reasoned public analysis.

Until the Trump presidency, the Supreme Court, while not escaping controversy, largely avoided ideological crises in recent decades. Trump ran for president vowing to transform the Supreme Court and overturn earlier decisions, particularly *Roe v. Wade*, the 1973 opinion that women had a constitutional right to choose whether to terminate a pregnancy before viability.[62] Then he won, and the Republican leadership helped him accomplish that goal. Trump handpicked for confirmation three nominees who, it would appear, agreed with him despite precedent and popular support for an almost fifty-year-old right. Few citizens—or pundits—anticipated how far right the Supreme Court would turn and how its new majority—Trump's appointees along with two sitting justices—would deepen the national polarization over abortion and other highly emotional issues.

In the 2022 majority opinion invalidating *Roe* and the other major abortion rights case, *Planned Parenthood v. Casey*, Justice Samuel A. Alito Jr. argued that "the Constitution makes no reference to abortion, and no such right is implicitly protected by any constitutional provision."[63] Alito grounded the decision in *originalism*, itself a controversial theory endorsed by a minority of jurists and lawyers who believe in interpreting laws, particularly the Constitution and its amendments, by their meaning *when first written*. In its extreme form, originalism examines emerging constitutional challenges through a narrow window of the past. In overturning *Roe*, the new majority's arguably tendentious reading of the historical record accomplished an apparently political objective—it ruled that women never should have had a constitutional right to abortion in the first place. David Cole, the legal director of the ACLU, said that "never has the Court overturned precedent on such a transparently thin basis."[64]

After the Supreme Court departed so drastically from *Roe*, questions arose: What can we now count on as inviolable Constitutional rights? What other protections established by historic Supreme Court decisions might face reversal? Such questions apply to both liberal and conservative courts as they interpret the Constitution. In view of recent behavior, the Supreme Court and other contentious courts, for that matter, bear watching by citizens and journalists.

## A Postscript for Troubled Times

If the First Amendment belongs to the people, then the people ought to be alarmed when Americans fight over whose rights prevail. Even a nation born of dissent might flinch at armed men who scream "f— you" when asked to put on a mask, hecklers at a public meeting who threaten school officials who endorse approved vaccines to protect public health, overzealous protesters who accost outdoor diners while screaming "defund the police," or a resurgence of book bans and the removal of literature from school libraries and classrooms deemed "too liberal" about subjects such as sexual orientation and American slavery. That, however, is what we have come to.

But it is worse than that, as we now know. Recall how the Supreme Court dealt with expression that posed a "clear and present danger" to civil order and national security. Beginning in 1919, a series of the Court's rulings established tolerance for incendiary speech up to the point of "imminent" lawlessness. So, marches through Jewish communities by swastika-bearing neo-Nazis, oratory by self-styled circuit-riding preachers damning female college students as whores, or pro-life and pro-choice showdowns outside abortion clinics were permitted until the speech crossed whatever nebulous line separated protected from punishable speech—at that moment. Usually, impermissible speech arises in close proximity to an audience that could quickly act on a speaker's inciteful language—in the extreme, an anarchist addressing a crowd while holding a Molotov cocktail and reaching for a Zippo lighter. That type of clear and present danger remains, but perhaps a far greater danger comes from a speaker who incites a near boundless online audience of potential bombers, assassins, or domestic terrorists. Consider, particularly, a speaker with the means to address gatherings of thousands of true believers at in-person rallies and to reach millions more via Twitter. A clear and present danger? Not by himself, but the Supreme Court of the early twentieth century never envisioned speech becoming so powerful, so pervasive, and so enabled by communications technology.

In normal times, our review of free speech ought to be reassuring and perhaps uplifting. But not now. After 233 years marked by the gradual expansion of expressive rights, our forty-fifth president incessantly denigrated the First Amendment unless it served his interests. He stifled opposition speech and speakers at nearly every turn. Inexcusably, he used the pulpit of the White House to demean foes and propagate lies. No citizen can ever underestimate the potential power of selfish leaders who are willfully unfamiliar with or indifferent to our nation's democratic traditions, who advocate "shooting when the looting starts,"[65] who encourage followers to beat up journalists, or who praise "patriots" armed with assault weapons. Free speech comes with an ever greater responsibility to use our rights with great care. The nation has seen enough bloodshed and violence spurred by speakers who abuse freedom of speech and political actors who falsely villainize peaceful dissent.

If the First Amendment is allowed to be treated with contempt or indifference, expect it to melt at our feet. In chapter 4, we examine freedom of the press, the provision that the Founders expected to safeguard the other first freedoms. Under the aegis of the First Amendment, journalists now benefit from a range of statutory, administrative, and judicial rulings. Citizens share in those benefits. The next chapter shows how the rights of journalists to gather and report news promote citizenship and public discourse—and protect us from those who would do us harm.

## CHAPTER 4

# An Epic Battle, Then a Victory for Press Freedom

Fifty years or so before Donald J. Trump declared war on the news media, another president wrote the first draft of the script Trump weaponized.

In the late 1960s, the Vietnam War occupied the American consciousness. The peace movement, finding its voice early in the decade, grew steadily and reached a crescendo in 1971. On college campuses, in city parks, and even outside the White House, protesters clashed with riot police. Government buildings, ROTC offices, and military research centers came under attack around the country, including by means of sit-in occupations and deadly bombings by fringe anti-war groups, notably the Weather Underground. At Kent State University, nervous National Guardsmen fired into an anti-war crowd of students. Neil Young immortalized the tragedy in his soulful song with the repeated line, "Four dead in Ohio." Elsewhere, a loose confederation of Catholic priests, nuns, and laypeople targeted draft board offices, stealing records they burned or defaced with animal blood.

For a week in April 1971, Vietnam veterans camped on the National Mall near the Capitol to demand an end to the war.[1] With a cinematic touch of drama, the 1994 movie *Forrest Gump* had its hero in uniform wearing his Medal of Honor, speaking before a throng of protestors encircling the Lincoln Memorial Reflecting Pool. In real life, on the last day of the protest, a collection of ragtag veterans, one at a time, threw their medals, discharge papers, and military paraphernalia onto the steps of the Capitol. Thousands of miles away, around a table in Paris, U.S. and North Vietnam diplomats parried in agonizingly long negotiations to end the war. In Southeast Asia, the death toll of American military personnel topped 45,000, but as summer approached, troop withdrawals began and the flow of body bags arriving at Dover Air Force Base diminished.

Then came a bold act of anti-war resistance from a scholarly man named Daniel Ellsberg, who decided Americans deserved to know the truth about U.S. decision-making and military operations in Southeast Asia—a story he knew intimately. Ellsberg, a former Marine platoon leader, returned from Vietnam to earn a PhD from Harvard and found himself working as a military analyst for the Pentagon. He joined a team assigned to produce a voluminous military-diplomatic history of the war commissioned by Secretary of Defense Robert McNamara. Operating under strict secrecy, the team gathered a trove of records, reviewing and organizing them into a classified narrative that later came to be known as the Pentagon Papers.

As Ellsberg ventured deeper into the material, he uncovered evidence that conflicted with Pentagon public pronouncements minimizing details about U.S. losses and missteps and, more important, lying about military "successes" in Vietnam, deceptions that both the Kennedy and Johnson administrations knew about. In Ellsberg's off-hours, he copied the report, one page at a time, seven thousand in all.[2] In several tense trips, he removed documents in a stuffed briefcase, walking pass the front guards at the California offices of the Rand Corporation, a Defense Department contractor. Ellsberg had tried to get members of Congress to disclose the study but to no avail. He finally turned to the press and convinced *New York Times* reporter Neil Sheehan, a former war correspondent and friend, to consider publication. As Sheehan reviewed the study, he realized he held an explosive exposé. He also knew Ellsberg feared being prosecuted and imprisoned and had vacillated on whether to turn a full set of documents over to Sheehan. Finally, Ellsberg told Sheehan that he could read the papers and take notes but not make copies. Most books and articles about the Ellsberg-Sheehan relationship suggest they worked in harmony. They did not, apparently. When Sheehan, at age eighty-four, died on January 7, 2021, the *New York Times* published another version of the story that it agreed to withhold until after Sheehan's death—a story based on an interview Sheehan gave the *Times* in 2015. Contrary to previously published accounts, Sheehan decided that Ellsberg posed too great a risk of getting caught with the documents or surrendering them to government officials who, in turn, would lock them away perhaps forever. Sheehan deceived a trusting Ellsberg and, with the help of his wife, *New Yorker* writer Susan Sheehan, feverishly copied the report at print shops in the Boston area. The Sheehans booked an extra seat on a flight from Boston to New York, safeguarding the photocopies in several suitcases strapped next to them.[3]

With approval of publisher Arthur Ochs Sulzberger, a team of *Times* staffers worked from suites at the New York Hilton to wade meticulously and warily into the documents they knew were stolen goods.[4] Sheehan's first story based on the Pentagon Papers appeared on the front page of the *Times* on Sunday, June 13, 1971, topped by a sedate headline, "Viet-

nam Archive: Pentagon Traces 3 Decades of Growing U.S. Involvement."
At the White House, President Richard M. Nixon and his family relaxed
after the Rose Garden wedding of daughter Tricia the day before. On the
lazy late spring day, other administration officials overlooked the story,
too. But not for long. Nixon, prodded by his advisers, moved forcefully
to quash what he perceived as a direct threat to national security. Nixon
believed a traitor leaked a top-secret government report and the *Times*—
and the *Washington Post*, which ran its own news reports based on material obtained by Ellsberg—acted as accomplices. The U.S. Department
of Justice, under orders from the president, obtained temporary court
injunctions to halt publication of all stories based on the leaked documents. The newspapers complied but sought an expedited appeal from
the United States Supreme Court.

In a matter of days, the Supreme Court reviewed the record, heard oral
arguments, and reached a controversial decision that did not sit well with
several justices who wanted more time to fully consider legal positions
and ramifications. The majority of justices believed the gravity of the clash
warranted haste. Justice Hugo Black described the showdown starkly: "For
the first time in the 182 years since the founding of the Republic, the federal courts are asked to hold that the First Amendment does not mean
what it says, but rather means that the Government can halt the publication of current news of vital importance to the people of this country."[5]
Black knew the injunctions constituted a prior restraint of the sort the
Founders hoped to avoid with the First Amendment. On June 30, the Court
assembled to announce its decision through a 241-word joint ruling called
a per curiam opinion, normally unanimous and straightforward; this one
was neither. By consensus rather than unanimity, the justices concluded
that any prior restraint by government to block freedom of expression was
presumptively unconstitutional and that the government, therefore, faced
"a heavy burden" of justifying such drastic action. Two federal courts earlier held that the government had not met that burden. The Court's opinion said: "We agree."

For the moment, journalists worldwide breathed a sigh of relief. But
there was far more to the case, officially titled *New York Times Co. v. United
States*. Each of the nine justices wrote a separate opinion, highly unusual
compared to the Court's normal procedures. Those separate opinions
revealed a range of interpretations and reactions. Yes, the majority of justices ultimately sided with the press, but several did so with reservations.
The dissenters, too, took different stances, and one, Justice Harry Black-
mun, said, "I strongly urge, and sincerely hope, that these two newspapers

will be fully aware of their ultimate responsibilities to the United States of America." He added a concern about national security in wartime:

I hope that damage has not already been done. If, however, damage has been done, and if, with the Court's action today, these newspapers proceed to publish the critical documents and there results therefrom "the death of soldiers, the destruction of alliances, the greatly increased difficulty of negotiation with our enemies, the inability of our diplomats to negotiate," to which list I might add the factors of prolongation of the war and of further delay in the freeing of United States prisoners, then the Nation's people will know where the responsibility for these sad consequences rests.[6]

Some observers believed that in rushing to complete separate opinions on a grave constitutional issue, the Court yielded to expediency. Law professor Laura Krugman Ray later wrote, "With so little common ground, the majority justices in *New York Times* found in the *per curiam* a convenient form to contain the message of their diverse concurrences: we stand together as a Court and emphatically reject the government's claim for prior restraint of the press." By Ray's analysis, "The Court majority believed the result more important than the theory that supports it."[7] It was not a neat decision, but it was momentous.

While journalists and legal experts watched the unfolding drama with apprehension, a majority of Americans went to work, picked up their children after school, caught the local TV news, and dozed off watching Johnny Carson's *The Tonight Show*. After all, with U.S. involvement in the Vietnam War winding down, the political, diplomatic, and martial heat had already spiked. A dull-sounding "scoop" and the reaction of the White House seemed significant but not *that* significant. But it was. Here we stood at the brink of an unprecedented attempt by the president of the United States to emasculate the constitutionally guaranteed rights of a free press in order to protect politicians' lies to the public. In 1971, many Americans shared Nixon's disdain for the "media elite."

Consider what happened within the context of the Constitution: As a nation wages war, an anti-war advocate steals classified Pentagon documents, which the nation's two leading newspapers publish, only to cease publication by order of the president, setting the stage for an epic legal battle played out before the United States Supreme Court, which tells the president the First Amendment prevails over his authority as the commander in chief. Had it not actually happened, the scenario seems grist for the great American novel. The exceptional nature of the Pentagon Papers case is hard to overstate. Freedom to print ensured under the First Amendment dwarfed the president's authority, even in wartime, even when absconded classified records went to the heart of the matter.

A short time after publication, Sheehan and Ellsberg crossed paths, Sheehan related in the 2015 *Times* interview. Ellsberg said, "So you stole it, like I did." Sheehan said he responded, "No, Dan, I didn't steal it. And neither did you. Those papers are the property of the people of the United States. They paid for them with their national treasure and the blood of their sons, and they have a right to it.'"[8]

Reflecting on the case from a 2016 vantage point, Dana Priest, a two-time Pulitzer Prize-winning national security reporter at the *Washington Post*, agreed: "This heroic act of journalism, and the legal ruling it forced the US Supreme Court to make, still stand today as the most powerful legal and moral weapon in the American media's battle against government secrecy."[9] And David Rudenstine, author of *The Day the Presses Stopped*, applauded the courage of the Supreme Court:

> The Court's decision in the Pentagon Papers is a guidepost for any democratic society to follow as it daily resolves clashes among competing claims that implicate freedom and security. Distilled, the decision represents the judgment that democracy must tolerate risks—even potentially serious risks—inherent in freedom because freedom also strengthens democracy's fundamental security.[10]

In the decades since the Pentagon Papers, scores of observers have pondered the practical importance of the decision. Several conclusions stand out. First, the Supreme Court did not ban prior restraints outright as unconstitutional. The government continues to use prior restraint, but, thanks to the Pentagon Papers, the freedom of the press clause vastly limits that power. Second, had the press been silenced in 1971, the relationship of journalism and government would be far different today. As you watch or read the news, consider the implications if the content *only* reflected what the current administration approved. What if latter-day presidents wielded broad power to pull the plug on disfavored news and journalists? Had Nixon won, it is not far-fetched to imagine far wider use of the "classified" stamp to withhold government records, ranging from safety reports at a nuclear power plant to travel logs of presidential excursions to play golf. Had Nixon won *decisively*, today the First Amendment might not prevent secret surveillance of journalists' phone and digital records, government investigations of news organizations for publishing stories criticizing government deception, politically based scrutiny of media banking records and tax returns, and arrests of journalists for true stories that government officials simply claimed to be threats to national security.

Although tenuous in the scope of its protection, the Pentagon Papers decision emboldened print and broadcast journalists who, for example, insisted on access to scenes of breaking news, filed lawsuits to unseal public documents, and chose jail rather than disclose the identities of confidential sources. A Sheehan contemporary, Andrew Pearson, recently described how the Vietnam War and the Pentagon Papers shaped generations of reporters to follow: "The best young reporters have learned from the Vietnam War to question authority and find out for themselves what's really going on. And that's how it's supposed to work in a democracy."[11]

Forty-three years after the Pentagon Papers, the Pulitzer Prize, journalism's highest award, went to British-based *The Guardian* and the *Washington Post* for their work in exposing a massive secret surveillance operation by the National Security Agency that included monitoring the telephone records of tens of millions of Americans and spying globally on allies and adversaries alike. The exposé was based on documents leaked by CIA analyst Edward Snowden, whom the U.S. attorney general later charged with espionage. In the Snowden case, as with the Pentagon Papers, reporting legitimate news meant the publishers knowingly risked retaliation aimed at reputations, earnings, and, in fact, their ability to function. The journalists who wrote and edited the stories knew they might be branded as traitors themselves. The Obama administration investigated a number of reporters linked to the leak and threatened legal action but, in the end, chose not to use injunctions to block publication or file criminal charges. Later, Daniel Ellsberg said Snowden deserved thanks for forcing Congress to change U.S. surveillance law. While both men are notable whistleblowers, Ellsberg sought to expose *actual* falsehoods that supported a war fought largely by draftees. Snowden warned of *potential* evils caused by secret government surveillance. In both cases, they put themselves in personal jeopardy to alert citizens about the conduct of their government, as did the journalists who put those disclosures into public circulation.

## "A Sacred Trust and Great Privilege"

The press freedom clause undeniably protects journalists. But just as significantly, it serves all Americans by supporting and reinforcing the press with a legal rationale to gather and report the news, an immense benefit to citizens who care about democratic roles. Press freedom belongs to anyone who expresses truthful information by tweet, social media post, blog, or other means of mass communication. Remember Margaret Gilleo and her yard sign. In an essay from August 2018, the editors of *The Atlantic* magazine provided a context:

> The freedom of the press is an individual liberty, not the peculiar privilege of a profession or an industry. It is *your* right as an American to read what you will, to write what you think, and to publish what you believe. The press is neither the enemy of the people nor its ally, but rather its possession.[12]

Citizens, whether journalists or not, ought to appreciate the Pentagon Papers decision as a decisive moment for our collective liberty to read, discuss, and share information that truly belongs to us—our "possession"—even if we question the methods or motives of some journalists and news organizations. We "possess" the news in another sense, meaning that journalism *belongs* to us because the Founders undeniably linked the press to the public's *need* and *right* to know. In turn, responsible news organizations since the founding have committed themselves to public service. We would say to the editors of *The Atlantic* that the press *is* an ally, too.

An ally is on your side and backs you up. It does not observe from a safe distance. In 1971, as the sound of high-speed presses reverberated through their buildings, Kathrine Graham, publisher of the *Post*, and Arthur Ochs Sulzberger, her counterpart at the *Times*, understood that the First Amendment would not spare them from liability for the conduct of their publications. They purposely challenged the power of government and infuriated a segment of citizens, including subscribers and financial backers, who thought they acted recklessly. Both Graham and Sulzberger—among society's elite—risked imprisonment and the demise of two family-owned journalism dynasties. Few other chief executives in fields like banking, law, aeronautics, or Big Business would risk all on a constitutional principle as did Graham and Sulzberger. They held true to the vision of Madison, Jefferson, and other Founders who staked the future of the young nation on the ability of newspapers to inform a diverse collection of citizens about the conduct of their leaders. Jefferson's attitude was striking: "Were it left to me to decide whether we should have a government without newspapers or newspapers without a government, I should not hesitate a moment to prefer the latter."[13]

In a post-Pentagon Papers moment, Justice Potter Stewart spoke of why the press occupies an exalted position within the First Amendment protections:

If the Free Press guarantee meant no more than freedom of expression, it would be a constitutional redundancy. . . . For centuries before our Revolution, the press in England had been licensed, censored, and bedeviled by prosecutions for seditious libel. The British Crown knew that a free press was not just a neutral vehicle for the balanced discussion of diverse ideas. Instead, the free press meant organized, expert scrutiny of government. The press was a conspiracy of the intellect, with the courage of numbers. This formidable check on official power was what the British Crown had feared—and what the American Founders decided to risk.[14]

Jefferson and Stewart—separated by hundreds of years—shared the same respect for a free press as the bedrock for democracy. They knew the First Amendment never *obligated* the press to perform in service to the republic. But they correctly trusted that it would. Graham and Sulzberger, as have generations of journalists before and after them, assumed a role described by fellow publisher Nelson Poynter (1903-78) as a "sacred trust and great privilege."[15]

## Marginalia

President Nixon's obsession over the Ellsberg leaks led the White House to create a team of ex-CIA and ex-FBI agents called the Special Investigations Unit. It set up shop in the basement of the Executive Office Building under the supervision of presidential aides. One charter member of the team jokingly called himself a plumber, tasked with plugging leaks, so the slang term "the Plumbers" unofficially replaced the unit's formal name. In its first major operation, the unit burglarized the office of Ellsberg's psychiatrist in search of material to discredit Ellsberg. The Plumbers later transitioned to covert operations to reelect the president like wiretaps and dirty tricks. Early on June 17, 1972, police apprehended five intruders at the office of the Democratic National Committee in the Watergate complex. It turned out that four of them formerly had been part of CIA attempts to overturn Fidel Castro in Cuba. The fifth, James W. McCord Jr., was the security chief of the Committee to Re-elect the President. Assigned a seemingly routine police incident story, two young *Washington Post* reporters, Bob Woodward and Carl Bernstein, doggedly tracked the Plumbers' shenanigans until the trail led them to the White House. Caught up in a large-scale scandal, Nixon refused a court order to turn over secret Oval Office tape recordings. Once again, the Supreme Court thwarted him. In a unanimous opinion, the Court decided that no citizen—not even the president—was above the law. He must comply with the subpoena and surrender the tapes. Facing impeachment, Nixon yielded and resigned. Two major motion pictures—*All the President's Men* (1976) and *The Post* (2019)—dramatize the Watergate case and the Pentagon Papers, respectively.

## Jim Crow Meets the Press

As the Pentagon Papers case firmly established, if freedom of the press means anything, it means freedom against direct government censorship. But the right to publish freely, as essential as it is, depends on a subset of protections that allow journalists to ferret out news to begin with—news citizens need to read, hear, and consider, no matter where they might stand on a particular dispute or issue.

Before the Civil War, people knew "Jim Crow" as a popular minstrel character portrayed by white actors in blackface. During the Reconstruction period, Jim Crow referred to state and local laws enacted by southern states to deny basic freedoms to former slaves and stymie federal attempts to integrate public places. In the late 1870s, Southern segregationists, some of whom held high state or local office, stepped up Jim Crow enforcement. Over the course of two world wars, the Great Depression, and the Franklin D. Roosevelt years, Black Americans living in the South—and elsewhere, too—learned through painful experience that the Constitution and the Bill of Rights seldom applied equally to them. The segregationists prevailed until the mid-1950s, when Blacks and whites moved generally in peaceful ways to right wrongs. Journalists reported about courageous women, men, and children who marched and led various protests to eradicate Jim Crow. (No one should assume, however, that the civil rights movement weeded out white supremacy. America may yet again have to face down Jim Crow–type laws.)

By the 1960s, TV correspondents and newspaper reporters had spread across the country to document an era of racial injustice. News reports entered family rooms, sports bars, and other gathering places. They required the nation to examine and reexamine its values, attitudes, and behavior. Overt and systemic racism permeated American life, even where laws had been passed to supposedly guarantee equal rights for all citizens. In the South, especially, persons of color carefully navigated a world of separate restrooms, whites-only hotels, back-of-the bus transportation, off-limits lunch counters, segregated schools, and voting rights based on passing bogus literacy "tests." Klan bombings and terror attacks threatened anyone who challenged segregation, including reporters. Besides using such tactics as beatings and tear gas, public officials strategically filed defamation suits for alleged damage to their reputations. Mainly, they wanted to discourage news coverage by northern interlopers.

In 1961, L. B. Sullivan, the police commissioner of Montgomery, Alabama, joined the ranks of the aggrieved—but not over a news story. Sullivan's case centered on a full-page advertisement printed in the *New York Times* with the heading, in large type, "Heed Their Rising Voices." An organization calling itself the Committee to Defend Martin Luther King and the Struggle for Freedom in the South had paid $4,800 for its publication. The committee's officers included actor Sidney Poitier and singers Nat King Cole and Harry Belafonte. Sixty other prominent public figures were listed as sponsors. The committee alleged that Sullivan, although not named, and other Alabama police and public officials brutally suppressed peaceful protests and persecuted civil rights activists. Sullivan sued the committee, its listed sponsors, and the *Times*.

The ten-paragraph advertisement contained errors, trivial at best, such as misstating that King had been arrested seven times when it had been four times. (Police in the South often questioned him without filing charges.) The evidence of defamation seemed flimsy, but not in the Alabama of 1961. The trial judge, a devotee of the Confederacy, submitted the case to a twelve-man, all-white jury with instructions that the accusations were "libelous per se," meaning inherently defamatory. He told the jurors they need only determine the parties responsible for publication and whether the commentary was "of and concerning" Sullivan and other officials, a threshold that meant "the average reasonable person" would recognize whom the story was about, even when a plaintiff was not mentioned by name. In most tight-knit communities, any number of identifying details, such as a physical description, job title, or an address, would be telling. Two and a half hours later, the jury reached its judgment to award Sullivan $500,000, the full amount of damages he sought. In related lawsuits, other Alabama officials sought damages that totaled $3 million.

Folks in Montgomery jokingly said the advertisement probably enhanced Sullivan's reputation rather than harmed it. The *Times*, of course, found nothing humorous about the judgment. Defamation lawsuits were serious business, and this one, coupled with other cases against the *Times*, threatened the newspaper's very existence.[16] Being sued for defamation also reinforced the common perception that journalists ought to be held responsible for all information they publish, no matter if the story or opinions enhance the public's right to know.

Sullivan filed his lawsuit at a time when defamation fell strictly under state law; there was no federal defamation statute then or now. Prior to the mid-1960s, each state defined and administered defamation law as it saw fit. The Founders, while opposed to seditious libel with its criminal penalties, generally saw no reason for the First Amendment to shield the press from liability in private litigation. English common law, transplanted to the colonies, defined defamation as a false communication (picture, image, words, depiction) that exposes persons to hatred, ridicule, or contempt; lowers them in the esteem of others; causes then to be shunned; or injures them in their business or calling. Before we became such a litigious society, the defamed party might challenge an editor to a duel or storm into a newspaper office for a face-to-face confrontation. In the twentieth century, defamation become a weapon of choice against political foes, largely journalists engaged in investigative and social justice reporting. Big-city newspapers and TV networks possessed deep pockets and libel insurance, making them tempting targets. Judicial application of state laws overwhelmingly tilted in favor of those suing the press.

On March 9, 1964, after four years of legal wrangling, the U.S. Supreme Court overturned the lower court's verdict on the defamation suit. It ranks among the most significant decisions in Supreme Court history. In the majority opinion, Justice William J. Brennan Jr. stated where he stood on a free press and where he believed Americans stood as well: "We consider this case against the background of a profound national commitment to the principle that debate on public issues should be uninhibited, robust, and wide-open, and that it may well include vehement, caustic, and sometimes unpleasantly sharp attacks on government and public officials." Errors, said the Court majority, are "inevitable in free debate." To require critics of government officials to prove the truthfulness of every utterance leads to self-censorship. For freedom of expression to survive, let alone flourish, the justices concluded that "breathing space"—a tolerance for human error—was needed in defamation cases. Thus, the Court established a federal standard applicable in every state that prohibited public officials from recovering damages for a defamatory falsehood relating to official conduct *unless* they prove the statement was made with "actual malice"—that is, "with knowledge that it was false or with reckless disregard of whether it was false or not."[17] If you hear mention of the "actual malice rule," it stems directly from *Times v. Sullivan* and how the case dramatically reshaped defamation law.

The Court set a high standard decidedly advantageous to the press. *Times v. Sullivan* required that public officials suing for defamation produce evidence that the news organization went beyond mere carelessness, beyond negligence, and even beyond evidence of ill-intent by the reporter or executives of the news organization. The standard applied to elected officeholders and a broad category of officials with clear administrative responsibility over government affairs. The burden of proof shifted from media defendants to public realm libel plaintiffs who had to (1) *prove* they were defamed, (2) *prove* the alleged defamation was false, (3) *prove* demonstrable harm, and (4) *prove* the alleged defamer acted with actual malice. Before *Times v. Sullivan*, if a small-town newspaper published a fact-bound, verified investigation accusing the mayor of theft from the city and the mayor sued, a judge applying pre-*Sullivan* law was likely to instruct jurors to *presume* both the falsity of the publication and the injury it caused. State law left jurors with little to decide other than the amount of compensation for actual damages and punitive or exemplary damages, often exceptionally high monetary awards, at times amounting to millions of dollars, intended to deter others from committing similar acts.

Under such conditions, why would journalists risk careers, and publishers their businesses, to report wrongdoing by public officials in the first place? As much as editors in the South and elsewhere might have wanted to expose corruption and injustice, they often chose the safer route to report on subjects unlikely to provoke a lawsuit. Hence, the importance of *Times v. Sullivan*. It told journalists around the nation that the balance point on the scale of justice had shifted. The decision was meant to encourage reporters to investigate, editorial writers to harshly criticize, and cartoonists to skewer. *Times v. Sullivan* rested on the proposition that news organizations that held authorities accountable did exactly what the Founders and citizens expected of them. *Times v. Sullivan* fast became both a defensive and an offensive strategy for the news media.

In subsequent rulings, the Court expanded the actual malice rule, applying it to public figures, defined "as people in the news or public eye by virtue of fame or notoriety." The vagueness of *Times v. Sullivan* and its progeny required the Court to clarify its definitions. Eventually, the Court identified "all-purpose public figures" who occupied positions of "persuasive power and influence." The category included top-tier entertainers (e.g., broadcaster and activist Oprah Winfrey), elite professional athletes (e.g., professional basketball star Steph Curry), and the heads of major corporations (e.g., Facebook founder Mark Zuckerberg). The Court also recognized "limited-purpose" public figures—individuals who "have thrust themselves to the forefront of particular controversies in order to influence the resolution of the issues involved" (such as Alicia Garza,

Patrisse Marie Kahn-Cullors, and Opal Tometi, cofounders of Black Lives Matter).

Moreover, the Court clarified "reckless disregard for the truth" in *Curtis Publishing Co. v. Butts*. The multimillion-dollar lawsuit arose from an article published in the *Saturday Evening Post* that accused two prominent college football officials, Alabama's legendary coach Bear Bryant and Georgia's athletic director Wally Butts, of fixing a 1962 football game between the two schools. In examining the trial court record, the Court found evidence that "cast serious doubt on the adequacy of the investigation underlying the article." The story, the Court concluded, amounted to an "extreme departure from the standards of investigation and reporting ordinarily adhered to by responsible publishers."[18] The most serious offense? The magazine built its article on the dubious account of insurance salesman George Burnett, who overheard a phone conversation between Bryant and Butts. In those days, long-distance phone calls required an operator to connect the caller and the person being called. On occasion, wires would literally get crossed, which happened in Burnett's instance. As he attempted to call a friend, the operator accidentally cross-connected him into a call between Butts and Bryant. Instead of hanging up, Burnett listened in for fifteen minutes during which he said he heard the men discuss game strategy and play calling. Burnett took notes, which he eventually turned over to the magazine for a reported $5,000 payment.

When the Court ruled for Butts, it listed examples of how the magazine failed to interview a person with Burnett when the phone call was overheard, view the game films, or check for any adjustments in Alabama's normal game plans. The writer assigned to the story was not well versed in the sport and never asked an expert to critique the article in advance. The actual malice test, *Butts* demonstrated, would not spare journalists who grievously violated the newsgathering and verification norms of the profession. It cost the *Saturday Evening Post* a reported $750,000 and sent the magazine, with roots tracing to Benjamin Franklin, into a death spiral.

The actual malice rule applied to officials and public figures for good reason. But what about ordinary citizens drawn into the news—someone, for instance, incorrectly identified in a news report as arrested for DUI or possession of cocaine? In addressing that question, the Court recommended a less strict "negligence" standard for failure to take a "reasonable level of care" expected of journalists. The new test considers the prepublication steps taken by a news organization to research, edit, and fact-check a story. These "private individuals," the Court reasoned, warranted special consideration because they held "no substantial responsibility" over matters of government and public life and were more likely to suffer appreciable injury. A majority of states have incorporated the negligence standard, as well as the actual malice rule, into their defamation statutes.

## When the News Intrudes on Private Lives

Not long after the Court addressed defamation, it turned its attention to the emerging rights of personal privacy, then a relatively new phenomenon. You can scour the Constitution and the Bill of Rights and not find explicit reference to a "right of privacy." In 1965, the liberal-leaning Supreme Court broke ground in a 7-2 decision that ruled that individual protections in the First, Third, Fourth, Fifth, and Ninth Amendments implied a constitutional right to privacy. The Court cited a key part of the Fourth Amendment: "The right of the people to be secure in their persons, houses, papers, and effects, against unreasonable searches and seizures, shall not be violated." The case, *Griswold v. Connecticut*, challenged a state law that read: "Any person who uses any drug, medicinal article or instrument for the purpose of preventing conception shall be fined not less than fifty dollars or imprisoned not less than sixty days nor more than one year or be both fined and imprisoned." Another section of the law said: "Any person who assists, abets, counsels, causes, hires or commands another to commit any offense may be prosecuted and punished as if he were the principal offender." Justice William O. Douglas put the issue bluntly: "Would we allow the police to search the sacred precincts of marital bedrooms for telltale signs of the use of contraceptives? The very idea is repulsive to the notions of privacy surrounding the marriage relationship."[19] States once criminalized the use of diaphragms and birth control pills even inside the privacy of the home. *Griswold* paved the way to *Roe v. Wade*, the 1973 Supreme Court ruling affording women the freedom to choose abortion, a decision overturned by another generation of justices nearly fifty years later.

*Griswold*, however, opened a privacy land rush of sorts, as the lawyers and lawmakers staked out claims in a vast, unexplored territory that included litigation over privacy-invasive news coverage. Lawyers drew upon a noted law journal article from 1890 for guidance. Written by Samuel Warren and Louis D. Brandeis before Brandeis's ascension to the Supreme Court, the article damned practices of newspapers that, in competition-fueled quests for readers, sensationalized and, at times, fabricated the news. Historians called it the era of "yellow journalism," and today's critics of journalism have resurrected the term to characterize objectionable news coverage. The arguments Warren and Brandeis laid out continue to influence invasion of privacy disputes and statutory law. In everyday language, these include rights to be left alone, to decide how much of ourselves to make public, to avoid physical intrusion by the press, and to preclude disclosure of private information "about which the public has no legitimate concern."

Elements of defamation overlap privacy law, with one significant difference: The defense of truth, used successfully in defamation cases, does not apply to a majority of privacy cases. Truth does not justify unauthorized publication or broadcast of accurate but private details, such as a personal diary, medical records, and intimate details of family relationships. But when private matters become "newsworthy," the Supreme Court and lower federal and state courts have been more likely to uphold media disclosure. As a result, truthful news accounts that name, for example, a pool boy linked to a sex triangle involving a prominent president of a Christian university get published. But responsible journalists do not intrude on the lives of private people without legitimate reasons.

Another distinctive feature of privacy law involves the conduct of reporters and photojournalists pursuing stories that can be invasive to personal physical space. A celebrated case that bounced around New York state and federal courtrooms between 1970 and 1981 began when the Secret Service arrested Ron E. Galella, a pesky freelance photographer notorious among celebrities. The agents filed charges over his alleged stalking of Jacqueline Kennedy Onassis, widow of President John F. Kennedy, and her two minor children, Caroline and John. After Galella won an acquittal on the criminal complaint, Onassis sought a permanent injunction that set distance limits when Galella approached family; over the course of various court petitions by Onassis and counterpetitions by Galella, the limits ranged from twenty-five feet to one hundred yards. Rarely do courts set specific and permanent limits on newsgathering. Galella was an exception, and the order still allowed him to photograph Onassis and her children with a zoom lens. Galella, however, failed to win his argument that the First Amendment established an absolute immunity from any liability while he gathered news. Galella, facing contempt for repeatedly violating the injunction, eventually gave up and focused on targets like Sean Penn and Madonna. The Galella-Onassis duel offers little in precedent-setting importance, but it illustrates that judges will step in to mitigate egregious journalistic behavior. Moreover, the First Amendment rarely insulates journalists from general criminal and civils laws for property trespassing, online hacking, and other illegal ways of obtaining the news.[20]

At a time when millions of Americans post self-revealing details on social media or invite scrutiny when applying for a loan or shopping online, court battles over privacy rights may seem pointless. We tend to accept a lack of privacy as the new normal. Nevertheless, privacy lawsuits against media continue to be filed, particularly by celebrities, some of whom shamelessly self-promote until they find the publicity backfiring on them. Then they sue, with supermarket tabloids a common target. Responsible professional journalists delve into private matters rarely, and when they do, it is with care. The extensive coverage of the extramarital liaisons of Bill Clinton and Donald Trump, seldom pretty and occasionally salacious, raised germane questions about good judgment, fidelity, decision-making, and truth telling of public people. Journalists seldom lose privacy cases brought by prominent government officials, business leaders, or entertainment figures when coverage involves the public's right to know.

A particularly sensitive privacy zone involves sex crime victims. Under a professional standard honored by a vast majority of journalists and news organizations, news stories will not identify a rape victim, period. But media disclosure occasionally happens by accident or through story details that inadvertently identify someone by association, such as naming the middle school where a sexual assault of a sixth-grader occurred. A small newspaper in Florida unwittingly published the full name of a rape victim obtained by an inexperienced reporter from a police report left out for reporters to read. The victim started getting calls from the rapist, who threatened to attack her again. The woman successfully sued, citing a Florida law, also common in other states, that made it unlawful to broadcast and publish a rape victim's name no matter the circumstances. On appeal, the Supreme Court overturned the verdict and set a condition that applied to other privacy protection laws that punished media disclosure. The Court said, "If a newspaper lawfully obtains truthful information about a matter of public significance, then state officials may not constitutionally punish publication of the information, absent a need to further a state interest of the highest order."[21] The opinion, *Florida Star v. BJF*, established precedent in other cases involving publication of sensitive personal information—to name a few, child abuse cases and juvenile court records. The Supreme Court and lower courts gradually placed newsgathering rights and the public's right to know above the interests of victims and stakeholders. Again, though, responsible news organizations tend to protect privacy regardless of what the law says they can or cannot do. On occasion, the press overly safeguards individual rights by withholding identities of vulnerable persons swept into the news.

## Marginalia

In early 2020, as the deadly coronavirus destroyed lives and closed down the economy, privacy concerns took on greater urgency. Does the public have a right and a *need* to know the identities of Covid-19 victims, including where they live, where they work, where they have traveled, and who they have had contact with? The Health Insurance Portability and Accountability Act (HIPAA) of 1996 became federal law to protect the medical history of each of us from disclosure, even after death. Does our right to know outweigh HIPPA and privacy rules, as citizens try to protect themselves against a pandemic and avoid people and places of danger? Can we begin to reconcile the privacy of Covid-19 victims against the need of others to stay alive? Let us hope we avoid such an unfortunate collision of competing rights.

## *The Right to Know Put to the Test*

The pace of press freedom cases accelerated under the Warren Burger Court (1969-86). The docket notably included the Pentagon Papers case and several others pitting the First Amendment against constitutional rights, particularly those involving the Fourth and Sixth Amendments. The Court, for example, dealt with whether journalists could be barred from criminal trials at the request of the accused who claim protection under the Sixth Amendment. "Yes," the Court first said in *Gannett Company, Inc. v. DePasquale*, raising the specter of wholesale secret tribunals.[22] When critics berated the Court for ignoring a national commitment to open courtrooms dating to well before the Constitution, it reversed course in the next term and said the First Amendment required openness for the benefit of the press and the public. Chief Justice Burger's majority opinion surprised legal experts: "The First Amendment goes beyond protection of the press and the self-expression of individuals to prohibit government from limiting the stock of information from which members of the public may draw."[23] Burger cited the First Amendment right of assembly when he observed that "people assemble in public places not only to speak or to take action, but also to listen, observe, and learn." This recognition is especially important for our discussion of the centrality of everyday talk and citizen dialogue in democratic practice.

Boxed into a corner when it initially allowed the closure of criminal trials, the Court ended up promoting the First Amendment as a *vehicle* by which citizens "listen, observe, and learn." In his concurring opinion,

Justice John Paul Stevens stressed the larger importance of the *Richmond* case: "For the first time, the Court unequivocally holds that an arbitrary interference with access to important information is an abridgment of the freedoms of speech and of the press protected by the First Amendment."[24] The record of Court opinions over the years contains ample acknowledgment of the *importance* of freedom of information and an informed public. But it appears the Court prefers that Congress, state legislatures, and the executive branches of government determine the extent to which the right to know applies to freedom of the press and other public interests, such as requiring nutritional labeling by food manufacturers.

In theory, the right to know applies to information necessary for citizens to self-govern. Are there useful distinctions to be made among *need to know, nice to know,* and *essential access to knowledge*? Can we determine the difference between news reports that advance self-governance as opposed to those that satisfy our curiosity? Material that fills news columns and evening news programs contains its share of trivial occurrences and oddities. Can we judge the value between news that sustains the republic and that which is pabulum? Media scholar James Carey offered a perspective that might help guide discerning citizens:

> The press justifies itself in the name of the public. It exists, or so it is said, to inform the public, to serve as the extended eyes and ears of the public. The press is the guardian of the public interest and protects the public's right to know. The canons of the press originate in and flow from the relationship of the press to the public.[25]

We agree with Carey and assume that, by its language and decisions, the Supreme Court does, too. News that clearly *serves the public* receives the highest status. But the more news media might drift from a mission of public service, away from substantive and fair reporting about public affairs, the less likely citizens will believe the profession serves the right to know.

Under the Warren Court, journalists prevailed in many cases, but they lost their share, too, as they fought for access to jails and penitentiaries; challenged military policy that restricted covering troops in war zones; and contested widespread government attempts to interpret public records narrowly. The number of press freedom cases heard by the Supreme Court declined when William Rehnquist succeeded Burger as chief justice in 1986. After Rehnquist's death in 2005, John Roberts Jr. succeeded him. The Rehnquist-Roberts era has been known for its more conservative, judicially restrained approach to cases. Its record on the First Amendment reflects a preference by Roberts and like-minded colleagues that privileges freedom of *speech* but not necessarily freedom of the *press*. A vivid example comes from Roberts's majority opinion in *Snyder v. Phelps* (2011). The Phelps family headed tiny Westboro Baptist Church in Topeka, Kansas, notorious for picketing at hundreds of military funerals, including one for Marine Matthew A. Snyder. Many observers thought the church exploited private moments of grief to promote its campaign against homosexuality in the armed services. At the Snyder services, held in Maryland, church members stood across from the cemetery, reciting Bible verses and holding placards with the messages "God hates fags" and "Thank God for dead soldiers." Matthew's father sued, and a trial jury awarded him more than $10 million in damages. The U.S. Supreme Court took the case on appeal. Despite public opinion strongly in support of the Snyder family, Chief Justice Roberts came to a conclusion that troubled him but that he believed was right:

> Speech is powerful. It can stir people to action, move them to tears of both joy and sorrow, and—as it did here—inflict great pain. On the facts before us, we cannot react to that pain by punishing the speaker. As a Nation we have chosen a different course—to protect even hurtful speech on public issues to ensure that we do not stifle public debate. That choice requires that we shield Westboro from tort liability for its picketing in this case.[26]

The Court held 8-1 that Phelps and his followers engaged in speech on matters of public concern on public property and therefore were entitled to protection under the First Amendment. It was a difficult decision, questioned by Justice Samuel A. Alito Jr., who said in dissent: "In order to have a society in which public issues can be openly and vigorously debated, it is not necessary to allow the brutalization of innocent victims."[27]

In terms of defending freedom of the *press*, neither Rehnquist nor Roberts appears as motivated as the Warren and Burger Courts. In his 2019 book, law professor Ronald J. Krotoszynski Jr. chided both chief justices for failing to issue any landmark First Amendment decisions that expanded the right to gather news.[28] Then again, cases decided decades ago remain in force, so freedom of the press case law essentially has stood pat. But even precedent established in landmark Supreme Court decisions can erode and, on occasion, be overturned as the ideological composition of the Court shifts or social conditions warrant. Justice Clarence Thomas's comments about the 1964 *New York Times v. Sullivan* actual malice rule hint of turbulence ahead for hard-hitting reporting and, consequently, the public's right to know. In a 2019 concurring opinion, Thomas described the actual malice standard as "almost impossible" for defamation plaintiffs to satisfy. He said *Times v. Sullivan* was one of several Warren cases that "were policy-driven decisions masquerading as constitutional law." Thomas called on the Court to cease "reflexively" applying the actual malice rule and consider abandoning it.[29]

No other justice immediately supported him, but the door opened a crack. "His concurrence provides momentum for critics of *New York Times* [*v. Sullivan*] and room for courts to reexamine the standard, as the press continues to face increased scrutiny," wrote attorney Natasha Cooper on the American Bar Association website.[30] In July 2021, Justice Neil Gorsuch joined Thomas in questioning the efficacy of *Sullivan*: "Not only has the doctrine evolved into a subsidy for published falsehoods on a scale no one could have foreseen, it has come to leave far more people without redress than anyone could have predicted."[31] They both recommended that *Sullivan* at least be reconsidered. That prospect led Floyd Abrams, a prominent lawyer who assisted in the Pentagon Papers case, to react:

> When the Supreme Court decided the Sullivan case 57 years ago, Alexander Meiklejohn, a leading First Amendment scholar, exclaimed that it was "an occasion for dancing in the street." If the court agrees to hear one or both of the libel cases before it, that would be an occasion for us all to hold our breath.[32]

The *Sullivan* rule developed when newspapers were still the predominant forum for news and commentary. In the anti-*Sullivan* camp, critics of actual malice argue it gives news media a license to lie. That stance echoes then-candidate Donald Trump's promises at a presidential campaign rally several years earlier, at which he said:

> I'm going to open up our libel laws so when they write purposely negative and horrible and false articles, we can sue them and win lots of money. We're going to open up those libel laws. So, when the *New York Times* writes a hit piece which is a total disgrace or when the *Washington Post*, which is there for other reasons, writes a hit piece, we can sue them and win money instead of having no chance of winning because they're totally protected.[33]

A retreat from the actual malice rule would certainly chill if not silence investigative coverage of public officials who already show a propensity to file meritless lawsuits against news media. Weakening the actual malice rule would hit hardest on hometown news already operating on the tightest of budgets. The actual malice rule does occasionally offer shelter to liars trying to harm others, but the reporting it enables also can expose the liars and blunt their impact. If politicians and public figures call for abolishment of the rule, they need a better reason than "we can sue them and win lots of money."

**FYI**

In April 2019, Representative Devin Nunes (R-California) sued the *Fresno Bee* for $150 million over a story that accurately reported Nunes's part-ownership in a winery that hosted a charity auction aboard the company yacht. The newspaper reported that a witness said the event featured cocaine and prostitutes. Nunes did not attend and denied knowledge of the event, but in the lawsuit, he alleged the story falsely *implied* "that he was involved with cocaine and underage prostitutes." The case, still active as of early 2020, was filed in rural Virginia against a publication twenty-six hundred miles away. Why there? Virginia libel law, legal experts say, enables plaintiffs to pursue litigation that the courts of other states would dismiss as groundless or frivolous. According to the website Roll Call, between March and December 2019, Nunes had filed a half dozen defamation lawsuits outside his home state. The practice has become known as "libel tourism."[34]

## *The Imperfect Alliance of the Press and Lawmakers*

Despite the often adversarial relationship between public agencies and news media, occasionally the two sides align when lawmakers propose press freedom protections beyond those provided by the courts. A dilemma, however, arises whenever journalists solicit or accept statutory protection. The First Amendment states that "Congress shall make no law" abridging First Amendment rights, so journalists, sometimes in consultation with lawmakers, weigh the pros and cons of statutory protections and ask themselves, "Do we open the door for restrictions by supporting laws we might come to regret—boundaries and conditions we must subsequently live with and abide by?" The quest for open meetings and records demonstrates the dilemma.

## Open Meetings and Records

In the mid-1950s, Representative John E. Moss thought that as a member of Congress he would have no difficulty obtaining files he needed to investigate Senator Joseph McCarthy, infamous for his vicious smear campaign to expose Communists in government. After hitting one bureaucratic brick wall after another, Moss concluded the country needed strong, enforceable legislation to unlock the federal government's immense depository of records to the public and the news media. It took more than a decade, but Moss finally convinced his colleagues to pass the Freedom of Information Act (FOIA). To win passage, Moss agreed to nine broad categories of records exempt under the law. They included "national security," "trade secrets," "personnel records," "law enforcement investigations" and the near bottomless "personal privacy" category. The FOIA went into effect on July 4, 1966, and it fast became the go-to model for open meetings and open records law now commonplace in every state.

### Marginalia

The FOIA became a comic footnote in the Trump impeachment hearings when the president's longtime personal lawyer, Jay Sekulow, rebuked Democrats. "Lawyer lawsuits?" he shouted. "We're talking about the impeachment of a president of the United States, duly elected, and the members—the [second impeachment] managers are complaining about lawyer lawsuits? The Constitution allows lawyer lawsuits. It's disrespecting the Constitution of the United States to even say that in this chamber— lawyer lawsuits." Sekulow evidently misheard "foiyuh" (FOIA) as "lawyer" or was unaware the expression was shorthand for the FOIA.[35]

Moss knew that if *he* lacked the clout to extract vital information, the average American had no chance to access documents a government official or office arbitrarily decided to put off-limits. Moss believed he served the public good in pressing for the FOIA, but he encountered stiff opposition, including from the White House. President Lyndon B. Johnson considered a veto and refused to hold a signing ceremony for the FOIA. But he suppressed personal disapproval to issue a supportive written statement that conceded that the law "springs from one of our most essential principles" in a democracy—citizens must understand what government does, without undue secrecy that shrouds decisions. "Government functions best in the full light of day," the statement asserted.[36]

The federal FOIA indirectly imposed openness on city councils, county boards, and government bodies accustomed to conducting public business in private and keeping records locked away. Several important expansions to the FOIA were added in 1974—setting deadlines for government offices to answer a FOIA request, sanctioning officials who wrongly withhold information, and establishing criteria for waiving copying and service fees for journalists and public interest groups. Federal and state officials across the country, however, often resisted FOIA requests from the media, citizens, and open-records advocates.

State legislators particularly continue to stymie access by adding exemptions well beyond the nine included in the original federal FOIA. Florida, for example, enacted its Government in the Sunshine Act in 1967. While praised initially for its expansiveness, lawmakers crippled it with more than 250 exemptions by 2020. One prohibits release of firearm ownership records, including names of Floridians granted a concealed weapons permit. In 2019 alone, Florida lawmakers passed twelve new exemptions, including measures to block public access to building plans for healthcare facilities, data used by a state-run insurance company to pay claims, and documents revealing the value of surplus properties held by water management districts. On the surface, these may seem like insignificant steps; their significance, however, is the trend toward lawmakers weakening existing laws and special interest groups pressuring legislatures to designate particular government records as exemptions to openness.[37] Some lobbyists readily find new crops of legislators willing to trade influence for a campaign contribution.

Occasionally, efforts to restrict access are well intentioned but in some ways misguided, such as "Marsy's Law." California became the first state with a Marsy statute, named for a college student murdered by her ex-boyfriend. Marsy's Laws typically include nondisclosure of the names of crime victims, information once commonly available under the state open records law. The young woman's family lobbied for legislation and launched an organization dedicated to extending Marsy's Laws across the nation. More than a dozen states adopted comparable laws, mainly through popular vote on ballot initiatives that amend state constitutions.

A concern for victims is generally shared by journalists, who voluntarily withhold hurtful or embarrassing details. But a growing number of law enforcement agencies have cited Marsy's Laws for other purposes, such as nondisclosure of the identity of officers involved in arrests and physical encounters with civilians. In Florida, according to a *USA Today*-ProPublica investigation, officials used its law to shield officers who, for example, fired bullets into moving cars and released K-9 dogs on drunk and mentally ill people. Kentucky placed a Marsy's Law before voters while the state was still reeling from the botched raid that killed Breonna Taylor, a twenty-six-year-old Black medical worker in Louisville. "Had it been in place this March," said *USA Today* and ProPublica, "the public may not have learned the identities of the three white officers who opened fire."[38] On November 4, 2020, 63 percent of state voters passed the amendment.

Restrictions, exemptions, and noncompliance obviously complicate the work of journalists. They deter citizens, too, such as Linda and Mike Raymond. In the early 2000s, they were taking a walk when they noticed several huge trucks loaded with debris headed to the city landfill, long dormant, or so they thought. The Raymonds live in Woburn, Massachusetts, where a protracted, costly, and emotional lawsuit brought by residents accused local industries of polluting the town's drinking water and causing a spike in leukemia deaths. A book and movie, *A Civil Action*, graphically detailed Woburn's ordeal. The Raymonds, understandably on alert for threats to public health, asked city officials to explain activity at the landfill. Spurned repeatedly by the city, the couple turned to federal and state freedom of information laws to uncover records and, eventually, convinced the city to shelve its plans to reopen the landfill.[39]

The privatization movement of the 1980s added to access problems. Officials at all levels of government became convinced that hiring for-profit companies to manage government facilities and functions would save money and increase efficiency. Cities from Los Angeles to Sandy Springs, Georgia, "outsourced" responsibilities. Privatization expanded to nearly every corner of government—prisons, sewage plants, ambulance service, medical clinics, building inspections, budgeting, and accounting. Perhaps the most significant side effect was the loss of local control and accountability. A reporter seeking details on how the regional branch of Waste Management, Inc., deals with disposal of hazardous material can knock on doors and leave voice messages until the point of exhaustion. A public relations official might eventually respond—or not. Journalists cannot expect full disclosure from a for-profit company, nor can the public; open government laws usually do not apply. Though seldom its original goal, privatization essentially negated existing open government laws by removing management records and organizational decision-making from public view. As a consequence, much of what was at the center of the public's business goes unreported and is unreportable without tips or whistleblowers, especially in news deserts.

Court decisions have not been particularly helpful in fighting access battles. A series of cases heard by the Supreme Court helped set a pattern for federal and state courts dealing with access contests that cannot be resolved by negotiation or goodwill. The Court has ruled consistently that the First Amendment affords journalists no special right of access despite the historic role journalists play as surrogates and watchdogs for the rest of us. With or without court backing, journalists rarely hesitate to remind public officials who they should be serving, but they seldom accept denial of a request for information without a tussle either. Like a perpetual tug-of-war, news media and advocates of open government push back against efforts to erode access. None of these laws, including the federal FOIA, was ever meant to ensure absolute access to meetings and records of government. The restrictions, however, creep up like crabgrass and choke off facts important for citizens to know.

Journalists hate secrecy and dig hard to uncover public information blocked by government officials. They turn resourceful and go through back channels rather than filing time-consuming legal requests. If the town clerk dallies over the release of safety code inspections of a local heavy industry, a reporter's good relationship with a town board member might get results. She knows a bit of calm persuasion can succeed when a righteous demand might trigger resistance. Government officials often are quite willing to fulfill requests, provided someone asks them with justification. But who will ask? With fewer local newspapers and waning civic engagement, in many places no one steps up to hold public officials accountable for adhering to open government laws. As records requests decline, officials come to assume people no longer care much about access, and local residents become less likely to request it, precipitating what communication researchers call "feedback loops" or, more commonly, downward spiraling negative outcomes—known as "vicious cycles." Inquisitive citizens and journalists can make a difference in keeping a community better informed and connected.

## Shield Laws and Journalist's Privilege

The Reporters Committee for Freedom of the Press was created in 1970 when journalists faced a wave of government subpoenas ordering them to name anonymous sources. The crackdown reflected the Nixon administration's mistrust of the press and involved misuse, at times, of law enforcement power to harass journalists. At the time, U.S. attorneys and state prosecutors from coast to coast investigated so-called dissidents and agitators—the Black Panthers, antiwar militants, marijuana advocates, and women's liberation activists. Using the investigative power of grand juries under their control, prosecutors compelled journalists to appear behind closed-door sessions and pressured them to reveal names of confidential sources or surrender information the reporters obtained through a promise of confidentially.

The subpoena spree threatened to diminish a vital flow of information to the public. Reporters traditionally have relied on anonymous or confidential sources to provide tips, documents, and insights upon which to base important stories, particularly investigative reports. Journalists, however, also prefer on-the-record comments and records provided with no strings; they know how much transparency boosts the believability of an investigation. So, reporters usually try to convince sources to identify themselves voluntarily. A pledge of anonymity is serious business, and reporters generally only follow that route for the sake of a particularly vulnerable source with information that bears directly on a significant issue, unobtainable otherwise. The classic figure in journalism is Deep Throat, the shadowy figure who assisted Bob Woodward and Carl Bernstein in the Watergate investigation that lasted from June 1972 to President Nixon's resignation in August 1974. The reporters steadfastly protected the identity of their source, but in 2005, W. Mark Felt, associate director of the FBI during parts of Watergate, outed himself.

Although a renowned example, Deep Throat bears little resemblance to anonymous sources typically used by journalists. A majority come from the ranks of secretaries, clerks, and hourly employees they meet while assigned to news beats, like city hall or the courthouse. A vitally important source could be a low-paid aide at the town nursing home who sees elderly residents strapped untended in wheelchairs for hours at a time. The aide knows that complaining to superiors will do no good, but her nephew suggests, "Talk to a reporter I know. She will disclose conditions and protect you from retribution." Anonymous sources place their trust in journalists to protect them at all costs. And journalists seldom betray that trust. Reporter William Farr, covering the murder trial of Charles Manson, spent forty-six days in jail for refusing to tell the trial judge who leaked sealed witness depositions to him. Farr died in 1987 at the age of fifty-two without naming who provided him the documents.[40] Of late, jailing of reporters is uncommon, but veiled and even explicit threats from judges and prosecutors give reporters pause before pursuing stories that might land them behind bars.

Use of anonymous sources is an effective reporting tool, but only if it is not abused. From ethics classes and professional folklore, journalists know about Janet Cooke, who won a Pulitzer Prize in 1981 for her moving story of Jimmy, an eight-year-old heroin addict. The story relied heavily on anonymous sources and blurred details, including the identity and whereabouts of Jimmy. Cooke's editors never insisted she reveal her sources to them—with everlasting regret, it turned out. Under routine media follow-up for her Pulitzer accomplishment, several reporters checked out Cooke's background and found inconsistencies in her résumé. They searched further, and a pattern of deception emerged. Under pressure from the *Post* and her newsroom peers, Cooke confessed that Jimmy was a composite character derived from the experiences of several children. The Pulitzer Prize board stripped her of her award. Today, even editors born after the Cooke scandal move cautiously and usually insist that reporters reveal their sources to them. Conscientious journalists typically police themselves and keep editors well informed about their sources and methods.

The mounting use of subpoenas in the 1970s led to a concerted response, as a loose coalition of the ACLU, press associations, media corporations, and civil libertarians campaigned for something called "journalist's privilege" against forced testimony. Testimonial privilege traditionally applies to husband-wife, lawyer-client, priest-penitent, and doctor-patient relations. Now, free press advocates sought to exempt reporters and editors from the long-standing common law principle by courts to compel testimony and produce evidence central to a legal issue. Could the First Amendment, through judicial interpretation, countenance a testimonial privilege for reporters? The 1972 case *Branzburg v. Hayes* (1972) seemingly settled the matter. In a 5-4 ruling, the Court declined to recognize a First Amendment-grounded privilege for journalists. It appeared to be a defeat for journalists.[41]

But *Branzburg* was a plurality decision, which means that a clear-cut majority of the justices could not agree on both the rationale and the holding of the decision. The concurring opinion of Justice Potter Stewart gave latitude to lower courts as they confronted their own journalist's privilege cases. Stewart proposed that before forcing journalists to reveal sources, the plaintiff or prosecutor seeking disclosure should meet three preconditions: establish the relevance of the information to the legal question at hand; demonstrate that no other alternative source for the information is available; and show a compelling and overriding need for the information, such as when a journalist is the only witness to a murder or holds evidence that could determine whether a criminal defendant goes to jail or not. *Branzburg* has worked for and against journalists, as judges applied the decision to the issues before them, and some courts have been more sensitive to the role of journalists than others.

The *Branzburg* decision fell well short of journalism supporters' expectations, but it boosted another movement to protect journalists' sources—shield laws. The Court made clear that state legislatures, like the state courts, were free, "within First Amendment limits, to fashion their own standards" regarding a reporter's privilege. In other words, they could pass statutes that clearly protected journalists from forced testimony via subpoenas. Seventeen states had shield laws in place at the time *Branzburg* was decided. More followed. As of 2020, forty states along with the District of Columbia, had shield law statutes. In April 2020, West Virginia enacted a statute that provides journalists with a nearly absolute journalist's privilege. The law stipulates that state courts may compel disclosure from news professionals *only* if "necessary to prevent imminent death, serious bodily injury or unjust incarceration." Most shield laws are not that sweeping.

Shield laws also both help and hinder journalism's professional responsibilities. Yes, they spare reporters and news organizations from fighting constant subpoenas. But the laws often set parameters and conditions that journalists find a hindrance to newsgathering. Bad experiences with state shield laws prompted a broad contingent of the journalism community to pull back from efforts to enact a federal shield law. Their chances were better, they decided, fighting for testimonial privilege case by case in the courtroom.

The overall picture for journalists, though, has improved substantially since the 1970s. While offering limited protection, the combination of shield laws and post-*Branzburg* pro-journalism court opinions serves the public's right to know and without overly restricting investigative reporting. The legal status of journalist's privilege assures wary confidential sources that reporters enjoy a degree of protection from being coerced by courts or prosecutors to reveal identities. Sometimes a reporter's word alone suffices. Journalists who have served jail terms rather than unjustifiably revealing sources have helped the profession build a reputation for trustworthiness.

"Anonymous" and "confidential" sources are not necessarily interchangeable terms. They both refer to sources who want to keep their names, positions, and other identifying details secret. The motives, though, differ, as do the consequences of disclosure. Journalists protect certain sources for good reason, but an unbridled practice of promising anonymity leads to a problem editors call "sourcery." Sourcery's roots are in Washington, DC, where story after story cites "high-ranking officials" or "sources close to the White House."

Like a lava flow, sourcery has spread from the Washington press corps to local newspapers, weeklies, and broadcast news. Journalists who too readily allow news subjects to hide their identities in return for juicy quotes or inside dope do a disservice to readers and viewers, leaving them unsure about the reliability of the story, the reporter who wrote it, and the news outlet that disseminated it. Journalism's use of unnamed sources can be exploited. Public officials, in particular, benefit from floating ideas ("trial balloons"), spreading accusations, and planting information without accountability. Some of them even rail against "the leakers," as if they were not leakers themselves. Journalists take the hit when caught in such hypocritical gamesmanship. The ultimate loser is the public, which is denied the opportunity to judge the credibility and motives of these nameless, faceless "insiders." President Trump discredited anonymous sources during a heated coronavirus briefing on April 18, 2020:

> And they make up—I said it today; they make up words. "Sources say . . ." Most often used: "Sources say" . . . You know what "sources say" means? "Sources say" means they have nobody. And they make it up. Okay? They should really be mandated, and I mean mandated to use a name. If there is a source, use a name. . . . And you'd find out that the—number one, the source wouldn't say it. The sources don't exist. I don't believe the sources exist.[42]

He knows they do exist, having called out former employees and a few more within his own administration for consorting with the news media. Leakers, though, can lead the profession into quagmires. News organizations that rely too casually or regularly on anonymous sources invite claims of fake news. Before granting anonymity, responsible reporters and editors ask of themselves: How does the source know this information? What's the motivation for telling us? Has she or he proved reliable in the past? Are there ways to corroborate the information independently? Do we need to protect the source's identity in the first place? Assessing and answering such questions helps set guardrails to prevent reporters from going overboard with promises of confidentially. The worst kind of anonymous source? One pitching gossip or a rumor for self-serving ends. Good journalists will not bite.

### Quotables

"Any mope can pick up a phone . . . and pass along a rumor. It happens to me all the time. The first thing I ask is: 'Who told you?' They almost always say: 'I can't tell you, but it's true.' So I say: 'Okay, if it's true, give me your name and I'll attribute the story to you.' Click. Most don't bother to say goodbye before hanging up."[43]

—Mike Royko, legendary reporter and columnist

## Privacy Protection Act

Law enforcement and criminal prosecutors discovered that subpoenaing journalists was costly, time-consuming, and futile as journalists accepted punishment rather than reveal sources of information or documents. Police and prosecutors had another weapon to bypass subpoenas that news media invariably contested. It was a big deal that journalists clearly noticed even if the general public did not.

Police officials turned to no-notice search warrants to obtain information they knew journalists would never willingly turn over. Such a warrant requires a judge to review and decide on whether its use is justified. Usually that presents no great hurdle for prosecutors. Known in some jurisdictions as a delayed-notice warrant, it authorizes law enforcement officers to enter, search, and, in some cases, seize material on private property without the occupants' permission or advance notice. The tactic proves useful when authorities fear evidence, such as illicit drugs, might be destroyed or moved before it can be confiscated. The fairness and legal reach of no-notice warrants remain contested, particularly when the practice conflicts with Fourth Amendment search and seizure protections. Used against dope dealers, few complained. But howls of protest arose when prosecutors began to use them against news media.

The prototypical newsroom search case developed in April 1971. Stanford University officials had called on local police and sheriff deputies to remove demonstrators barricaded in the administrative offices of the campus hospital. When the police forcibly entered the building, demonstrators armed with sticks and clubs fought back. In the melee, several officers were injured, one with a broken shoulder. A few days later, the student newspaper, the *Stanford Daily*, published articles and photographs that documented the violent encounter. Seeking evidence to identify suspected assailants, the county district attorney ordered a squad of police to enter the *Daily*'s offices to seize negatives, film, video, and other documentary material. When the police simply walked in the front door, they shocked the staff, several of whom objected but shut up after being threatened with arrest. The police searched widely, opening desk drawers and combing through notebooks and Rolodexes. They departed with several photos and negatives but little of value in making arrests.

Aided by pro bono lawyers, the newspaper sued, arguing the search violated both the First and Fourth Amendments. The case, *Zurcher v. Stanford Daily* (1978), ended up in the Supreme Court seven years later. In a decision written by Justice Byron White, the author of the *Branzburg* opinion, the Court majority skirted the First Amendment implications to rule narrowly on whether under the Fourth Amendment the warrant was properly obtained and executed. White said the Constitution gave the press no special protection from valid search warrants, which this one was.[44] The decision prompted wide condemnation. It so upset President Jimmy Carter that he directed Vice President Walter Mondale to lead a bipartisan congressional counterattack that produced the Privacy Protection Act of 1980. It offset the damage done by *Zurcher* and amounted to an extremely rare legislative rebuke of the Supreme Court.

The law applies to workplaces and work products, including unpublished material, such as video outtakes, digital files, reporter's notebooks, and internal correspondence.[45] Its passage indirectly safeguarded confidential sources and effectively halted a pattern of police searches and seizures in newsrooms. The law reasonably excludes from its protection journalists suspected of criminal activity or information that is immediately needed to prevent loss of life or serious injury. It covers searches by all government and law enforcement officials, both federal and state. In practical terms, the law means that when prosecutors or police *anywhere* demand documents from journalists, they must justify in a judicial proceeding why their need for information outweighs contrary arguments from lawyers representing news organizations.

Another controversial method of rooting out confidential sources occurred during the Trump administration. At the behest of the White House, the Justice Department began secretly subpoenaing the records of members of Congress and their families under the guise of national security. Apparently the probes found nothing improper, but when reporters learned about the clandestine investigations, backlash erupted. "Good God," journalist Jennifer Rubin tweeted. "They were running a police state."[46] At one point, the Justice Department gagged *New York Times* lawyers from revealing attempts to seize emails and phone records of *Times* reporters that might expose leakers. In other words, under White House pressure, top officials at the supposedly independent agency entrusted with upholding the laws of the nation not only went after the private correspondence and phone calls of journalists but also tried to stop the news media from publicizing such tactics. In July 2021, Attorney General Merrick Garland, appointed by newly elected President Biden, announced rules to limit the department's secret seizures, but if the political climate changes, they might be revoked and the draconian rules reinstated.

## Whistleblower Laws

Recently, President Trump's colloquial use of the term "whistleblower" suggests it is synonymous with a "rat" in an organized crime family— someone who leaks secret details to a rival mob or the police. That assumption is dangerously and destructively wrong. It misrepresents the purpose of federal and state whistleblower laws. The most prominent whistleblower law, the Whistleblower Protection Act, applies to most federal employees who disclose information internally or externally that they reasonably believe to be evidence of a legal violation, mismanagement, waste of funds, abuse of power, or substantial and specific danger to public health or safety. The intent of these laws is to ensure that misdeeds, often in government, come to light and that those who provide helpful information to proper authorities do not suffer as a consequence.

Criticism of whistleblowing intensified when an employee privy to presidential phone records filed an official complaint that raised concerns about the president's misuse of his powers to solicit foreign interference to support his 2020 reelection campaign. The complaint eventually led to impeachment, after which President Trump retweeted a post that disclosed the alleged name of the anonymous whistleblower. In late 2019, he attacked the whistleblower in a press briefing. "They give this whistleblower a status that he doesn't deserve," Trump said. "He's a fake whistleblower, and frankly someone ought to sue his ass off."[47] Citizens might wonder about the future of the law's protections, given the reckless behavior from accused officials who directly threaten whistleblowers with no consequences to themselves.

According to the National Whistleblower Center, more than fifty federal laws, as well as an impressive collection of state laws, cover whistleblower rights. An estimated 95 percent of whistleblowers first raise their concerns internally, according to a 2012 study by the Ethics Resource Center; they seek external help only if their supervisors fail to act.[48] The study confirms that whistleblowers generally act responsibly and only as a last resort. Whistleblower laws vary in degree of protection, and they cannot ensure there will not be direct or oblique retaliation in the form of a job reassignment, bad performance evaluations, threats, termination, or ostracism.

Whistleblowing poses ethical and practical complications. Similar to steps taken before accepting news from anonymous sources, journalists, for the sake of the public and their reputations, must act with abundant caution and focused skepticism. Responsible journalists accept information when they are confident the source of the leak or tip truly believes their information belongs in the public arena. Responsible journalists also report on public officials who out or punish people trying to be conscientious citizens.

## Our Stake in the Press Freedom Clause

Nowhere does the First Amendment grant a license for the news media to operate carte blanche. No responsible journalist assumes this. Nonetheless, in today's media-bashing climate, people tend to believe journalists can get away with just about anything. Television dramas and movies reinforce the stereotypes of callous reporters sticking microphones and cameras in the faces of stunned citizens, of a detective at a gory murder site upbraiding a young reporter for her lack of decency, or of a distinguished judge lecturing an editor for putting newsstand sales ahead of concern for victims. Does the image fit? Yes, on occasion, but not as an all-purpose accusation of a profession. The public usually observes journalists at work only in the ritual of the press conference, news briefing, or, in journalism jargon, the "presser." Their questions seldom yield information of great substance, but reporters show up, like those assigned to the White House, take their licks, and come back the next day. The news briefing may appear to be a nasty game of "gotcha," but that seldom is the case. For the most part, newsmakers—especially politicians—benefit from the publicity of a presser. Playing to the cameras, they might pretend to be annoyed and put upon. But most relish the attention that boosts their profiles for fans or voters. Reporters seldom benefit from pseudo-drama staged by politicians and celebrities. They tend to prefer to work behind the scenes, where they can ask questions under more low-key circumstances.

The routine give-and-take of public officials and the press went off the tracks, though, with the election of Donald J. Trump. No other American president has ever sparred so vociferously with journalists as Trump did in face-to-face insults and tweet storms. Public officials long have resented tough questions, but with President Trump setting the example, more public officials followed suit. In Florida, a suitable microcosm for foreshadowing other states, Governor Ron DeSantis banned a statehouse reporter from a coronavirus briefing because she earlier asked why social distancing was so lax in his crowded news conferences. The ouster by DeSantis ignited criticism from other journalists and civil libertarians. A columnist for the *Tampa Bay Times* spoke directly to citizens when he said: "Understand, this is not a journalist's whine about favoritism or payback. This is about your right to get answers from your governor."[49]

Complaining public officials and figures get help from imposters posing as journalists to undermine the reputations of honorable journalists actually producing legitimate news and disseminate fake, disruptive, and dangerous news, frequently online. In the form of news "stories," they peddle conspiracy theories, miracle cures, and bogus reports designed to confuse and divide. Their impact appears substantial and harmful. According to research conducted by the reputable nonprofit group Avaaz, the top one hundred fake news stories on Facebook in 2019 were viewed over 150 million times—enough, said Avaaz, "to reach every registered voter at least once." The deception spanned most of the political spectrum. The second-most read story carried the headline "Nancy Pelosi diverting Social Security money for the impeachment inquiry." The headline on the top-read story was "Trump's grandfather was a pimp and tax evader; his father a member of the KKK."[50] No matter their motivation, these assorted foreign and domestic disrupters abuse free speech protections of the First Amendment to inflict damage on the credibility of American journalism and, by extension, harm democratic principles as well.

### Quotables

"It doesn't really matter how much freedom journalists have if no one believes them. A discredited press plays no role in shaping democracy and holding power accountable. And a public that finds a press contemptible holds no stake in defending First Amendment values and standing up for press freedom. Why would it? The civic instinct is to do just the opposite. It is a very short half-step from not believing the press to not believing in press freedom."[51]

—David E. McCraw, newsroom lawyer for the *New York Times*

The First Amendment gives journalists neither superpowers nor immunity from legal consequences. But they report and edit the news with a degree of confidence that the Constitution stands behind what they do. They earn paychecks, usually modest, and seldom abuse their positions by letting their personal beliefs influence their work. They ask lots of questions but usually politely, not trying to annoy or intimidate. Citizens depend on their inquiries far more than we often realize. They ask questions about police use of chokeholds, perhaps to save our children from harm. They check out government bills and invoices to see if anything looks amiss, such as the mayor awarding his son-in-law's company a lucrative contract for city employees' health insurance. They question nursing home operators about coronavirus conditions, seeking answers the residents' families and the surrounding community desperately need to know.

No doubt journalists enjoy immense, constitutionally protected power. If abused, that power can do great damage to reputations, businesses, institutions, social controls, military operations, diplomacy, and other facets of a well-functioning republic. No other profession assumes a comparable social responsibility. Media misdeeds occur, but in nearly all cases the profession corrects itself with a near religious devotion to truth, fairness, and accuracy. Watchdogs inside and outside newsrooms expose the profession's wrongdoers to protect the overall reputation of journalism as an institution; when these watchdogs growl, journalists pay attention and get a stern reminder of professional obligations.

As journalists go about their jobs, they know others resent them, damn them, and might attempt to silence them. Recently, defamation and invasion of privacy lawsuits filed against the news media seem designed to inflict financial injury and chill coverage rather than redress wrongs. A freedom of the press guarantee is meaningless if wealthy individuals can stifle public discourse with their checkbooks. The leading figure among billionaires bankrolling anti-media lawsuits is Peter Thiel, founder of PayPal. Thiel underwrote legal aid that helped professional wrestler Hulk Hogan win a $140 million jury verdict against Gawker, a popular blog featuring news and gossip about celebrities and media moguls. Gawker later settled for $31 million, filed for bankruptcy, and sold its online business at an auction. Thiel believed he had good cause to take Gawker out. In 2007, the website identified Thiel as gay, and, in reaction, Thiel said Gawker "ruined people's lives for no reason."[52]

People familiar with Gawker's style and tactics knew its rambunctious staff often tested accepted journalistic norms and ethics. To some critics, Gawker's demise was good riddance. But others lamented its passing and feared for the precedent of a billionaire burying a popular publication. Gawker represented an iconoclastic approach to news coverage, and while traditional news media dared not pursue some of its topics, a good number of reporters applauded how Gawker applied heat to the powerful. In other words, Gawker acted in the tradition of colonial editors as they lambasted public officials and the elite.

The First Amendment belongs to the public, and journalists draw strength and leverage from judicial decisions, administrative rules, and laws enacted in the name of the public's right to know. When citizens tolerate the constant battering of the press, generalize about media bias, or retweet news and memes known to be unreliable, they diminish journalism and the democratic ideals of communication. It is somewhat like living in an urban neighborhood and then denouncing everyone trying to keep you and your home safe, from alderpersons to police, trash collectors, crossing guards, firefighters, and your local newspaper staff. Each attack on journalism reduces public confidence and renders the press less effective and less present in the nation's dialogue. With journalism missing in action, citizens go without a guardian of their right to know and without protection from wrongdoers.

In chapter 5, we examine the values and practices of journalists and challenge numerous misconceptions commonly held about the profession. We sketch, too, how journalists put into practice newsgathering rights won by their predecessors and resist attempts by public officials to dictate the terms of freedom of the press and tamper with the prerequisites of responsible citizenship.

# CHAPTER 5

# Inside the Newsroom,
# Behind the Story

Journalists mostly work as if anonymous. Their names might appear on story bylines and photography credits, and news websites sometimes include a thumbnail-size photo of the writer. Even more operate "backstage" as copy editors, researchers, section editors, photography technicians, graphic artists, and "stringers"—part-time staffers. The faces of television and cable anchors become known to local and national audiences, and some of them get recognized when eating out or grocery shopping. Generally, though, you would not recognize a reporter or editor sitting in your pew at church or checking out before you at Pick 'n Save.

Yet millions of Americans believe journalists work against them, spread lies, and conspire against conservative causes. Until relatively recently, the public thought it "knew" journalists from dramatic portrayals in movies or prime-time programs known to stereotype them as callous, nosy types who pander to readers and viewers. In reality, journalists pretty much represent a cross-section of American middle-class professionals. When the Covid-19 pandemic forced most people indoors, broadcast reporters accustomed to reporting from news scenes filed reports from home. Viewers had a glimpse into their dens or kitchens—settings that revealed slices of private lives through photos on the wall or books on the shelves. Journalists sometimes depicted by politicians as barbarians at the gate were revealed to be fairly ordinary—even-tempered and civilized. Like so many other Americans, they, too, worry about stretching the household budget, finding a babysitter, or getting laid off.

Journalists, though, differ from average citizens because they provide a vital service to communities, perhaps the one you call home. They cannot understand why they must bear the stigma "enemies of the people." The expression gets repeated by leaders in Congress, by state governors, by county sheriffs, and in many enclaves of partisan politics, including coffee klatches at Kim's Café.

To counter stereotypes and politicized talking points, citizens need a fuller picture of the daily—and largely ordinary—responsibilities of American journalists on duty from Washington state to Washington, DC. Consider two journalists whose contributions are representative of many. Most likely, you have never heard of either, but learning something about them humanizes the ordinary-extraordinary roles journalists play in a democracy.

One is nomadic, untethered from the demands of daily reporting to cover stories and topics outside the conventional. He blends photos and text in portraits of people frequently overlooked or shunned by general society. Chris Arnade, author of *Dignity: Seeking Respect in Back Row America*, specializes in unconventional reporting that takes him across the country—he estimates more than 150,000 miles to research *Dignity*—mainly by car.

Arnade carries on the photojournalism tradition of Jacob Riis (1849-1914) and Walker Evans (1903-75). Riis documented conditions in the working-class slums of 1880s New York City, and his images and reporting later became the basis for a best-selling book, *How the Other Half Lives*. Evans teamed with writer James Agee for a series of pieces about share-croppers in the Great Depression. The series led to another nonfiction best seller, *Let Us Now Praise Famous Men* (1941).

Arnade gives voice to citizens struggling to survive, some in the shadow of massive high-rises and others in trailer courts at the outskirts of town—places he calls "the back rows" of America. When they can afford it, the people he meets eat at McDonald's or other fast-food hangouts, for many the only restaurant option. To passersby, many of his interviewees might appear to be life's designated losers. "Despite being stigmatized, ignored, and made fun of," Arnade said, "most of the people I met were fighting to maintain dignity."[1] He listens carefully to them.

His own road to the "back rows" was unusual, to say the least. A PhD in theoretical physics who never studied journalism formally, he worked on Wall Street as a bond broker. Living a middle-class life in Brooklyn and sending his children to private schools, he still found himself increasingly restless and unfulfilled. In off-hours, he began taking long walks through unfamiliar neighborhoods, including several considered unsafe or unsavory. One place drew him back often—Hunts Point in the Bronx. At first, Arnade intended his walks as casual explorations to relieve work-related stress, but something changed his intent and outlook. As he walked, he unwittingly fell into the news collection methods of observing, asking questions, meeting strangers, taking notes, and snapping photos. He fed a nagging curiosity common to journalists about worlds outside their own.

During his walks, Arnade fine-tuned another journalistic trait—a respect for human diversity. He came to know sex workers, married couples who slept under bridges, and drug dealers who cajoled customers at street corners. All of them were persons to him, not just urban problems to be solved. When, with permission, he photographed someone new, he would ask: "How do you want to be described?" One responded: "As who I am. A prostitute, a mother of six, and a child of God."[2]

Arnade practices a journalism that changes or deepens perspectives. It raises questions about biases and preconceptions. He does not tell you what to think; he concentrates on communicating what he sees and hears. A few critics have accused him of exploiting people by giving them money or buying meals in return for personal stories. Arnade acknowledges he built relationships through small gestures of kindness and respect. In his travels, he encountered pain and despair that touched him deeply. But he also encountered people quietly engaged in community outreach to feed, clothe, and comfort those in need. They gave him a rejuvenating dose of optimism, which he passes on sensitively to readers for whom America's back rows *are* news. Journalists like Arnade illuminate people and places that the larger community might otherwise never get to know.

Eric Eyre, introduced in chapter 1, followed a more traditional route. He earned a master's degree in journalism and settled in Charleston, West Virginia, where he began a long career as a reporter for the *Charleston Gazette-Mail*. He crafted an array of stories as a general assignment reporter—the infantry of journalism—who get their marching orders from editors: "Find out about that pileup on the interstate." "There's a dedication of the new city library; get some highlights." "The publisher is speaking to the Rotary at noon. Cover his speech, but focus on what he says about downtown projects." Like firefighters answering a 911 call, general assignment reporters such as Eyre speed to the action, not sure of what they will encounter. Indeed, news about fires is part of the job. Most reporters will only rarely receive touchy and highly politicized assignments.

Eyre later reported from the statehouse, a position that gave him greater leeway to pursue stories on his own initiative. One of them proved exceptionally elusive and taxing on his body and spirit. It started, though, routinely enough. A combination of tips from acquaintances, families of victims, and public interest lawyers drew Eyre to the center of an epidemic of misery and death throughout West Virginia. He found staggering amounts of Vicodin and other addictive painkillers being sold at hometown drug stores, among them a small pharmacy in Kermit, West Virginia, population 382. Over a span of two years, giant pharmaceutical companies had shipped nearly nine million opioid pills to just this single store, which drew a daily stream of customers from across the state and from as far away as Ohio, Florida, and North Carolina.

Eyre's investigation took years. He scoured thousands of court records, interviewed CEOs and medical examiners, filed dozens of freedom of information requests with government agencies, and traveled across the state to listen to victims and their families. Eyre wrote hundreds of stories about them, earning him the 2017 Pulitzer Prize for investigative reporting. In 2016, a tremor that hampered his ability to use a keyboard was diagnosed as Parkinson's disease, a neurological disorder with no known cure.[3]

Journalists do not seek thanks or praise. They would, however, like to think that people at least *value* their work. If people knew how meticulous, caring, civic-minded, and pro-democracy journalists are—qualities not found in all professions—the reception toward them would likely improve. You do not risk your life, go into danger zones, or work yourself sick to concoct fake news or promote conspiracy theories you know to be false. While others called to public service—teachers, clergy, social workers, firefighters—do rightly earn thanks and praise, many in journalism hear only slurs and complaints.

A majority of citizens know little about journalism and the women and men who bring them the news. This chapter focuses on those who research, write, and edit "hard news"—information with significant consequences for citizens. In journalists' vernacular, hard news comprises a range of human experience, from home invasions to increased property taxes to bridge repairs, with particular emphasis on government offices and activities. Hard news can happen spontaneously, as with industrial accidents or other unplanned or unexpected occurrences. "Soft news" includes celebrity profiles, travel features, and restaurant reviews, interesting but somewhat less essential to democracy when compared to news about lawmaking, policy debates, court rulings, and civil rights violations. Between hard and soft news, we find news analyses, editorials, columns, contributed opinion pieces (also known as "op-eds"), and letters to the editor—the stuff that often springs from public reaction to hard news developments. This in-between material contributes to civic discourse as well but frequently gets mistaken for "news" and generates accusations of political bias—"hit jobs," as an acquaintance puts it. To be clear, when we refer to "journalists," "reporters," and "editors," we mean those occupying a hard-to-define area where news, citizens, and civic life meet. It is ground patrolled by hometown journalism—where solid information is most immediately necessary for decisions that citizens must make. Our intent is to dispel misconceptions about an admittedly imperfect profession, but one too easily scapegoated and smeared.

## The Essence of a Journalist

Arnade and Eyre possibly know one another from the books each recently published. Otherwise, they are unlikely to cross paths. Yet even if they never meet face-to-face, they speak the same language and can relate to one another through a camaraderie outsiders find difficult to understand. It takes no genetics test for journalists to know their lineage or to identify other family members.

The ancestral roots can best be found in the values, beliefs, convictions, and sense of purpose shared by a majority of journalists. We distilled the descriptions of their worlds from what journalists reveal of themselves in autobiographies and personal essays, augmented by what historians, scholars, and fellow journalists observe about what makes newspeople tick.[4] Despite certain similarities, individual journalists remain unique in attitudes, tasks, and styles—even when much of the public imagines the profession shaped in the same mold. Journalists differ in education, social status, sexual orientation, and choice of music, hobbies, literature, and other factors that distinguish all of us as individuals. Journalists perceive things, including persons in the news, from diverse life experiences. A reporter from an Indigenous community might interpret discovery of a contaminated water supply through a prism of human respect for nature, or the daughter of a plumber may write about joblessness while recalling memories of a teenage kid hanging out in the workshop, waiting for a customer to phone.

We generalize, but we can safely and fairly say this about journalists: They get irked when encountering powerful people taking advantage of the powerless. They seldom take no for an answer from recalcitrant public officials who will not speak to their constituents. They seek the truth and strive for accuracy, with no detail too small to go unverified. They remind themselves to be open-minded and empathic toward the people they write about and those who provide them information and insights. They spend hours searching for material and tracking down details that may never get printed or broadcast. They filter out hearsay, sift through dubious claims, and prioritize their assignments, typically on the utilitarian ethical basis of the greatest good for the greatest number.

Successful journalists can be understood by certain occupational pre-
dispositions—as described here in an admittedly idiosyncratic list.

## Civil and Patient

Modern newspeople are far more professional than journalists in Jefferson's day or other historical eras noted for sensationalized, overly competitive journalism—perhaps the 1920s Jazz Age, when journalists were
known to go overboard to get a scoop or to satisfy an editor's demands,
such as the possibly apocryphal time when an editor ordered a reporter
to crawl through an open window of a murder victim's home to snatch a
family photo off a bedroom dresser. Today, you can expect news reporters
to respect personal boundaries and stay within the law while still aggressively pursuing the truth. A few still skirt professional norms and ethical
codes; they are exceptions. What has not changed, though, is how journalists remain steadfast in their mission. They ask tough questions and
pursue answers even when pilloried by politicians with agendas other than
the truth. To succeed, reporters need to keep cool and persist with their
inquiries until a source walks away, hangs up, or slams a door, which happens too often. When viewers of a televised press conference see a reporter
pressing a follow-up question, they should not consider it disrespect but a
professional dedication to the public right to know how a mayor, for example, evaluates policing behavior in her city.

By and large, reporters leave alone private individuals dragged involun-
tarily into the news—unless they agree to talk. When they do, these ordinary people might decide to contribute intimate details of grief and hardship, such as those found in the touching profiles of Covid-19 victims, best
exemplified by the *New York Times* series "Those We Lost."[5] When people
criticize reporters as pushy invaders of privacy, they may be unaware of the
expressions of sympathy and assurances of voluntary participation that
preceded the interview or the occasional thank-you notes reporters receive
for telling the story of a loved one.

### Quotables

"I am continually surprised by the willingness of people to talk about great
misfortune, even when they themselves caused it. They described what
happened in detail. They, the accidental, regretful perpetrators of serious
tragedies, the living victims, the survivors of plane crashes, house fires,
tornadoes, floods, boating accidents, rapes, shooting, you name it. They

were anxious to talk away their griefs, sorrows and guilt as though their words would erase the reality of the dreadful thing that had happened, not realizing how those words would sound on air or appear in the papers. They were not politicians or spin-doctors. They didn't have the proper words to sway the public in their favor, or know what not to say to a reporter. They were the innocents."[6]

—Joseph P. Ritz, *I Never Looked for My Mother and Other Regrets of a Journalist*

## Deadline Motivated

Journalists are clock-watchers. Without strict deadlines, the morning paper would not arrive on time and evening newscasts would start late. Journalists seldom work at a leisurely pace. They rush to line up interviews, dig up background material, and grasp facts, fast enough to write or produce a story in hours or minutes. Stress levels rise as the clock ticks, and the toll includes settling for what might not be their best efforts if given more time. Journalists take their frustrations home but, unless married to another journalist, usually try to spare partners and families. They go to bed knowing the next day means another set of deadlines under unrelenting conditions not faced by most other professionals. They or their editors pass over numerous stories worth telling because so many others are more pressing, and in journalism, time is always short.

## Grounded in Local Reporting

Investigative reporter Bob Woodward, former MSNBC news anchor Brian Williams, and Susan Page of *USA Today*, the moderator of a Trump-Biden debate, broke into journalism doing local news. Each of them, like so many other journalists, started out with small paychecks, long hours, and no overtime pay, chasing stories that laypeople would find unglamorous. They learned to read municipal budgets, wade through police incident reports, and stay alert during hours of dry government meetings. They slowly learned the basics and came to appreciate how important average people are to their reporting, because, for the most part, they grew up average, too.

## Neither Apolitical nor Partisan

Journalists usually avoid personal involvement in partisan politics, often by choice. But they are bound by professional standards, as well. Many news organizations limit political and special interest participation of employees, even during off-hours and unrelated to the stories or individuals they cover. Naturally, no corporate entity can keep journalists from voting as Democrats, Republicans, or Independents—or from not voting at all. A 2014 study reported that only 7 percent of reporters identified as Republicans. Does that mean the rest of the press corps leans to the left? The same study found that the number of journalists who identified as Democrats is shrinking and that 50 percent of the respondents described themselves as "independent." Based on memoirs by journalists and answers to surveys conducted by media organizations and political scientists,[7] journalists are not particularly interested in party politics, but they are preoccupied with public service—another facet of political life. As a rule, journalists keep their voting preferences removed from their news decisions.

## Altruistic by Inclination

The calling to do public service motivates journalists far more than the pursuit of fame or wealth. Ida B. Wells sought neither when she entered the profession, although she achieved both later on. Her public persona began in the late nineteenth century when she investigated the lynching of Black men accused of raping white women. Born into slavery and standing less than five feet tall, Wells, driven by conscience, pressed herself into the public arena and, possibly, into a few crosshairs. "Somebody must show that the Afro-American race is more sinned against than sinning, and it seems to have fallen to me to do so," she once said.[8] She wrote, lectured, and organized for civil rights and women's suffrage. Journalism history contains numerous accounts of editors and reporters who championed humanitarian causes for racial, legal, gender, and economic justice with no personal reward expected and regardless of personal risk.

## Rarely Saints, Occasionally Sinners

For a few journalists, a job is a job and collecting a salary matters more than being a do-gooder. On occasion, journalists otherwise committed to public service succumb to temptations to plagiarize or invent story details. Deadline pressure and ambition mainly lead them astray, not immorality or outright corruption. When one of its own commits an infraction, journalism, due to its public nature, suffers more than other professions—and public distrust increases, even when journalism almost

## Quotables

"It is one of the great failures of our profession that we assume that everyone inhabits our world. . . . We need to step behind our sources for a moment and imagine what we would see from behind the mayor's desk, from a bed in the charity ward, from a conference table in the corporate lawyer's suite, from . . . the prisoner's cell. If we can get out of ourselves and enter into the lives of those we interview then we may ask perceptive questions and may receive perceptive answers."[9]

—Donald M. Murray, journalist and writing coach

universally ostracizes its sinners. Journalists by nature and inculcation act ethically and honestly.

## Satisfied, though Seldom Fully

Journalists generally find their work satisfying and rewarding, although job insecurity and low pay dampen those feelings. They expect no applause or trophies. Occasionally a stranger emails or tweets to say "well done." Devoted journalists usually resist the call of greener pastures, finding corporate communication jobs monotonous and unfulfilling. If anything, the profession quits on them. They might seek better pay or hours within journalism, and many seek assignments with a public service emphasis. They push themselves to do more, to go further. A sizable number of journalists report on the arts, fashion, and, especially, celebrity, and they contribute to a brimming public cornucopia of information, from trivial to insightful. Journalism has long distinguished between "soft" and "hard" news, and more than a few traditionists shun assignments they consider too trivial. But people do not live in one world or the other, observes NPR host Sam Sanders. Such boundaries are arbitrary, he says, and signify that certain news need not be taken as seriously or examined as critically.[10] Journalists outside hard-news beats contribute to public life and find satisfaction in doing so.

## Increasingly Diverse, but Insufficiently So

From the late nineteenth century through the 1960s, journalism reflected blue-collar values and exuded masculinity. Back then, a high school degree was sufficient education to land a news job. Rookies often started as "copy boys" who—answering to shouts of "Copy!"—rushed typed stories from reporters to editors and finally to typesetters. A young man of ambition would usually get a chance to report on a minor story and prove his worth. H. L. Mencken, a political journalist, author, and essayist of the 1930s-1950s, scoffed at higher education, as did other colleagues, calling it "balderdash of chalky pedagogues."[11] Cigarette smoke and curses filled newsrooms, where women mostly did secretarial errands and non-Whites swept up the waste and emptied ashtrays. The Boomer generation of children of World War II veterans changed the demographics. The Boomers went to college, traveled well beyond the hometowns of their parents, and reached young adulthood during the 1960s and 1970s. The tumultuous period of the civil rights movement, the cultural awakening, the Vietnam War, and, especially, the Watergate scandal launched the careers of men and women driven to hold the powerful accountable and to expose injustices.

Newsrooms, though, largely remained a domain of white males for decades. Slowly, but under pressure, journalism opened its doors, and even more slowly, it acknowledged the value of ethnic and racial diversity and, to a lesser extent, diversity of physical abilities and worldviews—what came to be called "multiculturalism." Despite the industry's persistent efforts to recruit minorities, a 2018 Pew Research Center study found that about three-quarters of newsroom employees are non-Hispanic white, compared with about two-thirds of all U.S. employees. About half of newsroom staff are white men, compared with about a third of the overall workforce. Newsroom diversity remains far below the 1978 American Society of News Editors' goal "of minority employment by the year 2000 equivalent to the percentage of minority persons within the national population." Racial and ethnic minorities make up about 40 percent of the U.S. population, according to the Pew study.[12] Minorities find journalism a worthy profession that offers a chance to right wrongs and help the less fortunate. Greater diversity pays off in richer, more insightful stories beyond the world of the so-called usual suspects whom journalists once relied upon for interviews and expertise—predominantly white, male, and monocultural. Viewpoint diversity ought to be an objective, too, so that journalism becomes less likely to miss signs of unintentional political bias.

## The Mixed Meanings of "News"

In the world of journalism, "news" means the massive accumulation of information that writers, reporters, correspondents, students, and freelancers churn out 24-7. Not all of it is current or important or even interesting. Actually, no one on earth can keep track of everything that could be considered newsworthy. Millions of accounts escape us for assorted reasons: our media access, our level of interest, the time we can devote to news, and the innumerable instances when we simply miss what happened yesterday in New York. Often, people get the news secondhand, from a coworker, via a family member, or through social media. Once, it mattered little when, how, or why people accessed the news. They listened to NPR commuting to work, read the newspaper over coffee, watched YouTube videos, or tuned in the nightly news. But then almost daily accusations of liberal media slanting and fabricating the news reframed what was a normal part of our lives as a subversive activity.

Donald Trump did not create the term "fake news," but he made it a household phrase. Perhaps his most notable early use came in January 2017, just before the inauguration, when at a press briefing he avoided a question from CNN reporter Jim Acosta by dismissing it: "You're fake news."[13] After that, President Trump's numerous tweets spread its usage to the workaday vocabularies of world leaders, political operatives, journalists, and ordinary people. The president used "fake news" to deny stories published by major news outlets that exposed his administration's problems or challenged his versions of truth. He repeatedly told the nation that the negative stories about him were untrue and manufactured to poison his presidency and American values.

Trump's rhetoric eroded public trust in legitimate journalism, but, as we detail in chapter 6, demeaning the press has been a political strategy for many decades. Trump's approach, though, may be the most effective of them all. Millions of Americans *do* trust him and grew to believe that CNN, MSNBC, and the *Washington Post* conspired to mass-produce falsehoods. As fact-checking organizations repeatedly debunked bogus social media posts, open-minded citizens grew even more confused over what was fake or not—or wondered whether everything basically is fake. "This is a really complex problem," said Claire Wardle of the nonprofit research group First Draft News. "If we're going to start thinking of ways we can intervene, we're going to have to have clear definitions."[14] She worries about future iterations of fake news made possible by artificial intelligence—no need to hire someone or steal photographs to push false ideas or conspiracy theories. Just sit down at a computer and custom-build your own Proud Boy or Antifa puppet or create your own "deep fake" videos that appear to show public figures in places they have never been, saying words they have never said.

Distinguishing counterfeit news from the genuine article may someday require an expert authenticator and more research time than ordinary citizens can afford. For now, common sense and a questioning nature will have to suffice. If a story seems too preposterous to believe, assume it could be fake. Indeed, any information, whether in a news story or a social media posting that comes from a single source, should be considered suspect. Trustworthy news organizations will report whether they have been able to authenticate individual stories and how.

How can we identify trustworthy information outlets? For starters, university libraries usually publish and distribute tips and criteria online so students and the public can assess reliable websites and other medium platforms. Media literacy organizations—local, regional, and national—also provide online advice and conduct educational programs to help citizens find reliable information both online and in print. Generally, peer-reviewed scholarly journals (e.g., the *Journal of the American Medical Association*), long-standing and widely read magazines and newspapers (e.g., *Harpers* and the *Christian Science Monitor*), and respected civic organizations (e.g., the National Civic League) have well-established reputations for trustworthiness and fair treatment of cultural and political issues. In addition, train yourself to read carefully claims with which you disagree and compare them to fact-checking venues that apply evidence obtained from the public domain. And monitor you own belief systems and how they could shape your perceptions of the news.

Real news exists, and it far exceeds truly fake news. Those of us with high-speed Internet access or a nearby library can feast on well-written, detailed journalistic accounts about the law, community issues, sports, weather, business, fashion, technology, and entertainment. Neither Fox News nor the *New York Times* should be anyone's final authority. There is so much from which to choose and learn. For example, *Vanity Fair* profiled U.S. Representative Alexandria Ocasio-Cortez, with fashion as a backdrop.[15] *Golf* magazine revealed the story of Ann Moore Gregory, who grew up in Aberdeen, Mississippi, attended segregated schools, lost her parents in a car crash, worked as a live-in maid for a white family, and in 1956, at the age of forty-four, became the first Black female golfer to play in a U.S. Women's Open.[16] *Wired*, in print and online, reports on emerging technologies as they impact popular culture, politics, and the economy, recently running a story about a laid-off BuzzFeed reporter who started a newsletter called *Coronavirus News for Black Folks*.[17] These and hundreds of other media outlets expand our historic, civic, and cultural awareness. They provide a healthy balance and variety to citizens' news diets, which seldom sample, for example, how urban citizens may lack an understanding of issues impacting rural communities—and vice versa.

Increasingly in short supply, however, is the kind of news essential to the intertwined relationships of journalism, citizenship, and civic discourse—information upon which a republic such as ours depends. It is what we mean by the title *Democracy's News*. In another book, *The Conversation of Journalism*, written nearly twenty-five years ago, we conceptualized news as "cocreation." Anticipating that the term might cause head-scratching, we elaborated, suggesting that "all people are part of the news because news is a participative narrative that defines the culture in all its diversity. News is not what we receive; it is the culture's story, which develops as it is told."[18] A colleague and friend, John Pauly, wrote in the same vein: "Journalists help make public life what it is (or isn't). News stories summon the everyday world into public imagination."[19] The late James Carey contributed substantially to the journalism-as-conversation idea: "We have virtually no idea what it is we need to know until we start talking to someone. . . . The task of the press is to encourage the conversation of culture—not preempt it or substitute for it or supply it with information as a seer from afar."[20] The worlds of journalism, citizen responsibility, and everyday conversation are not separable; democracies work to the extent that we sustain their linkage.

Citizens determine what is news more than journalists when they are committed to communities, institutions, and each other. Together journalists and citizens can then better explore areas of shared and unshared interest. We say that with qualifications, of course. No person, group, or ideology should hold journalists captive or dictate the content of the news. We do believe, however, that people impacted by the news deserve a voice that journalists should carefully heed. Cocreation of news means that journalists at a minimum factor in the stakeholders of a story, particularly people they quote or interview. The story, then, is not strictly the reporter's; it is the subject's, too. In its final, ideal form, journalism is a cooperative community *achievement*.

Darryl Holliday, cofounder and director of City Bureau, a nonprofit news lab based on Chicago's South Side, expands on the concept of news as cocreation, "with journalists and communities working together to produce essential information as a public good." He proposes the "democratization" of journalism: "Let's build new newsrooms as civic hubs—and integrate existing newsrooms into community spaces. . . . Let's open up the field of journalism to include residents working alongside reporters on some of the biggest questions facing our communities."[21] He argues that news articles often are *about* and not *for* people most impacted by issues, such as tainted municipal drinking water or rising murder rates in poorer neighborhoods. Under his plan, news organizations would become part of an existing network of community information assets—block clubs, school newspapers, libraries, and social organizations—sharing ideas, resources, and, perhaps, office space. With more residents intimately involved, news becomes more representative, relevant, participatory, and successful as a tool of community building.

Viewed, then, as a mutual undertaking—a collaborative, communal activity—news accomplishes the following functions vital to a republic:

- initiates public conversations between citizens
- satisfies the civic body's need for reliable information
- stimulates substantive deliberation about common concerns
- introduces otherwise disparate groups to each other
- exposes issues and opinions that might otherwise never reach public awareness
- encourages participation in social movements and political causes that serve the common good

In these respects, news is less a "thing" than an activity. It resembles the modern version of the public spaces that predated the nation's founding. At early town commons, people, goods, and ideas intermingled and triggered more talk and transactions. Substantial journalism stands at the center of today's news commons, where its representatives observe, listen, and react to ongoing exchanges. While others come and go, journalism always shows up, unless an "out of business" sign goes up—which is why the crisis of hometown news bothers us so much.

What happens in a well-functioning news commons? Here is an example from St. Petersburg, Florida, a community we know well. In March 2006, citizens and news media converged when a developer proposed the construction of multifamily housing, professional offices, and a shopping center on a vacant eighteen-acre plot once home to Notre Dame Academy, a Catholic girls' high school. For the project to move ahead, the city needed to rezone the plot from "institutional" to "commercial." Word spread from neighbor to neighbor. Signs saying "Save Our Neighborhood: Say 'No' to Commercial Rezoning" sprouted on lawns and at intersections, stirring further reaction. An overflow crowd wearing bright red anti-rezoning T-shirts greeted officials the first time the issue was discussed at a city hall meeting. Citizens then turned out in force at each hearing or vote on the proposal.[22] Local print and broadcast journalists expanded the conversation by putting questions to public officials, the developers, and the larger community. Citizens in other parts of the city chimed in, as did neighborhood associations, civic groups, and social activists. The public heard and weighed multiple arguments—pro and con. Then the city pulled back on the development. As of early 2020, the property remains vacant, and for the neighborhood defenders, its emptiness symbolizes the marshaled power of civic discourse propelled by journalism.

Journalists who value a collaborative, cocreation approach emphasize listening to the opinions and experiences of everyday people. When, for instance, the city council announces draft plans for a new community park, the news exists at street level as well as in the offices of the mayor, the head of the parks department, and the project designer. The story includes all relevant facets and facts, but it foregrounds public dialogue with residents. A mother with a toddler in tow tells a reporter she thinks covering the playground with sand will create a giant litter box for stray cats, something the city officials had failed to consider. By focusing equally on residents *and* officials, journalists grow closer to citizens and learn more about the community assets they depend upon—such as churches, food banks, free tax services, legal aid, and neighborhood associations.

The street-level vantage point helps journalists acquire "local knowledge" and avoid writing a story that the community members later read and say, "That's wrong. That's not who we are." Disconnects between a reporter's limited vantage point and the community's lived-in reality do far more to erode public trust than a dozen spelling errors or contested details in editorials. Not all news organizations embrace the cocreation concept, but we find more evidence that it is taking root.[23] Journalism professor Andrea Wenzel advocates what she calls "community-centered" journalism that sees itself as a contributor to an "infrastructure for healthy communication," not an omniscient voice of authority. Jennifer Brandel, CEO of Hearken, a company whose clients include news outlets, uses the term "public-powered journalism" in describing how to involve citizens in deciding what is news. That includes asking residents what matters to them, what interests them, and what they themselves can contribute— story ideas, background details, and advice on sources to interview.[24]

## Marginalia

The website of the Department of Journalism and Digital Communication at the University of South Florida St. Petersburg features a "philosophy of news." It reads in part:

We focus on the community because we believe the needs and desires of the people should be communicated upward to government and public officials, not conveyed the other way around. . . . We encourage our students to seek out stories where people live, work, pray and relax. They find stories on buses, at parks and playgrounds, church halls and small businesses—stories that often raise issues every reporter can find at city hall or the courthouse, such as crime prevention, disbursement of tax money, economic development and race relations. But the perspectives are different. Even when their views are not that different from official viewpoints, the words of citizens are genuine, unrehearsed and natural.

Our "people-first" journalism does not ignore conventional news sources and events, including elections, government meetings and legislative action. But it always has citizens' interests in mind. That approach, of course, means that journalists must spend at least as much time among citizens and neighborhoods as they do with government officials and at public institutions. We further believe that not all news is bad. Journalists should report on what works as well as what is broken, what is healthy in society as well as what is ill.[25]

The language comes from the founding days of the department, in the early 1990s. It still holds true for a journalism that seeks to collaborate with citizens.

## "Mainstream" and Other Models of News

The cocreation concept can be adopted by news organizations wherever they are and whatever they do. Increasing evidence suggests it is making a difference. Older models exist that influence how we receive the news and in what formats. A simple glossary informally maps the vast territory citizens will recognize as the "news."

### Mainstream News

"Mainstream"—also known as "legacy" or "traditional" media—applies to corporate businesses of long standing with mass audiences drawn by a popular mix of entertainment and informational content. CBS is mainstream. So is the *Washington Post* and most other big-city newspapers and television stations. The term "mainstream" suggests information that appeals across many demographics. Donald Trump continues to recast "mainstream" as "lamestream," borrowing an expression popularized by former GOP vice presidential candidate Sarah Palin. Mainstream media merit criticism if profit-driven corporate goals override higher aspirations of reporters and editors—when stories get chosen based on what best attracts advertisers and subscribers who prefer a serving of ice cream over the spinach of hard news. Despite flaws, mainstream media fulfill several important purposes. Their financial stability sustains national and regional journalism upon which Americans form views of the world. They especially serve people living in news deserts and help create a generalized or common vocabulary for discussing complex issues. In addition, mainstream journalists provide information that influences coverage of related issues on the local level. Editors in Topeka and in your community, too, watch Lester Holt's *Nightly News* or similar general interest news programs and read major print outlets, such as the *Washington Post*. Some observers call that role "agenda setting," which suggests that mainstream news decides what is important in our lives.[26] There is some truth to that, but the news spectrum abounds with choices and alternatives. Perhaps most important, the power and reach of mainstream media counterbalance attempts by the powerful to manipulate or censor the news. Mainstream reporters roam the country and the world for news that impacts our lives, using resources—private pilots, interpreters, expert advisers, and First Amendment attorneys—no local news outlets could muster.

Mainstream media largely deal in "general interest news," a category that applies across the news ecosystem, from small-town weeklies to CNN. As the word hints, general interest media focus on events and stories with broad appeal. Network and local newscasts fall under this category, as does most hometown news. Local outlets draw people of a community to the same page, website, or channel, heightening public awareness of common problems, such as a steady drop in student achievement test scores or rising mortality rates at the community hospital. This is especially important when a single major issue, such as racism or loss of industrial base, must be addressed from multiple angles simultaneously.

If American journalism has a lodestar, it is the *New York Times*, founded in 1851. When it comes to a comprehensive and dependable source of news, commentary, reviews, investigations and other elements of a full-service newspaper, nothing in the world matches the *Times*. It employs an estimated 1,750 people charged with producing an array of print and online editions. Juxtapose those figures against the fact that total employment for the entire U.S. newspaper business dropped to just under 35,000 as of 2019.

The *Times* survived the online revolution by joining it. Its weekday print circulation, once more than 900,000 daily in pre-online days, now stands at an estimated 375,000. Its online user growth, however, boggles industry analysts. As of mid-2021, the *Times* reported a total of 7.8 million subscribers across both print and digital platforms, including its popular apps, such as "Cooking" and "Crosswords."[27] Online subscription revenue now far exceeds that of print, but declining advertising income continues to be a concern. Still, growing readership helps offset advertising losses. Despite false characterizations, it is far from being "the failing *New York Times*." Industry observers, however, caution that the *Times* may grow too big—the Netflix of journalism—although its publisher, A. G. Sulzberger, considers its success as "rising-tide-lifts-all-boats dynamism."[28]

The *Times*'s online subscribers enjoy for seventeen dollars a month more information than the typical user can consume. Most of the content comes from its own expert staff or well-paid contributors. Some critics wrongly accuse the newspaper of being a vehicle of pro-liberal propaganda, partly because its prime audience is heavily Democrat, white, college educated, and affluent. A quick scan of the online homepage, however, reveals significant stories far removed from partisan politics. Many originate from the *Times*'s network of foreign correspondents, science journalists, bureaus in major national and international cities, special in-house investigative and visual journalism units, and statistical analysts. Due to the newspaper's internal protocols, stories and multimedia reports are as reliable as could be expected from a complex news organization that daily aims for worldwide accuracy across continents and multiple editions. Its news accounts are presented in detail, placed in context, and fact-checked thoroughly. At the end of many stories comes an editor's request: "The Times needs your voice. We welcome your on-topic commentary, criticism and expertise." The *Times* gets what its asks for. Keen-eyed subscribers— sometimes numbering in the thousands—scrutinize a featured story with pithy observations and from varied experiences. The comments section represents a passage into the newsroom through which ideas flow between press and public.

The *Times* struggles to live up to its ideals and slips up on occasion. Its nickname, "the Gray Lady," was not particularly complimentary in the past, nor is it now. It implied a certain decorum, demeanor, and aristocracy evidenced by dense news stories, a dignified editorial page, and an unadorned format of long columns of type. In appearance and tone, the newspaper projected a message: We mean for you to take us seriously. When the *Times*'s behavior departs from its well-maintained self-image, the incongruence can seem almost scandalous. In June 2020, the newspaper published online and in print a commentary contributed by U.S. Senator Tom Cotton of Arkansas in which he urged the president to send troops into American cities to quell clashes promoted, he suggested, by liberal radicals. *Times* news staffers, led by African American journalists, denounced the editorial decision that gave Cotton a forum for encouraging violence against protestors. Swept up into the internal revolt, editorial writer Bari Weiss resigned, citing a hostile work environment for conservative employees, such as herself. She blamed a permissive approach by executives: "A new consensus has emerged in the press, but perhaps especially at this paper: that truth isn't a process of collective discovery, but an orthodoxy already known to an enlightened few whose job is to inform everyone else."[29] The episode has a positive spin, too—the *Times* remains a place where even the dirty laundry of in-house politics gets an airing.

The *Times*'s influence is immense. Its news, features stories, and columns circulate to other news organizations through the New York Times News Service and Syndicate. Journalists around the world consult its print and online editions daily for ideas. Foreign and domestic leaders subscribe. Corporate giants seek its attention—or hope to avoid it. Its innovative approaches of blending 3-D photography, data sets, music, video, and graphics in explaining complicated issues are models for other news organizations. As of 2020, its trophy case held 130 Pulitzer Prizes, far more than any other news organization. Incredulously, the world's most esteemed news source remains tagged by partisan opponents as the enemy of the people. A caveat: The *Times* resurgence solidified its role as a powerful public influencer whose perceptions of issues can dominate civic conversation. Chang Che, a writer from the Australia-based online magazine *Quillette*, wonders if such dominance is good for democracy: "Even if loyal readers trust these outlets, there is still something wrong with a public whose news consumption is dependent on the personal decisions of a few journalists."[30] He reminds citizens not to put too much faith in any one news source.

## Digital News

Digital news websites at first essentially republished stories, primarily from tradition print publications, a practice reminiscent of the early days of radio when "newsreaders" simply repeated excerpts of newspaper articles into a microphone. Digital news has matured and gained legitimacy, producing its own reliable content as well as starting to reimburse traditional news outlets for republication of their material. For example, Apple News Plus subscribers can access hundreds of print publications. In return, those publications get a slice of the $9.99 monthly (as of 2021) Apple subscription fee, the amount determined by how many users read a particular story.[31] The arrangement advances journalism in a general sense, because a story from the *Wall Street Journal* gets circulated beyond its subscription base and into the hands of news-savvy readers. Even citizens who abandoned or never connected with mainstream news receive bulletins and highlights of news via smartphones and social media apps. Axios, a website founded in 2016, prides itself on summarizing the news in breezy stories of fewer than three hundred words, easily scanned by readers on the go. Axios well serves those who prefer quick reads; its mission statement says, "We aim to make the experience more substantive and meaningful—and therefore more valuable."[32] Axios is a compact, daily news workout for preoccupied, multitasking citizens.

The popularity of Internet and streaming services enabled digital news providers such as BuzzFeed, Politico, and Vox, along with Axios, to launch and grow successful. They and other start-ups put aspiring journalists to work when they could not find jobs in newspaper journalism and rehired experienced newspeople laid off by print and less prosperous online news outlets. Blogs, tweets, text messages, and a host of other Internet-based methods of communication make news of one sort or another readily available to nearly everyone with a smartphone or any digital device. To be sure, digital news damaged print publications, large and small, by luring away audiences and advertising. It took a while, but traditional media adapted to digital news and its technical ability to incorporate video, audio, and complex graphics impossible in print alone. Online editions of major daily newspapers finally attracted paying customers, and the print giants, especially the *New York Times*, began earning a profit.

Online operations spawned a host of auxiliary ventures, notably Storyful, a news agency founded in Dublin whose journalists monitor social media, foraging for popular user-generated content, usually action videos of everything from a massive interstate pileup to firefighters rescuing a cat trapped in a sewer.[33] If the individual content provider agrees, Storyful licenses the material and puts it through a verification procedure to weed out pranks. Major news organizations, including ABC News and the *Washington Post,* pay Storyful a monthly fee for access to its worldwide inventory of news and human interest stories. Storyful supplies the lighter fare of online journalism but on occasion delivers valuable hard news contributions from nonprofessionals.

## Niche or Specialty News

The model of niche or specialty news includes magazines, weeklies, podcasts, and online websites that narrowly focus on particular news subjects, such as aviation regulation or solar technology. Their editorial staffs typically include journalists whose résumés include jobs at daily newspapers, magazines, or broadcast news stations. Now they operate within a smaller frame of reference. A reporter for *Stars and Stripes* knows she writes mainly to a veterans community that includes those who fought in Vietnam or Afghanistan and, as well, to retired or active military in government or the private sector. Such publications plug gaps in the flow of general interest information. For example, a court decision that CNN cannot squeeze into its programming gets covered by the *National Law Journal* (law.com). The niche category also describes specialized publications represented by the likes of the *Smithsonian* magazine (smithsonianmag.com) and *Foreign Affairs* (foreignaffairs.com). Niche journalism supplements mainstream media, whose editors and writers often scrutinize specialty outlets for story ideas and background details. Journalism in all forms tends to operate in a far-flung symbiotic relationship.

## Independent News

The Internet accelerated the development of independent journalism, which requires no printing press, cable system, or TV transmitters. By "independent" we mean generally journalists who work on their own without the safety net of full-time employment at a news organization. With traditional news jobs vanishing, some freelance journalists found it an avenue to enter the field or reestablish themselves in meaningful journalism. For others, independence gives them greater flexibility to choose where and how they do journalism. The category includes the relatively recent term "citizen journalists," who often are part-time unpaid volunteers. They show up at protests, disasters, and other sites of breaking news, self-publishing or posting visual and audio reports online for social media. Traditional media might pick up citizen-generated reports to augment staff reports or those from wire services, such as the Associated Press. Independent journalism allows journalists to partner in nonprofit ventures and pursue stories and subjects free of corporate restraints.

Thousands of young journalists find newsletters and blogs to be viable options. The online service Substack, established in 2017, offers a home for writers and reporters to publish email newsletters such as *Coronavirus*

*News for Black Folks.* Substack distributes the newsletters, helps set up the mechanics, and collects fees from subscribers.[34] Writers can focus on the content and leave the logistics to specialists. Independent journalism has expanded the scope of news and brought nonprofessionals into the mix, usually with good results. That has been especially true for Heather Cox Richardson, professor of nineteenth-century American history at Boston College, who found a large audience for her "Letters from an American"—or, rather, an audience found her. In a profile, the *New York Times* said:

> Dr. Richardson's focus on straightforward explanations . . . comes as much of the American media is going in the opposite direction, driven by the incentives of subscription economics that push newspapers, magazines, and cable channels alike toward super-serving subscribers, making you feel as if you're on the right team, part of the right faction, at least a member of the right community. She's not the only one to have realized that a lot of people feel left out of the media conversation.[35]

Independent journalism serves a substantial number of Americans who prefer news in analytical context and unsensationalized.

## Hyperlocal News

Hyperlocal news generally covers online-only content that concentrates on a specific geographic zone—a neighborhood, a city, or sometimes a particular state. For example, Eric Eyre found a professional home at the *Mountain State Spotlight*, where he continues coverage of West Virginia's opioid crisis. His small, nonprofit, online newsroom collaborates with Report for America, a Job Corps-type national service program that places journalists in local newsrooms, where they specifically report on undercovered issues and communities.[36] The hyperlocal approach is seen as a less expensive way to somewhat compensate for the demise of hometown newspapers.

Before digital-only, localized nonprofit news operations popped up from coast to coast, most urban regions already featured so-called alternative print weeklies in a tabloid format. Many came on the scene in the late 1970s—colorful in design and content and irreverent in coverage of government officials and policies. As the Association of Alternative Newsmedia characterizes the publications it represents:

They all share these attributes: an intense focus on local news, culture and the arts; an informal and sometimes profane style; an emphasis on point-of-view reporting and narrative journalism; a tolerance for individual freedoms and social differences; and an eagerness to report on issues and communities that many mainstream media outlets ignore.[37]

The alt-press, too, has experienced journalism-wide struggles for advertising revenue and readership, and several, such as the St. Louis region's *Riverfront Times* and Tampa Bay's *Creative Loafing*, laid off staff or suspended print editions temporarily during the pandemic. Those that survive appeal to younger audiences and tell stories with verve not always found in traditional media or on mobile devices.

## Documentary News

Documentary news combines script, audio, and visuals (still photographs, digital video, film) to report layered stories of people, conditions, and issues. It stresses long-form journalism and provides deeper context than the normal news story. Of late, print publications with enhanced graphics and video have ventured into documentary reporting, but the genre once was a staple of high-quality network journalism. Edward R. Murrow's classic *Harvest of Shame*, broadcast nationally by CBS the day after Thanksgiving in 1960, opened with a scene of overseers calling out to recruit field hands in rural Florida. The narrator says:

> This scene is not taking place in the Congo. It has nothing to do with Johannesburg or Cape Town. It is not Nyasaland or Nigeria. This is Florida. These are citizens of the United States, 1960. This is a shape-up for migrant workers. The hawkers are chanting the going piece rate at the various fields. This is the way the humans who harvest the food for the best-fed people in the world get hired. One farmer looked at this and said, "We used to own our slaves; now we just rent them."[38]

CBS, NPR, and others news organizations revisited the Murrow documentary as recently as 2018, finding little significant improvement in the plight of itinerant laborers in search of crops to pick. On occasion, a network, PBS, or a cable program produces comparable work.

Today, practitioners of documentary journalism tend to be young, idealistic, and limited by tight budgets, although Ken Burns and Michael

Moore are notable and successful exceptions, and powerful public figures such as Barack and Michelle Obama on occasion become prominent producers. As a result, the documentary has undergone rejuvenation evident in a diverse catalog of subjects available on streaming services. In 2019, Netflix produced *American Factory,* a gritty report on a clash of work cultures when a Chinese billionaire reopened an abandoned General Motors assembly plant in Ohio to produce automotive glass. An Amazon Prime documentary in 2021, *The Dissident,* detailed the apparently premeditated murder of journalist Jamal Khashoggi inside the Saudi Arabian consulate in Turkey, where he went to pick up paperwork for his wedding.

Controversy sometimes falls unfairly on the documentary genre when people confuse it with the *docudrama* format that blends factual reporting with recreated dramatized scenes or dialogue. Responsibly produced documentaries based on immersive up-close reporting frequently touch emotions and inspire reactions in ways print and short broadcast news stories cannot duplicate.

## "Wire" News

To veteran journalists born before 1980 or so, the "wires" refer to those stories and features distributed around the world by news agencies that still retain the name "wire services" even in a wireless world. The most renowned is the Associated Press (AP), which began in 1846 when five New York City newspapers collaborated to fund a pony express route through Mobile, Alabama, to bring news of the Mexican-American War north faster than the U.S. Post Office could deliver it. In 1861, coverage of the Civil War reaffirmed the importance of the AP in keeping the country quickly informed from the battlefront via telegraph reports. The wire services no longer boast a speed advantage, but the AP and other major news agencies, particularly its closest rival, Reuters, supply reliable news when and where traditional news media cannot. Journalism outlets everywhere depend on material from wire service reporters and photojournalists who, in a way, shape impressions of millions of events occurring across the world.

The AP calls itself a "cooperative" because its members—nearly all categories of news operations—contribute stories to a large kettle of news from which they all share. Nonmembers can pay an annual, prorated fee for access to news stories, photographs, audio content, graphics, and election data. The fee for mid-sized daily newspapers might run into six figures, although the financial arrangements seldom get disclosed. In the case of

the AP, its member journalists, along with its own staff of editors, designers, reporters, and visual journalists, number more than ten thousand
worldwide.[39]

The AP and most other wire services focus on breaking news, and
often the first reporting on an airline disaster or deadly tornado comes
from a news service. From there, major news media—networks, cable
news, regional and national daily newspapers—usually take over. Smaller
news organizations—at least ones that can still afford a wire service—now
rely more heavily on wire content when layoffs and cost-cutting newsroom budgets prevent staff-originated reporting from the state capital, of
out-of-town sports events, or about breaking regional news. News services
also provide relatively inexpensive content to feed the perpetual demands
of cable and digital journalism.

As local news continues to dwindle, the wire services become even
more essential—and problematic. Northern European researchers recently
questioned whether the "omnipresence" of news agency content might
lead to a homogenization of the news—more formulaic, conventional,
and generalized, lacking in local viewpoints and context.[40] That concern
applies particularly to America's hometown news crisis.

The wire services influence the shape of news worldwide so familiar to
most newspaper readers. In the early days, a partisan-free emphasis made
it easier for news services to market to newspapers of varied editiorial
page viewpoints. Big-city newspapers followed a similar path of impartiality to avoid alienating party loyalists among their subscribers. The
"inverted pyramid" model of writing news, born in the age of the telegraph,
loaded the story's top lines with the most relevant "who, what, why, where,
when, and how" basics, with additional details presented more or less in
descending order of importance. Editors at other outlets could slice less
important material from the bottom at will, saving printed space and, in
the case of broadcasters, airtime.[41] In a variety of ways, the "wires" remain
integral to journalism.

## How Journalism Defines Its Roles

Over the years, dozens of adjectives have been affixed to the word "journalism," such as "ambush" (intentionally catching a news source off guard);
"literary" (stories that stress a narrative, storytelling style); and "gonzo"
(characterized by an iconoclastic, "gotcha" style of reporting and writing).
But these are special-case *labels* as opposed to *orientations,* some of which

have long guided news organizations in finding their civic bearings. The orientations also help laypeople understand what motivates journalists as public servants.

## Monitorial Orientation

We rely on monitors in daily life to detect leaks, see who is at the front door, regulate the AC temperature, and check on the babysitter. We monitor to stay alert and make adjustments as needed. Monitorial journalism is similar. We trust reporters to go where civic monitoring is most needed— government meetings, courtrooms, and police headquarters, for example. And we trust them to have more resources and a more fine-tuned sense of relevant context than most everyday citizens. Their scrutiny extends, as well, beyond the obvious to include nondescript offices responsible for water-quality tests or collecting public health data. Reporters encounter both cooperation and resistance in their monitorial activities. They cannot be everywhere and naturally occasionally underestimate or overlook something important. Public officials may also succeed in diverting their attention. The presence of reporters, however, discourages those being monitored from trying to keep public issues hidden.

## Anticipatory Orientation

Journalism tends to be reactive rather than proactive, which is understandable because so much news erupts spontaneously. Reporters never sit at a city fire station waiting for the alarm to sound. They do, though, read history, recent research into social trends, magazines, and blogs, anticipating that news elsewhere could create potential fallout in their own backyards. A school fire in San Jose, California, kills six children who were trapped because exit doors were locked to keep intruders out. It prompts a reporter in Hoover, Alabama, to consult with local schools so the same deadly error is not repeated. Routine assignments often leave less time for anticipatory reporting. Yet society needs journalism that sees beyond the moment and beneath the obvious.

## Explanatory Orientation

The formula for traditional coverage relies on the "who, what, where, and when" of the news. A fifth element, "why," gets reported often enough, but usually less thoroughly than the other *w*'s because it requires follow-up digging beyond the initial facts. A sixth element of the formula—"how"—can be the most elusive of all yet the most significant. When a Kenosha, Wisconsin, white police officer evidently fired seven shots into the back of a Black man being questioned in a domestic dispute, demonstrations escalated at night into fires, looting, and physical assaults. Two men were killed by seventeen-year-old Kyle Rittenhouse, who left his nearby Illinois town to turn up in Kenosha earlier that night. He carried an unlicensed assault weapon and a medical kit—one to control violence and the other to offer aid, he later said to police. The killings, widely covered and critiqued, left the public and journalists with as many questions as answers.

A handful of news organizations with uncommon resources sought fuller explanation. They investigated past the five *w*'s and an *h* for a seventh element—what else? One of the most comprehensive accounts came from the *Washington Post*. Its newly formed Visual Forensic Unit combined public records searches, video grabs from security cameras, and data from cell phones to document what happened before, during, and after the killings. It included interviews with Rittenhouse (who admitted the shootings but pled not guilty to murder charges), his mother, police officials, and dozens of other sources and witnesses. The *Post* published the multimedia report in print and online on November 19, 2020, under the headline "Kenosha: How Two Men's Paths Crossed in an Encounter That Has Divided the Nation."[42] It provided factual and verified information to compare with contradictory and incomplete narratives and falsehoods spread by outsiders with ideological motives.

Reporters with fewer resources also produce excellent explanatory journalism when circumstances permit. In April 2020, the NPR podcast *Planet Money* detailed how General Motors swiftly mobilized its vendors to answer the urgent call for ventilators during the worldwide pandemic. The story focused on Ventec, a small manufacturer in Bothell, Washington. Before Covid-19, Ventec produced a few hundred ventilators a month. It now needed to increase its monthly output to twenty thousand. About seven hundred custom components from eighty different suppliers went into each ventilator. General Motors used its global connections and clout to convert its production of auto parts for a more delicate purpose.[43] The story revealed a herculean accomplishment and directly responded to prevalent questions about why industrial America seemed incapable of meeting the Covid-19 challenge.

## Advocacy Orientation

Some news media critics assume journalists who care deeply about the community they serve cross a line. "Just report the facts," they admonish newspapers, for example, as though journalists should ignore ways to improve life in the towns and neighborhoods they understand so thoroughly. The *St. Louis Globe-Democrat* conducted hundreds of advocacy projects between 1955 and 1967, and most of them led to legislative reforms or other concrete results—cable crossover barriers on a stretch of road known as "dead man's curve," a multilane toll-free bridge across the Mississippi, and passage of a state law requiring front seat belts on new cars sold in Missouri. The *Globe* slogan, "Fighting FOR St. Louis," was emblazoned on newsstands and delivery trucks. Its publisher, Richard H. Amberg, liked to say that newspapers fell into two categories—thermometer and thermostat: "A thermometer simply tells you the temperature and does nothing about it. The thermostat, on the other hand, tells you the temperature, but converts that information into terms of effective action." He elaborated: "A newspaper should be the leader in community thinking and action, and it should translate news and opinions into forcible action whenever and wherever it can, by whatever means are at its disposal."[44] A newer rendition of the advocacy model goes by the name "solutions journalism." It means confronting a problem through solid reporting on strategies that might work best in resolving it. The Amberg-style crusade identified the problem and rallied the community. Solutions journalism concentrates on objective reporting and a hands-off stance. The difference in the two approaches is explained in the mission statement of the Solutions Journalism Network organization:

> When the daily news product makes people want to tune out and disengage, it doesn't bode well for the news business—or for democracy. We believe that journalism can do better. It can provide a view of the world that's faithful to reality. It can strengthen engagement with audiences and rebuild trust. . . . We help reporters, producers, and editors bring the same attention and rigor to stories about responses to problems as they do to the problems themselves. Doing so, we believe, can elevate public discourse, spur citizen agency, and reduce polarization. It can strengthen democracy. When added to the mix, it improves the overall quality and impact of journalism.[45]

The solutions methodology meshes well with our belief in news as a cocreative activity.

## Humane Orientation

To balance out news about exploitation and inhumanity, citizens need stories that restore the spirit. CBS correspondent Steve Hartman, a specialist in the genre, communicates compact stories that celebrate our relatedness. In "The Little Patriot" he tells about Finn Daly, a six-year-old with Down syndrome and autism. Finn spent hours a day transfixed by an American flag attached to a neighbor's tree that he viewed through a glass storm door. Touched by the sight, the neighbor hand-built "Finn's bench" out of scrap wood and put it at the foot of the tree. It became Finn's first stop on family walks.[46]

Humane reporting invites us to experience the lives of people outside our commute to work or a shopping trip to Whole Foods. Greg Jaffe of the *Washington Post*, assisted by a videographer and photographer, reported a story headlined "A Pandemic, a Motel without Power and a Potentially Terrifying Glimpse of Orlando's Future." The motel's owner had abandoned the property, situated down the road from Disney World, before Covid-19 invaded. Street people, addicts, and the homeless moved in. But the influx also included grandparents, single parents, school-age children, and the disabled, all left in desperation caused by unemployment, drugs, fate, and then the pandemic. In an incident Jaffe observed, a few residents walked room to room to scrounge $1,500 to keep the power on.[47] The story caused citizens in Orlando and across the country to ask how this could happen in the land of Mickey Mouse and Cinderella.

"Civilization," the historian Will Durant believed, "is a stream with banks. The stream is sometimes filled with blood from people killing, stealing, shouting and doing things historians usually record; while on the banks, unnoticed, people build homes, make love, raise children, sing songs, write poetry and even whittle statues. The story of civilization is the story of what happened on the banks."[48] These are also the kinds of stories journalists can often tell best. Citizens should mourn what they miss when journalists no longer come around to seek out stories.

Good journalism grabs us by the collar and forces us to focus on portions of the community—the riverbanks—where people struggle almost unnoticed. A focus on people trying to cope with economic or personal hardships elicits "warm and fuzzy" feelings, observes Kali Holloway, writing for *The Nation*. Her examples include a boy, age fourteen, who spent his summer vacation selling homemade popsicles to help buy groceries and raise funds to purchase a motorized wheelchair for his mother. But feel-good stories, Holloway says, tend to frame *societal* dysfunction as *personal* misfortune. "Only in a society inured to heart breaking inhumanity of a capitalist culture could they be passed on as heartwarming."[49] Her message is directed to journalists and citizens alike. Anecdotal reporting seldom gets close to the heart of deep-rooted social problems.

## Investigative Orientation

American journalism history provides many early examples of investigative reporters at work: Ray Stannard Baker on racial injustices; Ida Tarbell on John D. Rockefeller's stranglehold on the oil industry; and Upton Sinclair on the wretched working conditions in big-city stockyards. They belonged to an era of reform-minded journalism that President Theodore Roosevelt branded as "muckraking." He borrowed the term from the seventeenth-century allegory *The Pilgrims' Progress* and its "Man with the Muckrake . . . who could look no way but downward," fixed on the vile, dark side of life. Contrary to Roosevelt's pejorative assessment, the muckrakers ushered in the Progressive Era, roughly from the 1890s to the 1920s, marked by widespread social activism and political reform to confront problems introduced by industrialization, urbanization, immigration, and political corruption.[50] Generations of investigative journalists followed in their steps. Some are well known, such as the *Washington Post*'s Bob Woodward and Carl Bernstein of Watergate fame and many more whose contributions received less notice. The public, for instance, owes gratitude to journalists like Morton Mintz, who in 1962 warned about thalidomide, a drug almost approved by the Food and Drug Administration for morning sickness—but suspected in Europe for causing births of children without arms or legs.[51] Under an intense media spotlight, the agency backed down and spared thousands of American families from tragedy.

When journalists refer to "investigative reporting," they usually mean a systematic and carefully researched examination of a serious, neglected social problem or a case of gross malfeasance. Police, scientists, and bank examiners conduct investigations, but unlike journalists, they often keep their findings confidential or anonymous. Journalists usually tackle investigations of people, events, or conditions to support citizens' right to know and protect the well-being of the community. They do not target individuals or organizations to settle scores or peddle scandals. The vast majority of investigative reports support the journalistic goal of public service. Only rarely do mistakes occur after the meticulous research and fact-checking that typify investigative journalism. If journalists err, most often either the offending reporter or news organization suffered a lapse in judgment or the normal methods of care were compromised. *Rolling Stone*'s 2014 "A

Rape on Campus" article centered on a purported gang rape during a fraternity initiation ritual at the University of Virginia. The shocking report sparked public outrage. The investigation, however, fell apart under scrutiny by other journalists doing subsequent reporting about sexual abuse at this and other universities. The alleged victim, the primary source for the story, eventually admitted lying. *Rolling Stone* retracted the article in 2015, later settling several million-dollar-plus lawsuits. Investigative journalism overall took a hit for the article as well, which played into critics' narrative that journalists engage in witch hunts and spread gossip under the guise of reporting the news. Interestingly, the *Rolling Stone* episode prompted another round of investigative journalism, but this time the subject was the magazine's handling of the original story.[52]

Investigative journalism, while honored by and important to the public, poses legal risks if it goes wrong, as *Rolling Stone* painfully learned. Litigation aside, the expenses of conducting records searches, traveling long distances to track down sources, and tying up top reporters in time-consuming projects add up quickly. Without deep pockets and fortitude, few news organizations can afford it, and when they take the plunge, these days they can expect accusations of "fake news." The future of investigative reporting looks less bleak thanks to partnership initiatives that unite traditional news media with online-only news operations supported largely by foundations, philanthropists, and citizen contributions instead of advertising and circulation numbers. The investigative resurgence has been documented by the Investigative Reporters and Editors organization, which circulates a weekly newsletter, *Local Matters: The Best in Local Journalism*, that recognizes journalists following the example set by early muckrakers.[53]

## Engaged Orientation

"Engaged journalism" harkens back to the "public journalism" debates of the 1990s. Public journalism proponents, primarily editors at mid-market newspapers, faulted news organizations that treated readers as consumers who were given little input over the products they received. The relationship, the reformers contended, should be grounded in community involvement and awareness. For a while, experiments popped up uniting journalists and residents at forums, in focus groups, and at neighborhood cookouts where strangers met and talked in a relaxed setting. The movement stalled, but journalists and academics retained a belief that journalism as an institution needed to do more than report and wait for letters to the editor. Media observers Mark Coddington and Seth Lewis see engaged journalism as an extension of public journalism: "Public trust in news will improve as the public has a more active, rather than passive, part to play in the news agenda."[54] Engaged journalism works best where citizens really want a voice in the news on a regular basis and where journalists welcome a collaborative relationship.

Often enough, these seven orientations overlap and coexist within the same news organization. CBS News gives us Steve Hartman, 60 Minutes, CBS News Investigates, and especially CBS Sunday Morning, where over the course of a ninety-minute program you might find examples of each orientation. News media do not commonly use terminology like "anticipatory" or "engaged" in mission statements or "About Us" sections on their websites. Indeed, journalists might find talk of "orientations" something only academics find useful. Yet citizens who hope to understand what journalism *accomplishes* can profit by considering carefully how the performance of a news organization reflects its motivation and values.

## How News Becomes Journalism

A journalist can be quite versatile. The editor of a small local weekly, for example, may deliver newspapers, sell advertising, write stories, answer phones, and take out the trash at day's end. Usually, journalists work with others in a team—even a small one—with the common objective of getting news to the public. Roles depend, in part, on the media "platform," meaning the technical system of communication used to transmit information. The print newspaper is one kind of platform. TV is another, and so is a website. Lately, journalism is moving toward large multi-platform operations that might deliver news by combinations of print, video, audio, live broadcasts, podcasts, apps, and social media.

The twentieth-century newspaper created the jargon and organizational structure for other media platforms to follow. The newspaper provided terms such as *byline, front page, copy,* and *cut and paste,* as well as job titles like *managing editor, general assignment reporter, columnist, press foreman,* and *typesetter.* Each modern platform, though, has made modifications to the newspaper template. Broadcast news recast *photojournalists* as *videographers* and developed fresh roles such as *news anchor* and *content manager.*

Rather than describe journalists by platform or job description, we suspect most citizens are interested in the process that brings "news" into being. "Process" suggests transforming raw material—statistics, quotes, descriptions—into informative and helpful accounts. The news process comprises three primary stages: researching, writing, and editing. Unlike a series of automated steps of an assembly line, journalism requires craftmanship, one special-order item at a time. To the uninformed, the news process seems uncomplex. It is not.

Journalists usually call the research they do "newsgathering," a simplified term that suggests the collection of bits and pieces of information—the ingredients of a story—that they then arrange in a readable form. More is involved. Journalists tend to conduct research in ways roughly similar to those of historians, social scientists, and anthropologists, although they operate on a smaller scale with far tighter deadlines.

### Quotables

"In our field, journalism, I trust only those with scuffed shoes. The nicks in the polish, the ground-down heel, the mud and dust on the instep, all of these attest to the act of reporting. Scuffed shoes are evidence of enterprise. . . . There was history before Nexis, and there is research beyond Google. The very ease of online reporting makes it seductive and dangerous. . . . I see a version of reporting that eschews human contact and firsthand observation, two things that have an inconvenient way of complicating or contradicting one's preexisting opinion."[55]

—Samuel G. Freedman, *Letters to a Young Journalist*

In-depth and investigative stories, freer of deadline demands, allow time for writers and editors to question whether a subject, personality, or event warrants close attention. Journalists, similar to the culling done by scientific researchers, discuss whether a proposed story is needed, significant, or original. The assessment includes practical and logistical factors, including the resources available. Would undertaking this project be too expensive? Is it less important than other alternatives? Do roadblocks hinder its pursuit? Are some essential facts, for example, physically unavailable, guarded behind the gates of a chemical plant? Has a competitor already told the story? If every consideration adds up to "go," the process moves forward.

The research methods most often used by journalists include personal observation, document searches, background reading, and interviews. Research may go like this: An experienced reporter gets assigned to cover a popular restaurant shut down by the health department for code violations. She likely will consider what she needs to know prior to making phone calls or visiting the scene—like jotting down a shopping list. She might choose to research: a copy of the code violation citation; procedures for on-site inspections; the full ordinance that sets requirements for local restaurants; state incorporation records to identify the legal owner; any records documenting customer complaints; background data through online sources like Intelius.com (a public records business that tracks down, e.g., police records, state business incorporation data, and employment history); and in-house digital archives of previous stories about the business, its employees, customers, and owner. Digitized public records, along with troves of information circulated online, enable journalists to pursue stories impossible to conceive of much less accomplish in a pre-Internet era. Armed with documents and particulars, the reporter usually begins to frame questions, schedule interviews, and, as reporters used to put it, "work the phones." In the process, the reporter undoubtedly will think of other people to interview, such as the public health inspector or customers upset by the closing, and conclude she needs extra background information.

If that seems like a lot of work for a single story, it is. Slapdash preparation, a couple of quick phone calls, and a few scraps of fact do not cut it. At each step, details in the story need verification; unclear comments by interviewees need clarification. If the owner says, "I've been targeted because I'm Muslim," another layer of inquiry unfolds, and the reporter's assignment expands to confirm or refute his claim. The research often goes deep, the norm in a profession that prides itself on getting the complete story, although achieving that goal is never entirely possible.

For breaking stories, deadlines necessarily limit the completeness of available information. When a nursing home fire breaks out or a prominent public official unexpectedly resigns, reporters respond with little if any time for pre-story research. They must move quickly, making phone calls, leaving text messages, asking rapid-fire questions, and conducting rudimentary Google and archival searches. Technology greatly hastens and enhances newsgathering. Reporters at a breaking news scene communicate with newsroom-bound colleagues who track background information, collect reports from any citizen journalists who have checked in, and do basic fact-checking.

Journalists deal with the realities of shape-shifting news occurring in the midst of chaos, confusion, and conflicting witness accounts. As deadline pressure mounts, so do frustrations, such as tracking down someone in authority to answer questions or working with corporate or government media spokespeople who generally are guarded in their remarks. News done on the run naturally increases the potential for errors. Supposed facts turn out wrong, damage estimates are overstated, victims are misidentified, and addresses get copied incorrectly. Mistakes usually get corrected quickly, especially at news outlets that can post updates online. Journalists can sometimes avert errors by such precautions as check-back interviews to reverify dates, names, and the bones of the story. But not always.

Of all the journalistic research methods, the interview most frequently reveals the heart of the news. Reporters spend a substantial portion of every day interviewing to collect information from public officials and everyday people, such as a convenience store clerk who experienced a holdup or a neighbor who sponsored a resolution on the town board agenda. The success of interviews depends heavily on face-to-face communication skills and the willingness to build relationships with conversation. Little of value emerges from an interview that a reporter treats as a simple task of asking a few questions and recording the first thing an interviewee says. Interviewing is far more complicated, and while some journalists are excellent natural interviewers, others flounder. The inexperienced interviewer might, for example, fail to elicit a fuller account from those who are reluctant, shy, or deceptive.

The cocreation concept enhances journalistic interviewing by reminding reporters that interviewees are indispensable partners. It is a mindset that reminds a reporter to listen intently and ask questions nonjudgmentally. Sometimes, skillful interviewers will abandon persistent questioning in favor of thoughtful silence or empathic responses (a nod of the head, a smile, an "I hear you") that indicate how well the partner has been understood.

As the clock ticks, the reporter approaches the inescapable point when research ends and writing begins. It is time to inventory a stockpile of reporting artifacts—recorded interviews, public records, handwritten notes—from which to create a story. The word "create" is appropriate. A blank canvas awaits. Occasionally, a reporter-writer freezes, fingers poised over a keyboard. Writer's block happens to all types of authors—from skilled novelists to students writing a term paper. Journalists on a deadline cannot wait for it to pass. In 1949, sportswriter Walter "Red" Smith said writing daily posed no problem. "Why, no," he said. "You simply sit down at the typewriter, open your veins, and bleed."[56] On occasion, journalists will tell you, stories "write themselves." That happens when a writer has a clear vision of the beginning, middle, and end of a story and the raw material to match. It is seldom that easy.

Needing to move quickly to meet deadlines, journalists often try to visualize the story taking shape while still reporting and collecting information. They seek what is variously called the "angle," "news peg," or "frame." Imagine a reporter who interviews witnesses to a driver who ran into a family of tourists trying to scurry across a busy beachfront street. She recalls that a month earlier, the city council rejected a proposal to install flashing-light crosswalks. A possible angle: Had the city acted, the family might be enjoying a walk along the ocean instead of pacing outside an emergency room. Once a reporter settles on an angle, asks relevant questions, and collects details, the end product, no matter how well done, represents a somewhat selective piece of what usually is a much larger reality. That does not mean the news is inherently flawed or slanted; it means news writers, especially on breaking, deadline-driven stories, must employ methods helpfully efficient in creating—often from scratch—coherent, readable, *and* truthful representations of newsworthy occurrences.

With every assignment, the best journalists try to remain open to alternatives and resist defining news in ways that merely confirm their existing but perhaps mistaken beliefs, which editor Donald Murray calls "cliches of vision" or academics call "confirmation bias" (we tend to see what we expect to see or already believe).[57] Confirmation bias can poison the entire news enterprise, from misjudging the credibility of a source to letting stereotypes about gender or ethnicity distort a story. It can occur when, for example, an inexperienced reporter assigns meaning to an interviewee's tone of voice or facial expression, describing her as "tense" or "disturbed" when, had she been asked, she might say, "No, your question didn't bother me. I was concentrating on my answer." Citizens, of course, also can succumb to confirmation bias in judging news organizations and news articles. And they do.

Selecting an angle or frame also influences the tone and structure of the story. It often inspires an opening—in newsroom jargon, the "lead," sometimes spelled by professionals as "lede," a practice that started in order to remove confusion over the lead (pronounced *led*) once used to produce metal type. A lede alone never wins a Pulitzer Prize. But journalists love it when a story opens with a sentence or paragraph that readers, listeners, or fellow journalists cannot resist: "His last meal was worth $30,000 and it killed him." It was one of hundreds of grabbers from *Miami Herald* reporter Edna Buchanan, winner of the Pulitzer Prize for police beat coverage. It topped a story about a drug smuggler who died when cocaine-filled condoms he had swallowed leaked into his stomach.[58]

Ledes like Buchanan's invite readers like a midway barker at a carnival. Step right in. With news reports so frequently tragic or momentous, a pun or teaser seldom fits. The most traditional type of lede summarizes the who, what, where, why, when, and how of the news—the five *w*'s, one *h*, plus *what else*. For impact and appropriate tone, few ledes surpass what United Press reporter Merriman Smith produced in minutes on November 23, 1963: "President Kennedy and Gov. John B. Connally of Texas were cut down by an assassin's bullets as they toured downtown Dallas in an open automobile today."[59] Compact, stark, and shocking, it resounded across the globe. Smith's story stood out among thousands detailing the death of a president.

A good lede not only invites us into a story; it captures one's attention and signals what news lies ahead. A reporter cannot admire the lede and then rush through the rest of the story. The next paragraphs lay out the supporting details in a clear and cohesive order. The writing stage requires an organizational structure, attention to syntax, correctness in grammar and punctuation, clarity, cohesiveness, context, and, most of all, attribution. Attribution is the footnote of journalism; it identifies and authenticates sources of factual material in a story. The weakest form of attribution: "Sources close to the secretary of state say . . ." It leaves unsaid whether the information comes from a custodian or an ambassador. Journalists stand accused of relying too heavily on anonymous sources and thereby eroding public trust in the news. Nearly all journalists prefer that their sources be named and vetted. But they also know that an administrative assistant can be a more talkative resource than a cabinet-level secretary, and masking an identity is paramount if the story is to be told and its main source shielded from retribution.

The credibility of journalism rests on what media historian Mitchell Stephens refers to as "veneration of the fact."[60] But in our so-called post-truth society, do facts still exist? We think so. Facts include concrete goods and materials: an ounce of gold, Grandma's rocking chair, or a 1957 Chevrolet Bel Air Sport Coupe. A fact can be an accurate quotation. When a news story reports, "The president said today that Covid-19 will disappear when warm weather comes," the statement seems factual when witnessed, recorded, and preserved. It happened. Even then, a president can deny the claim by saying, "No, I never said that," and the denial is interpreted by supporters as the latest "truth" or "alternative fact" from a trusted leader, even though medical researchers point out that the claim itself is wrong. Covid-19 is still deadly in hot climates. Trump was factually wrong on that score, but for citizens, the central issue should be whether the president actually made the statement. He did, and he lied when he denied his own words.

Verifying a fact can become the news in itself. Was President Obama born in the United States? He produced an official birth certificate from the state of Hawaii. Still, it was contested by thousands of Americans, led by a future president. We live in a time when what we thought was an indisputable fact becomes disputable. Facts stand up best when based on what researchers call "primary sources." These include official documents—a will, a court opinion, and a birth certificate—tangible forms that might be authenticated.

Before voters went to the polls in 2020, opinion writer Farah Stockman analyzed a list of more than one hundred accomplishments a supporter credited to President Trump and circulated on social media. One item claimed, "Low-wage workers are benefiting from higher minimum wages." That is true, Stockman reported, and she then provided fact-based context: "But that's because activists have fought for state laws that raised the minimum wage, not because Mr. Trump did it. The federal minimum wage hasn't budged in over a decade." Her conclusion: "Facts are vital. But they are insufficient. A bit of context is usually required to produce the truth."[61] Facts presented without qualifying context allow politicians and other influencers to shape interpretations to their advantage. When squishy facts arise—those that, in media talk, "can't be pinned down"—they often get tossed, true to the journalism adage, "When in doubt, leave it out."

### Quotables

"After an article is published, the first hour or two is some kind of exquisite torture. You're waiting to find out if somebody will come back and say, 'You got this wrong,' or, 'You misstated my position.' Those are the same worries I had when I was starting out as a journalist at 23, only now it's worse. . . . People are going to be reading very, very closely."[62]

—Michael Powell, veteran reporter

Final assembly of a story involves multiple choices about, for instance, which direct quotes from interviewees to use, what details are expendable and can be left out, how to position one paragraph to best transition to the next, what paragraphs need more revision for clarity, and which ones sorely need more detail. Typically, news writers spend more time polishing an article than writing its first draft. They rewrite, revise, and return to reporting when they find "holes" in a story, meaning missing or incomplete key details. When they submit a story, journalists are habitually unsatisfied with their work.

From inception to completion, every story is unique. Any two reporters could work with an apparently identical set of facts but produce accounts that differ in writing style, organization, and, ultimately, quality. Press Watch, a nonprofit with the mission to encourage "political journalists to live up to the highest standards of their profession," examined actual ledes and compared them to alternatives from other publications. One example: A story published in September 2021 by the *New York Times* headlined "United Airlines to Fire Workers Who Refused to Get a Vaccination." Its lede:

> United Airlines said it would terminate about 600 employees for refusing to comply with its vaccination requirement, putting the company at the forefront of the battle over vaccine mandates as the economy moves through a bumpy pandemic recovery.

Press Watch juxtaposed it with a headline and lede from NPR about the same events. The headline: "United Airlines Says Almost All Its Workers Are Vaccinated; Some Others May Be Fired." The lede:

> United Airlines is touting the success of its COVID-19 vaccine mandate, saying that more than 99 percent of its U.S.-based employees have met the company's requirement to get vaccinated, or have applied for a religious or medical exemption.
>
> But the fewer than 600 United employees who did not get vaccinated by the airline's deadline of Sept. 27 now face termination.[63]

What to conclude from this informal experiment? You could say that one story emphasizes the negative, the other the positive—a possible sign of bias. For now, let us say that neither story is deliberately slanted. But something *subjective* happened. Here we have two experienced reporters with significantly different emphases, both factual, that could lead readers to quite different interpretations of corporate vaccine mandates. Unless artificial intelligence takes over journalism with story-writing robots— and pray that it does not—news reports remain handcrafted, not manufactured with assembly-line precision and uniformity. Journalists do not approach a story subject from identical experiences or vantage points;

human idiosyncrasies come into play. Citizens who understand the variables and limitations of story building and storytelling can better evaluate news reports objectively and knowledgeably, not based on "fake news" conjecture.

That observation applies as well to the editing process, which occurs out of public sight. Much of what we describe here applies to editors who work with written material meant for print display, either online or in magazines and newspapers. But no matter the platform or format, the job still boils down to working skillfully with words and writers.

Bringing a story to life is a team effort. In newsrooms, the title "editor" is common and applies to various areas and types of supervision—executive editor, managing editor, city editor, foreign editor, enterprise editor, design editor, and so on. Regardless of title, nearly all editors work with other staffers and subeditors who enhance the bare-bones story with headlines, photographs, and, increasingly, audio, video, and graphic elements.

Laypeople might assume that editing begins when reporters hand off their stories to editors, who then catch factual errors, correct misspellings, and fine-polish sentences. Editors do far more and far earlier. They are expected to come up with story ideas in the first place; in fact, nearly everyone on staff stays alert for potential news. An editor's curiosity about the growing number of for-sale signs she noticed on a drive across town may result in an important story about the real estate market and the impact of rising property values. Reporters propose their own story ideas, but in many cases, it is the role of editors to approve, assign, and supervise major stories and, on a smaller scale, to send one reporter to the scene of a multicar interstate accident and another to the courthouse for the sentencing in a murder case.

Editors and reporters coordinate and, ideally, collaborate. For breaking news, they may quickly discuss how to approach the story, when it will be needed, and where it fits in a priority ranking of stories already underway or expected from other reporters working in the newsroom or in the field. Editors handle multiple tasks that include recommending sources to interview, suggesting questions to ask, and providing less experienced reporters with background insights. Writers often fail to see their own mistakes, particularly those based on faulty thinking. Editors step in to catch logical fallacies, like false dilemmas (those presented as black-or-white absolutes without consideration for gray areas) or hasty generalizations (conclusions drawn with too little evidence). They also stay alert for what the story does not say—for missing particulars or unanswered questions. The job involves coaching as well as correcting.

The best editors view stories with the audience in mind. Jia Lynn Yang, who supervises the *New York Times*'s national reporting, explains her approach:

> If I'm editing a piece, particularly if it's ambitious in a way where the writer and I are having to discover its meaning together, I like long conversations where I immerse myself in what the reporter has learned and is trying to say. As I'm listening, I'm trying to act also as an advocate for the reader who will be encountering the piece when we are done.[64]

Editors, though, who simply *assume* they understand their audiences usually do not. They try to look into the world *they* know—into their communities—and decide what events, people, occurrences, and conditions deserve attention. How they determine what is newsworthy can resemble guesswork, and it should not. An editor's insights should penetrate the crevices of everyday life. Diversity in the newsroom helps overcome institutional or individual myopia over truly newsworthy matters.

Few news stories include an editor's note to inform audiences that what they read, listen to, or watch is the work of many hands. For example, the headline may get written by a copy editor on deadline unable to consult with the writer; the photojournalist for a story might never talk to the reporter, either at the scene of the news or back at the newsroom; or the photos or video accompanying a story may come from a news service, not an in-house staffer. The newsroom ideal of face-to-face collaboration cannot always be achieved.

With others in the newsroom contributing to a story's overall appeal and understandability, mistakes can occur, such as a headline that fails to capture the main point of a story or, worse still, one that is outright inaccurate. The online *Paste* magazine criticized the *New York Times* headline "Eight Bullets Struck Sacramento Man as He Faced Away." The story reported on the killing of Stephon Clark, a Black man police shot to death because he was holding a cell phone they mistook for a gun. The headline missed the main point. In a later edition, the *Times* rewrote the original: "Sacramento Police Shot Unarmed Black Man Eight Times in The Back."[65] Even the best-edited news outlets make mistakes in judgment or fact, although because of their exacting standards, big errors get corrected—and pointed out.

## Marginalia

Among the most persnickety newsroom staffers are copy editors. Once in a copy editor's hands—sometimes the final stop before dissemination—the story undergoes a line-by-line review. By that point, others in the editing chain have caught the most obvious errors, but no copy editor takes that for granted. Each platform has its own variety of copy editors, whether they use that title or not. Deep cuts in news organizations have reduced the number of copy editors but not their dedication. If a mistake gets into print, is broadcast on air, or is posted online, the first head on the block usually is the copy editor, regardless of how many other editors previously had inspected the story.

At every stage, conscientious journalists do everything humanly possible to ensure that the news that reaches the public meets standards as demanding as those of any profession. When news organizations stumble, as they do, journalists who are responsible are already in the spotlight, already exposed to public critique, some of it from other professional colleagues.

If a particular article or report fails to meet your expectations, recall the process. Good journalism takes time—when available. It requires attention to detail, but errors slip through. It seeks the truth, as best it can be ascertained. Remember, too, that major stories generate follow-ups that expand upon the original story and correct earlier mistakes. Rarely is a solitary news report the last word. Once in the public arena, a story, like dough rising, can expand, spawning additional coverage. A minor traffic accident involving a school bus may get sparse treatment at first, but under closer examination, the circumstances and consequences emerge, including identities of the drivers, witness accounts, toxicology reports, and public records searches. An accident that caused a few bumps and bruises could evolve into an extensive investigation into school bus safety, driver-screening protocols, maintenance procedures, and employee background checks.

The collapse of the Surfside, Florida, condominium in June 2021 that claimed ninety-eight lives triggered hundreds of follow-up stories. An important one was the *Miami Herald*'s report about a city building inspector who, knowing an engineer's report had flagged the condominium for "major structural damage," still told a meeting of residents that the building was "in very good shape."[66] Elsewhere, journalists launched investigations of high-rise regulations and inspection procedures in their communities. Local news outlets routinely used to do follow-up reporting, but severe cutbacks mean fewer journalists to report on government offices—such as a building code department tucked in a corner of the municipal building.

Journalism can never produce all the news citizens need, but it does not usually settle for far less, either. Nor should citizens expect it to identify, investigate, and solve all their problems. The best journalism relies on members of the public, including government officials, CEOs, and civic leaders, to sound alerts. If a community is suffering, its people should speak up and reach out to local journalists. Correspondingly, local journalists need to listen and respond. Rather than admonish journalists for their alleged failings, realistic citizens should consider newspeople as *partners* in defining, reporting, and acting upon the news. Working together increases the odds that broader truths will come out. What might have been the outcome had insistent residents at the Surfside condominium reached out to local journalists when they first learned of problems at the building?

## What Keeps Journalism Strong

Journalists worthy of the name protect the news environment and leave it in better condition for future generations. They self-police through ethical codes and strict enforcement of professional guidelines. Usually, they are their own harshest critics. Good journalists reflect on their work, read widely, strive for self-improvement, and welcome opportunities for professional development. They get support from other professionals and organizations dedicated to exemplary journalism.

### Professional Organizations

Journalists often belong to strong professional organizations such as the Society of Professional Journalists, the Radio-Television News Directors Association, Associated Press Managing Editors, Local Independent Online News, the National Press Photographers Association, and the Online News Association. These organizations do not exist to cheerlead or engage in public relations. They exist to assist journalists with advice, training, and constructive criticism. The Society of Professional Journalists, for example, sponsors a race and gender hotline for journalists, publishes a quarterly magazine with online updates, conducts seminars, and publishes *News Media Ethics*, a handbook now in its fifth edition. Each of these organizations contributes to the professionalization of journalism.

## Journalism Education

Journalism is a profession without all the prerequisites and stipulations of law, medicine, or even certified public accountancy. Becoming a journalist requires no written examination or professional licensure, although some critics have recommended both. A majority of journalists hold college degrees, but no specific education background is strictly required. Instinct, innate ability, language skills, and general knowledge count for job qualifications. News outlets, though, usually prefer a BA in journalism or the social sciences or a professional graduate degree. The best journalism programs belong to the Accrediting Council on Education in Journalism and Mass Communications (ACEJMC). Thousands of institutions teach journalism, but only 115 or so meet the rigorous requirements demanded by the ACEJMC.[67] Some critics, even in the profession, dismiss journalism's academic programs as trade schools. They are not. Students receive a grounding in media ethics, communications law, and research methodology along with practicum or internship experience in reporting and editing. The ACEJMC requires that students take three-quarters of their total coursework outside journalism. Faculty in journalism schools conduct media research, publish professional and academic articles and books, deliver invited lectures, and provide practical and scholarly advice to professionals.

## Auxiliary Resources

More than a dozen exceptional organizations support the practice of journalism. The Nieman Foundation for Journalism at Harvard University, the Committee to Protect Journalists, the John S. and James L. Knight Foundation, and the First Amendment Coalition are especially well known. The nonprofit Reporters Committee for Freedom of the Press (RCFP) reports in detail on freedom of the press issues. Its staff attorneys and law school fellows offer pro bono services to journalists and news organizations drawn into the courtroom. At times, the RCFP takes the lead in advancing lawsuits against government agencies. The RCFP operates a reporters' hotline; produces comprehensive guides, notably on securing access to records and meetings; and publishes a print and online magazine.

## Internal Controls

Top-tier publications and news organizations follow detailed guidelines for fact-checking and newsgathering. A few operate under their own code of ethics. The newly revised *NPR Ethics Handbook* (2021) is a notable example.[68] Other means of professional self-regulation include reader advocates and media criticism columnists assigned to explain newsroom decision-making to nonprofessionals and to respond to public complaints directed to the newsroom. A leading voice among in-house critics is Margaret Sullivan, introduced in chapter 1, previously media columnist for the *Washington Post* and public editor of the *New York Times*. Outsiders may also contribute. When facing serious allegations of malpractice, news organizations have hired independent experts to investigate and issue detailed critiques.

Ultimately, journalism stays strongest when it is "of, by, and for the people"—borrowing, of course, from Lincoln's Gettysburg Address.[69] "Of the people" means that news inhabits the lives of everyday Americans. "By the people" reminds citizens that journalists cannot report the news alone; they depend on others to share their fears, hopes, aspirations, frustrations, and deeply held opinions. "For the people" acknowledges that journalism provides citizens better knowledge by which to govern themselves; as the Founders intended, journalism protects their rights and livelihoods.

## CHAPTER 6

# Untangling Accusations of Journalism Bias

Suspicions of bias in public life seem almost as common as breathing. But one assumption overly influences many everyday Americans: major news media are dominated by liberal bias, a perception that appears to be growing.[1] Liberal bias supposedly rigs the news, and conservatives must fight uphill battles to get a fair shake. Citizens did not always assume this. Our story is about how the belief took hold and the quaint notion of whether it is true.

Bundled up in this controversy is a strong hint about why our democracy has had trouble lately encouraging people to talk thoughtfully with each other.

Although for some observers the case is closed—liberal bias infects news media—a search for evidence can be unexpectedly complex. Simply defining what we mean by "bias" is daunting enough. Psychologists consider bias to be the mental attitudes or inclinations that could influence someone toward or against an idea, behavior, or person. It refers to attitudes that are somewhat partial, but perhaps in a benign or helpful way. Parents are often biased in favor of their own children but may be biased against the next-door neighbor who swears loudly at night in the adjoining backyard. Other people's children might be nice, too, but mine are especially important to me. If I got to know the neighbor better, my negativity might turn into friendship. Bias in this common-sense interpretation is natural in the human experience, and humans consistently adjust for it as new situations emerge.

In the high-stakes world of political rivalry, however, "bias" has become a swear word, an epithet used for accusations. In everyday partisan rhetoric, normal usage can get murky, blame is stirred into the mix, and the tone starts to imply intentional unfairness. Is political media bias, for instance, something that one knowingly *possesses*, like a gym membership, or can the concept of bias be more amorphous, wafting along on someone else's *inference*? Was *New York Times* columnist Tom Wicker right when he slyly noted that unfair slanting of news usually "is in the olfactory organ of the sniffer"?[2] Is journalism tainted by bias whenever it reports actions unfavorable to a political group? Or could accusations of news bias, as Wicker might have suspected, often be a strategic move, a projection by partisan opponents?

## Accusations and Actualities

For decades, the profession of journalism has been both courted and targeted by political interests—including think tanks, parties, pundits, candidates, and talk radio celebrities. Citizens who follow such things are undoubtedly aware that the most serious and sustained critiques are directed not at sources that more or less *announce* their partisan preferences, such as special interest websites or cable television networks of self-cultivated ideological purity, but at traditional or legacy news organizations, which do not announce political and policy preferences except for editorial commentary traditionally walled off from the newsroom.

At least since the Barry Goldwater campaign adopted the generic blame-the-media rhetorical strategy in the early 1960s, conservative politicians have pressed the point that influential newspapers and television networks deliberately and consistently scheme to be unfair to conservative ideas and their representatives.[3]

Widespread public assumptions of mainstream journalism's liberal bias are rooted in examples and surveys gathered by conservative groups over the years, often presented as *facts* that prove the bias. For example, as accusations from recent conservative literature suggest, people should already *know* intuitively that liberal media bias victimizes conservatives. The claim often is accompanied by a rhetoric of sarcasm and disdain: scholars whose research fails to support the accusations of bias "sound like they never read or watch the liberal media"; a political scientist's conclusions can be rejected because he "sounds dumber than a grade schooler"; another researcher who found virtually zero backing for liberal media bias "doubles down on the idiocy" and "should be teaching geology because, clearly, he is living under a rock"; "suspicion prevails" that social media firms are "biased leftward"; "media is all-in on non-criticism of socialism"; the media "fact-check" infrastructure [is] suspect, as its function appears to be that of providing cover for liberals"; and "we know liberals think their authoritarianism is harmless."[4]

Of course, sarcasm is not evidence that the accusers are wrong. But the shadow portion of an "everybody knows" rhetorical style is the *certainty* of the accuser, which is itself presumed to reinforce the validity of accusations. Professed certainty is itself subject to suspicion. The eighteenth-century political sage Artemus Ward reminded us that "it ain't so much the things we don't know that get us into trouble. It's the things we know that just ain't so."[5] Citizens owe it to themselves to try to distinguish things we think we know from what "just ain't so."

The issues of bias are too complex to settle for simplistic and thin political accusation, the repetition of which may lead to squelching citizens' civic participation, access to truthful information, and thus the inclination to hold leaders accountable. You do not prove another's unfair bias by how you complain about it. What actual evidence justifies political claims of liberal bias in major journalistic institutions?

A fairer examination, we believe, will not hold journalists blameless—but should clarify the differences between actual professional responsibilities and supposed political goals. Our own position on the liberal bias question will be obvious: it is to listen carefully to accusations, evaluate them thoroughly, but trust reliable evidence. Citizens should understand clearly what reporters and editors actually *do* before endorsing politicized explanations about their dishonesty—which is why this chapter complements the previous one. We will spotlight newly available evidence that is largely overlooked in public discussions of the controversy. You might not be persuaded, but a careful consideration of less politically inflected studies should provide much to think about. The answer to this problem will not be someone's slogan.

Deeply rooted attitudes will not change immediately, if at all. Attitudes change slowly and incrementally, for logical reasons and emotional ones. Persons consider their opportunities, the plausibility and practicality of new attitudes for their lives, and the traditions they value. Conversations with what sociologists call "significant others" are also decisive. We often learn more about what we believe by listening to ourselves talk to others we trust. Many citizens zealously protect their attitudes, as part of who we consider ourselves to be or how we relate to friends and supportive communities. Similarly, journalists who have honed skills and practices throughout their careers are unlikely to drop their professional commitments simply because they are accused of something like liberal bias. Our goal for the chapter is more modest than winning an argument: we intend simply to highlight pesky reminders about media bias that have had a hard time pushing through curtains of political mistrust.

Citizens can expand the terrain for discussing media bias by improving the tone of public deliberation. Each of the potential "sides" in a conflict can benefit from more perspective and less dismissiveness. Like most moral conflicts, this one lingers because dialogue can seem such a distant option. According to the founders of the nonpartisan Public Conversations Project, in such situations "each side considers its own position to be so vital, and that of the adversary to be so dangerous, that neither seems mindful of the costs of the battle. . . . The whole system suffers."[6] Although the media bias controversy often reflects predictable conservative-versus-liberal skirmishing, listening well can be an antidote to misunderstandings or overheated nastiness that arises from conflicting worldviews. We explore in the remaining chapters the relationship between citizenship and the skills of everyday speaking and listening. A simple request to "listen," by itself, resolves few conflicts unless listening critically makes sense at a personal level. Citizens must value knowing what other citizens believe.

## Quotables

"For conservative media activists, the concept of 'liberal bias' was both a lived reality and a rhetorical argument. . . . They taught a generation of conservatives to reject nonconservative media and to seek out right-wing news sources. . . . Conservatives took up this battle against the dominant journalistic mode of midcentury America: objectivity. American journalists who were invested in the ideal of objectivity claimed the trueness of their stories could best be evaluated by how well they adhered to standards of disinterestedness, accuracy, fairness, and less overtly but no less importantly, their deference to official information and institutional authority.

Conservative media activists advanced an alternative way of knowing the world, one that attacked the legitimacy of objectivity and substituted for it ideological integrity."[7]

—Nicole Hemmer, media historian

Basic newsroom practices and stories often fail to satisfy fully all the goals of a conservative establishment, a liberal one, or, for that matter, any organization. Fair and effective journalism intends to play no role in advancing the political goals of specific groups. Its goal is to serve a democratic mission of supporting citizens in their roles of meaningful self-government. A suspicion of deliberate liberal bias might be justified if newsrooms actually plotted corrupt and unfair reporting. Or a suspicion of deliberate conservative bias might be justified if newsrooms systematically praised only the ideologies of the political right. Or, maybe, a plague on both of their houses, if both are scheming and lying about it. Pay attention. Citizen judgments are best made on the basis of real events and comprehensive knowledge of fact, not by sarcastic put-downs or taken-for-granted political allegiance.

For whatever reasons, though, citizens assume that liberals control mainstream journalism. A 2017 Gallup poll showed that, among respondents who believed partisan bias influenced news reporting, 64 percent thought "the media" is biased toward Democrats, while only 22 percent believed it favors Republicans. But just fourteen years earlier, also in a controversial political moment, almost half the respondents said *neither* party benefited from journalistic bias.[8] Note the assumption embedded in the more recent antiliberal impression: that the word "media," actually a plural form, is equivalent to a singular thing with a coordinated set of moving parts. Yet the media sources currently under attack show a plural and vigorous mix of thousands of information and entertainment sources, national, international, and local, many of which share almost nothing in common except perhaps for how deeply they are motivated by competition with each other—and by the desire to maintain democratic accountability. Just as there is not a unitary "media," there is no single "liberal" or "conservative" viewpoint. Intense partisans, dissatisfied with news coverage, might have their own reasons to portray traditional news organs as monolithic enemies. What might motivate them?

## Politicians Want to Win, Journalists Want to Report

Pointing out an obvious oversimplification can, by way of surprise, explain something important about the media bias controversy. Politicians and journalists see news from vastly different angles, with often different ethical emphases. Politicians need to defeat opponents to accomplish their own objectives, however laudable they might be, and parties need to control seats in Congress, state legislatures, and statehouses. Journalists, however, operate in a different communication environment and avoid defining responsibilities in the language of winning or losing, although their for-profit owners inevitably focus on boosting readership, viewership, likes, and clicks. For the most part, professional responsibilities motivate journalists, while political success motivates politicians, and clashes between the two groups occur. But when political insiders routinely blame journalists for bias against them, the designated culprits seem surprisingly slow to argue back. Two of the most recent book-length surveys of contemporary journalism appear to downplay or even bypass the option that rhetoricians and theologians call *apologia* (defending one's own position), as if public hostility has become a normal feature of the territory that news professionals must traverse.[9]

David McCraw, deputy general counsel for the *New York Times*, once recommended that journalists let the constant attacks on their ethics roll off their backs while they continue to do their jobs. Now, though, after much of the news audience has decided that traditional sources fabricate stories because they "hate Donald Trump" or conservatives in general, McCraw is deeply worried. What happens to a journalism that loses credibility when citizens believe deceptive attacks? Given the press freedom built into the Constitution, is a mistrusted journalism that much better than an unfree one?[10]

Conservative political interests have turned accusation into an industry that extends well beyond the normal opposition research (What can we "get" on opponents?) used by most campaigns. Their persistence has paid off with agreeable public opinion polls. When public sentiment expects the inevitability of journalism bias, citizens are primed to look for it, to naturally "find" it, and to criticize journalists for it. They are ready to believe that news stories negatively portraying conservatives can be dismissed as fake news or hoaxes. "Don't Believe the Liberal Media," the conservative Media Research Center (MRC) advises without qualification in its umbrella slogan. Its website, in fact, is a clearinghouse of examples of allegedly proven liberal bias from major news media.[11] The MRC focuses on the personal political preferences of individual journalists, editorial stances and endorsements of publications and broadcast networks, content analyses of cases of variable treatment of similar events, and examples of media interpretations that conservatives find offensive.

An MRC offshoot, NewsBusters, reportedly keeps twenty digital recorders going to preserve eighty hours of selected television programs per day, each day of the year, in an effort to capture every slight or criticism of conservatives. It has archived more than 34,000 videocassettes, including nearly all news broadcasts dating back to 1988. NewsBusters's supervisor, Brent Butler, makes clear his organization's bottom line: "News media, the entertainment world, and academia are the enemies of conservative policies," and "we're just giving [people] the ammo to make the case."[12] MRC plays a high-stakes gotcha game, which helps explain blanket accusations of liberal corruption. If our description of the MRC seems harsh, consider an assessment by political analyst Thomas Frank:

> [The conservative] culture of closure also gives us the phrase "Don't believe the liberal media"—the slogan of the Media Research Center, an important player in winger Washington. When you consider that, by the standards of the MRC, virtually *all* traditional media is liberal media, you begin to understand that the Center is calling for a deliberate cognitive withdrawal from the shared world.[13]

Professionals in journalism and communication studies are comfortable at the intersection of news media, citizenship, and democratic society. In such a neighborhood of public ideas, an overt frame of "politics is war and winning is everything" can seem especially jarring, if still common, in cutthroat politics. Democracies, of course, usually consider war a measure of last resort, not preferable to careful compromise or dialogue. A politics-as-war metaphor encourages actions that must be considered only when one knows that something utterly vital and irreplaceable could be lost. Citizens should assess very carefully the dangers of claiming other Americans are enemies, conservative or liberal. Metaphors can turn rabid and spread hate and polarization.

In a less bellicose conflict, for example, a muddle of interpretations and misunderstandings between good-faith communicators, differing opinions might be compared and addressed mutually. Participants could seek a ground of truth or proof on which clarification would be likely and resolution at least possible. But when multiple and almost unceasing accusations of intentional bias target a profession that stands on norms of truthful reporting, it pits two worlds of experience against each other in a moral conflict that resists dialogue or reconciliation. One world seems always aggrieved, verbally aggressive, and entitled to pursue a claim it considers strategically helpful. The other is largely restrained by a long-standing tradition of disinterested reporting and ethical guidelines. The conflict's asymmetry is confusing for much of the public and increasingly dangerous for the democratic concept of a free press.

Accusations of bias, repeated often, appeal to both playground bullies ("I only hit that little kid because he called me a name!") and political strategists. If a candidate complains often enough about media treatment, then it becomes easier for citizens—especially followers—to question or ignore what the media report. The familiar ring of a "poor me" strategy, too, can leverage better treatment. "Working the refs" is understood by sports fans worldwide as a tactic. By complaining about the opponent's horrible fouls, the poor victim expects more generous treatment from the referee and sterner monitoring of the opponent. A corollary of the "poor me" approach also amuses officials: "My following the rules puts me at a disadvantage!" In all these cases, the angst is cumulative, and that is the point. The accuser wants satisfaction from someone. In a democratic public, the refs being "worked" are citizens—you, me, us.

Do the refs fall for it? Sorry to say, we do. Recent developments of political mistrust aside, basic features of public life probably have changed little since a systematic study showed how rapidly assumptions about liberal bias emerged more than two decades ago, mostly in the 1990s. Media researchers analyzed different polls covering a dozen years, during which conservative rhetoric about unfair liberal bias intensified. Over those twelve years, citizens' belief in liberal media bias quadrupled and, with it, presumably their mistrust of journalism. Had journalists become four times as unethical that rapidly and only to support liberals? Researchers concluded that ironically the increased reporting in various news media about persistent *claims* of news bias reinforced public perception that liberal bias was actually on the rise. In other words, journalism was dutifully *covering* the stories describing conservative complaints—*about coverage*.[14]

Accurate reporting remains an ingrained practice in the education of journalists, making it hard for many of them to take bias accusations seriously. If it occurs, they say, intentional bias is aberrant, a flaw quickly renounced by other news professionals. A prominent media watchdog group, Fairness and Accuracy in Reporting, tracks corporate media for any "bias, spin, and misinformation," reporting critiques in its own research studies, newsletters, and weekly radio shows.[15] Journalists themselves are expected to report newsworthy accusations against them, sometimes at the risk of publicizing claims they often know to be false. Yet, when journalists make mistakes, the professional norm is to confess and pay penance. Why would the *New York Times*, by policy, run prominent corrections of mistakes when editors know that political accusers will then blame the newspaper's bias for the very mistakes it just acknowledged? Because it is in its organizational ethical DNA not to let errors stand. A generational concern for accuracy far eclipses journalists' defensiveness about being criticized. Do not bet that a presidential candidate—or any ambitious political figure—will voluntarily admit and correct a significant misstatement of fact.

History provides perspective for another perplexing contemporary phenomenon. Critics tend to argue ad nauseum about bias but usually focus on only one supposedly inherent type of political bias in American news media—liberal. Observers hear far fewer complaints about *conservative* media bias, almost as if Fox News and Breitbart are justified in fighting alleged bias with genuine counter-bias. Conservative critics work hard to assert that bias is baked into traditional media organizations' reports from ownership on down, while they historically have touted their own rhetoric as "fair and balanced." Conservative cable shows, talk radio, newspapers, and Internet sites objecting to liberal bias are coordinated, consistent, direct, passionate, and, above all, certain about conservative ideological commitments—but, we are supposed to assume, free from any stain of bias themselves.

The backstory of this tactical campaign is not shrouded in mystery. Roger Ailes and other media strategists working for Richard Nixon decided around 1970 to investigate the possibility of creating a television network with the goal of buttressing the Nixon administration. Their boss thought this was a great idea; he saw that it would be helpful for a network to provide "our own news" in order to enact "a brutal, vicious attack on the opposition." Much later, after Nixon's adventures in his Watergate scandal, Ailes finally got what he and Rupert Murdoch envisioned and more, with their version of "fair and balanced" journalism. Ostensibly, Fox News would stand up, bias-wise, to the liberal behemoths, which, by then, included CNN. In effect, aggrieved conservatives assembled their own propaganda counterbalance to what they argued was their enemy's propaganda campaign. "Our own news."[16]

Smaller outlets eventually emerged as ideological colonies of Fox, including the ascendance of the Sinclair Broadcast Group's local television stations spread across the country (as of this writing, 191 stations in 89 markets); Sinclair often requires its stations to air company-prepared political positions, which are disguised within what appear to be news segments and which after 2016 repeated Trump administration content such as accusations about liberal "fake news." The Fox phenomenon also inspired more mega-popular talk radio celebrity conservatives and hundreds of prominent social media sources like the *Drudge Report*, *Breitbart*, the *Daily Wire*, and others, such as *InfoWars* and *Gateway Pundit*, that are even more aggressive in their attacks on liberal media.

Critics from the right rarely define specific criteria for what constitutes *unbiased* reporting. Their working assumption, evidently persuasive enough for devoted audiences, is that they know bias when they see it, and it is only their enemies producing it. Searching for a solid *definition* of media bias is usually frustrating, even among communication researchers.

For example, the specialized handbook *Key Concepts in Communication and Cultural Studies* settles for describing why a specific definition is so elusive. Media bias, we are told, is

> a common sense term for presumed distortions in media representations that result from (i) deliberate prejudice against or (ii) unwitting neglect of an aspect of a story or a party to a dispute. The notion of bias is extraordinarily influential in public debates about the media, especially news. *But it is not in fact a very useful metaphor for the way media representations work.* It assumes that these representations simply "reflect" a pre-given "real" ("natural") world; and it assumes that this world is endowed with an essential truth that can be rendered without bias. Neither of these assumptions stands up to close inspection. Events are very different from representations of events, so these cannot simply reflect events; and *the idea that there is just one truth inherent in an event or a representation is usually a sure sign of special pleading—where one's own point of view is imputed to the event.*[17]

We will tease out the implications of such a description by discussing misconceptions about journalistic bias, which we later compare with the necessary practical biases of journalists. Remembering the adage of where there is smoke, expect a fire, some citizens evidently find accusations about liberal bias believable. You might find the following distinctions helpful in sorting out media influences on political life and political influences on media life. Of course, you can reach your own conclusions.

## Misconceptions about Media Bias

### Media Organizations and Sources Can Be Bias-Free

Not really. The answer is the same as if the claim was "*humans can be bias-free.*" Journalism can strive for total accuracy and fairness in its reports, but perfect self-awareness or total neutrality is not an achievable goal. Accusations of bias, however, usually point to a departure from an accuser's *desired* "real" and "unbiased" interpretation. Journalistic accounts of anything, for example, must by definition omit numerous details. Journalists must make judgment calls of importance, newsworthiness, and relevance for audiences. Truth does not announce itself but awaits interpretations, investigations, and comparisons from fallible human brainpower. Someone else's *choices* about reporting are not equivalent to *evil acts* designed to sabotage your life. Accounts of events can only be reflections or shards of real events; the map, as linguists say, is not the territory. Ambiguity remains and often invites projections of ego-involved readers and viewers.

Journalism means far more than transmitting daily parades of facts for public consumption. (And "What is a fact?" can be a surprisingly angular philosophical question.) Remember, too, that despite the common belief that a news organization should report only straight factual information without adding commentary, most readers understand the need for context in their own lives and expect journalists to place events and quotes in context. Context is an interpretive process that virtually every major national news organization endorses openly as a goal. It includes special sections of opinion pieces, commentary, and op-ed essays; in our experience, conservatives rarely complain about opinion columns in the *Washington Examiner* or the *Wall Street Journal* or about the conservative columnists and contributors who appear in the *Times* or the *Post*. Each media news source, of course, is aware of its audience and the many roles of news in community life, and each makes editorial decisions compatible with its audiences.

The *New York Times* is an especially relevant example. It earns a liberal reputation in part because of its reputation as a "paper of record" for social issues of national scope. Its scope is, in a nonpolitical sense, liberalizing— opening out the world in the same sense as educators acknowledge the need for a "liberal education." The *Times* also is known for its investigative reporting, its commitments to scientific and cultural reporting, its reputation for international reporting, and, in an emphasis that puts a target on its back, its sustained attention to social justice and individual rights consistent with the First Amendment. All of these tendencies have been painted by some readers as political biases, although each describes a clear and continuing interest of *Times* readership. If a traditionally "conservative" orientation that holds different positions is not a stain on the ethical reputation of other publications, and it should not be, then a traditionally wide-screen orientation to relevant news should not indicate deceitful bias in the *Times*.

## Perceptions of Media Bias Can Be Bias-Free

Again, no. Although some voters fantasize that their favored candidates are heroic and pure, squaring off against malign opponents out to destroy democracy, surely all makes and models of political actors have strong opinions, make mistakes, and hope to present themselves in a better light. That kind of bias describes the core goal of the political enterprise. It is reflected in rhetoric, aspiration, and attitude. Each political party is almost by definition convinced it is especially insightful and its opponents less worthy. When reporters are accused of bias by political opponents, under what conditions would a hypothetical disinterested observer assume only *one* of these groups is biased—the one trained in ethical and fair communication—while the other is pristinely objective despite its obvious political goals?

Citizens can observe the certainty with which accusers assert their well-publicized complaints about liberal journalists. Away from the spotlight, partisan insiders occasionally confess doubts about their strategy: "I don't think it's good for democracy that we're branding an entire industry as an enemy. But is it effective? I think so. I'm not saying it's right," said Sean Spicer, Donald Trump's first press secretary. Of course, he was willing to accuse; after all, it is "effective," he thinks. Not exactly a profile in courage from a man who later, back in the spotlight, danced with stars.[18]

Accusers in Congress and on the street, however, appear unwavering, sure that each news cycle weds *CNN*, the *Washington Post*, and *CBS* in one big cabal, willing to bring all hands on deck from ownership on down to favor Democratic party candidates and lie about conservatives. Accusers fail to explain obvious examples that question why liberal cheating is baked into mainstream journalism while conservative media bias is no issue at all. Why did large media "liberal" conglomerates, including the *Times*, voluntarily cover in minute detail each day's status of Hillary Clinton's email server investigation ("What about her emails?"), making it the most closely reported and impactful political story of the 2016 campaign? Did liberal editors overlook their options? They could have lied about it (they are not above that, we are told), or made up quotes, or invented alternative stories from fictitious sources exonerating her, or simply buried or ignored the story. They did not. If anything, mainstream news went hard on Clinton, perhaps to quell anticipated complaints about pro-Clinton bias.

A major study of journalism's election choices, sponsored by the Berkman Klein Center at Harvard, "document[ed] that the majority of mainstream media coverage was negative for both candidates, but largely followed Donald Trump's agenda: when reporting on Hillary Clinton, coverage primarily focused on the various scandals related to the Clinton Foundation and emails."[19] This indirect but real cumulative choice of "liberal media" extended distinct advantages to the Republican candidate. The Clinton coverage in so-called liberal media was so negative overall that "in just six days, *The New York Times* ran as many cover stories about Hillary Clinton's email 'scandal' as they did about all policy issues combined in the sixty-nine days leading up to the election."[20] The neglect of policy issues undoubtedly harmed the candidate with vast political experience as secretary of state and U.S. senator, compared to the opponent with no experience running for public office. At the same time, the allegedly dishonest liberal media in broadcast and newspaper stories again and again demonstrated or described delirious fans at Donald Trump rallies chanting "Lock her up!" as if she had already been convicted.

Advocates of bias conspiracies might also consider why such a supposedly biased liberal headquarters as MSNBC's *Morning Joe*—must-see TV for many political junkies—granted vast carte blanche airtime to Donald Trump during his presidential campaign. The hosts encouraged his phone calls and rants again and again, amid an exchange of friendly banter and political innuendo while ensuring free softball publicity for one candidate. He later complained he was victimized by bias.

To some extent, reporters dealt with journalistic vertigo when trying to present a clear picture of a presidential campaign for high office in which one candidate stressed detailed, if not boring, policy discussions while the other packaged celebrity charisma armed with macho denigration of government, various scandals, and miscellaneous threats to upend a "deep state" that no one could define. Attempting fair and equivalent coverage, reporters often seemed to settle for the false equivalence kind. Such a disparity of coverage and tone easily could have been a major factor in the election result—in which Donald Trump lost the popular vote by almost three million and eked out only thin majorities to carry crucial states for an Electoral College win. But thanks to a media system unable to decide how to frame his campaign, he cemented in place a deeply loyal and almost unmovable base. Was his "enemy," the liberal press, more of a Trump ally? He continued to complain about bias.

More than a few thoughtful critics say the traditional news media often favor conservative politics. In other examples, mainstream media hitched a ride on the George W. Bush conservative bandwagon after 9/11, boosting his agenda of patriotism, and it decided to run quite positive coverage of that administration's prewar certainty about Iraq's purported weapons of mass destruction. A resulting public climate of certainty evidently helped propel the country into war on misrepresented grounds, as historian and head of the National Security Archive's Intelligence Documentation Project at George Washington University, John Prados, showed. Prados analyzed the documentary record to demonstrate that the gov-

ernment deceived the American public about what it knew when deciding to go to war, while hardly a whimper was heard from most investigative journalists before the documents came to light or after.[21] In fact, the
*Times* and its star reporter Judith Miller had much to explain after it was
disclosed that many instances of misinformation were missed or ignored
by the paper's surprising submissiveness to, or de facto complicity with,
the Bush administration plan. Miller enabled a source, I. Lewis "Scooter"
Libby, chief of staff to Vice President Dick Cheney, to plant stories anon-
ymously, including one in which a covert CIA agent, Valerie Plame, was
outed because her husband challenged administration claims about weapons of mass destruction. Libby, convicted of lying about his involvement,
received a full pardon from President Trump in 2018. In chapter 4, we analyze how reporters can get too cozy with anonymous sources.[22]

No one can prove there is *zero* political bias within various news outlets. But journalists might be better monitors of their own biases than
many of the rest of us (it is part of their training). If bias implies partiality *toward* a goal, then all committed judgments exhibit partiality to some
degree. The inclinations might be toward protecting civil rights, toward
holding government officials accountable, toward ensuring the well-being
of citizens in need, or toward submitting accurate stories on time. Or from
other perspectives, the partiality might be toward ensuring that Barack
Obama was a one-term president, toward getting Mexico to pay for an
expensive border wall that a candidate promised, toward favoritism for
one's family or religion, toward deregulation of harmful chemical industries, toward encouraging citizens to neglect wearing masks during a pandemic, or toward cutting the federal deficit (or not). Sometimes bias cuts in
favor of conservative plans, sometimes not. Journalism's most persistent
biases, we have noticed, incline it toward public service.

## News Must Be "Balanced" to Be Considered Bias-Free

No. Balance is a shaky criterion, especially when applied to politics. The
contemporary news business is inevitably tied to the unsurprising criterion of *what actually happens*; politicians are not. Even publishing an
exacting and coherent balance of conflicting positions is impossible, given
the multiple connotations of words. Reality itself usually refuses to balance itself in any particular way; a crime wave in Chicago does not necessarily occur in equal measure with an outbreak of generous volunteerism
throughout the city. They are essentially different events, each with multiple causes.

Furthermore, good deeds and bad do not necessarily balance daily on any scale of which we are aware. How would good and evil be defined and measured for categorization? Journalists overall would rather commit in principle to reporting each newsworthy event on its own terms, within its own context, without pre-calculating how to allot news space or whose reputation needs sweetening while another's should be left for dead. What we know as real life presents itself as a mosaic or grab bag of trends and tendencies usually unrelated to each other. More attention to some might reflect reader or viewer interest in why they are happening or a civic need to know about them, rather than a balanced endorsement or criticism of them. Prosecutors and defense attorneys do not start with "equal" evidence to work with in handling cases. They are not playing a board game in a parlor.

Even the word "balance" is fuzzy at best if we hope to find criteria for our historical moment of polarization. Consider your responses to a series of questions about what is implied by the term. What criteria should be used to gauge journalistic balance? Covering the same number of stories about conservatives as about liberals, while remembering to include equal numbers for Libertarians and the Green Party as well? What if the "liberal" stories are thought to be less complimentary than an equal number of "conservative" ones? Is the balance still intact, or is there a metric for positivity that must be figured into the equation? Should there be a political equivalent to sport's somewhat dubious phenomenon of the "make-up call"? Is emphasis on equal coverage true even if a Tea Party leader's or a progressive Green Party leader's speech was relatively non-newsworthy on a particular day? Does balance commit a journalist to report obvious falsehoods equally prominently with accurate descriptions of public controversies? Or maybe balance should be journalist based, requiring that each time a columnist criticizes a politician's actions, that journalist should balance the criticisms with praise for similar actions of that same politician? Should balance be measured by column inches of print, or frequency of mentions, or perhaps airtime devoted to friendly banter between a celebrity candidate and ingratiating on-air personalities? Citizens should find it interesting that we need after-the-fact studies and examples, such as those we cite in this chapter, to highlight the not so startling fact that liberal media also treat *liberal* issues negatively.

Journalists typically would rather invoke the simple criterion of public interest when deciding about newsworthiness: if it happened and is important, report it accurately as soon as possible, devoting the appropriate space, impact, and context.

The old phrase "evenhanded" describes a useful if rough approach, similar in some ways to balance, that most journalists would recognize. It clarifies how news stories are chosen and envisioned. A mayor accused of bribery, for example, is clearly a newsworthy event from which an opposing candidate will profit. Does the local newspaper *owe* the readers a conjured-up equivalent negative story about the opponent, or a positive mayoral one, that might level the playing field a bit for the upcoming election? This makes the journalist clearly a player in the election, not a clearheaded observer in the press box. Maybe the paper will find in the challenger's past a list of unpaid parking tickets from 2009. From the standpoint of citizen choice making, does a lame attempt to maintain equivalence help or confuse the public? If journalists should care about balance at all, they would do better to see it in terms of evenhandedness: if I write a major story about X's bribery, would I also write the same kind of story about Y if he did the same thing?

Imagine that a president assumes power and ignores existing laws, acts erratically abroad by insulting international allies while showing love for dictators, and shifts previously advocated positions apparently on a whim. He mocks and demeans individual reporters who ask questions in press conferences and misrepresents or lies outright about facts in plain sight, later to deny the falsehoods. Reporters observing these behaviors find them relevant to engaged citizenship and include them in news stories, in fair context. Do citizens deserve to know them? Yes, and they ought to know, too, if the president's critics are guilty of similar ethical lapses.

Let us play out this point a bit further. Does CNN escape the tag of "liberal bias" only when reporting problems of a Democratic president, or should journalists assume the public needs to know of problems regardless of the party of the president? Should the *Washington Post*, for example, include only enough negative stories about a candidate, assuming they can identify them as such, to balance out the positive stories it has run in the past? Must a newspaper or network uncover equally scary transgressions of a party's previous presidents in order to justify negative reports on that party's current president's problems? These are largely rhetorical questions; we suspect you will not need to spend much time puzzling out reasonable answers.

Journalism has waged its own internal debate recently about what appears to be concocted "balance" to satisfy different political groups, an issue that became known as "false equivalence." Were newspeople so fearful of appearing too tough on a scandal-drenched candidate that they had to gin up negative coverage of Hillary Clinton to appear appropriately unbiased? Most journalists are guilty of nothing more sinister than doing what they are trained to do; they use news skills to report *what is new and important* that citizens need to know. Individual stories about government leaders cannot be evidence of negative (or positive) media *bias* toward an entire political perspective if the stories are founded on specific political actions that a leader performed. It is a sad commentary on our recent political climate that this needs saying at all. Accusations about balance and bias have to be seen in the context of the *actual events* being reported; if more of them happen on one particular side, then the "even-handed" news stories can seem "unbalanced" at first glance.

A recent example of applying an "actual events" criterion might sharpen the point. The usually liberal-progressive online site Media Matters argued that a study of news stories from the *New York Times* and the *Washington Post* demonstrated that "mentions" of Republicans were about two and a half times more common than mentions of Democrats. Some on the left took this as evidence that the papers could be *favoring Republicans.* Others concluded that notoriously liberal papers must be more balanced than stereotypes would suggest. But enter the political communication scholar Dominik Stecula, who levelheadedly explained what could easily be an event-related result. Stecula checked the data in context. It had been collected in May and June 2018, a period in which Republicans controlled most aspects of the government. He compared it to how three previous administrations were covered, two of which were Democratic. You might have guessed the result. When Republicans are in power, Republicans are "cited in a higher proportion of news stories," and the same goes for Democrats in power. "There's nothing unique," Stecula shows, "about the party that dominated elected offices across the country also dominating news coverage. This has been the case for decades and is not evidence of partisan bias in the media."[23] It is nonsensical to equate fairness with equal treatment without considering the context of actual events.

## American News Content Is Rigged to Reward Political Liberals

No. This assumption is dangerously false, for reasons we have previously suggested and a few others. We should survey recent evidence carefully and not just rely on previous analysts' suggestions that this kind of generalization sounds weak. Our basic response to accusations of liberal media bias is based on the certainty with which they are advanced: how can accusers be so *certain* of systematic deception and widespread unfair bias? Now it seems we can extend that reaction to another level. Contemporary evidence just does not support a claim of systemic liberal bias in American mainstream media.

Obviously we cannot argue that journalism is incapable of mistakes or deceit, some of which may negatively affect one political view or another. Like all professions, there will be occasional problems of unethical behavior from rogue employees. The same applies to financial planners, psychotherapists, plumbers, linebackers, teachers, and elected public officials—respected careers, all. Nevertheless, few professions devote more attention to developing, stressing, and policing its guidelines for practitioner conduct, which "encompasses," as media ethicist David Craig says, "accuracy, honesty, lack of distortion or misrepresentation, and fairness."[24] Strong codes of ethics guide—and rebuke—members of the Society for Professional Journalists, the Radio-Television News Directors Association, and the National Press Photographers Association.

Assuming that news is slanted by design or fabricated by liberal journalists for partisan gain over time implies intricate logistical coordination beyond the capabilities and competitive instincts of media organizations. Asserting that mainstream journalism involves *business as usual* malpractice does not pass the simplest of common-sense tests. Newsrooms are busy, active places, and journalists move often from assignment to assignment and employer to employer. The newsroom rhetoric of truth and public service generally creates a far too open and airy climate for concocting conspiracies of lies, much less coordinating them with hundreds of outlets large and small.

Evidence proving systemic liberal bias in traditional media institutions is thin, strained, and exaggerated at best, for several reasons. First, in mainstream newsrooms, committing deliberate misrepresentation, lying about a story, or making up quotes from phony sources would be, and has been, a firing offense. By contrast, it is evidently not a firing offense for political advisers to claim wrongly that an opponent lies or to insert deliberately falsified videos in campaign ads. Major media outlets have reputations to protect and do so by running corrections, retractions, and clarifications after printing any factual errors that they discover or that get pointed out to them. When you see a notice that a newspaper, for example, says it "stands by our story" after a complaint questions it, this means in all likelihood that an internal review has verified its reliability and the paper still has confidence in the story. A president who accuses journalists and editors of "making stuff up" should be expected by citizens to back up the accusation with evidence, not with repetition, name-calling, or dismissiveness. Journalists for whom intentional deception is business as usual will soon be preparing new résumés, probably for a different career. Should deceptive politicians specializing in spurious accusations do the same?

Second, partisans often point to out-of-date surveys of journalists' own political preferences as evidence of dishonest and intentional news bias in media they dislike. It is seriously misleading to treat an inference as proof, especially after a decades-long one-sided political strategy of claiming news bias. A 2014 survey found that journalists increasingly self-identify as "independents" (50 percent of all journalists surveyed in an *American Journalist* study).[25]

Accusers might admit that individual party preference may not override professional practices in public service careers such as journalism. Citizens typically know many elected officials across the political spectrum who commonly help constituents in need without regard to political affiliation. Indeed, this is one of the common tropes of campaigning—"I will be the representative for *all* the people." Judges readily rule in favor of lawyers and clients they dislike and even distrust if the law justifies doing so. Secret Service agents who dislike a president personally will still sacrifice their lives to respond to their duty when danger arises, and public school teachers who go to mass on Sundays will still treat their Muslim students honorably. Professional action fundamentally reflects the acceptance of ethical responsibilities—to interpersonal caring, professional standards, and the law, not to raw ideology. Something disturbing is happening in public life when so many citizens appear to exempt journalists almost automatically from this quite common and generous assumption about professional integrity.

Even if rogue journalists are tempted to violate professional ethics, those employed by a traditional news organization are not free agents. They operate within an organizational structure in which editors assign reporters to do interviews and stories while overseeing their work. Various levels of scrutiny are built in. Other safeguards include team reporting, as the 2016 Oscar-winning film *Spotlight* demonstrates in its depiction of how the *Boston Globe* exposed a massive cover-up of sexual abuse of children by Catholic priests. Team projects make systemic ethical lapses even less likely and thoroughness and fair play even more likely. Everywhere in a typical newsroom, staff writers and editors—often with years of professional experience on education, local government, or police beats— monitor the reporting of colleagues. If they see something amiss in a story, including signs of unfairness or inaccuracy, they seldom hesitate to inform a supervisor or directly confront the writer in question.

Third, attributing political bias in media tends to depend on who you ask. Conservatives are upset about undue liberal influence in major papers, networks, websites, and blogs, as if hundreds of diverse leftist media plot together and coordinate their "wars" on Christmas, family values, patriotism, unborn children, masculinity, and law and order. Newsroom journalists, though, tend to fear biases that can be exerted by the corporate side top-down, perhaps motivated by non-news issues of corporate decision-making styles, government pressures, or a financial bottom line. In his panoramic survey of social trends and practices in journalism, Michael Schudson reminds us that "almost all influential media institutions are owned and operated by large, profit-making corporations, and every one of them depends on government officials and representatives of other powerful, established social institutions as news sources."[26] There is more to it than that. Major news outlets are part of a largely conservative business and political establishment and can feel pressure to align with owners' political or financial interests or an entrenched status quo.

When corporate interests collide with newsroom values, often those in authority stand up against outside interference. David McCraw, the legal voice of the *New York Times,* considers himself a "raging moderate." He acknowledges the possibility of unfairness and describes guardrails in the journalism of what many call the best paper in the world. McCraw maintained a wait-and-see attitude at first about the Trump administration and its relationship to professional journalism, but the president's factual inaccuracies about the *Times* mounted. After mostly empty threats of legal action from government lawyers, McCraw decided to document the newsroom process carefully to correct the public record. Throughout his book, he emphasizes the careful attention reporters and editors invest in story fairness and factuality, as well as the politically inspired complaints of critics.[27]

But we do not have to rely only on denials, professional logic, and internal defenders. Independent scholars systematically study the phenomenon of attributing political bias. Recent scholarship clearly casts doubt on the extent of biased partisan practices within allegedly liberal media. Interdisciplinary studies focus on *perceptions* or inferences of bias rather than *evidence* of bias—and *perception by observers* is not evidence of *intentional bias in the observed.* One analysis done about a decade ago set the stage for research to follow. Tien-Tsung Lee found the evidence "suggests that audiences' ideologies and partisanships affect how they view the media. Strong conservatives and Republicans are more likely to distrust the news media, whereas the best predictor of a media bias perception is political cynicism." Partisan readers and listeners, in other words, tend to impute partisanship to media they dislike but not necessarily to themselves.[28] (This feature of a conservative political approach, of course, is what most people would call a bias.)

An additional implication of the study, although unstated, is also worth considering in light of complementary evidence cited later in the chapter. A campaign strategy of political polarization that intensifies partisanship by demonizing sources reporting truthful news likely increases attacks on media, shifts blame, reduces public faith in the concept of a truthful journalism, and declaws "watchdog" functions of traditional journalism. The tactic succeeds for anti-journalism partisans by planting widespread cynicism about politics and civic participation. Diminished participation in government subverts our constitutional rationale for a conversational republic of fair listeners to others' positions.

S. Robert Lichter, himself an early activist in the criticism of media elites, provides a summary of media bias research in a recently published handbook for political scientists: "Assertions of liberal bias," he found, "draw on surveys of journalists' attitudes and content analyses of news coverage. . . . However, numerous content analytic studies have failed to find a liberal bias. This has led to efforts to explain public perceptions of liberal bias in terms of cognitive psychology and elite manipulation."[29] "The central point," Lichter continues, "is that people's perceptions of media bias are shaped *more by their own perspectives than by actual media content.* The public's increasing belief in liberal media bias has also been explained as the product of a rhetorical strategy of conservative political elites seeking to gain a partisan advantage by delegitimizing the media."[30] Lichter is careful not to be definitive about causation but clearly does not now embrace conspiracies about liberal bias.

Other researchers from different disciplines have been busy investigating the same problem. Well-known journals in political science, public opinion, political psychology, and communication have published relevant studies of why political actors might *perceive* media bias, but none of them in our survey find that liberal bias is inherent or systemic in national political journalism.[31] At the very least, the definitive certainty advanced by conservative media critics is not supported by what serious researchers consider solid evidence. As with most research, Lichter and other scholars urge that we keep our minds open to further research, and that is our recommendation as well. Social science research offers little support for bias assertions based on individual journalists who self-identify with liberal causes. Despite all the rhetorical outrage, critics' accusations are difficult to prove. In fact, "the increasing public perception of liberal media bias has been linked to audience biases and strategic efforts by conservative elites."[32] Strategies are political tools, not bias detectors.

## Quotables

"The institutional commitment to impartiality of media sources at the core of attention on the left meant that hyperpartisan, unreliable sources on the left did not receive the same amplification that equivalent sites on the right did."[33]

—Rob Faris et al., "Partisanship, Propaganda, and Disinformation"

"It appears that the degree of media bias perceived has become almost a proxy for political ideology. The existence of media bias may have become a political issue unto itself, putting it in the company of the stark ideological divides over abortion, taxes, and . . . gun control."[34]

—Carroll J. Glynn and Michael E. Huge, "How Pervasive Are Perceptions of Bias?"

The results of several other studies deserve a closer look, because they are so at odds with the ironclad conservative certainty about liberal media bias and because they probe deeper than simplistic attributions or propaganda. To summarize them, we pose three everyday questions in light of their findings.

*Question 1: Are self-described conservatives and liberals different types of citizens?* At one level, apparently not. Both conservatives and liberals generally love their families; have spiritual lives; worry about the safety, health, and well-being of others; express support for community outreach; take pride in being good neighbors; and value many of the same freedoms and rights guaranteed by the Constitution. At another level, they are strikingly different. The Pew Research Center, a valuable resource of journalism and media studies, recently examined political polarization between citizens, including its apparent increase and variant forms.[35] As part of the project, Pew staff issued a subsidiary report on how America's conditions of polarization relate to media habits. They found differences that could easily impede conversations citizens otherwise could have about politics: "When it comes to getting news about politics and government, liberals and conservatives inhabit different worlds. There is little overlap in the news sources they turn to and trust."[36]

Research from Rob Faris and colleagues ties this "different worlds" finding more closely to how different sources of news were consulted by polarized citizens in the 2016 presidential campaign. "On the conservative side, more attention was paid to pro-Trump, highly partisan media outlets," they discovered, while "on the liberal side, by contrast, the center of gravity was made up largely of long-standing media organizations steeped in the traditions and practices of objective journalism."[37] The personal differences between citizens on the right and left are mirrored in the structures of media they frequent. One audience segment tilts toward highly partisan news. The other leans toward a journalistic tradition of objectivity. Yet the "traditional objectivity" media get blamed for unfair bias, while those who rely on news from highly partisan media on the right are primed to do the blaming.

Energized polarization along these lines discourages normal, non-defensive political conversation. When liberals and conservatives disagree, we might be basing our positions on different issues, different language, different goals, and, strikingly, different news. In personal political conversations, too, "those on the right and left are more likely to largely hear views in line with their own thinking." Still, according to the same research, we are not always shut off from each other and can find some optimistic openings for dialogue. Nearly half of committed conservatives who discuss politics have occasional discussion partners with whom they disagree, and that figure rises to almost 60 percent of committed liberals and almost 80 percent of those with "mostly liberal and ideologically-mixed" views. Although many citizens inhabit well-defined news enclaves and often distrust news sources not their "own," it seems many of us are still open to disagreements with others of different views without dismissing their ideas.

Discussing partisan bias openly means evaluating the worth of another person's information, no easy task for people who rely almost exclusively on already-trusted sites and sources. Tunnel vision and selective listening derail too many conversations before they can develop. Citizens deliberating together could easily underestimate the importance of establishing a mutual information base or understanding each other's linguistic land mines. Citizens capable of strong conversation risk misinterpreting or dismissing even the most basic information available to all, simply because it appears in a politically distant, unapproved, or blacklisted source. "That article in *The Atlantic*? I refuse to read that liberal rag." "I'll never read another Hugh Hewitt column again; he's just a conservative shill." Clearly, our caution about unfair dismissiveness should apply to all points along the political spectrum.

*Question 2: Does liberal media bias affect journalists' choices about which stories to cover?* The question appears to arise from various sources: (a) the belief that journalism is a profession attractive to liberals, (b) the conservative claim that liberal bias directs journalists' decisions, (c) the long-standing existence of journalism norms inconsistent with biased decision-making about coverage, and (d) the contemporary crisis of public faith in honest news dissemination. If the conservative critique is valid, the public would expect journalists to prioritize stories that make liberals look good and exclude others because of their animus toward conservative causes.

Does this happen? Researchers Hans Hassell, John Holbein, and Matthew Miles, against the backdrop of similar accusations, studied whether American journalists consistently choose stories that exalt liberal thinking—that is, whether a "gatekeeping bias" prevails. Their study, published in *Science Advances* in April 2020, was titled as if to reply to the question at hand: "There Is No Liberal Media Bias in Which News Stories Political Journalists Choose to Cover." The authors argue in the article's summary discussion:

> Regardless of the exact reasons for a lack of ideological bias, our results provide *concrete evidence that counters popular narratives* by political pundits, academics, and even President Trump himself. Despite repeatedly claiming that the media chooses to cover only topics that are detrimental to his campaign, presidency, and followers, *we find little evidence to comport with the idea that journalists across the United States are ideologically biased choosing what political news to cover.*[38]

The study offers a "relatively positive view" of professional journalists that partisan critics seem to resist. Even if journalists might identify with liberal positions, they do not necessarily translate their own preferences into negative bias against conservative stories, for several reasons.

The Hassell team studied national and local news outlets that had different perspectives and reporting priorities and found decisions verified "with a mix of self-policing of journalists or oversight of newspaper managers," a condition of journalism consistent with previous research. Their research further suggests that bias failed to influence news because previous studies perhaps have underestimated "the ethos of ideological balance that is often discussed in journalism training programs."[39] The Hassell study, in other words, reinforced David McCraw's experience at the *New York Times*—that "guardrails" of journalistic training, ethics, and practice enforce a level of evenhandedness that should encourage even dubious citizens.

These social scientists—hardly political operatives—offer an even more explicit conclusion of their empirical research: "While the nature of politics encourages politicians to undermine negative coverage through claims of bias, our research suggests that ideological bias in U.S. newspapers is largely nonexistent."[40] Millions of citizens who have already decided that liberal bias taints mainstream journalism should at least question the certainty with which they hold and project their own assumptions. Insights from the Hassell research build trust rather than suspicion for the journalistic enterprise, and it is only one of many objective studies with a similar message. Even in abnormal times, evidence that confirms a journalism of basic fairness seems to us good news for democracy.

*Question 3: Can both conservative and liberal citizens trust the national media?* Two recent studies shed light on this question of overall trust. One, reinforcing other research, implies that *both* conservatives and liberals are well advised to distrust themselves as objective analysts of partisan bias. Bias can be an equal opportunity condition, in which conservatives and liberals exhibit bias similarly. In a second study, different authors explicitly contradict this finding of relatively equal levels of liberal and conservative bias. They suggest that the bias problem indeed haunts one particular perspective.

Again, we do not insist that journalists are always unbiased. We only object to the right's certainty, both in its blanket accusations of liberal media bias and its stance of near total dismissiveness. Neither justifies persistent attacks on institutional journalism that ignore public evidence, exaggerate divisiveness, and ultimately limit citizens' access to reliable information.

The two research studies particularly relevant to our third question deal with social cognition, a research area in psychology that studies how people think, process information, and act socially because of how we think. The first is a meta-analysis, an academic way of describing a study of previous studies. It analyzes their conclusions, looking for common threads. The focus in this case was broad, identifying fifty-one different recent studies of political bias and involving more than 18,000 participants. The research particulars—definitions, criteria, methods—are available in the original article, but here we need only summarize.

On the whole, research does not show that liberal bias is a unique problem in politics. For example, a large study by Peter Ditto and colleagues found that liberals and conservatives are both biased and each favored information that supported its own ideological beliefs. Each group even exhibited a similar degree of bias. Moreover, it evidently only takes an indication that a policy comes from an ideological opponent to trigger a kind of bias, an expectation that the opponent's policy has serious bias problems. This is a critical observation for understanding effects on audiences that expect politicized bias. Each side believes bias in the other side is clear, while failing to recognize its own. The bias critique is more or less a toss-up, equally distributed across the spectrum of left and right. We might just have to live with it as a feature of human psychology. It sounds, however, like bad news for conservative critics who overlook their own bias as they accuse journalists of a liberal bias.[41]

Another study in social cognition quibbled with the Ditto team's explanation that "each side thinks the other side is biased." The new critique, by Jonathan Baron and John T. Jost, reads a bit like a brewing intellectual tiff, complete with sly digs at the other study. But Baron and Jost's work of critique attempts to build constructively on a platform of previous knowledge. The critique is a serious, thoughtful, and potentially controversial contribution capable of starting strong conversations.[42] Upfront, Baron and Jost say it is "false equivalence" for the Ditto researchers to conclude that conservatives and liberals are equally biased across the political landscape. The earlier study's method, the response claims, was slanted toward *not* finding significant differences of bias that are present. Baron and Jost, however, cite significant differences between liberals and conservatives in their processing bias and therefore in their discerning journalistic bias as well. But conservatives should not celebrate; the target of predominant bias points in the other direction. Conservatives' reasoning about liberal media bias is far from airtight when evaluated by experts in the field of psychological bias.

Cognitive variables (how people mentally process information and make decisions based on it) also get addressed by Baron and Jost, who cite evidence that liberals tend to score higher than conservatives on measures of integrative complexity, cognitive reflection, need for cognition, tolerance for uncertainty, cognitive ability, and cognitive flexibility. Conservatives outscore liberals on personal need for order and structure and for self-deception. In a comment directly relevant to political polarization, they generalize that "social scientists are increasingly finding that conservatives are more likely than liberals to spread 'fake news,' political misinformation, and conspiracy theories throughout their online social networks."[43]

Still another recent publication brings us even closer to identifying sources of ideological bias in media. In a study of "false" news, "four of the U.S. news/opinion sources that contained the highest proportion of false statements (the *Rush Limbaugh Show*, *Glenn Beck Program*, *Fox News*, and the *Sean Hannity Show*) were highly trusted by a strong majority (51%-88%) of 'consistent conservatives.' Conversely, *The New York Times*, which received the second-highest score in terms of statement veracity, was highly trusted by 62% of 'consistent liberals' but only 3% of 'consistent conservatives.'"[44] Independent peer-reviewed research suggests that ideological bias is not symmetrical across the political spectrum. All political positions surely exhibit some bias. But liberals apparently are less likely to display it—making conservative accusations about liberal media bias clearly less credible.

The cognitive approach seems to reinforce our "actual events" approach to understanding media communication. When accusations of bias arise from strongly partisan motives, counting or comparing offending instances (e.g., "This is just another witch hunt from liberal media that hate me" or "Of course they're against my legislation; Republicans will deny me a 'win' at any cost") should not be trusted to prove bias. The context of events always will play a vital role. Actual events are the phantom variables: *what actually happened* to stimulate the different portrayals, and how true were these events? Comparing differences between instances only will tell the obvious—that they are different. It cannot lead to conclusions about bias—what causes the difference. To justify accusing another of intentional bias, critics should need to show intent, plus comparisons between similar events of similar newsworthiness and context, considering which actions are compared. In other words, something like evidence. It could be that a president might be receiving flak *not* because of journalism bias but because of identifiable mistakes, incompetence, and ethical lapses. Thoughtful citizens expect that accurate news should reflect actual events within a clear context.

Despite the difficulties people have in pinpointing bias, Baron and Jost conclude with two guidelines that could apply equally well to academic research and daily journalism's ethical coverage of news. First, in a controversy, "if, in fact, one side is closer to the truth—and the other is more deserving of epistemic scrutiny . . .—then a preponderance of criticism of the latter is not the result of bias but, rather, the desirable outcome of an impartial decision-making process."[45] Second, "if the application of [a standard of open-mindedness and fair treatment] leads to the conclusion that conservatives in the United States and perhaps elsewhere are more rigid, dogmatic, and epistemically fallible than liberals (on average), this is not bias."[46] We should consider carefully research into differences in how conservatives and liberals appear to process information and how those differences could influence perceptions of journalism.

## Journalism's Persistent Practical Biases

Despite the difficulties of defining bias precisely, it is a persistent human reality everywhere, as journalists must understand. The profession even accommodates practitioners who proudly let their values show. Douglas Kellner, one of the biased-by-my-values types, proudly admits and exalts a type of personal commitment. His writing, he says, is "engaged and partisan and I readily admit to being partial toward democracy, social justice, accurate information, and good journalism."[47] Kellner believes that he, like any citizen, can take a partisan position, but he does so by supporting a bias that favors democratic values. He does not load the deck with doctored data or unverified information sources to prevail over people or ideas he dislikes. It makes good civic sense that self-aware journalists support democracy, social justice, and accuracy.

Another form of conscious bias can be found in what journalists or news organizations define as their areas of special interest to citizens. While mainstream journalism mostly covers news of general interest, a few practitioners specialize with a tighter coverage focus—for example, on accentuating positive stories of individual accomplishments and goodwill rather than failure or disintegration of a community. Even within those "good news" stories, however, ethical journalists try to remain true to a standard of impartiality, such as not glossing over higher crime statistics.

### Marginalia

"People seldom want to read or hear what does not please them; they seldom want others to read or hear what disagrees with their convictions or what presents an unfavorable picture of groups they belong to. When such groups are organized, they let the press know their objections to remarks concerning them. The press is therefore caught between its desire to please and extend its audience and its desire to give a picture of events and people as they really are."[48]

—Commission on Freedom of the Press, 1947, "Hutchins Report"

Journalists are not all programmed with the same software of professional values. Some value commitments that reflect best practices in making equitable newsroom decisions, while others emphasize ethical standards of trust and compassion in relationships with readers, viewers, and news sources. While considering allegations of unfair bias against conservatives, remember also the many biases that daily journalism must *depend on*. Journalists cannot be free of all biases. Because we devote an entire chapter to typical newsroom practices, here we will only briefly discuss whether some practices constitute biases that should worry citizens.

## Media Coverage Is Biased toward the Truth, inasmuch as It Can Be Verified

Yes. General interest journalism values truth, admittedly an elusive and often abstract concept, and its cousin verification, a more pragmatic and concrete one. Verification usually involves more than happening onto a smoking gun of proof. More typically, it involves procedures of fact discovery that include multiple sources and interviews, two-source corroboration, documentary research, eyewitness experience of reporters, comparison of different narrative accounts of the same event, extensive notes and recorded backup techniques, additional eyes on draft copy, levels of editorial oversight, in-house fact-checks, and prominent and timely corrections of errors and mistaken inferences.

Kathleen Hall Jamieson and Paul Waldman are committed to what we consider a truth bias, labeling it as a "custodianship of fact."[49] Because journalism provides an ongoing record of public life, custodianship encourages journalists to be biased also toward defining terms and events clearly for citizens while verifying details of public events. But journalism also maintains and protects a quite real archive of facts, definitions, and context clarifications that can be accessed by the public through search engines, as needed. If journalists shirk this task, an "if" similar to the issue of "if citizens *let* them shirk this task," expect our future to coddle more dishonest leaders and revisionist histories.

## Media Coverage Is Biased toward Official Sources

Yes, but not to skew the news ideologically. By longtime practice, news organizations assign reporters to places where lawmakers and government officials gather and often make important decisions. These coverage zones, commonly called "beats," mean that some reporters have regular routines and normal informants in particular geographic or topic areas, analogous to police officers who still walk a specific beat on assigned city streets and neighborhoods.

On the federal level, key news beats are the White House, Congress, and the Supreme Court. A few specialists cover regulatory agencies and cabinet departments, particularly the Department of State and the Department of Defense. State capitals draw beat reporters, too, and before newspaper closures, layoffs, and retrenchment, dozens of reporters from across the state maintained full-time bureau offices within the capitol building. Certain local beats receive regular, if not daily, scrutiny, including city hall, the county courthouse, police headquarters, and school districts. The beat system ensures a degree of efficiency and convenience. But it is a pattern of alertness fraught with blind spots. When news organizations focus their limited resources on government buildings, the news that emerges might constitute a thin slice of all newsworthy government events in a community. Newsgathering based on beats and other routines nearly guarantees stories that reflect a narrow, top-down point of view from elite bodies vulnerable to shifting political winds and not necessarily committed to representing citizens' best interests. There are other helpful ways to assign reporters, but where reporters should go is a constant concern for editors. Reporters could wander around neighborhoods or apartment complexes waiting for news to break out, but it rarely works that way on deadline. Usually, news outside the corridors of power occurs—from the perspective of editors and reporters—by happenstance, like a lightning strike during a grade school soccer game or a spontaneous protest over a police arrest.

A bias favoring official sources and regular beats extends to cultivating relationships with experts whom reporters consult regularly for insight, depending on a particular subject or development. At most newspapers, for example, when a story touches on the history of the city or town, a reporter might call a college professor already well known among readers for being a reliable and quasi-official source on local history. Advantages are obvious, as are the occasional drawbacks. Journalists learn to seek greater diversity in their sources, but when deadlines loom, the choice might boil down to who is available and, from previous experience, thoughtful and trustworthy. The expertise factor might produce an unfortunate side effect: occasionally, interviewees will produce only soundbites and pithy remarks on demand rather than react spontaneously.

## Media Coverage Is Biased toward the Immediate

Yes, but with a disclaimer. In general, readers and listeners are more likely to encounter pieces about *yesterday*, *today*, or *now* than ones that provide broad historical context for current events or future projections of trends. This tendency may stem from difficulties verifying retrospective and prospective stories and depends on the essence of such news traditions as "breaking news" or "scoops" in which one source outdoes others or demonstrates to its audience that it is especially alert and resourceful. People are attracted to the raw newness of news and to what introduces them to the exciting or unexpected. In one critic's description, journalism usually works from a "reactive" perspective to what just happened, but it is more devoted than it thinks to "proactivity." That is, it knows that the public expects news stories to focus on the immediate *while* anticipating future events. These dual expectations can create cross-pressures on journalistic resources, leading to tight deadlines, oversights, mistakes, and unfulfilled speculation.[50]

Another challenge to contemporary journalism's priority of the immediate is that a large percentage of mainstream media's audience has been lost to, or shared with, the lure of what could be termed the *access culture* of electronic media, especially mobile devices. Facebook, YouTube, Twitter, and similar information destinations have changed reading and listening habits. Accessing news immediately is a compelling alternative that encourages a range of options users can control with their thumbs, but it can also reinforce haphazard or excessively habitual sampling behavior and more dependence on superficial or less reliable news reporting. Access culture is a psychologically distinct choice from the older transportation model of news media, in which evaluated and curated news was "brought to you by . . ." some network or another. Scholars could debate the differences between the older transportation model and a newer access model, but both depend on the attraction of immediacy for news organizations and their audiences.

## Media Coverage Is Biased toward Conflict

Yes. Several issues accompany this bias. Accusations, arguments, spats, feuds, and fights all energize public interest. "When it bleeds, it leads" became a cliché among journalists for a reason, and reporters or editors do not need to be ghouls to understand that the bias has roots in human nature. A three-car crash at Damon and Irving Park immediately draws spectators, who anticipate disagreement, blaming, and perhaps the clash of differing accounts. Journalists are expected to be attuned to conflict because citizens are.

However, journalists can become enamored of confrontations in unhealthy ways. They breach the public trust by helping to create either-or faceoffs or conflicts to boost public interest artificially. For example, a reporter hears from a source that the local mayor wants to hire a new "law-and-order" police chief whose primary reputation is based on being tough on protesters and demonstrations while staunchly advocating for police unions' protections. A news story lurks within this tip, she knows, and she will definitely call the mayor to get more information. When considering who else to interview, she thinks about an alternate point of view and calls a city council member with a social justice reputation and a personal history of criticizing the mayor. She does this to get "both sides" of the story. What seems like open-mindedness, though, can become a problem.

Linguist Deborah Tannen's research into interpersonal communication explains that our reporter is *thinking in twos* and that she might create conflict herself, even while she believes she is simply covering the story objectively. Before she even understands how many "sides" there are or should be, she has predecided there would be two: for and against the mayor. The two-sided frame somehow makes the story cleaner and more involving, she reasons, and perhaps easier to organize and write. Therefore, a reporter who assumes she is being fair may in fact be unfairly ratcheting up polarization, making it harder to compromise on the new hire while oversimplifying the issues. Thinking in twos also can preempt the perspective from readers, making creative solutions less likely to be considered or deliberated. Experienced journalists have learned, in fact, that us-versus-them scenarios of political accusation present the same problem.[51]

Anthropologist and teacher Mary Catherine Bateson asked her class discussion groups to compare three cultures, not two. She found that by discussing two, students tended to think in terms of one versus the other, as if they were in opposition. Adding a third means class members "are more likely to think about each [culture] on its own terms."[52] Her realistic approach to dialogue is not only an object lesson many interviewers learned long ago but one that citizens can emulate. Broadcasters' on-air interviews need not be artificial face-offs between two sides but, following Bateson's lead, a more exploratory dialogue. In some cases, a reporter even could play the part of "a third," not to intervene in the story but to enhance its likelihood of generating interesting and truer detail. Dialogue still should welcome conflict, but in the sense of exploring realistic alternative choices. The for-or-against model facilitates dismissiveness and ego involvement, thus failing to serve democracy well, however convenient it seems for ideological commentators. Citizens would be smarter to assume, along with journalists, that there are numerous sides of a social issue, not just two. Then investigate.

## Media Coverage Is Biased toward Tasty Pudding When Possible

Yes, thankfully and regrettably. Media critic Eric Alterman believes that some journalists think of the tasty pudding bias as the choice of *pudding* (tastes good, goes down easily) versus *spinach* (good for you, challenging, and maybe kind of gaggy at times).[53] This is not exactly an either-or question (thinking in twos), and a pudding bias does not necessarily ignore hard news. In making news choices, however, digestibility and audience receptivity often become major criteria. *USA Today* was founded, at least in part, on the advantage of packaging news in ways that were less dense and intimidating than other national papers. Its news section could be scanned by most readers in a matter of minutes, providing a ready sense of catching up on the day's events. *USA Today* also pioneered other innovations that made the news more accessible, including more color in its format, informational graphics, and complementary takes on editorializing. The merging of the elements of news and entertainment by broadcast and cable networks was thought to make staying informed more palatable for citizens, as did adding looped chyrons of information fragments floating on the bottom of television network screens, augmenting the primary news content for viewers. On-air television journalists are now hired not as "news readers" (a vintage term) but as "personalities" who refer to colleagues or interviewees as "my friends" and supplement news accounts with their own emotions and personal vignettes.

Some might point out that these changes engage wider audiences and make news more relevant and humanized. Others believe that they trivialize the news and make it harder for citizens to uncover the important but deeper information that they need to participate in productive civic dialogue. We understand both positions, favor a blend of straightforwardness and accessibility, and remain suspicious of a position that claims a "one or the other" solution. A serving of pudding can help the spinach go down.

## Media Coverage Is Biased toward Keeping News Organizations Financially Healthy

Yes, not to mention alive. The profit motive is not always the most powerful decision-making factor for news professionals, but it would be naive to overlook it. Money does not always talk, but it can stave off a silencing of the presses. According to figures reported by Jill Lepore in 2019, five hundred or so daily newspapers went out of business during the years roughly corresponding to the four-decade teaching careers of each of your authors. "The rest cut news coverage," she writes, "or shrank the paper's size, or stopped producing a print edition, or did all of that, and it still wasn't enough." That's not all; in less than a year and a half, layoffs occurred at a third of the nation's largest newspapers and a quarter of "digital-native news sites."[54] As those of us who live in rural America have learned, community papers fare worse. They either disappear or are bought up by news conglomerates who then merge several local papers, keeping the nameplates while excising local coverage and replacing it with somebody else's news and bylines even a careful reader might fail to recognize.

News that enhances democracy cannot flourish in an environment of pink slips and budget cuts. Without solid fiscal support from subscribers or advertisers, journalism will look to donors, philanthropists, foundations, and, possibly, government funding. However, news is best, arguably, when independent, and many of the proposed solutions come with strings attached. At the same time, the public cannot expect thorough and impactful news reporting from part-timers and volunteers. Even fire departments and libraries require public subsidies.

Companies now work hard to provide reliable news for citizens disinterested in paying for it. More fluff, more entertainment, more conflict, and more diluted stories are easier to sell. Journalism is not a get-rich-quick scheme and struggles when confronted with the power of wealthy political donors who try to undercut it for their own purposes. Understanding the power imbalance might begin to make the whole "fake news," "enemy of the people," "all-powerful organ of liberal bias" scenario seem like someone's convenient mythology.

## Media Coverage Is Biased toward Digging

Yes, naturally. Politicians and CEOs often try to hide information that could harm or embarrass them or their causes. And all manner of cheaters would rather you not discover their misdeeds. Journalists learn that information vital to citizens is hard-won only by persistence, healthy skepticism, and long hours without overtime pay. Journalists might be stereotyped as leeches, weasels, or predators in films and television shows. Are there such people? Surely there are. Is it a norm? Of course not. Even when faced with social avoidance, deception, and slurs, most journalists understand that their reports could be the only possibility for many citizens to discover political corruption and coverups. Information crucial for public decision-making eludes voters if journalists leave details uninvestigated. Citizens should want reporters to be dogged in their interviewing, to double- and triple-check the veracity of responses, and to track down obscure documentary records. Watchdogs of democracy do more than growl. They dig.

Tracy Grant, deputy managing editor of the *Washington Post*, replies to accusations about liberal bias by pointing out that a clear bias indeed motivates journalists, who have "a sense of mission about shining light in dark places. I think there is a sensibility among people who feel that calling and if there is a commonality of people who go into journalism, it is people inspired by things like . . . that idea of telling stories that need to be told." Perhaps this can look like liberal bias to illiberal causes being investigated. Yet "anybody who thinks that the mainstream media—the Washington Post—didn't make Hillary Clinton's life miserable or Barack Obama's life miserable by holding them . . . accountable is just not looking at the record," Grant counters.[55]

## Media Coverage Is Biased toward Compassion

Yes, we say gratefully. David McCraw knows that journalists harbor biases, but not necessarily ones that most people expect. "They believe," he said, "all other things being equal, that the little guy is getting screwed." A journalistic bias toward treating personal difficulties in their fully human dimension is justice based. Here is a refreshing take on politically convenient conventional wisdom. While "enemy of the people" accusers loudly complain about unfair media bias, journalists' deeper bias is a concern for the exploited and voiceless of society. We citizens should not confuse the latter for the former.[56]

Bias toward compassion characterizes a history of crusading journalists who worked to ensure that journalists empathize with the suffering and pain of real people who would not necessarily appear in headlines or breaking news. The long list includes Lincoln Steffens, Ida B. Wells, Dorothy Day, and more contemporary reporters like Bill Moyers, Charlayne Hunter-Gault, David Halberstam, John Siegenthaler, Jane Mayer, Eugene Robinson, Richard Engel, Masha Gessen, and Nicholas Kristof. Over time, their values have established compassion as a journalistic ethic. Compassionate journalism assumes that news reporting is a quality-of-life issue, a relationship of mutuality and recognition. Often journalism is the only voice available for citizens who have been forgotten amid daily obsessions with ball scores, Dow Jones averages, Paris fashion shows, or the latest meetings of the president's Homeland Security appointees. An especially influential book in communication ethics is Christians, Ferre, and Fackler's *Good News: Social Ethics and the Press,* which carefully describes a philosophical ethic enhancing the dignity of dialogue in community.[57]

Journalist David Craig interviewed sixty successful working journalists from three city newspapers, including Pulitzer Prize winners, and included their experience in his book on journalistic ethics. For his interviewees, truth, with all its complications, was their touchstone. Yet, they also stressed a principle of compassion, which complements the respect for context and perspective in news decisions. A journalist with compassion does not act by being bound to a list of official *do this* and *don't do that* commands but by asking, "Who will my story affect?," "What kind of reality does that person or community inhabit?," and "How will my actions care for, or discount, others?" "The ethical value of compassion is also connected with the notion of minimizing harm," Craig writes, similar to the principle in medical ethics of "doing no harm" or—technically—"non-maleficence."[58]

## Marginalia

Journalists should:

"Give voice to the voiceless."

"Show compassion for those who may be affected by news coverage. Use heightened sensitivity when dealing with juveniles, victims of sex crimes, and sources or subjects who are inexperienced or unable to give consent. Consider cultural differences in approach and treatment."

"Realize that private people have a greater right to control information about themselves than public figures and others who seek power, influence or attention. Weigh the consequences of publishing or broadcasting personal information."

"Consider the long-term implications of the extended reach and permanence of publication. Provide updated and more complete information as appropriate."[59]

—Society of Professional Journalists, "SPJ Code of Ethics"

## Old Ball Game, Played with New Rules

Deliberating freely in public is a democratic right many other countries will not and cannot guarantee. Contemporary citizens might have become insufficiently grateful for it over the years. For constitutional scholar Cass

Sunstein, American life promises what he calls a "public forum doctrine" implicit in the civic goals of our Bill of Rights. Speakers should have access to a wide range of diverse audiences, including those with whom they might have conflicts and complaints. Listeners should have access to a wide range of speakers and ideas.[60]

Sunstein understands the importance of free spaces in which citizens can gather to test ideas together, and this is interdependent with effective journalism. Naturally, some will bypass these opportunities because they lack interest or because they cannot attend specific events. If they do participate, citizens usually cannot ensure personally that the information provided by their dialogue partners will be accurate ("I read somewhere the other day that . . .", "Don't quote me on this, but . . ."). Thus, a democracy creates a niche for a trusted journalism. In another sense, journalism itself can become more than a commodity; it is a *place* providing a valuable free space for dialogue—an idea we and others articulated more than twenty-five years ago.[61]

It is nearly impossible to imagine a factual and robust civic dialogue without the common vocabulary and knowledge journalism provides. Citizens will never completely agree on how to evaluate controversies in Washington, DC, but many citizens will avoid talking about them, except to the like-minded. This is the threat of unnecessary polarization, to which citizens should respond with one especially important question: "Who benefits?" Critics demeaning journalism might believe they have won a battle by eroding public faith in it. But when dismissiveness alienates and polarizes citizens, a culture of automatic accusation becomes a shared problem for all citizens in a republic. Where reliable journalistic authority vanishes, truth matters less and lies fill the void. Undercutting the concept of healthy journalism is not a battle to be won by dismissive political infighters. It is a lost opportunity for us all.

Citizens complicit with the bias-accusation industry trivialize citizen dialogue. Sociologist Katherine Cross, surveying the lies attacking journalism and other institutions, answers the question by describing a frightening result: "It's becoming increasingly acceptable to give up on the truth altogether. . . . Accommodating this in a liberal democracy, or in a free press, where exchanges of ideas are seen as vital is like admitting a virus to the very heart of our system." If American citizens minimize the importance of truth, substituting strategic propaganda in news deserts, we grow more like one of the third world autocracies in which we have tried for decades to introduce democratic ideals.[62] The anti-truth virus that worries Cross is still infecting us, still gathering strength.

Perceptions and accusations of liberal political bias have become more or less wired into the media experience as a normal expectation. Citizens need more perspective to understand how a bogus stereotype changes the tone and potential of public communication, along with how we might develop a shared sense of what to do about it.

## CHAPTER 7

# Journalism, Everyday Talk, and the Future for Public Life

People lead busy lives sorting out budgets, kids, neighborhood meetings, and whether the plumber will really show up this afternoon. The big picture of democracy's story, not surprisingly, might seem to be someone else's problem compared with the more immediate decisions arising at home. The faucet is still leaking, the baby is crying again, and rent is overdue. Besides, schools stopped teaching civics classes decades ago.

Seyla Benhabib understands the many dilemmas of citizenship, and her guidance is important for the rest of us. Born in Turkey not long after World War II ended, she rose to the top tier of social critics who acknowledge both the promise and the fragility of democratic public life. Fittingly, she connects journalism to stories of ordinary lives and thus to democracy's necessary recognition of those citizens ordinarily overlooked by elites:

> I'm interested in the way in which more structured narratives or public narratives and story-telling can aid in the formation of an enlarged mentality and in the ability to take the standpoint of the other in deliberative processes. This is where there is a special role for the right kind of journalism and media because journalism is really what makes present to us—re/presents—those whose stories we cannot hear or share first-person.[1]

It does not take a political theorist to understand Benhabib's enthusiasm for journalists' mission to help citizens participate in government. She has learned firsthand that citizenship involves more than marking ballots for candidates we like.

For her, public communication choices are interdependent in creative ways: the power of public stories to shape our impressions; the practical value of speaking across differences; the potential for an "enlarged mentality" that respects the ideas and customs of citizens we have not yet met; and the complementary effects of journalism as it introduces citizens to each other through a wide world of daily news.

The institution of journalism is democracy's Velcro. It grips citizens to common causes while reminding us all how easily we can be pulled apart. Done well, it functions as a supplementary public listener, recorder, organizer, and cultural travel guide. Done poorly, it devolves into corporatism or isolated private clubs of entitled membership. Potentially, it offers far better resources than most ordinary citizens can consult. None of society's other major institutions contribute more than a responsible journalism to fueling civic commitment—not the corporate world, the entertainment industry, government bureaucracy, or, sadly, even formal education or the church. Journalists are able to connect citizens' stories, fully aware that not everyone will approve of, or agree with, every report.

If journalism does not devolve into an array of mouthpieces for bickering special interests and ideologies, the spirit of an enlarged mentality can improve everyday conversation among citizens, clarifying everyone's civic responsibilities. For Benhabib, the immigrant, democracy is too precious to assume we can leave it only to elected officials to implement fairly. It is not a set it and forget it thing.

## Marginalia

Benhabib borrowed the term "enlarged mentality" from another borrower. Hannah Arendt, the political philosopher who studied twentieth-century totalitarian movements, famously said that democracy depends on its citizens' "enlarged mentality": the ability to expand their perspectives by imagining what other citizens are thinking and feeling instead of relying wholly on individualized judgment or self-centered motive. Arendt herself borrowed the term from Immanuel Kant's earlier philosophy of aesthetic judgment. It resembles empathy—the willingness to get out of one's own head and sincerely try to imagine the reality experienced by other persons.[2]

American journalism (in the beginning, the "press" of the "free press") merited special protection when the Framers articulated the First Amendment in the Bill of Rights. Its set of protections, they decided, must be grounded by faith in the wisdom of everyday experience, and this in turn depended on a faith that citizens will continue to talk with other citizens. Dialogue and deliberation anchor a robust public life, and the rationale for both was written into the Constitution. The Founders decided that a vast *direct* democracy—in which voters would approve or disapprove specific actions and laws—would be unworkable and risky as the country grew. A republic provided a more effective alternative: the form of a *republic* is not top-down in procedure or spirit but broadly shared, held in common for the common good, by citizens. "We the people" energize shared self-government, not only by electing representatives but by taking seriously direct and indirect political conversations that could contest thin civic judgments and enhance citizens' valid claims—if we listen well enough. Democratic responsibility is propelled by a kind of attention that takes others' differences into full account. Whatever or whoever forces citizens into silence or divisive separation does democracy no favors.

Mutual accountability explains how journalism and politics overlap to form a commitment to uphold a citizenship through communication. Each provides social and civic context for the others. In the next chapter we develop an ethic for citizenship based more on commonplace experience than on complex political theory. For now, however, consider the importance of something usually considered trivial—talking informally with other citizens.

The original goal of the language of the First Amendment, according to James Carey, was to "create a conversational society: a society of people who speak to one another, who converse."[3] Working within their particularly intolerant eighteenth-century conditions that denied full personhood to citizens of color, women, Indigenous Americans, and others, the Founders nevertheless planned a foundation for vigorous communicative participation by and for citizens. Contemporary citizens assume *individualized freedom of choice* was the primary message bequeathed by the Founders. However, given the clear evidence of First Amendment language and the deliberations that led to it, *interdependent communication* is the not so secret sauce stirred into the rationale for a Bill of Rights.

"Democratic conversation" means far more than small talk with neighbors, chitchat that avoids conflict, social exchanges to enhance friendships, or talk that occurs in private places. Even the term "conversation" can annoy people who consider it a contemporary fad—who misunderstand or underestimate its role in forming and sustaining a nation. Public conversation is not an incidental *result of democracy*. More significantly, it is an energizing *attitude for ensuring it* by assisting both exploratory dialogue and goal-oriented deliberation. History tells us that the Framers of our Constitution had this broader view in mind when they put faith in a republic and afforded citizenship true agency. Unless citizens believe political and public affairs are worth talking about—and arguing about—with friends, neighbors, family, and public officials, the potential for democratic life begins to fade.

The First Amendment supports democratic conversation but in more ways than the unadorned language of the freedom of the press and free-dom of speech clauses. The "establishment clause," for example, explic-itly prohibits government authorities from declaring an official religion or banning disapproved sects—a move other governments worldwide have used to marginalize entire groups and restrict their freedom to commu-nicate. The First Amendment is also a blueprint for facilitating citizen participation in other important senses: speaking freely about issues of public concern; publishing, disseminating, and reading those concerns; the freedom to assemble peaceably even to protest government policies; and the ability "to petition the government for a redress of grievances." Citi-zens should speak, yes, but with the assurance that the new country would be committed to clearing spaces for listening too—another vital prereq-uisite for political decision-making. Such assurances, Carey argued, were the essential backdrop that illustrated the self-confidence of a republic. The First Amendment is far more than a list of do's and don'ts for the gov-ernment; it symbolizes what contemporary society refers to as "voice"— serious verbal engagement among citizens when evaluating government. Its communication emphasis even suggests, however faintly, an ethic of change through which the new country's blemishes of racial and gender injustice might later be addressed. Within this often challenging ideal, a genuine public was constituted politically through relying on persons' willingness to converse.

### Quotables

"The Court has developed a theory it calls the 'bundle' of First Amendment freedoms, with speech and the press dominant. In these decisions the freedoms of assembly and petition are often used interchangeably. Actually, that is understandable from simply reading the words of the amendment. The Founding Fathers envisioned assembly in order to petition."[4]

—Robert J. Wagman, *The First Amendment Book*

To call our political system a *republic* is to say that the country has been spoken into existence and ideally maintained by monitoring and strengthening it through unscripted and open talk in block parties and over backyard fences. If we forget that the country's strength relies on relationships, even with strangers of different political loyalties, our grip loosens. A republic is a constructed expectation—an architecture of words. Its genius is that it regulates and renews itself, stays current, enlists new participants, asks difficult questions of established ideologies, and is agile enough to respond to unexpected social challenges of subsequent generations. Stated differently, it relies almost precisely on what a responsible journalism provides. It needs *news*, a constant connection with the new.

The quest for democratic conversation can be prolonged and time-consuming, but the rewards are impressive. William Caspary, an insightful guide to John Dewey's defense of democracy, describes conversation more as a public contribution than a governmental task. Dewey saw its democratic effects "in informal settings, in formal meetings, and via electronic media—in response to direct experience and to journalistic reports. Conversation topics include daily events, trends, policy issues, electoral campaigns, governmental proceedings, and protest actions." Beyond this, "citizens in discussions with one another and in responding critically to mass media, may develop complex and differentiated views on what is at stake," later to contribute them to the public dialogue or compare them with views of experts having their own deliberations. "Public judgment," though, is usually reached gradually and in stages in democracies and in some ways is dissimilar to the work of experts: "Experts may have formed judgments early and concluded that the public is hopelessly adrift—only to find responsible public judgment emerging when they least expect it." Expert-based public discourse, according to Caspary and Dewey, is more impersonal and "favors the ethical perspective of the judge over that of the agent."[5] Citizens need not wait around for heroes and experts to reach definitive solutions. We learn *with* others in democracy's version of cooperative homework, perhaps eventually influencing elected representatives but nevertheless clarifying where we stand and how we can contribute.

## A Republic of Conversation

Talk, some people say, can be cheap. Small talk, too, is supposedly just a way to fill time. But beware the tendency to underestimate its potent and concentrated power in political life. In an influential modern commentary on public life, the moral philosopher Alasdair MacIntyre claims that conversations are "the most familiar type of context" in which our "purposes are rendered intelligible." Conversation, so deceptively ordinary and common, does not rivet the attention of most philosophers, educators, or city planners. But in fact, "conversation, understood widely enough, is the form of human transactions in general." MacIntyre wanted conversations to have their due; they are best understood as informal joint-authored narratives that assist us in "placing a particular episode in the context of a set of narrative histories, histories both of the individuals concerned and of the settings in which they act and suffer."[6] This same description might apply to the social contributions of serious journalists.

Typical examples illustrate what MacIntyre is getting at. Teachers at all levels of education understand the value of students talking with each other. Through talking, which reinforces their self-confidence, students often learn in unexpected and creative ways that stick with them. Rookie teachers who try only to drill the right answers into a class eventually realize they have missed the whole point of education. Students might react by conforming, but often they will avoid thinking creatively, and the same goes for teachers. Dictators also fear occasions of uncontrolled citizen talk and often clamp down viciously on open conversations. Poet Czeslaw Milosz, whose homeland Poland was long dominated by the Kremlin's Communist regime, learned that "what is not expressed does not exist." Choking off informal conversations trivializes creativity, cultural memory, and a sense of social possibility.[7]

"Talk is cheap," you see, only until it proves to be invaluable. New ideas float to the surface of committed conversation far more often than by self-centered introspection. Informal idea-trading and testing allows sincere citizens to surprise themselves even while listening to their *own* replies. Propagandists, publicists, or spokespersons try to deposit slogans in listeners' brains. But, usually, free citizens appear to listen best for new ideas when discovering positions that challenge our own and that seem to invite reply. Conversation is crucial for understanding context because it nudges us beyond our own brains and perspectives toward considering multiple perspectives of others—and maybe the genuine difficulties of comparing perspectives.

When MacIntyre suggests that persons coauthor stories together, he is onto something important about the human experience. Coauthoring builds strong bonds that can accommodate divergent beliefs. We learn to live in this tension because conversational challenges may arise from loved ones and friends who are impossible to dismiss as hypocrites or shills. Context widens and deepens. We are less likely to hear from friends that "it's not all about you, you know." We tolerate differences more readily, cooperate better, maybe at times find ourselves compromising or, at least, having more productive disagreements.

Hannah Arendt also knew how conversation enhances thinking-in-context, even when it does not alter existing beliefs:

> I form an opinion by considering a given issue from different viewpoints, by making present to my mind the standpoints of those who are absent, that is, I represent them. . . . The more people's standpoints I have present in my mind while I am pondering a given issue, and the better I can imagine how I would feel and think if I were in their place, the stronger will be my capacity for representative thinking and the more valid my final conclusions, my opinion.[8]

Arendt was a careful student of authoritarian politics in the mid-twentieth century, when autocratic leaders and copycats mocked and limited person-to-person talk because they feared its threat to their power. Communication that spans viewpoints and transgresses taken-for-granted frames helps citizens imagine, and probe together, political alternatives.

W. Barnett Pearce's research into interpersonal communication processes explains why this is so. As people interact, "'gaps' appear between the participants," and the gaps *help* citizens continuously adjust their social worlds—a role for communication similar to the Founders' faith in an evolving republic. Most people assume that gaps derail communication ("What will I say to him? He's an Arab, and I avoid them") but fail to realize that gaps are open invitations that can lead to *aha* moments. Conversations in one sense are negotiations between two or more selves, each with the other person's realities to account for.

Scholars of dialogue respect the territory of the "between," a social territory belonging to neither speaker nor listener. "The specific responses within particular contexts to the utterances of another with an utterance of our own creates a unique, nonrepeatable event," Pearce said.[9] If citizens are sincere, the gaps experienced in our interactions, elements of our strangeness to each other, are far more productive than feel-good agreement or even studied civility. An honest disagreement could feel uncomfortable in the moment but might contain the key to softening future conflict. A limp agreement or insincere politeness can wallpaper over a festering conflict, only later becoming an ugly resentment or deferred blowup. Political implications for citizen self-rule are obvious—beware of hanging out exclusively with people who already agree with you. Good communication lurks in the gaps of the human experience, in our differences—if we are alert to them.

Good advice comes from Christian social critic and educator Parker Palmer, who urges a constant renewal of democracy through informal public communication. In fact, he nominates *the stranger* as "the key figure in public life."[10] "When we meet the stranger, we are engaged in public life, and through such engagement, according to Scripture, gifts of the Spirit will be brought into our lives."[11] Palmer's practical experience reaffirms the bases for public life, regardless of our spiritual commitments. He notes that most organizational consultants have discovered an important way of seeing others:

A slight change in angle of vision can open up a new truth. A group may be blocked by a simple problem which the outsider can see and remedy, a problem which the group had taken as a given simply because they had lived with it so long. This function of the stranger in our lives is grounded in a simple fact: truth is a very large matter and requires various angles of vision to be seen in the round. It is not that our view is always wrong and the stranger's is always right but simply that the stranger's view is different, giving us an opportunity to look anew upon familiar things.[12]

Reading Palmer helps to explain why our politics so often accents "the public." In *private* spaces, we tend to interact with, and depend upon, the comfort and safety of the familiar—in family life, for example, or among close friends we already trust, in tightly knit neighborhoods with long histories, and within clubs or groups, formal or informal, where expectations about people basically ride on the same time-honored relationships. In private spaces, too, we can more or less regulate what we do and say, and we can keep outsiders out. The world seems more predictable and tamer.

*Public* life, however, especially within the worldviews of Madison and other Founders, is somewhat wilder. It requires being out there, meeting others who do not know you and might not want to know you. They might not dress like you or talk like you. Although you think of yourself as normal and likable, they could react as though you are strange, as in "Is she trying to pick a fight?," "Is he ignoring me?," or "I'd give them a chance, but they seem so odd." When trying to talk over important issues at neighborhood association meetings or book club gatherings, unanticipated attitudes or closely guarded experiences might lead to arguments, arguments to dissatisfaction, dissatisfaction to new resentments, and resentments maybe finally to a retreat from public involvement.

Strangers can be a lot of trouble to get to know, more trouble than some might fear they are worth. It is far more comforting to stay with the safe familiarity of privacy, where what we know is what we always knew and people you mistrust always seem to lack your own brand of "common sense."

Nothing is wrong with privacy; its restorative comforts might even help

244 / DEMOCRACY'S NEWS

citizens tackle new challenges or stave off others' intrusions or manipulations. But privacy, which is worth protecting, can also become a shell. The Constitution, in a sense, shaped a republic of communicators willing to be productive strangers for each other: "I think I understand why you say that, but I also find myself disagreeing." Thoughtful disagreement plants many seeds. This approach has political implications that were, in the context of eighteenth-century thought, intentional and courageous. Freedom of speech as a concept encouraged confrontations between the aggrieved and their unpersuaded listeners. From those exchanges could come revolutionary social and political insight—and change.

## Readings

A recent example of the challenges of encountering strangeness is *Rising Out of Hatred: The Awakening of a Former White Nationalist*, by Pulitzer Prize–winning journalist Eli Saslow. It tells the story of Derek Black, a young man groomed as a rising media star among white nationalists, one with his own hate-filled radio show with a committed following. Based on months of interviews following Black's original decision to prefer privacy and anonymity, Saslow's book highlights at least two ways Black's tale will resonate with citizens even of vastly different persuasions. At one level, it is the experience of a zealot in contact with new experiences of learning, fairness, and loving commitment on an unfamiliar college campus. The book, then, is a good reminder if you believe people never change. On another level, Derek Black's story also captures how anti-racist activists themselves can begin to empathize and change. His resources were ultimately stronger than his hate, and reading about his upbringing forges a better sense of his basic humanity.[13]

The story of the United States is long and fascinating—a near mythic tale of starts and stops, achievements and disappointments, ethical courage and disgusting shortcuts, cultural invitations and nearly unbelievable bigotry. It is difficult to keep it all in perspective. But Seyla Benhabib, the immigrant as teacher, not only welcomes but supports journalism in its persistent mission to offer historical context, knowledge, and urgent reporting to buttress humble attempts to cultivate the public life of the republic.

Americans share the benefits of public conversation, but, especially in times of political divisiveness, we could do more to assert and protect its traditions. The remainder of this chapter is a weave of several options for doing this. First, we discuss several examples and reminders—specifically, speech as important action, political and otherwise, and such communication-based insights as speech acts, context, framing, empathy, and the effects of interpersonal polarization. Next, we suggest two forms of citizen conversation that lead to effective participation—finding opportunities or spaces for *dialogue* and developing norms of informed *deliberation*. Third, extending the premise that public citizenship and journalism are intimately related, we dig deeper into journalism's challenges in a newly toxic climate of political distrust, a time in which the credibility of news is suspect at best and increasingly demeaned outright. Finally, we end the chapter with a glance ahead, previewing how and when journalism can, by enhancing its communication mission while maintaining traditional values, ensure a more active public.

## Are You a Talker or a Doer? Yes

Occasionally we hear comments like "Some people are talkers, but I'm a doer," or "He's all talk and no action," or "What she said was just rhetoric, plain and simple." Many people assume talking and accomplishing something are mutually exclusive—one or the other. Sometimes they seem separate, of course. If you often tell neighbors you care about them or say you will help them with tough tasks, your words are not the same thing as actually pitching in to unload the furniture from the van. As the old saying goes, 90 percent of life is showing up. Promising you are going to be there does not get the new showerhead installed.

Exceptions aside, though, words themselves can be important actions. As communication research shows, speech can *accomplish* goals. Saying you care might be just the reassurance your friend needs at a given time and for practical purposes *is experienced as* the caring itself. "I do" is not merely two empty words: it is the central performance *act* defining a wedding; a swearing-in of a witness about to tell the truth, the whole truth, and nothing but the truth; or an elected president's oath to "preserve, protect, and defend" the Constitution.[14] On these occasions, a speaker is not just *saying* something but *doing* and *affirming* something central on which others rely.

Even apart from official ceremonies, the right words at an appropriate time accomplish far more than "just talking," like calling a child abuse hotline when you suspect mistreatment of the toddler next door. More than just talk, it is an act of civic responsibility performed with words.

Journalists interviewing people under the condition of "deep background" are also not "just talking" but acting to promise a skittish interviewee that any information she provides is only to help the reporter understand an issue and will not be published. Linguists have long studied such *speech acts* and conversational *rules*—occasions when speakers' words "count" as *doing* something. The idea of "speech acts" explains why we know how to respond when a family member asks, "Could you pass the potatoes?" You do not say, "Yes, I *could*" and continue to eat; instead, as a normal cooperative listener, you recognize that in the immediate context, the seemingly mundane *question* should be interpreted as a *request* that the potato bowl be picked up and passed around the table. Everyday conversations are loaded with speech acts. When your sister asks, "Are you sure?" her intent might be not to ask a straightforward yes-or-no question but a way for her to act, to intervene, to make a statement similar to "I'm not sure I agree."

Language is like interpersonal weather—always with us, always forming contexts for interpreting events. While listening to someone's speech cues and word choices, we decide when and how to attribute motives, recognize insults, offer apologies, clarify ambiguities, repair misunderstandings, model ethical behavior, rethink our personal interpretations, explain ourselves, or—as journalists know well—provide historical background necessary to understand connections between apparently isolated events. Effective journalists are speakers and listeners in addition to being accomplished writers, editors, and analysts. Their words ratify their faith in readers and viewers, an oath of responsibility. Think twice before telling a dedicated beat reporter, for example, that a long-sought-after interview with the mayor is unimportant because that is "just" two people talking, no big deal.

The republic's implicit model for governing is that when citizens talk, even about ordinary life, we act, committing to the civic work of maintaining a politics we can live with. We keep the lines open, in case of crisis. Conversations matter.

Journalists, although hard to categorize, are a particular brand of everyday communicator, yet they are still citizens themselves. This populist notion has long been nurtured in the literature of the profession; local journalists, particularly, do not simply "cover" or "report on" their community from a distance. They live within its weather of talk, because it is their home. Their ongoing role is to anticipate and answer citizens' implied questions. Neighbors want to know more than the bare bones of "what happened?" They are curious to hear how it happened, why and to whom, while wondering if it might keep happening. They deserve context. They want to talk about it over the backyard fence. Are there drug deals happening around here or not?

Yet, as we have explained, journalists are citizens with more crucial deadlines for their words than most of us have, and no story can be the full story. Occasionally, they must sacrifice an elaborate explanation of context when rushing toward a hard deadline. Or several stories compete for front-page attention that day. Meeting deadlines is another of journalism's acts, necessarily stitched into its role and messaging. The commitment to explain issues and facts in context, however, remains a cornerstone of journalistic practice. Textbooks in the field often designate richer context as a goal for improving everyday stories. ("Long form" journalism, such as that published by the *New Yorker* or *Foreign Affairs*, has fewer constraints but also usually fewer, if more serious, readers.) The bottom line is that no fact, no circumstance, is context free, just as no expression can be totally free of partiality, no word free of connotation. Despite such a recognition, the general public might be shocked to overhear the frustrations of editors when reacting to articles that take even small quotes *out* of context. Without context, citizens might assume that the sliver of a story they have heard *is* the story or that a generalization can double as a fact, without further explanation. Journalism's context-reinforcing role clarifies conversations that help professionals, in fact, all citizens, understand the limitations of the information system.

Communication researchers use the metaphor of *framing* to explain people's mental methods as they organize and define what social acts mean for them. Just as a picture frame might decorate and set apart a photo from the wall surrounding it, a perceptual frame is a special or preferred contextual definition of a situation reflected in language and set off from other possible definitions. For example, wealthy people might frame daily news reports in terms of profits and losses particularly germane to them, while marginalized minorities might be more likely to frame news in terms of its implications for broader issues of social justice and economic equity. The same process applies to large corporate media as they decide how to present or package daily news reports. For example, "reporting a politician's problem accurately" could be a journalist's frame for writing a story, while exactly the same piece for the politician might be read as "yet another example of media bias undercutting my credibility." A regulatory change might be "named or labeled *as* ecological destruction or *as* economic development" depending on who you are listening to, and "expectations and evaluations are framed accordingly."[15] News professionals cannot ignore framing as a contextual reality of vernacular speech; "facts" are not shiny objects easily separated from interpretations.

Kathleen Hall Jamieson and Paul Waldman have studied political framing in an impressively wide context.[16] Their book, *The Press Effect*, is an eye-opener for citizens curious about behind-the-scenes news media practices. They found that politicians consistently favor perspectives or contexts that imply friendly, self-serving interpretations of what is true or real. No surprise, right? One candidate's "willingness to go where the evidence leads me" is an opponent's "flip-flopping." Neither is a fact, but both are frames. The behavior can be the same, while the framing is conveniently, or inconveniently, different. Listeners and readers are left to analyze not the raw "truth" but the frames. Ideally, they will evaluate with relevant evidence probably provided by journalists. Of course, frames also can be relatively benign. Everyday citizens often wonder how to explain or put into context an argument so that it is more persuasive or how to frame a compliment so it will be understood as sincere, as intended. Journalists might use their own professional frames to package the news readily with speed and accuracy, as when the Bureau of Land Management announces a plan to open more land for oil and gas exploration when it borders a Native American reservation. The news story that follows might fit different but familiar news frames, depending on who is assigned to the story. One frame: another step by the administration to undo environmental law. An alternate frame: a boon for the local economy. A third: a predictable clash between Indigenous culture and an insensitive bureaucracy. The stories that emerge might emphasize a dominant frame or some combination of several. Political dramas are always a stage for differing contextual emphasis. Framing is real and consequential, but no court of appeal will tell you which is the "right" frame. Journalists typically do not explain how they decide to shape a story, nor do citizens fully grasp the significance and consequences of frames.

Whether or not citizens appreciate or adopt the "framing" terminology in everyday talk, its explanatory power should not be ignored. Persistent frames can amount to shortcuts for making sense. Politicians, advertisers, and other influencers use frames to reduce complex issues to sloganeering, preparing messages in terms the public would be likely to remember and repeat. If the framing is intentionally dishonest, it can work as effectively as frames scrupulously true to existing fact. Consider some examples from news coverage, as applied by Jamieson and Waldman in *The Press Effect*.

> During election campaigns reporters see themselves in part as unmaskers of the hypocrisy of those who seek office. That perspective carries with it a frame that is ironic and often cynical, focusing on strategic intent, motives, and appearance. A candidate's missteps are featured as signs of a defective character or questionable competence.[17]

Such a frame might be helpful for a journalist when motivated by a watch-dog role. It also could mislead readers and viewers if the political context shifts or if the evidence suggests not malign intent but rather a simple mistake that could have led to Jamieson and Waldman's hypothetical example of "a candidate's missteps."

When the country is at war, as in the immediate aftermath of 9/11, the cynicism-skepticism frame can fade into the background for reporters, and they risk becoming absorbed by a "patriotic" lens and frame. Reporters began to take U.S. leaders "at their word" and to "assume truthful and honorable motives" in political and military leaders. Jamieson and Waldman discovered that reporters even "overlooked, even compensated for, [leaders'] missteps."[18] Reporters who rely too readily on a government's version of information and framing risk being co-opted by officialdom and become auxiliary mouthpieces for government messaging. Coverage of the Iraq War reaffirmed the importance of journalists developing their own independent sources and means of investigating evidence.

The process of framing is still not necessarily either factual or false. It just *is*. Frames obviously create different context expectations, though. Their contributions (or the facts we assume are true because of them) depend on where you sit or how much power or credibility you might have. Mental frames seep into messages of writing and speaking, often unobtrusively. At times, one sort of framing results in messages that appear to be "spin," or as reasonable public relations, or just as plain old innocent civility designed to avoid ruffling feathers. But since framing is such a natural inclination, a journalist attempting to produce the most objective reporting possible is not framing free. In the "cynical election" frame described earlier, certain candidate flaws or inconsistencies might be emphasized because the reporters are more attuned to them and expecting them. Their news stories might never acknowledge exceptions.

Thanks to decades of social science research, much of it stimulated by the early work of sociologist Erving Goffman,[19] professionals are increasingly attuned to the effects of framing. Alert reporters and editors will understand that framing biases might be lurking and attempt to counteract them by constantly reminding themselves that many assumptions and expectations lie underneath the surface of what we like to imagine are plain facts. As citizens, we could encourage and support such journalists more effectively than we typically do. One candidate is not evil because she or he uses a *small government* frame to view legislation, while a political opponent instead could justifiably see legislation through a *social justice* frame. For some citizens, a pick-yourself-up-by-the-bootstraps frame is meaningful and natural in discussing social assistance programs, but others just as commonly frame the problem in terms of care for the helpless, a spiritual obligation of charity, or basic human respect. All are interpretive frames, not literal *truths*. Citizens are wise to investigate evidence to account for differences and possible overlaps if democratic deliberation is a goal. Frames influence issues even when politicians do not mention them, and the term might not even be in the vocabulary of voters.

A free press concept made it far easier for citizens to stumble upon news frames that represented strangers' positions that could be compared with the more comfortable niche of one's private affiliations. One of the primary ways citizens learn of strangers' ideas is through "general interest intermediaries," media that report information of wide appeal.[20] Previous chapters highlight the advantages of interest-broadening news, such as providing shared bases for large-scale public engagement and possibly consensus. This goal, in many ways a presumption behind the idea of a republic, can be at odds with the emergence of narrowly audience-targeted news sources designed only to advance particular interests or issues, often for the purpose of indoctrinating biases and preferences. Sometimes termed "news silos" by journalists who cover politics, these networks, papers, websites, magazines, and talk radio programs package lots of stories, repeatable and persistent, about single-focus perspectives. They are not known for breadth of analysis, fresh ideas, or toleration of dissent. Within such socially comfortable "news" settings, readers and viewers may not know in advance exactly which events will be reported, but they can readily predict reporters' or anchors' attitudes about them. Persistently partisan news sources discourage audiences from exploring new spaces to challenge their ideas and bypass opportunities to acknowledge, much less credit, opposing arguments.

The practice of partitioning off public concerns subverts journalism's traditional role of providing information to help the full range of citizens when they encounter strangeness—that is, what they do not know but could. It encourages general interest news sources to alter their own best public judgment, becoming more specialized with targeted messages. "We the people" veers toward, sadly but more accurately, "we, some of the people, who are disinterested in discussing other people's reasons."

News anchor Shepard Smith, who resigned from Fox News in 2019, witnessed competing philosophies of news organizations for many years. After departing Fox, he explained his concerns at an International Press Freedom Awards dinner. Smith said ruefully that a decade ago, the public believed the "online revolution would liberate us," allowing people the freedom to find their own best news sources on the Internet. Such a view, he said, "now seems a bit premature, doesn't it? Autocrats have learned how to use those same online tools to shore up their power. They flood the world of information with garbage and lies masquerading as news. There's a name for that."[21]

Just as disturbing in many ways, the public has witnessed a parallel attack on professional journalists who investigate and fact-check political rhetoric that could be untrue. In Smith's experience, the same autocrats— safe in silos with audiences in place—"dispatch troll armies after critical reporters, who are vilified and harassed. Their personal information, such as phone numbers, addresses and ID numbers, are posted and published as an invitation for even more attacks." The public itself is threatened when news-shy citizens appreciate news content only if it solidifies their own private partisan allegiances. Narrowly specialized news sources or politicians are fine and certainly protected under the First Amendment. But some of them undercut democracy by sponsoring attacks on political dialogue, such as branding normal fact-checking falsely as intentionally "one-sided" and mainstream news organizations as anti-American or corrupt. No wonder Smith finds that "intimidation and vilification of the press is now a global phenomenon. We don't have to look far for evidence of that."

News sources that primarily trade in us-versus-them strategies dampen citizen conversations about politics. It is our new segregation, our new journalistic bunker mentality; which cable news do you watch? This phenomenon is not new; the eighteenth-century philosopher Rousseau, who watched no cable news at all, reportedly observed that "keeping citizens apart has become the first maxim of modern politics."[22] Politicians who want to squelch citizen talk have no trouble using epithets and lies designed for that purpose—making another person's experiences appear to be threats to America itself: How can I trust *those* people? How can I work with *them*? How can I let them *do* this to us?

In spite of troubling trends, the value of communicating across differences remains politically practical—although you might not hear politicians recommending it. Citizens in conversation inevitably change as they take new contexts more into account. Ideas flow and shift. Frames seem contingent and negotiable, not locked in. Acknowledging the value of human difference is the basis of the "enlarged mentality" that Arendt believed was an antidote to totalitarian governments. The world gets wider and deeper, and so do its possibilities with it. Within this richer appreciation of context comes the ability to imagine, and internally acknowledge, potential validity in someone else's experience—while still standing on your own ground. It seems like a risk, and it is in some ways. To empathize sincerely is to take the chance that your cherished ideals might not fare well in direct comparison with others' experience. Empathy, however, moves citizens toward important objectives: they confirm others' worth as persons with something to offer, they enlarge their personal abilities to evaluate and "try on" ideas, and they keep the conversation going toward a future that trusts civic life again.

When good editors assess a story for fundamental fairness, they try to empathize with readers or listeners who could potentially feel diminished, excluded, or even victimized by the language of that story. Even if they do not use the term "empathy," editors remain aware that each of these audience reactions introduces noise that could interfere with understanding the news. Taking them into account has nothing to do with so-called political correctness. Journalists worth their salt who work for general interest media understand that their stories never touch down in a vacuum. A series of feature stories about homelessness surely will reach a diverse population living in different circumstances. The same series could reassure a single mother working two jobs and wondering if a warm blanket for her children will be on sale this week at Dollar General—or it could bore a millionaire investor who has just shifted money into an unexpectedly successful startup. The overall story is not inherently reassuring *or* inherently boring, not fundamentally a liberal issue *or* a conservative one. It is about communication in a republic of interests.

In our experience, some people narrowly treat empathy as a technique for having warmer conversations that leave all parties satisfied or too often think of it as a handy tool for "opening someone up" or for "keeping the interviewee talking so you get better information out of them." It would be sad if empathy implied only memorizing a set of "I hear you saying . . ." assurances that could be recommended by a corporate customer service trainer. Techniques might do some good sometimes, but usually pseudo-empathy is easy to spot.

Hannah Arendt, though, described something far more valuable than using empathy to mine data, and experienced journalists resonate to her point. Totalitarianism taught her to understand the selfishness of "I'm sure I'm right" narrow-mindedness, intolerance, bigotry, or dismissiveness when people are fearful or feel overlooked. But she also recommended testing personal ideas by widening intellectual or emotional boundaries. Empathy may not guarantee complete understanding, but it at least takes engagement seriously. It helps citizens realize *as citizens* that whatever our attitudes are about accepting immigration, for example, separating captured children from their parents in fenced compounds in a strange country—without a plan for reunification—for victims the policy is terrifying and inhumane. Millions of Americans, however, believed this to be a non-problem and ignored, downplayed, or doubted the stories. The Founders just could not have imagined a disengaged and context-free citizenry. Arguments about speech and public policy were not ornaments to them but civic virtues.

Why would Americans not be deeply concerned when a major avenue for communication like general interest journalism is being marginalized daily? Journalists, for all their human faults, enable the relatively powerless to imagine a productive civic life, justify a wider range of decisions for those who might overlook necessary facts or background, and discover options beyond identifying uncritically with someone else's political ideology or celebrity. People get outside themselves by reading and listening beyond our own prejudices.

Meeting each other across our differences and building a genuine basis for shaping the common good is a grand premise too readily compromised. Strangely, journalists themselves at times seem reluctant to explain something so basic about democracy or defend the concept justifying their role. Then the next narcissistic leader comes along, selling conspiracy theories (journalists are hacks, the *other* party hates regular people, "our" country is being invaded by un-American workers who refuse to accept our values, there is a "war" on Christianity that comes from godless socialist politicians, there is only one kind of "real" American, a "deep state" is secretly propelling the government to ruin).

Four years of an executive branch tweeting unsubstantiated claims and controlling information flow, while ignoring science, research, and news provided by a free press, potentially transforms any disagreement into a crisis of confidence. Instead of understanding disagreement as a learning opportunity for examining different political perspectives, we have now seen leadership—bolstered by strong strains of citizen support—that disdained values of public communication. It is now too easy to explain disagreement as treason. We may be living through what David Strauss calls "a slow-motion emergency" of ignoring norms and tolerating a politics of loophole legal interpretations—a disorienting public experience "unlike the more familiar kind of emergency."[23]

The summer of 2020 also brought threats of the more familiar forms of emergency, and two types of threat complicated each other. During the Covid-19 pandemic and increased racial tension after street protests,

America's president neglected opportunities to stress healing through interdependence and continued to sow distrust and, at times, make a case for hatred of demonized opponents. When public officials fail to promote our civic interdependence they fail, as well, to acknowledge a solid body of social science research. Attitudes of interdependence and common concern, according to William Julius Wilson, help to fulfill the American vision: "When people believe that they need each other they tend to relinquish their initial prejudices and stereotypes," he observes. In addition, such beliefs advance an awareness of "common interests, norms, values, aspirations, and goals."[24] The crucial step, evidently, is to encourage interdependent communication in which one group cannot fulfill its goals without the cooperation of others. Addressing differences by stressing common goals is a pragmatic response. Exploiting differences by taking sides and circling the wagons is not. How, then, has the basis for the Constitution suddenly come to sound so naive?

The institution of journalism is well positioned to take the lead in a renewed dialogic political culture, as we have argued elsewhere.[25] Before examining possible course corrections and glimmers of optimism, however, we should, first, distinguish between the concepts of *dialogue* and *deliberation*, two goals of citizen conversation with strong implications for how we are governed, and, second, consider how both public talk and journalism's role are jeopardized by politically motivated divisiveness and lies.

## Journalism's Environment for Talk: Dialogue, Deliberation, Divisiveness, Deception

We explored earlier why media historian James Carey believed that the Constitution affirmed the need for a "conversational" society. With this claim, he linked a republican (small *r*) government to the process of dialogue. Not surprisingly, he describes a *republic* not in terms of governmental decisions but in dialogic terms as "a tissue of relations in space and time" directly forming democratic citizenship: "To be a citizen is to assume a relation in space to one's contemporaries: to all, irrespective of class and kin, who exist in the same place under the canopy of politics as fellow citizens."[26] As Carey knew, the study of human dialogue is indebted to deep traditions in philosophy, social science, the arts, theology, and organizational studies.

In most of these traditions, everyday dialogue involves, as we have said elsewhere, "more than a simple back-and-forthness of messages in interaction; it points to a particular process and quality of communication in which the participants 'meet,' which allows for changing and being changed. In dialogue, we do not know exactly what we are going to say, and we can surprise not only the other but even ourselves."[27] Under such circumstances, even mundane small talk becomes an occasion for exchanging ideas, and an ongoing opportunity to wrestle with the ideas together, in argument or even opposition. Dialogue is not a permanent state or a strategy of persuasive rhetoric. It typically emerges as unforeseen moments of connection, insight, or newfound respect.

The Founders did not anticipate passive audiences merely observing or obeying government decisions. After their own verbal jousting, they put their faith in this republican model that applied dialogue that same way. Citizens would take on the messy job of taking seriously their lives in common and, in Jefferson's words, "have before [their] eyes [their] community as members of the same body." They would then be able to "see that it is their interest to preserve peace and order."[28]

In a true republic, citizens understand why they are "members of the same body" and participants, not a mass collection of spectators, receptacles, or ideologues. A republic lays the groundwork for, and invitation to, political dialogue. Political life generally works best when citizens marshal mutual resources of knowledge, history, current events, and insight, ready to, if necessary, grapple with policy issues. Reliance on dialogue is a necessary counterweight to individual blind spots, intolerance, rigidity, indifference, self-absorption, or rote dismissiveness of new or challenging ideas.

*Deliberation* is the additional step dialogue partners take when they commit to making plans or decisions. A clear distinction between dialogue and deliberation, for example, comes from the legal system. Jurors might meet and talk in the hallways of a courthouse, and the conversations could well be dialogic. They could be building mutual trust, finding shared experiences, learning to accept each other, all features of positive working relationships. But the obvious goal of jurors as citizens is deliberative. Working together, they must decide something. Their task is to listen carefully to the relative strengths of evidence and argument to later evaluate with other jurors. The goal is not simply to understand the facts but to reach some kind of group decision, even if agreeing on a stalemate. Most civic decision-making is similar. Community groups interested in urban renewal also deliberate, for example, when members meet to decide how to present complaints about city planning to the mayor. When the mayor convenes her advisers to consider possible responses, that, too, is deliberation.

Dialogue and deliberation are complementary forms of communication and depend on specific interpersonal skills: a willingness to engage even with those who disagree with you, an inclination to empathize even when disagreement remains, an invitational listening style, an emphasis on non-judgmental responses, an honest depiction of personal beliefs along with any tentativeness with which they are held, and a willingness to say, "Yes, your idea seems better than mine." Dialogue and deliberation also depend upon more generic habits: maintaining the fullest reasonable access to a knowledge base of historical context, scientific studies, and accurate accounts of contemporary events; the availability of conversation partners willing to talk; and convenient places to talk without undue interruptions.

On each of these criteria, twenty-first-century American political life has lost its way. For each problem, a stronger journalistic presence could provide a corrective.

In a recent and persuasive account of challenges to contemporary journalism, David Ryfe stresses that "our focus is no longer on 'the public' or on 'journalism,' but on the relationship between them. This relational approach has opened the way to rethinking journalism's connection to the public."[29] The central question is whether the journalistic role, essentially one of communicating credibly to enable subsequent public communication, can be enacted faithfully while its own credibility is under political attack and its own ethical integrity demeaned and diminished. Citizens who find the work of the *New York Times* suspect may extend that suspicion toward other news organizations. If that happens enough, journalism in general suffers a loss of reputation and impact. If, though, journalism can stave off suspicions and regain lost credibility, it stands a better chance of fulfilling its dialogical role. As a result, voters, elected representatives, and special interest groups are far more likely to have better public arguments as they deliberate a mutual future.

What is a "public"? Earlier in the book, even in this chapter, we stressed that with dialogue, a group begins to constitute itself as "a people," a distinct identity that binds them together. More than being bound, in fact, they identify with each other. The preamble to the Constitution of the United States marked a historic moment of identification with its three-word opening, "We the People." The Founders thereby signified the key to establishing a new country—creating an equally new sense of what it means to be a citizen. They knew the Latin term "res publica," which referred to that action and those people who are *public* in that they commit to identify with others in a common overall mission, even if their goals and beliefs seem to clash.

Casual use of the word "public" can cause citizens to forget what it implies, how the connection of person with person constitutes our government. "Public" these days often simply refers to what someone is willing to share with others, or perhaps it might refer to an amorphous mass that might or might not have similar commitments. America's founding documents theoretically welcomed differences between persons' ideas but advocated a common commitment to how we respect them.

We see a future for an *ecumenical journalism* that brings multiple voices to a shared, multicultural experience. "Ecumenical" comes from the Greek *oikoumenikos*, which means that which pertains to the world as a whole. In the Vatican's 1960s and 1970s emphasis on ecumenism, person-to-person dialogue was central to promoting widespread cooperation among different faiths, stressing fundamental personhood, commonality, and inclusion over spiritual competition.

An ecumenical journalism stresses collaboration over dismissiveness, and, as we wrote in 1994, it "expands the traditional focus on the 'public's right to know,' encompassing a broader emphasis—the 'public's right to be heard.'"[30] General interest journalism can be considered a shared meeting space—in older language, a commons. Through responsible journalism a public discovers a far wider swath of opinions and cultural experiences than individuals otherwise might have anticipated, insights often far afield from their own. Residents of wealthy neighborhoods in Chicago have access to vivid accounts of homeless encampments in other parts of the city, as well as to the plight of soybean farmers struggling through a drought in Wisconsin or Puerto Rican property owners whose homes no longer exist after a monster hurricane. Because of general interest media, multiple news audiences could find themselves identifying with young Afghan women whose opportunities for an education seem to have vanished along with the American troops stationed in their country. Print, broadcast, and online journalism affords men, for example, access to news that might otherwise appear confined to women's issues. Christians learn that Muslims love their children, too, and quite possibly the atheist on the city council is an ethically and spiritually motivated person in ways that resemble members of religious faiths.

The word *democracy* seems so friendly, so natural, so much like one of those "everybody knows *that*" assumptions, that Americans tend to be complacent about it. Many do not know how radical and experimental it must have sounded before America claimed its right to be free of autocratic rule. Greeks in Aristotle's time, for example, thought democracy might be worth a try but it would be risky. Plato evidently calculated that democracy could only work when governing fewer than 5,040 people. Beyond that, presumably, all bets were off. Supposedly, Socrates feared government in the hands of everyday poor people, because that would lead to violence and incompetent governance. Nevertheless, these fears did not prevail at the genesis of the United States, in part because of leaders' confidence in the power of information and a future of widespread communication.

Early American citizens, aided by a free press, would gather to trade opinions and argue in open forums and free spaces. Some opinions would prosper, some wither away, others adjust toward compromise or evolve to enhanced positions. But the Founders' worldview could not have included instant communication from afar. They had in mind conversation largely confined to local activities like property rights, religious doctrine, education, and local government. Conversation often blossomed in pubs, barbershops, or byways. These were the first "open spaces" for communication that were so important to early democratic theory, despite the existence of venues privileging membership on the bases of gender, race, religion, and wealth. These everyday exchanges remained important throughout the early years of citizen self-government, while too slowly the democratic impulse widened their inclusiveness. Over the decades, something else changed, as chronicled by historians: "open" or "free spaces" for public conversation gradually lost their influence on cultural life. Spaces devoted to political talk faded and, with them, a certain amount of popular faith in citizens' power to affect government.[31]

Recent trends in the complex journalism-citizen-politics relationship can be discouraging. Of course, no one should believe that American journalism has ever been politics free, for it has not. But the free spaces the Founders hoped would continue to attract political talk have evaporated further in the twenty-first-century media climate with general interest journalism now in economic decline. Elected officials encourage citizens to get their news from ideologically pure sources and not bother to research "the other side(s)" of an issue. Often, what is called "news" from such venues amounts to opinions, venom, endorsements, and alibis rather than facts, along with fake news about journalists allegedly trading in fake news.

The post-1990 online revolution had been so intriguing that media theorists hoped it would lead to a new democratization and personalization of opinion, conversation, and access to in-depth reporting and invigorating and accurate dissemination of news. Regrettably, according to the constitutional scholar Cass Sunstein, this expectation for a future of widespread public wisdom turns out to have invited more polarization than edification. And polarization, Sunstein argues, creates a "limited argument pool";[32] previously diversified news sources are ostracized, and group-think reduces the possibility of encountering important stories not already sanctioned within ideological safe spaces. Like-minded citizens may continue to meet but often only for comfort, reinforcement, or indulgent mutual therapy. In such a protected sub-public, ideas calcify, complaints are savored, and talk is directed to already-receptive ears. Diversifying influences of new alternatives go dark and with them realistic opportunities to credit strong reasoning from positions diverging from one's own. "If the group's members are already inclined in a certain direction, they will offer a disproportionately large number of arguments going in the same direction, and a disproportionately small number of arguments going the other way."[33]

In such a climate, arguments naturally tend to fortify themselves, self-reinforce, reject alternatives, and ultimately become more dismissive and extreme. As a result, we see Internet sites, once thought to be the latest media saviors of democratic life and citizen talk, often fueling storms of hate speech and spreading unevidenced accusations. Some citizens now willingly welcome and believe "news" of public figures accused of being secret members of an international ring of pedophiles, operated from the dark confines of a pizza parlor. Public lying has now become normalized as a campaign strategy or tool for targeting highly specific groups. Political operatives understand that reputable fact-checkers could never successfully contradict the lies before the retweeting and forwarding begins in earnest. After all, thorough fact-checking is the province of only a relatively few general interest news organizations who have—sorry to say again—dwindling resources.

However, Sunstein's somewhat gloomy view of digital culture should not be the last word. He has reason to be worried about polarization and isolation fortified by news packages addressed only to tightly knit quarters anxious to fortify existing beliefs. But the final story of news access in the digital age has yet to be drafted, and our account would be incomplete without mentioning at least one significant reply to Sunstein.

In a recent collection about digital citizenship, Angel Parham and Danielle Allen point to digital media's ability to provide more access to unfamiliar perspectives and cultural assumptions. They could have excellent conversations with Sunstein. In "Achieving Rooted Cosmopolitanism in a Digital Age," Parham and Allen foreground the potential rewards of expanded news media technologies without downplaying the problems. In contrast to what Sunstein calls a diminishing "argument pool," for instance, they accent an obvious opportunity. Democracy's digital age invites citizens to explore personally directed media—leading to new approaches for aggregating, replying, replaying, refuting, and rearranging. At no time in history has more helpful information been available to more everyday citizens, even considering the real frustrations of a "digital divide" and the public pollution of outright lies. Collaboration, coauthorship, and cooperation all are potentially enhanced, even with strangers, opponents, or new cultural situations. There is no guarantee whose arguments will prevail in political life, but access to more trustworthy evidence, even if clouded by junk talk and gullibility in sketchier sources, cannot be a bad thing on balance. Productive arguments—and informational pools—can be enlarged by making the unfamiliar more familiar and by addressing the strange in ways that make it more accessible. Some recent research suggests that citizens who use blogs and social media actively for political talk are more likely to participate in forums and civic activities compared to citizens who are satisfied to read only the politically packaged content of silo or enclave sites or disengage from political discussions entirely. They also tend to be more likely to join civic groups or express their own beliefs to congressional representatives or news media. Of course, seeking out the bases for alternative ideas and arguments—and their validity—presumes public willingness to engage.[34]

Parham and Allen borrow the central term of their essay from Kwame Anthony Appiah, perhaps the most widely read and influential ethicist in America due to his weekly column in the *New York Times Magazine*. Appiah's work in what he terms cosmopolitan ethics and "rooted cosmopolitanism" provides a practical response to a world of cultural differences.[35] But he knows that those responses will not be persuasive to citizens bound only to a particular tradition or perspective. It is fine to be "rooted" in a place, a community, or a tradition of self-interest; we all need that, and it enriches our lives. At the same time, "cosmopolitan" describes the ability to participate in life beyond our own categories and the willingness to develop an *expanded* or ecumenical sense of citizenship that extends beyond our own usual borders. We need curiosity; it enables conversations—not to change strangers who disagree with you into converts but to understand their existing beliefs. Citizens genuinely open to this possibility will not reject their roots in favor of literally becoming citizens from nowhere, blank slates. But ethical citizens are not restricted to what they already prefer. Appiah says that effective conversational styles blend standing your ground *while* recognizing that others might validly inhabit different ground at the same time. As Appiah writes, "Conversation doesn't have to lead to consensus about anything, especially not values; it's enough that it helps people get used to each other."[36]

Consider the Internet as an inviting tool for getting used to each other. In the midst of an online temper tantrum about politics, it might not feel that way. You might use that moment to lash out. Or to clam up. Or to decide to use a search engine to recheck the evidence for your assumptions, or to investigate unfamiliar cultural assumptions, or to start fresh conversations.

Citizens frustrated with the challenges of online communication need a journalism capable of backing us up. We need information that is personal, public, trustworthy, immediate, and culturally diverse, all at the same time. If it is true that journalism and the public are best considered together, how does journalism fit into a downscaled landscape of contemporary open spaces for productive citizen talk, either face-to-face or digital? Are we squandering our opportunities?

## How Journalism Succeeds and How It Fails

Not long ago we enjoyed chatting with a couple about their son, who had graduated with a degree from a prestigious Midwestern journalism program. "He never used the degree," the mother said, repeating a refrain familiar to many parents who lovingly support their children's education despite possibly some ambivalence about the student's choices. After graduation, he chose another career path. But did he *never* use the degree?

As she talked, she listened well to herself, too. She quickly added that both she and her husband as well as their son agreed that journalism education clearly contributed to his professional career. The longer we talked, in fact, the more it sounded like his mom did not actually regret his choice, nor did he. In his major, he had learned to write clearly and succinctly, to read for nuance, and to interview important people to understand their stories as *they* experienced them. He learned to listen, to do thorough research, to test evidence and tentative conclusions against other interpretations, and to respect the differences between ego-involved opinion and actual events as foundations for publication. Beyond his mother's impressions, it seemed that he probably developed other important skills—for example, he likely internalized ethical standards of communication and could apply them to newsmakers' behavior as well as his own choices. He also must have discovered that there are more than one or two clearly defined sides to a story, especially a controversial one. He learned firsthand about covering political strategizing and how it can exploit everyday citizens who might not be aware it is sneaking up behind them. He certainly figured out hidden agendas and when people have information to share but might not disclose it because they cannot trust a reporter. And he surely had experience detecting the lies that powerful people think they can get away with.

The overlaps where public conversation and journalism affect each other will always influence the health of democracy itself. The architects of the country decided to assure citizens, in the *first* of many constitutional amendments, that the fundamental premise of a republic is best stated in terms of freedom for *public* communication. Secured by the prohibitive phrase "Congress shall make no law," this freedom embraced religious choice uninhibited by government control, individuals' free speech, a largely unregulated free press providing information and commentary, a right of peaceable assembly with other communicators, and an ability to petition the government if citizens need redress of grievances. Clearly, courts clarified the original amendment with a number of nuances and exceptions that balanced some rights with other rights. A republic needed wide latitude for citizens to communicate and wide availability to the truths that give that communication meaning for others. Communication guarantees and rights were expected to guide citizens' relationships with their government while facilitating responsible self-government.

Let us loop back to an earlier question of listening, approaching it from a slightly different slant. What might "free speech" or a "free press" actually mean, beyond the general freedom to speak your mind without being arrested or silenced by the government? Are unrestrained talking, printing, broadcasting, and tweeting the crucial democratic goals to be protected? Is there any broader advantage to free speech beyond verifying our "right" to say what we desire to say? The blend of journalism with broader fields of communication informs the feel-good personal rights that individuals like to think are forever—and all a democracy really needs.

Speech is far more complex than just exercising the vocal cords. It is exploring. It needs a place for listening and invitational turn taking as well. Apart from unfortunate or tragic pathologies, talk occurs when listeners have decided to pay attention. With the exception of *inner* speech, a topic long fascinating to linguists and psychologists, talkers talk *with* someone else, and that someone helps to regulate the communication. Each talker typically anticipates how their words might be heard, and perhaps responded to, by a listener—and they choose their language accordingly. We even interpret silences or micro-glances. Poor or unmotivated listeners can, without even knowing it is happening, squash a speaker's good ideas before they have a chance to develop. When another's commitment to listening is in doubt, speakers can be surprised, disappointed, self-critical, or angry: "I give up. How can you say you're listening when you're watching the game on TV?" Or, as our moms used to say, "Look at me when I'm talking to you!" Or "I want to tell you more, but it looks like you're late to an appointment or something." We hope journalists also internalize these ideas. If people are not listening, you are not speaking to them. If journalists are not listening to people, they will not really know what to write or say, or how to write or say it.

Many adults assume that communication is primarily about how speakers try to reach listeners: "How can I persuade him to stop smoking?" or "What can I say to console her?" They tend to overlook how listening regulates and stimulates speaking in the first place. Most of us have tried to have a delicate or emotional conversation with someone who, for example, keeps grooming the dog while claiming, "I'm listening!" When that happens, the speaker may decide to change the subject, wait for another occasion, or give up entirely. Listeners are more powerful than they usually believe.

Normal speech presumes a mutual willingness to be sensitive to conflicts that might be created by differences of opinion, culture, or vocabulary. We certainly expect that from teachers, clergy, social workers, and other professional communicators like journalists. For all of us, speech should involve a responsibility to stay open and aware to the content of another's talk, even if it fails to mirror our own conclusions. Or maybe *especially* when it does not mirror them. It is a challenging responsibility, even when conversation partners mutually accept it. Awareness is not just for "reading" other people. Through being aware of others and comparing our own opinions to theirs, we get a sense—however imperfect—of what those other people really believe and what we can say to them that is worth hearing or reading. Politically speaking, citizens who just talk to hear themselves blather never establish an awareness, possibly shared, of how their own attitudes fit within larger issues.

The authors of the documents that created our republic also understood a similar function for a free press—a journalism that does not need to beg for government permission, or even popularity, to publicize truths that ought to fuel public talk. Part of journalism's mission is simply to be competent enough in its listening mission to figure out what makes a difference to citizens and then translate this truth as best it can. This is the equivalent of tough love in families; sometimes stories are necessary even if unpleasant, but someone has got to say it. Offering the public new information, like giving advice, is a delicate negotiation that depends deeply on responsive listeners who tell you what they appreciate and what they do not.

Think of effective journalism as a form of supportive speech—informing, enabling, and enhancing everyday conversations and sparking other levels of conversation between journalists and their audiences. Print media, broadcasts, and online messages are symbolic "places" where democracy lives. Journalism allows citizens who have never interacted with national politicians or major celebrities—newsmakers—to meet them symbolically and evaluate their communication, too. Readers and viewers of news reports compare their own reactions to people they will never meet face-to-face. In a republic, citizens can participate indirectly in public issues of huge importance that could change how they live. They might opt out, preferring silence, or sit in a corner and snipe. Journalism as an institution preserves the choice, but the Constitution supplies a built-in rationale for fuller participation. If critics want to be heard in the public arena, other citizens should expect proof of their thoughtful listening as well.

While evaluating journalism's contributions, we describe a professional ideal that the so-called real world does not always enact. Some limits are obvious in how well the profession performs its many roles. Journalists have blind spots and character flaws like the rest of us. Some, unfortunately, have bent organizational rules and compromised their own ethical standards, making up stories to win praise or a prize, for example. Of course, similar lapses also occur in political candidates, factory workers, priests, CEOs, farmers, and Little League coaches.

### Quotables

"My colleagues who teach beginning journalism students say that they are intent on helping them learn to 'report against their own assumptions.' That is, whatever inclinations or presuppositions the students bring to a story, they should go about their research with inquiries that potentially call into question exactly those inclinations and presuppositions."[37]

—Michael Schudson, media historian

The basic social responsibilities of journalists in their professional roles are guided, we have seen, by rigorous codes of conduct about which most of its public remains unaware. Journalism's professional standards would inspire basic trust by all but the most skeptical or partisan citizens; indeed, it is hard to identify other public professions that specify, and enforce, ethical standards this aggressively. Many politicized organizations that brand journalists as dishonest enemies seem to be guided by no recognizable ethical code at all. The contrast is telling.

Of course, professional journalists' loyalties to support democracy can be challenged by conflicts with marketplace demands and strained because different companies have their own guidelines dictating what kinds of news (infotainment? celebrity gossip?) match their business model. But we find reassurance by their transparent behavior that a majority of reporters and editors have the Constitution, or broad-based civic welfare, foremost in mind. Nonetheless, a sizable number of journalists also fear that they will not have enough money to buy Christmas presents for their kids—or, worse, could find a pink slip on the desk tomorrow morning. Few college graduates see journalism as a get-rich-quick scheme. Some, thankfully, think it is a calling.

Even journalists working for large and weighty news corporations must realize that their best efforts are limited severely. Because "news" is what audiences find interesting and important, it exists in *potential*. A new drug might or might not earn a headline; dozens of factors confront editors trying to make the decision. What research confirms its effectiveness? Who wants it and for what reasons? A possible breakthrough on Alzheimer's disease or cancer treatment? What will a manufacturer charge for it, and who can afford it? What are the side effects? News, in one definition, is what people talk about, what matters to them. A newspaper or nightly news program cannot cover all potentially newsworthy events or implications for disparate audiences with detail or context they find satisfactory; judgments about priorities must be made. Someone will always be disappointed, or angry, or skeptical. Journalists' mission and goals are likely to be misunderstood, if not denigrated, by citizens on the street, as a recent report from the American Press Institute found.[38] Journalists can try to bring to the public the clearest, most comprehensive account of what they believe we need to know, yet what is omitted will always dwarf what they have the space and resources to include.

## Listening for the Next Journalism

Journalism can remain static or inert as it faces new events while anticipating tomorrow's headlines. As it changes to reflect the times, it becomes contemporary society's shape-shifter. Two of its central chroniclers, Bill

Kovach and Tom Rosenstiel, seem willing for their profession to adopt fresher perspectives right away, and many of their suggestions directly support the linkage between journalism and democratic conversation. In *Blur: How to Know What's True in the Age of Information Overload*, they celebrate much of contemporary journalism while considering new strategies for adapting to difficult conditions. Things are changing, and journalism is on the cusp of redefining itself. They call it the "next journalism."[39]

The flood of news sources on the Internet and ubiquitous social media platforms has deemphasized the traditional media practice of "gatekeeping"—journalism's long-standing function of selecting from mountains of potential stories the news most important to the public at a particular moment. "All the news that's fit to print," the storied slogan of the *New York Times*, is an artifact of this process of filtering facts and stories based on journalism's credibility and accurate reporting. It dates to a time when print journalism dominated as the authoritative source of information. Even in those halcyon days, no journalistic organization could ever provide *all* of the news that deserves to be known by a generalized citizenry, much less wisely sort it all out. Moreover, the old-style media gatekeeping model relied on the gut instincts and personal preferences of editors, often male, white, and middle-aged. It did not, and could not, demand or rely on much public participation. Today's abundance of news at least comes closer to *all the news*, although it clearly falls short of the *that's fit to print* part. A significant part of the news audience now acts like it does not *need* general interest gatekeepers because it has digital access to the whole news horizon and people can pick and choose on their own. Either that or they have discovered the only specialized niche they need to consult.

The "next journalism," Kovach and Rosenstiel believe, should adopt a different model for defining and providing news. Specialized news platforms are not just proliferating but becoming increasingly personalized, immediate, focused, specialized, hand-selected, targeted, unidimensional, and often, therefore, more ideological. As with all social developments, the results can be exciting and helpful, or discouraging and confusing, or, depending on whose interests are involved, something else entirely. However, new threats have emerged. With information fragmented within silos, it is even less likely that citizen conversations will share a common vocabulary or accurate knowledge about any particular topic essential for a dialogue about yesterday's events in Afghanistan, Atlanta, or Amsterdam—much less be broadly conversant with a shared understanding of democracy in U.S. history. What counts as verifiable fact sometimes seems utterly up for grabs, with commentators on some sites dismissing even a consensus of scientific researchers as simply an opinion that can be refuted by a politician's glib put-down.

Kovach and Rosenstiel identify eight crucial functions for journalism's next chapter of adaptation.[40] All seem intended to reinvigorate citizen dialogue while creating fresh responses to democracy's altered demands for news. Here we provide our own brief take on each recommendation.

## Authenticator

The explosion of special interest news platforms invites—and at times even rewards—truth stretching, bold lying, and willful ignorance of existing knowledge. Often, advocates of special interest groups disseminate "news," but they usually are neither trained to investigate public events thoroughly nor conversant in specialized fields of study. Institutional journalism must expand its role of adjudicating truth and falsehood, as well as clarifying why that difference makes a difference for citizens trying to discuss democracy together.

## Sense Maker

In a world of multiple sources of deliberate bias and deception, institutional journalism must bolster the factual context for complex stories that otherwise could easily be misjudged, stereotyped, or skipped.

## Investigator

As traditional gatekeeping recedes and news becomes more competitive and propagandistic, new problems of secrecy arise. Social mistrust and conflict compound the problem. Investigative journalism must redouble its attempts to discover important stories that are covered up by propagandists or other special interest actors. "Going after" or "taking down" bad actors is not the basis of investigative journalism; that would be the many lonely hours of digging in archives and public records in preparation for interviews and analysis.

## Witness Bearer

A powerful but often overlooked role for journalism is its prominent presence at public events. A reporter in the corner taking notes is a symbolic reminder that those town board meetings mean something. Through this witnessing, journalism monitors reality, legitimizes events, and reminds citizens that an honest public record can stabilize public processes and avoid unnecessary conflict.

## Empowerer

The next phase of journalism's growth will take increased responsibility for integrating the public into the news process, thereby establishing a mutual empowerment. Citizen voices are most powerful when they reach listeners while decision-making alternatives are being considered, not when the voices are deferred, muted, and retrospective.

## Smart Aggregator

In the future, institutional journalism should survey the far-flung news landscape more comprehensively beyond its own reporting, especially online sources. It can curate stories of special context and relevance, verify them, and perform a service that might be overlooked otherwise.

## Forum Organizer

Journalists can facilitate community conversation by organizing public dialogues on civic issues. These projects clear spaces—physical, virtual, and psychological—in which citizens of different persuasions exchange ideas. Journalism's presence at dialogue events represents the people's interests in listening. Declaring winners and losers in these events would be problematic, and becoming affiliated or associated with underwriting organizations, like the League of Women Voters, would create ethical problems as well. But organizing and supporting forums in the public interest should be readily distinguishable from sponsoring sports events or actively participating in political rallies.

## Role Model

It makes sense for journalism, through its civic commitments, to model effective community building. The goal should not be good public relations. Rather, it is to encourage informed outreach, open interaction, and other means for making people aware of how they and journalists can work *together* for common purposes. In the past, journalism often tried to set the agenda by its story choices and the subjects it covered; it tended to tell people what to think and do. But responding to controversy and issues with a goal of locally informed cooperation puts journalism where it should be—a caring community partner, not a detached observer. Vanessa Maria Gaber, director of the New Voices project at the nonprofit Free Press, represents journalists who advocate for change. "We are at a moment in this field where we're turning a corner," she says. "There is an awakening, people are advocating for themselves, communities are demanding more. And so we [journalists] need to capitalize on that momentum, and continue organizing, talking and collaborating."[41]

Propositions like these encourage a journalism that meshes with the tricornered intersection of news, citizenship, and dialogue we envision. Seyla Benhabib understood a homegrown citizen-based concept of a communicative republic, and, clearly, professional journalists are on board. Americans can respond to new challenges of technology, divisiveness, and cynicism without denigrating traditional roles of journalism. Citizens and journalists need each other for the sake of preserving the republic.

Our next chapter sketches a more substantive communicative role for journalism's listening public—citizens—and the political attitudes that restrain that vision. Then, in chapter 9, we ask whether our intersection metaphor could be imagined as opportunity or crisis, through lenses of optimism or pessimism.

CHAPTER 8

# A Citizenship Ethic for a Time of Diminished Journalism

Old advice can feel new again, even from a children's book. A good one was published in 1932 by Eleanor Roosevelt, who would soon become the First Lady of the United States.

*When You Grow Up to Vote: How Our Government Works for You* was written during the presidential campaign of her husband, Franklin Delano Roosevelt, amid the desperate days of the Great Depression's joblessness, soup lines, and bank failures. She hoped her message to young people and their parents would help restore faith in democracy. Thirty years later, she offered a companion piece for adult readers, *Tomorrow Is Now*—a fitting bookend for a life of civic engagement. She knew she was dying when writing it but persevered through fever, tremors, and fatigue so intense at times that she could not hold a pen. It was published posthumously in 1963, and in that edition we find these words:

> We have to take a new look at ourselves, at what our kind of government requires of us, at what our community needs from us; and then prepare to take a stand. In the long run there is no more liberating, no more exhilarating experience than to determine one's position, state it bravely, and then act boldly. Action brings with it its own courage, its own energy, a growth of self-confidence that can be acquired in no other way.[1]

*When You Grow Up to Vote* found a second life in a 2018 revised and updated edition. Its new editor and coauthor, Michelle Markel, included the 1963 passage because it so aptly expresses Roosevelt's style of active, take-charge citizenship—and perhaps because Americans now need the advice more than ever.

Some contemporary readers might be surprised that a First Lady of her time spoke out in the voice of an activist. Eleanor Roosevelt was her own person long before her husband became president. During World War I, she visited wounded soldiers, volunteered for the Navy-Marine Corps

Relief Society, and served in a Red Cross canteen. In the 1920s, she entered Democratic Party politics and joined the Women's Union Trade League and the League of Women Voters. She chose to lead by example.

Roosevelt modeled public participation for millions. Between 1932 and her death at age seventy-eight in 1962, she published twenty-seven books, including *The Moral Basis of Democracy*.[2] She became a global representative of the democratic experience. Her rhetoric expanded the concept of civil rights, especially those of women, African Americans, and refugees worldwide. As part of her special commitment to the United Nations, she became the first U.S. delegate and a guiding force in developing the United Nations Universal Declaration of Human Rights. Yet it was her 1932 children's book that best introduces an essay on citizenship. The book remains timely in another troubled millennium. Younger citizens still should grow up expecting to engage with each other to learn and compare political and moral values, not shrink toward cynicism. In a democracy, Roosevelt also wrote, leaders "will hold office not because it brings certain honors and considerations from . . . constituents" but because of "an obligation to perform a service to democracy."[3]

Her narrative about citizenship is indebted to journalism's role in keeping the country on course. She was true to a moral compass pointing toward justice, with a journalist's respect for truth and accuracy. In fact, she became the rare activist-citizen-journalist, responsible at various times for hosting weekly radio broadcasts and writing newspaper and magazine columns on current events. Her concern for youth growing into full citizenship still rings true; in a recent anthology on "understanding citizenship in a digital age," editors Danielle Allen and Jennifer Light decided that they too had to define their central concept from the standpoint of young people finding a place for themselves in a complicated world. For them, citizenship in a digital age cannot be explained merely by old patterns of political membership groups, which fail to account for the mixed roles of new media and communication—which have not "been well-integrated by the broader literature on political participation." Therefore, they reoriented the idea of "citizenship" around the deceptively simple process of how people with varied interests in democracy can influence the political landscape through *participation* rather than expecting the official machinery of government to take charge. Allen and Light define the core of citizenship as "civic agency"—getting things done. Being an agent of civic life means working on a human scale toward "shap[ing] their worlds together, especially in conditions of diversity, working both through and outside of political institutions."[4]

American culture is again experiencing wavering confidence in public life. Some citizens fear that the faith in public and political life that inspired the Founders might have run its course. Many no longer trust that citizen participation and reliable news media can be partners in the social architecture of a republic. Clearly, a citizenship ethic follows from topics we have emphasized to this point—from the founding spirit of the Constitution, to the discourse guidance of the First Amendment, to the irreplaceable role of journalism and dialogue in discussing information necessary to make justifiable political and moral decisions. The opportunity to vote and influence politics is not just a right that is nice to have. It is a gift with reasonable strings attached.

Understanding a citizenship ethic for the present moment begins by enlisting solid expectations for defining citizen *responsibility*, each in the context of accurate reasoning and healthy journalism. We then explore sources of disturbing and widespread citizen acceptance of, and complicity with, political lying and attacks on news media and information itself. Finally, we describe concrete possibilities for citizen responsibility. What citizens understand about citizenship shapes how we act to maintain and improve the nation.

## A Shaky Start for American Citizenship

Journalism is far more than a town crier. It is a community archive and time machine for citizens. Journalists understand better than most that what is newsworthy today has been developing over time and through events large and small, seen and unseen. Suddenly a wildfire or earthquake or surprise political resignation grabs your attention in the morning newsfeed. Where did that come from? What is its backstory? Truly understanding what is current is in some measure to recall the *previous*. Yet probing the previous on its own terms can be an elusive task. People easily forget that preceding generations dealt with their own issues of distraction, self-deception, short-sightedness, and even definitions of "normal." It is hard to be fully aware now of "how it used to be" as it was lived and experienced *then*. What passed for "common sense" in 1787 might be unrecognizable as common today. It helps, however, to see and hear *today* as at least a partial extension from a pattern of *yesterdays*. Scholars writing detailed histories and biographies make excellent contributions to the culture. Still, the most accessible public context work is largely the contribution of journalists.

The distinctly American notion that citizenship itself is a governing agency has a shrouded and, to the modern mind, disturbing or even hypocritical lineage. The Framers' definition of democracy was ambitious, but they harbored blind spots inherited from their own history, just as we all do and will. What the Framers negotiated through sustained deliberation, what they bequeathed to succeeding generations, was an impressive but flawed and aspirational Constitution. Their own assumptions, along with the need to compromise, perpetuated conditions that Eleanor Roosevelt and most twenty-first century citizens would consider unjust.

Schoolkids learn that the Declaration of Independence affirmed that "all men are created equal" and are "endowed by their creator with certain unalienable rights." Governments derive their powers from "the consent of the governed"—that is, citizenship constitutes governing, not the other way around. Did this eloquent affirmation and the subsequent Bill of Rights guarantee that *all* men had the same rights of full participation as citizens? Even male slaves? Even freeborn African Americans? No. Was American society in that time ready to affirm full equality for women? Not even close. Women were seldom considered even under an umbrella category of "men," nor were they presumed by fathers, husbands, brothers, or sons to be anywhere near equal as citizens. They were not expected to speak out fully in public and vote their own consciences. Nor were poor immigrants, women or men, regarded as full citizens. The elevated language of equality might be reassuring, but the political life of the mid- to late eighteenth-century colonies excluded citizenship for a majority of men, women, and children who helped establish and build the nation. The nostalgia we occasionally invoke for the good old days of rational debate among equals is also misplaced. It fades with just a casual reading of the work of historian John Hope Franklin, who tells harrowing stories of even freed Black men whom citizens tracked like prey and returned to slave owners in actions ratified by the courts.[5]

The often revered New England town meeting turns out to be somewhat mythical, according to historians of early citizenship such as sociologist Michael Schudson.[6] Colonial America did not fully prize equal opportunity, the equal right to speak, or, for that matter, reasoned deliberation.[7] Many town meetings resembled a private club of wealthy older men who owned property and were closely affiliated with the church. White males who paid taxes might be denied entry unless they were consequential property owners. Often, well-heeled members of the church called the meetings and decided on agendas for discussion.[8] The meetings primarily respected, and rewarded, affirmations of consensus and social order rather than productive differences of opinion that required serious decision-making. In this regard, meetings were more symbolic or honorific rather than vigorous forums for democratic encounters.

With so many voices left out of the civic conversation, rhetoric tended to be hierarchical and deferential, with high social status continually a marker of respect. In colonial Virginia, elections were "rituals for the reinforcement of gentry rule," which was identifiable not only by Episcopalian membership but also by "family name, dress, the possession of a carriage, a large house, and ample holdings of land and slaves."[9] Across the colonies, participation in decision-making often rested on one's social standing, while respect for fairness and justice was shunted to the background.

### Quotables

"In open and accessible public spaces and forums, one should expect to encounter and hear from those who are different, whose social perspectives, experiences, and affiliations are different. To promote a politics of inclusion, then, participatory democrats must promote the ideal of a heterogeneous public, in which persons stand forth with their differences acknowledged and respected, though perhaps not completely understood, by others."[10]

—Iris Marion Young, *Justice and the Politics of Difference*

Out of this environment of entitled, superficial, and monocultural citizenship emerged a turning point of vision. With determination, a new country can begin new traditions. It was not easy, and America is far from finished. Framers and concerned citizens needed to create documents to rely upon; they needed fresh expression of meaningful disagreements; and they needed a coherent path to a better future. They needed a constitution that might have sounded to many of their contemporaries like blue-sky wishfulness. They needed a reality-based rhetoric about government that justified far wider participation, full of practical possibilities for communication—a changeable rhetoric of *becoming* rather than static *being* mired in conventional wisdom. We previously described arguments establishing the responsibility of a republic to its citizens. They were presented in 1787 and 1788 by Alexander Hamilton, James Madison, and John Jay, a coauthorship collectively known by the pseudonym "Publius." Journalism was the vehicle for argumentation.

The Federalist Papers, as the Publius essays came to be known, launched much of the public support for the proposed Constitution and its relationship to citizens. The foundation was composed of words. Public life had to be energized by shared reasons. Journalism established its essential role by disseminating these ideas, starting with the New York *Independent Journal* carrying the Federalist Papers and continuing with various other New York newspapers.

The give-and-take of argument played a vital role. The Federalist Papers are among our best sources for understanding not only the early commitments of dedicated public leaders but also the value of direct conversations about controversial matters and, eventually, the trust invested in a broad electorate of diverse and quite ordinary Americans.

Despite a history of pervasive influences of privilege, wealth, exclusion, and simplistic bigotry, a country could be ruled through a different approach to citizenship. But there were implied "ifs": *if* citizens were committed; *if* a base of reliable information informed everyday life; *if* citizens conversed about differences in free public spaces; *if* citizens listened carefully to others' arguments; *if* citizens felt they were fairly served and addressed by elected representatives; *if* the seductions of excessive partisanship, ethnocentrism, and special interests did not debase basic premises of a republic; *if* a public could honor community goals rather than an elitism of property, wealth, self-dealing, race, and gender. So many "ifs" foreshadow many of America's contemporary problems.

The new country would renounce autocratic rule imposed from afar. But the soft ground for American citizenship, the privileged male-directed political world of racial exploitation, clearly fell short by today's social justice criteria. Wealth, gender, and ancestry granted access to power. We might ask, "When have they not?" The question is, in a sense, pivotal. Evidently it was the shadow fear of the Founders; without establishing, at least rhetorically, strong roles for everyday citizens, would they fail their own vision? To overcome privilege and unfair access, the nation's founding citizens were expected to participate in their own governance. Although the Founders could not anticipate and address all future problems, their oratory crafted a process through which future justice could be addressed.

Tracing the essence of citizen responsibility in more recent times remains complicated. Ethicists, political scientists, and community organizers have all tried to chart the relationship between citizens and democratic life. Next, we summarize several especially influential ideas, noting that each consistently depends on citizen communication as much as on literal laws of the land.

## Contemporary Models of Citizenship

Citizen-activists Eric Liu and Nick Hanauer understand that citizenship must have more meaning for democratic life than simple legal documentation. "We mean living in a pro-social way at every scale of life. We mean showing up for each other." Quite simply, they are talking about "the work of being in public."[11] "Showing up for each other" is a plainspoken but wise ideal.

Psychiatrist and teacher Robert Coles applied a similar definition in *Handing One Another Along*, his account of how literature highlights citizens' generosity with each other once they glimpse a larger purpose than personal well-being. *Service*, a key word for Coles, helps us escape the tiny traps of our individual desires. Citizenship is interpersonal. Coles's stories about literary reminders for living also suggest an ethic of citizenship that reinforces everyday civic participation: the world-famous author who worked as a migrant and accompanied indigent people into hospitals so he could discover how they lived, and died; the "writing doc" who wrote some of America's best poetry to help him translate the worlds of his patients; the writer whose studies in psychology at a small southern college interested her less than inhabiting the displaced citizens and misfits she encountered daily, often mired in segregationist traps; the singer, wasting away from drugs and exploitation, who still wanted desperately to "carry a tune" for listeners. Scholars and critics emphasize styles of, or models for, contributing to a self-reflective democracy; they are often distinctly worded but rarely mutually exclusive. Coles's stories help us to streamline the models somewhat arbitrarily to five, after which we speculate on roadblocks to an ethical arc of citizenship.[12]

### The Monitorial Citizen

A common baseline for democratic citizenship is accepting the responsibility to stay alert to the world, especially as events threaten the welfare of communities. Citizen awareness of public issues, controversies, and choices must often depend on contributions of journalism. Being at the center of social action might be better but is usually rarer. Monitoring is about staying as informed, current, and aware as possible or reasonable.

Citizens who appreciate a republic understand that government decision-making is not a self-regulating and automatic system. They do their best to attend to public interaction surrounding important decisions, considering not only occurrences—what happens—but also potential consequences. To monitor events (think of video monitors helping parents keep track of infants in the next room), they also imagine alternatives—comparisons to what could be more effective or safe. Is the baby restless? Should I get up and check her firsthand? In our broader communities, no one is expected to pay attention to all controversies. But what kinds of preparation do citizens owe society to justify their own opinions as meaningful and their own contributions as helpful? Citizenship requires us to check on public life and general media issues well enough, first, to know when the baby is in danger and, second, to learn how we can share knowledge about social choices and enable reasonable civic decisions.

The monitorial role is more like focused surveillance than official research gathering or political leadership. In Michael Schudson's striking analogy, parents watching their children cavort at a community swimming pool are enjoying the children's play, but they are also scanning the pool environment watchfully in case they need to take action. Careful monitoring is a fairly obvious expectation for citizens, although it also presumes a degree of trust in backstop social institutions like journalism that when necessary can supplement citizens' attention, much like a lifeguard.[13]

The adjective "vigilant" also describes this basic work of democracy. For example, in civil society, political philosopher John Keane writes, citizens "are obliged to exercise vigilance in preventing each other and their rulers from abusing their powers and violating the spirit of the commonwealth."[14] "Obliged," of course, extends the responsibilities of monitoring. A parent at the pool who sees another family's child flailing around in the deep end would not mutter, "I sure hope somebody's watching that little girl" and go back to his Michael Connolly novel. The stakes are too high to ignore danger.

When facing an impending diplomatic crisis or abuse of power, a democracy assumes a shared obligation of public alertness in its citizens. "See something, say something" goes beyond a catchy media slogan in response to threats of terrorists or active shooters. It captures a time-honored tenet of democratic citizenship. We look out for each other, in the spirit of "neighborhood watch" groups in big cities. Obligations of vigilance also justify whistleblower laws that ensure witnesses who observe and report organizational wrongdoing are protected from retaliation. Monitorial citizens keep their eyes and ears open, alert to what could go wrong, and cooperate with others to maintain democratic protections. It is like watching the road ahead but also checking mirrors and side windows to anticipate potential trouble.

## The Informed Citizen

A monitorial spirit contributes to a citizenship ethic, but "showing up for each other" often demands a heightened familiarity with the world as it is. Being aware and being informed are not quite the same thing. Perhaps influenced by Thomas Jefferson's comment that "information is the currency of democracy," some critics argue that even careful watchfulness is insufficient without strong civic education that includes focused journalism providing factual informational bases for action. If citizen self-rule is to succeed, it must rely on a proactive commitment from a significant percentage of citizens, a kind of herd immunity to autocracy. Without a citizen-grounded goal of operating with both general knowledge and specific factual preparation, dialogue becomes a faint hope and citizens remain hostages of their own beliefs and stereotypes.

Informed citizens equip themselves to participate in shared reflection about governing fairly. They read widely and listen across ordinary divisions of thought and preference. Reflection is neither noodling nor winging it. Reflection is not based on bumper stickers, quips, or talking points you heard at a political rally. Reflection cannot be a strategy to get your own way in a meeting. Information leads, as the word "reflection" implies, to forming oneself inwardly, toward introspection to aid observation. Informed citizens welcome new information to compare with knowledge that guided their past. They even consider the possibilities of holding seemingly conflicting information in tension with other things they believe—asking, for example, how it would be possible for a U.S. senator to reconcile new federal funding to aid frontline workers in a national health crisis, even though a particular bill conflicts with her long-held reservations about handouts, entitlements, and bootstraps.[15] Informed citizens do not wait for pundits and candidates to press their own accusations, rumors, or convenient interpretations. Seeking out and being open to new information from diverse perspectives is an underrated habit and skill of citizenship.

Public ideas require examination from a variety of angles. Ideas become meaningful because they are true to the best of your knowledge, born out of research, experience, and focused conversation. They are not truer or better because you have always thought that way or because Mom told you it was true. A friend of ours used to compliment students by saying they "speak from a well-stocked mind." It was his way of respecting inquisitive learners, those prepared for new possibilities because they continued to restock their mental shelves. Those of us who have worked in grocery stores can relate. Obviously, even reasonably persistent reading and cultural awareness describe a high bar for busy citizens. Yet staying at least reasonably current with the news can be considered a baseline social expectation if voters are to be partners in civic effectiveness.

Another fundamental informational goal is the ability to summarize important arguments *against* the political positions you presently hold. Try, in fact, to imagine your opponents' *strongest* information and arguments countering potential weaknesses in your beliefs. Opponents can be enormously useful in helping you shape and test your ideas. When Covid-19 struck, most citizens were woefully but understandably underprepared to discuss the national security implications of a global pandemic. Being informed means, then, having access to new learning and a knowledge base for conversation open to challenge and conflict. Informed citizens are wary of conversation partners who refuse to read an expert's relevant op-ed column because it was published in the *New York Times*, who believe that no one who works for a particular network can be trusted, or who cynically discount a science journalist's report of a climate change study without reading the story. It may seem harmless if the next-door neighbor is certain that scientific warnings about climate change are wrong (believe and let believe). It does not advance democratic dialogue if your neighbors—or you—refuse to *consider* being less certain or more willing to question the credibility of their own information sources. "They're wrong" does not suffice as either knowledge or argument.

## The Engaged Citizen

"The point of democracy is not perfect government," say journalism educators and critics Bill Kovach and Tom Rosenstiel, "it is self-government. Thus, journalism and the news are inevitably intertwined with engagement."[16] Engagement in our earlier Eleanor Roosevelt sense means not ignoring someone else's problem just because it is not *your* problem. Engagement means acting collectively to foster a sense of community. It is acting in public as a committed learner who cares about what other citizens think. It is caring whether your next-door neighbor will be able to get to work when her car is in the shop. And then offering to drive her.

Most engaged citizens will never run for public office or volunteer twenty hours a week at a homeless shelter or lead a campaign to recall an incompetent mayor. Many already are oversubscribed in complex personal lives. They might hold a couple of jobs, care for an ill grandmother part-time, and struggle to serve the family nutritious meals. However, citizenship does not depend on joining group after group or searching for the next volunteer opportunity. Engaged citizens occasionally care enough about an issue to fire off a letter to the editor of the local paper (if one exists). They fill in on a Saturday morning for a Little League coach who must work an unexpected shift at the factory. They run an errand for a homebound neighbor. They paint signs for an upcoming Thanksgiving parade. In public meetings, they overcome stage fright to speak up when their interests are ignored. They cannot always say "yes," but "no" is not their default response to public life.

Citizens with community building in mind might consider a way journalists think about engagement. Reporters and editors typically must make value judgments about public service priorities knowing they can cannot function as totally neutral uncommitted machines of pure impartiality. Neither can citizens. Journalist Stephen Ward's analysis of the objectivity-partiality issue can be applied to responsible citizenship as well. He stresses that journalists have to be committed to democracy. By the nature of the profession, they must be *partial* to some positive goals of "plural democracy," such as advocating open or transparent public communication when possible. At the same time, they must remain committed to impartial and objective *methods* for achieving those goals, including a commitment to truth, verification, and fairness to persons and groups in the news. Yet journalists' jobs presume value commitments to the community, and in that sense they cannot be neutral. "In contrast," Ward warns, "there are engaged citizens, such as extreme partisans, who use partial methods for partial goals." In other words, neutrality does not benefit society when it allows privileged or powerful people to get away with enriching themselves while manipulating others.[17] Ward's brand of journalistic ethical commitment applies to citizens as well; be partial toward community building in democratic life, and work to be impartial and scrupulously fair as you act to achieve those ends.

Broadcast journalist Bill Moyers clearly respects those moments when journalism should be impartial but also knows when it must act on what it discovers. Lincoln Steffens, a crusading beat reporter over a century ago, is a hero to Moyers. Steffens was famous for so-called muckraking stories in New York and other cities where graft, political corruption and rich business interests undercut public safety codes and citizens' rights. For most readers, schemes to fleece innocent people would usually fall into the category of "we'd like to know that." As Moyers tells it, however, Steffens found that robber barons and political bosses were not the only villains in the shadowy stories he uncovered. He also assigned blame to readers who sat back and accepted the corruption after they were aware of it. It was business as usual for them, rationalized with a sigh. What can we do? Steffens's tone toward public indifference was sharp and direct: "I am not a scientist. I am a journalist. I did not gather the facts and arrange them patiently for permanent preservation and laboratory analysis. . . . My purpose was . . . to see if the shameful facts, spread out in all their shame, would not burn through our civic shamelessness and set fire to American pride."[18] It was not enough that Steffens himself was engaged and committed, along with other journalists with his moral sense of public service. Citizens also needed to care and find ways to act.

Media ethicist Clifford Christians once said the goal of engaged, civic-minded journalism "is not readers and audiences provided with objective data, but persons who are politically and morally literate. News becomes an agent of community formation—not just informing the public but forming it instead."[19] Journalism can "form" a public, not by manipulating audiences or inducing them to think about social or political problems in a certain way. That would be propaganda disguised under a pseudonym. Rather, he was observing that news becomes civically useful when it enables a pluralized citizenry to form communities of common purpose across differences. Properly motivated, citizens in communities become less like consumers and more like problem solvers operating with resources and within a teamwork mentality. Journalists help, but citizens need to do the heavy lifting.

## The Reasonable Citizen

Citizens can offer reasons for why they believe what they do—truthful and evidence-based reasons that for them hold water. It is as simple as that, except for the complexities.

John Rawls's position on democracy is anchored by a clear statement about the place of reason within an ethic of civility and reciprocity:

> As reasonable and rational, and knowing that they affirm a diversity of reasonable religious and philosophical doctrines, [citizens] should *be ready to explain the basis of their actions to one another in terms each could reasonably expect that others might endorse as consistent with their freedom and equality.* Trying to meet this condition is one of the tasks that this ideal of democratic politics asks of us. Understanding how to conduct oneself as a democratic citizen includes an ideal of public reason.[20]

In Rawls's view, engaged citizens owe each other reasons as they interact about public decisions. Calling a person or their points of view "reasonable" is a meaningful compliment; reason-able citizens literally are *able* to explain why beliefs make sense to them. Reasons are neither opinions nor excuses. They do not simply parrot others' positions but articulate their own engaged positions in the context of issues and evidence.

**Marginalia**

Recall how we described the experience of Nobel Prize–winning poet Czeslaw Milosz in Poland. Most Americans are not fully aware of political tactics in repressive political regimes or how crucial it is for authoritarians to clamp down on everyday speech and the public exchange of reasons. Milosz knew firsthand about communist oppression; it started with repressing speech: "What is not expressed does not exist. Therefore if one forbids men to explore the depths of human nature, one destroys in them the urge to make such explorations; and the depths in themselves slowly become unreal." Reason is no longer public if citizens do not speak it.[21]

As we citizens speak our reasons, we justify what we believe in ways understandable to others. In the democratic context set by the Constitution's tone, citizen-based reasons usually reinforce broadly held attitudes of equality and freedom. Reasons set in motion an active dialogical commitment within a citizenship ethic, one that involves more than asserting an opinion. Reasoning involves a willingness to back up claims, your own as well as what others offer. In a democracy, citizens are also called to be political listeners: "Persons are reasonable," Rawls said, not only when articulating their own reasons but when they "are ready to discuss the fair terms that others propose."[22] Reasons are not personal sandwich board signs, advertising your own self-concept. When offering them, we are called to act publicly, as ourselves, but oriented beyond ourselves, too. Thoughtful citizens search for a truth wider than "That's what I believe." As reasons are communicated, their power becomes democratically mobile. Reasons can become light bulb moments for others' learning. Or they might fall flat, triggering listeners' rejection, and become moments for your own reconsideration.

The traditional way to describe reasoning is to distinguish between inductive and deductive approaches. *Induction* involves reasoning from specific instances to a more general conclusion about the observed group or phenomenon. ("I recently moved to Baltimore, but every time I try to start a conversation, people don't listen. This is an unfriendly city.") *Deduction* starts from a general premise or theory and proceeds by analyzing specific outcomes based on that theory. ("I've heard that Baltimore is unfriendly to new residents, so I'm testing that assumption by keeping a journal of my first meetings with everyone who lives in my apartment building. Later, I'll try to categorize what they say and do.") Obviously, the two processes can complement each other.

Literary critic Wayne Booth advises adding the term *coduction* to your vocabulary. Coduction depends on how well problem solvers coordinate experiences and conclusions with other observers, reinforcing conversational and dialogical approaches. Coduction is reasoning with other reasoners in mind, comparing one's judgments with another's, and steering away from the usual individualistic assumptions about reasoning or judging. It is not a way of justifying why you are "right"; it involves something like reasoning with other people's reasons—to supplement your own limitations. Conversation about contestable topics can produce conclusions that individuals would not have achieved on their own. Using attitudes like "What am I missing?" or "What does she value that I don't?," coduction gathers evidence, trusting creative intuition while sharing hypotheses and emerging interpretations with engaged partners. It is possible to study a given issue alone, but genuinely fresh ideas more often break through during interactions and comparisons—as organizational groups have learned with brainstorming. Taking each other into account, citizens can better reassess tentative conclusions, reflect on nuances after feedback, and advocate new conclusions when appropriate.

Real-life examples are easy to find. Reporters often cover complex social problems in teams and need editors for feedback. Scientists working in teams have won Nobel Prizes, and some writers prefer the stimulation and productivity of coauthorship and active editors to guide them. Interaction assists reasoning but cannot be, in Booth's term, "demonstrative." It does not prove, but it explains: coduction "will not persuade those who lack the experience required to perform a similar coduction. And it can never be performed with confidence by one person alone. The validity of our coductions must always be corrected in conversations about the coductions of others whom we trust."[23]

The U.S. Constitution brims with stated or implied reasons for democratic assumptions, developed through an intense process of evaluation—similar to Booth's coduction—by the Founders, which we describe in previous chapters. The reasoning begins with the very first lines of its preamble: "We the People of the United States, in order to form a more perfect Union, establish justice, insure domestic tranquility, provide for the common defense, promote the general welfare, and secure the blessings of liberty to ourselves and our posterity, do ordain and establish this Constitution for the United States of America." The reasons ("in order to") expressed what then was a theory—that "we the people" are collectively motivated and strong enough to establish a new and better union; that justice is a demonstrably vital political goal; that in a republic, divisiveness and polarization can be reduced by fair deliberation; that unified government can be defended for the common good; that general welfare (not just satisfactions of an elite class) can be achieved; and that liberty is a self-rewarding state of living.

In 1787, the country was an untested mixture of values, goals, and hope. Public discourse improves when citizens make their interests more *discussable*, with access to evidence that is empirical—directly experienced and reported—as opposed to hearsay, and a willingness to hear disagreement. Being accessible propels deliberation, as does the habit of depending on reasons. To say of a candidate, "I don't know—I just like her" or "I've lost confidence in him" might be true, but from the standpoint of those whose feelings differ, it can be a conversation stopper.

Reasonable citizens listen actively, with clarification as a primary goal. Here, we can learn from successful journalists who want to understand the intent and meaning of their interviewees. Rachel Maddow of cable TV's MSNBC draws insults from some critics. Nevertheless, she is an accomplished interviewer who models conscientious listening. After introducing her interviewees' views and background to viewers, she usually asks them if she got anything wrong or misrepresented them in any way. In the simple act of asking, she accomplishes several goals—she validates the person's presence, respects the guest's point of view, and encourages a level of trust that indicates she cares about accuracy and fairness. She is unafraid of being contradicted or corrected. Similarly, civic talk improves when everyday citizens informally check the quality of understanding in a conversation. Restate the reasons you heard from the speaker's perspective, not your own, to better ensure accuracy. "Did I hear that right? You distrust the jury system." Decide that you really want to prevent talking past each other. Double-check to see if the two of you are using a particular word differently or different words to mean roughly the same thing. Verbalize common ground or partial agreements that you sense are there, and see if your partner agrees. And if you are genuinely sincere about citizenship, avoid dismissiveness and put-down triggers when asserting your own reasoning to fellow citizens. As many community organizers have recommended, imagine that you and other citizens are teammates, even when you disagree. You both should be competing against your common rival—misunderstanding.

In the spirit of defeating misunderstanding, listening actively helps prepare citizens to investigate possibly uncomfortable issues, such as an unacknowledged "why?" that could be lurking in the background of disagreements. You might respond with a nonaggressive check back like, "I notice you often mention the unfairness of large numbers of immigrants and asylum seekers stealing jobs from neighbors and friends. I'm wondering if you could talk more about why this seems so important as a political issue." From the answer, you might learn that other speakers have read different statistical studies than you have or that you had not anticipated their personal experiences and deep immersion in a controversy. Workshops promoting effective communication typically remind people to "hold your fire" before accusing others of being narrow-minded, totally wrong, or misinformed. This alone can contribute to a positive tone and a better backdrop for the disagreement that may later seem necessary.

Democratic deliberation works when citizens stand for something *and* compare reasons for their positions. Those reasons, the Framers hoped, would be tentative and provisional steps toward a community of listeners, not final answers to unchanging questions.

### Quotables

"Because an open and inclusive public is itself an evolving political entity, the public voice is always provisional, subject to emendation, evolution, and even contradiction. The closure that comes with almost every exclamation on talk radio—a caller cut off, squelched, disconnected—is perhaps its most uncivil feature."[24]

—Benjamin Barber, *A Place for Us: How to Make Society Civil and Democracy Strong*

## The Inclusive Citizen

Benjamin Barber's idea of a democratic public being "open and inclusive" suggests a final model of citizenship—a shadow issue that has tested our country's values since its inception. Who belongs here, and who does not? Do all persons deserve the same rights and deserve them in equal measure?

Against the historical background of deeply entrenched racial tension and discrimination in major cities, especially her then home of Chicago, political scientist Danielle Allen sensed the opportunities sometimes overlooked by advocacy groups that distrust each other. How wide must the divisions become, and how long can we live with them, before citizens get serious about distrust, division, or willful ignorance? As one of the country's most accomplished interdisciplinary scholars, Allen brings impressive insight to such questions in one of her early books. She reminds us that the answers we fight about often depend on what kinds of questions we are willing to ask. Citizens can jump too readily toward defensiveness about answers without questioning the underlying values.

Inclusive citizenship takes strangers into account in their political calculations and in their goals. Inclusive citizens explain positions invitationally, in the light of objections, and without debating wins versus losses. This notion applies especially when historical imbalances of power and access to power award privileged groups great latitude to make and enforce political decisions at the expense of those who lack public voice and access to forums of dialogue and policy making. No wonder distrust so often disables dialogue, which is a vital antidote to distrust. Dialogue is no magic potion, especially when seats at the table are artificially restricted. According to Allen:

> [Democracy must] develop methods for making majority decisions that, despite their partiality, also somehow incorporate the reasonable interests of those who have voted against those decisions, for otherwise minorities would have no reason to remain members of a democratic polity.[25]

Is it a hallmark of democracy that outvoting and outspending someone else means you can get what you want without considering the lives of others? Or is it more like a stain?

Democracy thrives in moments when partisan infighting gives way to "the reasonable interests of others" who might vote differently. Allen, a classicist in addition to her work in political philosophy, draws on ancient Greek rhetoric for guidance.

Citizenship in a republic, Allen argues, is supported by Aristotle's concept that she interprets as *political friendship*, which differs from ordinary notions of getting along with others. By friendship, the old Greek teacher did not mean that good citizens must welcome everyone as intimate friends. (By contemporary standards, ancient Greece, despite its reputation as a birthplace of democratic thought, still welcomed slavery and many other inequalities.) Instead, Allen interpreted political friendship to mean that citizens engaged in politics ought to extend the same regard to opponents as they do to personal friends. In public rhetoric and its deliberations, each citizen values egalitarian listening and speaking, which in contemporary life we more commonly call respect. Disengagement or dismissiveness is not inevitable when people argue or even the necessary outcome of unequal distribution of wealth or social privilege. Aristotle recommended that citizens with different ideas and goals discuss politics with the attitude of "judging with." Stated colloquially, we are in this together. Some decisions inevitably create different winners than others. If more deliberations at times involved citizens willingly forsaking self-interest in favor of a wider provision of public goods, then the system overall emerges as more equitable.

Political friendship, therefore, tends toward the reciprocal and the inclusive. When addressed, citizens respond not with demands but with attitudes similar to friendship assumptions: "They needed help more than we did." "Yes, my time volunteering was a sacrifice, but it was my way to support neighborhood renewal." "The school referendum doesn't help my kids, who graduated years ago, but I'm all for supporting education anyway." "You're right—I didn't vote for her, but I sent her congratulations anyway." Under such a relational umbrella, friends can, as we often do, disagree strongly while living together cordially and even cooperatively.

## Quotables

"I . . . [am] eager for enlightenment, eager to learn new and better ways to manifest respect for the deep reverence for life that is our religion and our instinct. I hope that the public attempt to describe the problems as I understand them will give impetus to the dialogue in the Catholic community and beyond, a dialogue which could show me a better wisdom than I've been able to find so far."[26]

—Former New York governor Mario Cuomo, on his 1984 public position on legal abortion in a speech at the University of Notre Dame

Problems, however, can be glossed over by overly sugary and insincere appeals to the "common good," "rational dialogue," "impartiality," "collective sacrifice," "tolerance," or "empathic goodwill." Sometimes the moment seems to demand a salty, if civil, argument. It would be cruel irony if a phony feel-good dialogue overpromised social nirvana without examples of how inclusiveness works in a real-world clash of interests. Too much self-satisfied happy talk, even well-intentioned pity, also leaves marginalized groups in a frozen powerless status, unable to experience the supposedly equal treatment promised in the Constitution.

Part of this reasoning is based on instances in which women, for example, have pressed opinions about civic or organizational priorities but have not been taken seriously. Generic appeals to "equal access for all" or "treating everyone with compassion"—without specific institutional plans to invite specific role involvement by marginalized groups—can freeze out citizen voices the community most needs to heed. Inclusion needs active engagement that includes a variety of voices.

It also needs what Martha Nussbaum calls "compassionate citizenship," not achieved merely by platitudes but by an education in cultural difference. Only through understanding others' ways of knowing are we able to identify with their ideas, goals, or frustrations. Only then will citizens "cultivate the ability to imagine the experiences of others and to participate in their sufferings."[27] Dialogue does not work magic, but it can break through turmoil with moments of clarity about *us*, moments that transcend the *me*.

Cupertino, California, headquarters for Apple, provides an example of an inclusive approach that addressed the community's multicultural challenges. In the 1990s, the city experienced a shift from its former largely homogeneous culture to a multicultural blend when new residents, mostly from Asia, arrived with the technology boom. Local government officials faced new tensions of mistrust. When interviewed, both long-term residents and new arrivals cited ethnic and racial incidents, cultural misunderstandings, and widespread suspicions. About the only connection held in common by different groups was the realization that few residents knew how to talk about the problem.

Help came from a national group of professionals, academics, and citizens, the Public Dialogue Consortium (PDC), which offered its resources to the Cupertino community for a multiyear study of problem solving and public action. The group proposed more than a diagnosis of what was happening; it hoped to study in real time a coordinated plan for a community listening to itself. The plan would be generated through the involvement of citizens themselves. They would learn politics by participation, not by waiting for someone else to make their problems disappear. It was clear to the PDC that the old pattern of top-down governing (try something, wait a while, hear complaints, try something else, repeat) was not working. At the same time, residents and local politicians appeared to suspect that citizens are often passive and unlikely to be involved in problem-solving.

As the PDC's later case study showed, the goal was never to get everyone to buy into the same beliefs, solve everyone's problems, or encourage anyone to abandon strong cultural beliefs. The ultimate partnership, however, did demonstrate that citizen dialogue, working in concert with city administrators, trained facilitators, public school educators, high school students trained to do community interviews, and various civic leaders, can produce remarkable optimism about the future, along with significant agreement about the path forward. City manager Don Brown agreed to participate, but he had significant reservations at first. Local newspaper editors and reporters were also skeptical but covered the process. Brown's "light bulb" moment, he wrote later, "came when I realized that this project was not about changing people's minds, but . . . about giving people a way to talk about tough issues." In fact, he reported that his participation "has been among the most rewarding activities of my career. I am very proud of the Cupertino community. In many ways the city is becoming the model for a multi-cultural community."[28]

## Finding an Ethic in the Citizenship-Journalism Relationship

Our five contemporary models of citizenship point to an ethic for citizen participation in a republic. It rests on the public roles of citizens as informed by interpersonal communication research, the widespread public practices of journalists, and the demands of political decision-making. Think of an *ethic* generally as a set of principles to guide choices and judgments of right and wrong, but the philosophy of ethics and moral choice is a vast terrain, of course, and readily available elsewhere.

No ethical code can ever encompass, much less resolve, all dilemmas and choices of public interaction, but everyday citizens will find in journalism a pragmatic ally for negotiating gray areas. In 1923, the American Society of Newspaper Editors created the first code of ethics for journalists, followed by other journalism organizations and specializations including photojournalists, designers, and online and broadcast outlets. Professional journalism embraces codes of ethics, most largely relying on institutional self-enforcement. Self-enforcement does not necessarily imply loose standards, however. Reporters and editors might be tempted to cut corners, but over the years the unacceptable behavior of notorious corner cutters got them fired and professionally ostracized.[29]

Lapses by ethically challenged citizens usually do not cost them their jobs, but lessons for day-to-day citizenship can be found in how journalists attempt to enact ethical communication. Respect for factual accuracy certainly qualifies as a basic criterion for news reporting, but the demands of a democratic citizenry require a wider standard that some papers term "fairness." This contemporary sense of ethical fairness in journalism assumes factual honesty but also expects trickery-free stories without loaded language or hidden agendas, stories that lead without misleading, and stories that avoid conflicts of interest. Citizens might measure their concepts of fairness against those generally adhered to in journalism.

In his book *Committed Journalism*, Edmund Lambeth tagged "authentic interpretation" as a necessary element in news reports and the conduct of reporters and editors. For citizens in dialogue, interpretation is inevitable in providing context and perspective, as it is in news stories. Lambeth expects disclosure of relevant background information, evidence-gathering methods, and, of course, any personal involvement that might give the appearance of unfair bias. Authenticity, in Lambeth's sense, is needed as a truth-based check on interpretation. For example, Joe McGinniss, reporting on the 1968 Nixon presidential campaign and for his book *Fatal Vision*, and Michael Wolff, assessing Donald Trump's administration decades after McGinniss's work, evidently got access to interviewees and information by implying sympathetic motives or potentially misrepresenting their presence and intentions. Citizens debating public policies also have the reasonable expectation—especially in public forums—to assume, as with news professionals, that motives, reasons, evidence, and sources are honestly presented.[30]

Definitions of ethics are all over the place, but ethics often boils down to a particularly important distinction. Pragmatic thinkers will often focus on questions like "What works?" and "Why does it work?" Ethical inquiry, though, expands that focus to account for something beyond straightforward estimates of what works and why it works. An interpersonal ethic probes a "whether question" of right and wrong—that is, *whether* an action should be chosen, even if it might "work" or be "successful" (to persuade an audience, for example).[31] A guiding ethic is important if citizens hope to confront a public sphere that seems to encourage political deception and slanted decision-making. Looking through the lens of journalistic interpretation provides some clarity.

Journalists are citizens who take on extra professional responsibility for the health of public discourse. In doing so, they assume ethical responsibilities few expect from typical political leaders (or, for that matter, from typical citizens). One of the most vital responsibilities is a commitment to listening carefully for truth. As a foundational skill for preparing news reports, as journalists stay especially alert to racial, age, gender, economic, and ethnic differences that might influence them, listening is an ethic of respect. Effective listening is a positive regulator of speech; people do not normally communicate openly to others who seem uncaring. Listening helps anyone to keep the conversation going but is actually a prerequisite for journalists, who must prepare to ask questions, too. Recognizing the importance of listening, the American Press Institute recently began a program called Community Listening Fellowships, complete with mentorship resources, for journalists serving such communities as "Latino students and families in rural Idaho, a historically African American neighborhood in a large metropolitan area, Native American communities across a large rural state, and people experiencing homelessness in the nation's capital."[32] They know what John Dewey knew—"vision is a spectator; hearing is a participation."[33]

Effective listening is at the core of a healthy public ethic, a responsibility too easily forgotten. When elected officials notice large groups not paying attention or, worse, actually ignoring the need to listen to opponents or to new ideas, they are tempted to consolidate power, assuming no one cares enough to notice. Americans, bequeathed the world's most successful democracy, have too much to lose to invite complacency now. Assertive listening by citizens, and with journalism's public support, keeps our own government on its toes. It makes sure our government remains *ours*.

## Toxic Political Action: Diminishing Both Journalism and Citizenship

Journalists invite misunderstandings if they believe they can write completely factual accounts without discussing context or interpretation. "Communication is not merely a transmission-reception phenomenon," we wrote in *The Conversation of Journalism*, "but a complex interweaving of mutual influences, many of which are never formally or consciously acknowledged."[34] We support the overall journalistic mission, but we also encourage reporters and editors to listen even more deeply for mutual influences and notice how they might affect news reports.

An overly self-confident reporter, for example, might be tempted to report that a local mayor is nervous and will not talk about preparing to run for statewide office. Nervousness and reluctance could sound like *facts* or character traits in a candidate profile. But these are dangerous assumptions. It could as easily be true that she was not just "nervous"; she was nervous *with her interviewer*. Maybe she clammed up because she did not trust *the reporter* to listen carefully to details of her important decision. Or maybe it simply was a matter of timing; she is willing to talk and would do so with confidence—but just not today. Assumptions and superficial observations can cross up the most conscientious of listeners, a reminder that applies to us all.

Humans will never arrive at the one definitive and completely true conclusion about another person, much less know themselves completely. A different reporter—or a citizen—might have found the mayor talkative about her campaign decisions. Or the same interviewer posing questions differently could have made the difference. Facts reside within authentic interpretations, and interpretations are embedded in the stories of conversational partners, if allowed to emerge by patient listening.

While trust is important between news professionals and their audiences, it is rarely ironclad. Only a careless or gullible citizen places full trust in a particular story, a lone journalist, or a single news source for a bank-worthy account of news. Moreover, only gullible citizens place full trust in a politician's assertions when presented with no evidence or reasoning. Requiring evidence implies a further ethic of breadth, the responsibility to continue widespread surveillance of options. Even with a universe of information available online ("I'll Google it when I need it"), strong citizenship means doing basic research at least into the *patterns* of reporting across platforms—online, cable, print, left, right, popular, scholarly. Citizens who care about their roles in a republic must be suspicious of stories with hazy details that seem to pop up only in isolated sites, shows, or pronouncements—or on platforms like YouTube or Facebook, which "publish" virtually anything submitted to them. Apply the microscope of reasonableness scrupulously to sources openly flaunting ideological loyalties while making personal attacks. Some news outlets appear to ignore or downplay events that are pounced upon by others—be prepared also to *evaluate* these patterns, not just to be wary of them, identifying gaps in their accounts of events. Notice which sources are more likely to print or broadcast corrections and those willing to report successes of public figures they have criticized previously. It might be an interesting project for citizens to review published ethical standards of their favorite news sources compared with sources they mistrust. Finally, some news organizations openly appeal to readers or viewers by promoting polarization or even hate in the electorate; they exist for the polarization, not the news. Others more carefully reflect the ethic of breadth that characterizes much American traditional journalism.

Of course, experienced researchers can examine how audiences use media for political purposes. After the 2016 presidential election, for example, Harvard University and Massachusetts Institute of Technology scholars discovered that voters tended to fall into two relatively distinct audiences and that their tendency to polarize was "asymmetric." Voters favoring one candidate used a far wider spectrum of media and "were highly attentive to traditional media outlets . . . prominent across the public sphere." These voters chose more diversified news sources and perspectives. Audiences favoring the other candidate instead "paid the majority of attention to polarized outlets," creating for themselves an "internally coherent, relatively insulated knowledge community." They preferred a uniform voice that shielded them from journalism that might challenge the conformity of that community.[35] Citizens who read and listen to news comparatively, even if informally, can discover journalism's broad range of political interpretation. Those who choose to ignore that diversity lean toward polarization and thus away from fully informed judgment.

This study exposed a trend reinforced by a newly toxic political attack that argues mainstream journalism shuns the goal of authentic communication. The goal, as we outline in chapter 6, is to erode the trust that citizens have for even the potential for truthful journalism. It encourages millions of Americans to brand traditional news reporting as *inherently* corrupt and "rigged" to produce predetermined outcomes variously called evil, socialist, or Communist. The attack appears to come from an evidence-free zone that assumes citizens' basic choice for political news is binary: stay loyal to self-identified conservative media or sell out to the alternative, monolithic liberal media distortion. For reasons we discuss earlier, advocates for this claim have skin in the game—theirs is an ironically self-serving strategy: tune into only *our* version of news—that threatens the ethical ground of news reporting. It undermines the responsibilities of citizenship by denigrating their wellspring, openness to reliable, and diversified information.

A coherent citizenship ethic ought to motivate America's elected politicians, as well. They are citizens, too. As Martha Nussbaum urges, "We should demand political leaders who display the abilities involved in compassion," leaders who "take on in imagination the lives of the various diverse groups whom they propose to lead."[36] And compassion is not a possession held only by Democrats or Republicans. Citizenship, journalism, and political leadership form an interdependent democratic ecology of trust for improving public life. Trust, however, has been badly fractured, and citizens need to face up to why we have watched this happen in a nation founded on aggressive, participative citizenship. Several case studies, unfortunately, illustrate careless responses to violations of public trust.

## Lies and Trust

The highest office in America, and historically the one most trusted by citizens, is oval. The presidency has been treated as a basic symbol of trust even when embroiled in controversy and scandal. Even when he (always "he," so far) makes dubious decisions, the majority of citizens and elected officials customarily assume the president has the best interests of the country in mind and at least tries to represent unity, rational decision-making, and integrity. Maybe, they reason, he knows what we do not. Even disgruntled members of an opposition party over the years have responded to a president somewhat deferentially—as a symbol of trust in government, yes, but also in the spirit of res publica, a shared sense of civic togetherness, even while our conflicts are obvious.

Citizens, we like to think, trust government leaders because that is the presumption of republican governing, what distinguishes us from other countries, and because from the beginning the nation has trusted citizens to take care in choosing trustworthy leaders. Assuming meek submission to, or blind trust in, leaders' power or charisma is not in the same civic ballpark. In accepting our own responsibilities, citizens reasonably expect elected leaders to do the same, to assist and enhance our roles. Citizens like to assume, for example, that a basic goal for an elected government is to provide information to help citizens make political decisions. In fact, citizens have been assured that in matters of public concern, communicating accurate information is *required* of public officials.

To that end, the federal government has codified guidelines mandating its offices to disseminate only truthful and accurate information. The Information Quality Act of 2001 required that the Office of Management and Budget "issue *government-wide* guidelines that 'provide policy and procedural guidance to Federal agencies for *ensuring and maximizing the quality, objectivity, utility, and integrity of information.*'" The guidelines might sound like Washington bureaucratese. But they are consistent with the law's intended application: it should ensure that government information compiled "to share with, or give access to, the public" will be trustworthy. In other words, it serves us. In its plain language, the government is promising that every time you click on a government website, you will find objective, useful, and truthful information delivered from "a wide variety of government . . . activities that may range in importance and scope." If you want to know about the current status of climate change research funded by tax dollars over the past twenty-five years, you *should* be able to trust facts and figures there. The guidelines are explicit and "generic enough to fit all media, be they printed, electronic, or in other form." Disinformation supplied by the government to influence the public, therefore, would be prohibited even if in a tweet or even if it takes the shape of withholding strong counterevidence. The government promises each citizen "accurate, clear, complete, unbiased" information that is "not compromised through corruption or falsification." It should be shocking when political leaders decide to break such a trust for partisan reasons. It is more shocking still when they seem to get away with it.[37]

## Marginalia

"The disappearance of information about climate change from government websites is not the only evidence of the administration's effort to remove references to it. Anonymous civil servants at the United States Geological Survey claim that officials have prevented them from using the term climate change in press releases while press reports emerged in June that White House officials tried unsuccessfully to persuade NASA administrator Jim Bridenstone—a former climate change skeptic—to 'systematically sidestep' evidence for climate change coming from NASA programmes."[38]

—Peter Gwynne, "U.S. Government Websites Cull References to Climate Change"

Citizens deserve leaders who understand freedom of speech and the press and who work to protect the nation against calculated attempts to divide us into factions based on lies and deception. For their part, citizens should understand these same processes to avoid being duped or misled. No presidential election should devolve into a four-year campaign rally mobilizing disinformation to whip up supporters against opponents. These are minimum expectations, not pie-in-the-sky wishes. They are not conservative versus liberal expectations. National leaders represent the entire country, not just the portion that voted for them. A president represents, and is responsible for information provided to, all citizens on behalf of the federal government.

Public indifference to government lies and distortions eventually will create an unworkable impersonation of citizenship. The problem does not merely result from a single leader's name, party, brand, or celebrity. It is not about tarring and feathering one evildoer in a symbolic gesture to set politics right again. It is about what happens to public life when large numbers of citizens lose faith in realistic public consideration of what is and is not true. If the offending administration loses an election, its strategy of succeeding through falsehood and fabrication could easily tempt administrations to follow. Once a broken pattern is in place, many citizens might adjust to the result, without realizing that they themselves might be diminished in the future by those shattered norms of truth. Citizens, however, need not rely on the liar for truthfulness. They can go elsewhere.

After the 2016 election, boosters and aides excused a president's dishonest rhetoric, saying it merely reflected a real estate developer's strategic hyperbole as he inflated his accomplishments, boosted his ego, or courted cooperative friends here and abroad. We should give him a chance, they said; "liar" is such a rude-sounding accusation. We need his kind of strong leadership, they implored. Even some journalists complied for a time. But now we have moved beyond excuses and into repetitions, with falsehoods so blatant and habitual that, as Bob Woodward learned from insider interviews for his book *Fear*, the president's own lawyers evidently counseled him to avoid testifying under oath because they considered him incapable of avoiding perjury.[39] Later, the lies became business as usual throughout the administration. The president's insistence on loyalty took hold, and followers willfully reinforced a strategy of manipulating or contradicting the truth.

History warns us not to expect saintly forthrightness from national election campaigners adept at political spin. But strategic and thorough disregard for truth, combined with attacks on journalistic reporting practices, blows normal spin out of the water. It resembles normal spin only like debris resembles residential neighborhoods before a category 4 hurricane sweeps through. Mere spin is a framing process, familiar to most public advocates; it starts with a nugget of truth that is then interpreted in a direction convenient for the teller. The recent administration's strategy of exploitation starts with no such nuggets. Journalism's scrupulous fact-checkers have reported and corrected thousands of lies and obviously misleading statements warping history, science, public documents, health, conspiracy theories, personal qualifications, opponents' accomplishments, and other easily verifiable facts. Some fresh lies even provide air cover for previous ones or normalize public expectation of lying itself. The cumulative impact is an expectation that a hurricane of dishonesty has fundamentally damaged public discourse. Even political strategists who stress ethical communication have begun to wonder if perhaps they should reconsider playing playground softball when the other team's game is hardball.

The most dangerous effect of governing by political lying is not to fool the public on an important issue here or there. It is to numb listeners to the experience of being lied to. It destabilizes the intertwined social concepts of truth, knowledge, and thoughtful expectation. These ethical matters are no longer payday goals for the political liar, nor are they politically or socially useful to liars in governing or to their supportive audiences in decision-making. What is most useful to the liar is something far less tangible: conditioning citizens not to care, not to pay attention, and not to listen carefully enough to hold liars accountable. The dissembler seeks permission, a perpetual hall pass. Dedicated political liars make it impossible to be "caught" in a lie. They do not mind if listeners know something is untrue if they profit from it themselves, if they are willing to live with it or be entertained by it, or if they barter gullibility for a comfortable political La-Z-Boy lifestyle. Consumers who order a product online after reading rosy promises about its quality, but when they receive it discover something flimsy, unusable, and borderline worthless, have entered the domain of the shameless public liar. Marketing *promises* becomes the *product* and acceptable in a world where truth is up for grabs. The public liar learns that many consumers—and which ones—are less likely to complain or return the item than to shrug and chalk it up to the way things are in the real world.

Fact-checking may seem futile at times if it fails to scold or punish a perpetrator directly; "Oh, that's interesting. The administration is now saying the committee chair wrote the whistleblower's complaint for him." The lasting value of the fact-check, though, is to supplement and correct the historical record, subsequently inviting more thorough analysis. Skillful journalists apply criteria that citizens might recognize from daily living, such as comparing a moving company's ads with its Better Business Bureau complaints or noticing when a local school board president campaigned on an important pledge but ignored it after the election. Fact-checkers guard against imposing their own beliefs when evaluating claims but systematically compare public statements to verifiable events, historical context, setting, previous statements, and possible ambiguities.[40] They actively consider whether there are ways to confirm asserted facts, but they cannot be reticent about pointing out factual discrepancies or, for that matter, a context that *supports* the speaker's claim. The *Washington Post*, for one, has so much faith in its methodology that it opens its data files to academic researchers who study its methods and conclusions.

Deceptions might be justifiable in some extraordinary situations or interactions. When a doctor counsels loved ones about end-of-life decisions for a family member, she uses language that can seem both gentler and less explicit than the precision and blunt truth required when a suspect answers a police officer's question about her whereabouts yesterday evening. Although the American public develops a certain tolerance for truth-stretching in politics ("If they are white lies, how bad can they be?" "Everybody does it, right?"), an elected leader who lies continually to gain an obvious advantage *for himself* while pointing to falsehoods to support the lies, while simultaneously impeding democratic participation, is gaming the system of trust. That narrative is not the politician's alone but a story of muted citizens, some of whom sacrifice voice willingly. The liar whose primary faith is in his own ego focuses on believers only as he objectifies them and presumes their support. The liar could not care less about being everyone's president, and those not in the club, including mainstream journalists, just get in the way. Under such pressures, all citizens may doubt whether everyday political conversations and deliberations will make a difference, and the doubt can seem weirdly rational. People are tempted to give up—perhaps on the system or perhaps on the possibility of talking across differences with political opponents.

The role model for many citizens' attitude of "so what?" becomes the liar's own attitude, emboldened. He need not rebut factual corrections. Who cares if NPR is upset? "I can do what I want," and when a problem arises, trust me for my solution—"Only I can fix it." The government, to the liar, is his, not ours; he is convinced even the country's Department of Justice should represent his personal interests and pet projects. The lie therefore reappears at the next rally or press conference or court appeal. And the next. Historians understand how simple repetition has fueled "The Big Lie" strategy in totalitarian states. The German Third Reich's minister of propaganda, Joseph Goebbels, believed that the lie had to be so big that citizens could assume no one would be able to get away with inventing it, and it had to be repeated nearly ceaselessly without apology. In response to objections, the public is told equally persistently that the objections themselves are lies. Any question or dissent therefore can be dismissed by attacking dissent itself as treason or a failure to love one's country, and much of the public will grant implicitly either permission or a collective "so what?"

Even a liar's political supporters may unwittingly help to create an intimidating obstacle to an ethic of citizenship, by acting as if sacrificing or ignoring truth is not a real crisis. Lies, after all, do not directly silence opposing voices. Citizens remain free to protest, debate, and speak out. But while lies do not directly silence objectors or stifle inquiries in progress, they mask conditions that could otherwise stimulate valid protest. (If citizens realized that a government was withholding results of taxpayer-funded scientific studies of a promising cancer treatment, would we have an opinion about that?) Lies dishonestly suffocate the believability of protests or well-supported alternatives. Lies weaponize political talk through saturation attacks on an enemy's political positions and its channels of communication. The liar's advantages are obvious. Why talk things out when the "truth" is already known?

## Complicity and "Serious Reflection"

Beyond an "ain't it awful?" response to public lying, citizens with democratic (small *d*) morality should consider how they are validating a public culture of the lie by capitulating to it. Step 1 depends on questioning lying's pragmatic counterpart, truth. Of course, commitment to "truth" also can be a slippery ideal. But despite reasonable philosophical arguments about what constitutes truth in everyday life, you will not win an argument about a bank overdraft by asking, "What is truth, anyway?" The arithmetic wins. Neither can you fully diagnose a particular political liar just by labeling her or him immoral, evil, moronic, narcissistic, or unhinged. Dietrich Bonhoeffer asked what people meant by "telling the truth" and concluded that truth telling "is not solely a matter of moral character; it is also a matter of correct appreciation of real situations and of serious reflection upon them."[41] The difference is crucial. We do not diagnose failings simply by finding a culprit to blame.

Political leaders who refuse to reflect on what Bonhoeffer calls *real situations* betray citizens and build lofty proposals on a foundation of stubbornly selfish promises. If citizens let them, their undemocratic behavior redefines the playing field for determining what and who government serves, who it is for. The liar does not just "tell lies" but empties knowledge of its impact. Evaluating government's relation to its citizens must invoke a standard of *serious reflection*. Without taking real events seriously, a leader is drawn to the call and comfort of make-believe. Without seriousness, citizen reactions are superfluous. Lying becomes too easy, manipulation too manageable, accountability too thin, careful research too inefficient, and wrestling with difficult dilemmas too taxing for democratic decision-makers.

Stretching the truth does not seem flat-out immoral to most people, nor is truth telling automatically saintly. But the picture is bigger than everyday behavior. Bonhoeffer's notion confirms the practical value of political reflection when grounded in taking reality into serious account—

rather than accepting as normal a leader neglecting, bragging, deflating, rebranding, reloading, deflecting, dividing, and performing. Choosing dissembling over reflecting purposely degrades a public's sense of practical consequences while substituting something else entirely.

Hannah Arendt explains the "something else." When studying the roots of totalitarian regimes, she found that "consistent lying . . . pulls the ground from under our feet and provides no other ground on which to stand."[42] The precise words of a lie matter less than what cumulative lying from powerful positions crowds out of citizen conversations. Lies displace or subvert listeners' impulses toward participation and dialogue. Citizens quit talking about issues, which become inert, as if they are someone else's problem. Simply mentioning an issue becomes a flashpoint of undiscussable and angry conflict. "When we visit Uncle James, don't mention immigration or whatever happened to the border wall." Researching or explaining evidence risks becoming a futile exercise. Late in 2020, a common refrain of many conversations was not an issue but a plea: "Please let it stop." The normal "ground under our feet," so important for reflection on news, had vanished for many citizens, with no new ground in sight.

Lies from a White House that command a microphone or access to an influential cable channel displace a fuller consideration of complex social challenges. Even savvy voters can become spectators waiting to see if the coronavirus will indeed "go away" when summer arrives, or if the next tariff whim will work, or whether Mexico will pay for a border wall after all, or whether a president genuinely intends to do something about infrastructure during "Infrastructure Week," or whether a North Korean dictator is a friend instead of a foe. Leaders addicted to lies, especially those who consider themselves "chosen ones" or "stable geniuses," risk exploitation from opponents nervy enough to run scams on them. Liars in power cannot develop a working concept of genuine interpersonal or international trust, seemingly because trust requires a sensitivity to others' lives and meanings that liars lack. They are too busy listening for flattery, which other world leaders figure out rapidly. Lying, once it is exposed as nonserious reflection, becomes a national security issue.

A truer sense of honest communication comes from Martin Buber's philosophy of "imagining the real" that motivates other persons—by caring how *they* experience the world as we speak with them.[43] Buber's use of "real" is similar to Bonhoeffer's standard for truth telling—a serious reflection about actual situations. Buber's "imagining the real" describes relationships in which understanding others' meanings will not depend on your own projections of what you wish they would believe or what you want them to admit. But for ego-involved leaders who fancy themselves "strongmen," each negotiation, each interaction, is stirred into a soup of self-congratulation and a need for compliments that are themselves likely false. The liar revels in the capitulation of others, an achievement that must feel to him like strength. Actual deception is secondary to acquiescence. Common ground, national unity, the power of ordinary people, and social justice rarely surface in such a politics. The ground, as Arendt notes, is no longer under citizens' feet. The liar has won when we stop expecting politics to align with real situations—even if he loses the next election. A liar nudges listeners away from their own reflection, hogging the space for himself. Poet Adrienne Rich offered a similar point when she observed that lies are statements designed to make life easier—usually for the liar.[44]

In an authoritarian setting, the living lie is a style of feigning certainty, even when occasionally denying what had been said previously. Sometimes, however, even the liar loses track of his own lies, and aides delay acting upon his demands while hoping that he forgets again what he told them just last week. When a president succeeds with sustained lying, however, Arendt's disturbing prediction has come true; we citizens lose our bearings, and, with diminished journalism a less effective monitor, the civic ground promised by a republic has shifted. We settle for diminished freedom. It seems easier that way. Forget that nagging business of citizen responsibility for truthful politics.

### Quotables

"To a German grocer, not unwilling to explain things to an American visitor, I spoke of our feeling that something invaluable had been given up when freedom was surrendered. He replied: 'But you don't understand at all. Before this we had to worry about elections, and parties, and voting. We had responsibilities. But now we don't have any of that. Now we are free.'"[45]

—Stephen Raushenbush, an American writing from Germany in the 1930s

Blaming a liar's unethical behavior on a simple character flaw misses an important point. Political lying cannot succeed in the long run only as an individual quirk or moral failure. From the standpoint of communication research, lying and being lied to is a complex relational transaction in which an audience is more or less complicit. Actually, all conversations presume that listeners must offer some form of willing cooperation to achieve quality communication. A tacit agreement ties sincere communicators together. The intertwined acts of speaking and listening, along with writing and reading, are interdependent activities in which we need others to hear us but also to agree to develop meanings with us. What are the implications of the speaking-listening transaction, though, for the widespread acceptance of political lying within a supposedly democratic system?

Theorists of democracy praise free speech, but we must always return to the acts of listening. Without an expectation of serious reflective listening, speaking in public becomes a futile and empty gesture. Genuine communicative freedom requires more than merely *telling*. It requires *talking with* by being both heard and responded to, extended and changed, as were the readers of the 1776 Declaration of Independence. Americans invest social capital in such a transaction. When "conversation" is used as a metaphor for social change, it implies ongoing shared goals: keeping the conversation going, for example, along with clearing trusted spaces for future talk and the willingness to negotiate "conversational repairs" after misunderstandings.

Listeners are never passive receptacles; their sense making helps determine meaning and what works. Each successful speaker, therefore, has to adapt to others' listening styles, or they will be misunderstood and frustrated consistently. People who say whatever pops into their minds regardless of audience seem interesting in films but make poor conversation partners or committee members. They might encourage as much social disruption as socializing, despite occasionally being congratulated as free spirits. Celebrity free spirits (including some politicians) are probably not as whimsical as they appear, either. They too depend on calculating types of listeners or their fame vanishes. Listeners possess social power because their responses invite some kinds of talk and discourage others.

So it is also with many politicians, who read constituent cues to discover what audiences are willing to, wish to, or need to hear. Liars among them lick their chops when they see how readily listeners carelessly trust obviously dishonest public messages. Voters could reason that if politicians are on their side, then those candidates need to win. To some extent, most campaign speeches boil down to "*They* are against *us*." Within a committed base, who will renounce the liar when the lie advances beloved agendas?

Two often overlooked tendencies among listeners can help citizens answer such a question—*credulity* and *complicity*. Credulity describes the tendency of some listeners to believe that what they are told is true or real, even if supported by scant evidence—or none. Such a bias toward agreement with a speaker is troubling in public life but might be attributable to innocent conditions—such as naivete, inexperience, unfamiliarity, a need for social acceptance, or deference to an admired person. Credulous listeners can be exploited readily by grifters, lenders, and other powerful people ready to take advantage of them.

Complicity amounts to enabling or allowing another's problematic actions, seemingly reinforcing or contributing to them. It usually involves some awareness from listeners. Complicit support allows a problem to develop or even flourish, even though the complicit person might not have initiated the action. Systematic lying, an ongoing concern of serious journalists covering government, depends on generous helpings of listener cooperation. *Speakers most often lie when they have reason to believe the lie will work as intended* or at least be thought inconsequential. Any serious reflection on public lying must analyze the pragmatics of active audience receptivity. Public liars usually succeed when they tap into cultivated listener biases or expectations: "White men are the real victims in America," "Immigrants are invading our country," or "Climate change is a liberal hoax." True believers who are lied to might welcome insincere compliments and convince themselves that their plight is meaningful to someone important. They belong to something important, larger than themselves. Those lied to likely will be less motivated to seek information on relevant or complex subjects. They see no reason for fact-checking a particular claim. They excuse or even adopt the liar's reasoning: "He's different from regular politicians—he says what he means" and "I don't know why he would . . . lie to me." Listeners might even empower liars unwittingly when they rely exclusively on information vendors that help them convert current events into partisan complaints amplified by, for example, Fox News, Gateway Pundit, Breitbart, Newsmax, Infowars, or, in a different ideological frame, the Daily Kos or Media Matters websites.

Citizens' reliance on certain news providers does not mean that a political liar's supporters are stupid or ignorant or that their critics inherently possess shining insight. It means that all of us are human when welcoming and trusting confirmations of our own thought.

Our contemporary crisis of democratic trust, however, is fundamentally different. Heavyweight political liars demand unreflective audience response, with near immunity to opposing points of view. These rhetorical choices weaken the country's founding traditions of citizen participation. Political leaders with no interest in real or truthful reflection and the listeners they lie to play on the same team or they do not play. If those who are lied to grow cynical, they may leave the team but silence themselves through a benign form of complicity. Remember that Lincoln Steffens, the muckraker who exposed municipal corruption, thought his own readers contributed to the problems he investigated. They were not criminals, but through their tacit acceptance they allowed the corruption to flourish: "Of course big-city life is corrupt," "All politics is lying," and "What am I supposed to do about it?" The complicity of cynicism, certainty, and civic laziness remains a welcome mat for municipal dishonesty.

The rhetorical structure of the First Amendment blends interdependent clauses asserting the rights of religious choice, of speech, of the press, of assembly, and to petition government. Each of these rights rests on the *public* ability to hold powerful leaders accountable. Thorough, responsive news media are more than conduits for bare facts. At its best, journalism becomes democracy's go-to way of reinforcing the "real situations" and "serious reflection" that Bonhoeffer identified with truth telling. Journalism grounds situations in historical and social context. It facilitates the informed conversations through which citizens affirm civic identities, whatever their party affiliations. As Erin Carroll writes in the *Georgetown Law Technology Review*, "How we talk about the press" can affect whether we preserve the norms of democracy. Democracy prospers when norms of a free press "draw sustenance from the positive language of the courts, other institutions, and the public about how the press serves the democratic functions of truthful educator, trusted proxy, and fair watchdog." As more citizens begin to internalize and accept narratives without reflecting on their accuracy or shaky context, she implies, we face severe problems of credulity and complicity: "When labels or narratives are decontextualized and amplified, we begin to internalize and adopt them, sometimes regardless of their accuracy. . . . As a label, fake news is arguably becoming so entrenched and normalized that it might ease the way for other terms that rhetorically marry the press to falsity, bias, and laziness . . . to slip into our everyday discourse."[46] A citizenship ethic includes a responsibility to protect a free press that respects the truth; if we ignore it, we are complicit.

## How Systematic Attacks on Journalism Damage Citizenship

Not long ago, it felt disorienting to even mention a widespread acceptance of presidential lying within the world's most powerful democracy. The allegedly biased American press would shy away from the word "lie," substituting such euphemisms as "dubious claim." More commonly, we heard about lies and deceit spread by established authoritarian regimes or perhaps emanating in newly minted states without secure traditions of citizen rights. Political lying in America today is happening in plain sight, backed by millions of citizens, and often to delirious cheering of "Lock her (or him) up!" or similar chants. To borrow a line from an old horror film, *When a Stranger Calls*, this call is from inside the house. No need to scream in distress? When U.S. citizens suspect governmental lying, they at least can count on authentic general news institutions of the world that include, as we note frequently, the *New York Times* or the *Washington Post*. Although readers might disagree with overall content in these sources, and despite occasional but inevitable errors, in contrast with what passes for news across the planet, the *Times* and the *Post* enforce tight professional criteria for factuality and fairness. Americans who mistrust even these media, while feeling insulated from reality-bending third world authoritarians, might want to reassess.

Washington journalists recognized long ago that presidents set the tone for other officials to imitate. A particularly instructive case study in the distinction between assertion and actuality began with Mary Louise Kelly of National Public Radio and her 2020 interview with the sitting secretary of state, Mike Pompeo. After the interview, Pompeo accused Kelly of lying to him and "violating basic rules of journalism and decency." Pompeo complained that she had agreed not to question him about the White House firing of the U.S. ambassador to Ukraine and accused her of breaking her word. The president, Pompeo's boss, weighed in with a threatening tweet suggesting that NPR might not deserve government funding, because it is a "big-government, Democrat party propaganda operation." In other words, NPR is not one of "us" and better mend its ways—or else.[47]

Pompeo's press release, issued by the State Department, relied on a familiar frame of media bias accusers: the powerful man is the victim. He asserted that his experience revealed an "unhinged" media. "No wonder that the American people distrust many in the media when they so consistently demonstrate their agenda and their absence of integrity," the statement read.[48] It offered no evidence and of course did not mention that Pompeo shouted and swore at Kelly privately after the interview, according to the reporter. NPR said it stood behind Kelly, an experienced and highly respected national correspondent.

Fortunately for Kelly and NPR listeners, facts still matter in skirmishes like this—thanks to journalists' habit of keeping notes and records. NPR defended its reporter for the right reasons; her saved email record proved Kelly had clearly informed Pompeo's staff that he could expect questions on the Ukraine situation. The intimidation strategy did not work on Kelly or her employer. However, because of the carefully coordinated false attack against the messenger, it probably reinforced stereotypes held by millions of listeners that National Public Radio is a left-wing propaganda machine willing to lie about the administration. The president did not follow through on his implied threat to NPR, nor did the secretary of state initiate legal action. To our knowledge, Pompeo never apologized for the false accusations. Most citizens are unaware of the sneak attack on an honest reporter.

In May 2020, the Committee to Protect Journalists (CPJ) issued a report on the administration's attacks on news media, accompanied by an open letter to President Trump decrying the attacks. Both the report and the letter referred to the dangers that false accusations create for press freedom around the world and asked the president and his administration to cease their threats against journalists. CPJ listed ten areas of special concern: (1) using the "fake news" epithet and lies to discredit and vilify reporters in the absence of evidence, (2) trying to restrict reporters' access to the White House for punitive reasons, (3) eliminating relevant information of interest to citizens from government websites, (4) having Customs and Border Protection officials search reporters' electronic devices at the southern border, (5) threatening owners of media corporations with legal regulatory actions, (5) ending daily press briefings, (6) filing lawsuits against media corporations for defamation based on opinion pieces, (7) making less information available to the press about officials' travel schedules and White House visitors, (8) threatening the broadcast licenses of television and radio networks, (9) selectively withholding Freedom of Information Act requests filed by certain journalists and news organizations not in favor with the administration, and (10) having federal agents question journalists about beats, political opinions, or contacts, among other requests.[49]

If listeners allow it, a rhetoric of deception and dismissiveness delegitimizes journalism's basic principles while planting deep suspicions of democratic values even among citizens who consider themselves patriots. If it is true that genuine attempts to speak across differences support mutual reflection and the ability to deliberate on difficult public issues, to what extent does an emerging culture of lies reinforce division and civic decay? The traditions of American pragmatism, deliberative democracy, practical innovations in journalism, and dialogue studies help provide answers.

In the American pragmatic tradition of philosophy, established by John Dewey and others, individual decision-making cannot be divorced from interconnected social influences, and ultimately the *meaning of any idea is best understood through the effects it initiates*. The meaning of pervasive lying from national leaders can be documented by the actual effects that are produced in the relations of "we the people," broadly defined.[50]

The evidence of democratic damage is clear. A 2018 Marist/PBS poll found that nearly 80 percent of Americans believed that civility declined after the 2016 election, adding to an increased threat of violence. Another 2018 study reported in the *Scientific American* suggested that the president's tweets about Islam "may be directly related to an increase in anti-Muslim hate crimes over the past few years," although evidence is based more on correlation than on causation. Still, according to the author, there is a "strong case" that the president's tweets encourage anti-Muslim crimes.[51]

After President Trump's "fine people on both sides" comments about the Charlottesville riots in 2017, prominent white supremacist leaders cited him as inspirational. Asked by the moderator of the first presidential debate in October 2020 to condemn white supremacists, he could muster only this enigmatic message for the Proud Boys hate group: "Stand back and stand by," which the members evidently took as an affirmation of his support and a heads-up that they may be needed to mobilize. Millions of families over the past several years have experienced friends or relatives who, in a climate of intense polarization, now refuse to talk about political values. Around Thanksgiving, television shows and websites offer tips about orchestrating a turkey dinner without a helping of rancor. (Helpful hints include strategically seating guests to bypass hot spots of tension or changing the subject to college football, family recipes, or how you might switch dentists this year.) Given this level of discomfort, people taking sides could feel justified in skipping small talk about politics when a slice of pecan pie awaits. "What good could it do? I'm not changing my mind, and she is dug in, too."

Motivated by avoidance, friends and relatives never discover how many *sides*—plural—might actually be involved in the shadows of these non-meetings. Citizens who applaud falsehoods or avert interpersonal contact because of them especially need accurate and fair journalistic accounts. Those who believe the *Washington Post* editorials are always on target could also benefit from a broader range of information sources. Lively conversation is being numbed further at the precise moment we are being threatened by its absence.

## An Ethic Tested: The (Current) Big Picture

The commonality implied by res publica comes from mutual engagement with the reality of our historical moment. Democracy does not cause equality but is a stated and continually restated commitment to equality. It functions best when citizens freely argue, and an engaged journalism reports good news and bad with a respect for truth. Disagreement can signal citizens to talk more with each other, not less, matched by more reflective and generous listening. But our recent experience of normalized public lying shows that the potential of citizen conversation is fragile indeed. Instead of admiring a long tradition of citizens and journalists confronting conflicts directly, we increasingly fear polarized camps of angry people unwilling to talk or listen across differences.

In their classic *Democracy and Disagreement*, Amy Gutmann and Dennis Thompson wrote that effective deliberative conversations lead to an "economy of moral disagreement." They mean that citizens certainly should press their own moral positions, but at the same time they should "seek the rationale that minimizes rejection of the position they oppose." The best deliberative moments "may encourage citizens to form views not merely of what they want for themselves but also of what they want for their society."[52]

Eric Liu and Nick Hanauer's view of democratic citizenship diagnoses the alternative more bluntly: When voting only to satisfy our own personal needs, "we've convinced ourselves that a million individual acts of selfishness magically add up to a common good."[53] Responsible citizens stay alert for traces of common ground, acknowledge and support common access to basic facts, and cut one another some slack. Yet empathic response is nearly impossible when leaders falsify facts to cultivate voters' disdain for demonized enemies and, worse, encourage disdain even for the possibility of agreement.

Occasions for deliberation are commonplace. Couples discover values of give-and-take as they struggle over a budget decision before deciding to remodel the kitchen. A civic group or club deliberates as it rewrites its mission statement. Members first assess what seems unclear or inaccurate in the existing one. A company's hiring committee deliberates when deciding which of four strong candidates to recommend to the personnel director. The committee assesses varied perceptions of the kind of employee the organization most needs at this moment. The Founding Fathers envisioned cooperative deliberation of this kind but to serve the *public* good, not just a club's or a company's interest. They anticipated willing citizens would work in dialogue to shape and, when necessary, reshape democracy. They knew not to expect a clear and unchanging blueprint for a new country.

In the decades following World War II, Arendt advocated the "enlarged mentality" necessary for public judgment. This way of thinking does not grow from personal conclusions, private analyses, or administrative orders. It begins within social conversations connecting citizens who care about democratic roles. Enlarged mentality "needs the presence of others 'in whose place' it must think, whose perspectives it must take into consideration, and without whom it never has the opportunity to operate at all."[54] Attempting to understand political problems without taking citizen dialogue into account opens the door to dismissiveness. It is suspiciously like waiting to be told what to think by someone addicted to lying to you. In therapy, those who consistently allow others to lie to them about addictions are called enablers. The enablers and the addicts both suffer.

Ultimately, a citizen ethic depends mightily on shared social awareness, receptivity, critical thinking, listening, a willingness to hear opposition, and other abilities employed in careful observation and person-to-person talk. Journalism contributes raw material for citizens to reason, question, and decide together. Beyond that, journalism serves to stimulate and safeguard citizenship, most clearly as a lie detector and reality checker. So much more, though, is left up to ordinary people willing to care actively and conscientiously about democracy.

We found it helpful to revisit an aging landmark, sometimes forgotten even by news professionals. Reading the 1947 Hutchins Commission report *A Free and Responsible Press* again, this time *with citizen action especially in mind*, gives it fresh meaning. Charting a course for what was then called "mass media," Robert M. Hutchins and his colleagues described five requirements, to which we add brief links to responsibilities of citizenship:

> "A truthful, comprehensive account of the day's events in a context which gives them meaning." A citizens' ethic respects truth, but isolated facts without comprehensive context do not help citizens understand fully what they must decide.
>
> "A forum for the exchange of comment and criticism." A citizens' ethic is empowered by active disagreements on how policies and ideas might better reflect truthful context.
>
> "The projection of a representative picture of the constituent groups of society." A citizens' ethic necessarily depends on conversations

that introduce us to each other, while including and acknowledging the wide cultural range of American experience.

*"The presentation and clarification of the goals and values of society."* A citizens' ethic clarifies how everyday people can understand overall value differences and how they sometimes must be reconciled with each other through difficult choices.

*"Full access to the day's intelligence."* A citizens' ethic means that in a republic, intelligence thrives only through *access*—to general interest news sources, to fact, to options for reconsidering cooperative decisions in an era of political conflict and intentional falsehood. And we must not forget the implications of *full* access in a political moment of organized, targeted, and relentless lying.

The Hutchins Commission report, although dated in some ways and still criticized for some of its recommendations, does an excellent job of reminding us of the proper relationships within our historic intersection of journalism, citizenship, and political life.[55]

CHAPTER 9

# Assuming Responsibilities for the Republic

When emergencies arise, ordinary people often respond before the Federal Emergency Management Agency or the National Guard arrives on the scene. They show up in pickup trucks pulling johnboats, in rusted RVs, or as part of an impromptu caravan. They donate clothes, hand out food and water, and help pick up the pieces. That spirit still prevails in our sometimes broken civic life. Across the country, individuals, donors, and ad hoc groups pitch in, and the helpers include those in need of help themselves. They are known within their communities as "solid citizens."

Without much fanfare, local organizations, foundations, and individual community members are mobilizing, providing financial assistance and know-how to preserve both local news and civic life. In Connecticut, the nonprofit, online-only news site the New Haven Independent offers a model of citizen-journalism partnership. The Independent reports on neighborhoods, city government, schools, and public health, filling holes in the depleted coverage of the community's for-profit daily newspaper. The stimulus for New Haven's experiment in local news came from the combined forces of local philanthropy, volunteerism, and civic pride. Rather than leave solutions to chance, the community took matters into its own hands. The Independent partners with several organizations— NewsMatch, the Institute for Nonprofit News, and News Revenue Hub, among them—that match community-based donations with those from foundations and corporate donors nationwide. Now fifteen years old, the Independent demonstrates that nonprofit local journalism can succeed where and how commercial journalism has not.[1]

In this capstone chapter, we offer an overview of the efforts of journalists and citizens now working together to create a new environment of reason-based civic involvement, productive dialogue, and shared responsibility.

After the Founders signed the Constitution in 1787, the elder statesman among them, Benjamin Franklin, encountered a group of citizens waiting outside the historic Philadelphia State House where the delegates met. What kind of government could the people expect, they asked of Franklin. His answer: "A republic, if you can keep it." Constitutional scholar Richard R. Beeman provides contemporary context by observing: "The brevity of that response should not cause us to under-value its essential meaning: democratic republics are not merely founded upon the consent of the people, they are also absolutely dependent upon the active and informed involvement of the people for their continued good health."[2]

Here, then, is a smorgasbord of citizens' stories for rebuilding journalism, especially on a local scale, and journalists' stories for reestablishing the historic role of civic discourse, both offered in the spirit of "keeping" our republic intact.

## A Reemerging Alliance of Citizens and Journalists

In 2018, Alabama businessman David Preston took a chance and joined a new group quite different from his daily life. Preston was already an active citizen in his local community; he could have played it safe and stayed at home. We suspect he got involved because civic responsibility guided him. As he described later, Preston worried about citizens becoming disconnected from public life, succumbing to short-term seductions of putdowns or this-isn't-my-problem attitudes.[3] The group, he believed, presented an opportunity for members to share personal stories with other worried citizens. It might even provide a small step toward addressing that problem. Why might Preston have thought so? What happened? What did he learn?

Preston volunteered for one of a growing number of recent journalism-fueled projects that confront calcified political divisions and apparently intractable social issues. Many people shy away from discussing controversies until they know that listeners will endorse their opinions. On such safe ground, talk often leads to mutually reinforcing complaints that retread old ground and echo stale sentiments. People have heard them before and seemingly want to hear them again, like greatest hits replays of "I'll reinforce you, and you reinforce me" and "Aren't those other guys terrible?" The problem Preston sensed is that these pseudo-conversations never really satisfy; the gap separating our own "truth" from our critics' remains at least as wide, and the concerns of strangers just as alien. Predatory politicians crave supporters who form a predictable base to be mined for contributions, applause, ego stroking, and unswerving loyalty.

Yet the gaps separating different perspectives could also be opportunities. Gaps are where change lives. The group Preston joined, "Guns: An American Conversation," probed a volatile controversy dividing citizens in every corner of the country. Its objective was neither a theoretical exercise about conflict nor a catharsis or talkfest for airing individuals' gripes and fears. The conversation that ensued did not attempt to influence political beliefs, teach how to conquer the opposition's power, or make a specific conflict disappear. It simply allowed strangers to gather and hear different stories as they each told them.

Being agreed with is a tempting conversational experience, and persons often seek it out to affirm the value of their own beliefs. It is an effective conflict-management skill only for those who believe managing conflict means ducking serious problems by ignoring others' sincerity or dismissing them as too stupid or biased to be worth one's attention.

## Marginalia

"The term dialogue affirms the notion that journalists ought to think of themselves as communicators, while recognizing the importance of storytelling as a communicative practice. . . . [Dialogue] treats information gathering and storytelling not as ends in themselves but as moments in a larger social process. To think of journalism as dialogue is to insist on richer standards of mutuality, such as being present to others, accepting otherness as an opportunity for learning, and refusing to set agendas that exclude others' deepest concerns."[4]

—John J. Pauly, media historian and researcher

Preston's account of what he learned in group conversation, published a year later, does not embrace a "side" in the controversy, nor do readers learn much about the personal attitudes he brought to the group. Twenty-one participants from across the country met at the Newseum in Washington, DC, for an experimental program advertised as "dialogue journalism."[5] Reporters from Advance Local Publications, *Time* magazine, and the innovative journalistic start-up Spaceship Media were there to observe, support, and report on the event. The interaction was facilitated by one of the most experienced public dialogue organizations in the country, Essential Partners (formerly Boston's Public Conversations Project). About 120 people then extended the group's communication in a private Facebook discussion on the same topic.

For Preston at least, the online communication component never developed the rapport of the face-to-face group. This may or may not be surprising, perhaps depending on expectations about Facebook-style exchanges. But the story of his in-person experience certainly should surprise skeptics who assume that virulent partisanship is inevitable or that journalism is irrelevant for the well-being of citizenry. Here are his takeaways:

- "For me, the biggest takeaway . . . is to remind me and reinforce the fact that there are real people on the opposite side of a political debate from me."
- "People on both sides usually want to achieve the same goal, they just differ on how to achieve that goal. Moreover, there are relatively few people that even come close to the characters that political operatives try to portray on all sides of an issue."
- "Very few, if any, NRA members are gun loving psychopaths and on the flip side, very few pro-gun [control] advocates want to take all your guns away."
- "Political operatives highlight or mischaracterize only the most extreme, on either side, for political effect."
- "Learn to listen to the other side and instead of talking at the other side, talk to them."
- In one exchange that would "normally set me off," the group "gave me the confidence to reach out to one of the members for a better understanding of the history of blackface and why it is offensive during the recent political scandals in Virginia. The history of blackface just wasn't taught when I was in grade school."
- Facilitators help participants to "develop rapport with people that disagree with us politically," a change that "continue[s] to this day."
- "While certain media organizations and national media personalities can seem to have an agenda, journalists, for the most part, are very dedicated hard-working professionals who want to get the story right and present the facts in the most honest way possible. Contrary to popular opinion, most of the media is not the 'enemy of the people,' nor are they 'fake news.'"[6]

Preston encouraged others to participate in similar groups. He predicted the result would be "better insight and understanding of yourself, your community, and others" in ways participants previously thought unattainable.

We introduce David Preston not because his group experience is rare or extraordinary but because occasions for listening across differences are far more common and rewarding than most citizens realize. The well-spring often is a refreshing willingness of journalists to reinforce citizen dialogue in a common trajectory. Joint ventures like the one Preston experienced have obvious potential, and their emergence at this fraught political moment also is noteworthy and encouraging.

## Journalism and Its Evolving Role in a Republic

Media critic Jeff Jarvis sees public dialogue as a bridge to a different tone and task for journalism—a mission not entirely new but newly relevant and optimistic. The joint AL.com-Spaceship Media project—even its social media aspect—was his touchstone for an *Atlantic* magazine commentary in which he encourages political adversaries "to meet, listen to each other, find where they disagreed, and—here's the good part—call on journalists to help them combat misunderstanding with fact." Media professionals "can no longer expect every citizen to come to us and our content as the destination, as if we alone are the solution. We must go to the people where they are having their conversations to listen and then bring value."[7] Jarvis is not naive; this is not a "reset it and forget it" kind of social problem. Something beyond newsroom practice has to change.

Citizens serious about improving democracy now can find "free spaces" for civil conversations absent of verbal altercations. The new opportunities usually involve face-to-face meetings moderated by independent organizations. Some are mediated by online technologies. Journalists are particularly well qualified to help citizens, in Jarvis's words, "combat misunderstanding with fact." Several historical projects gave structure and purpose to hundreds of other local and national initiatives now remaking democratic communication in America.

### Journalism's Conversation with Citizens, Refreshed

Recent political polarization has been demoralizing, especially when rooted in hate speech and dismissiveness toward underprivileged and marginalized minorities. Partisan sniping in general still dominates headlines and "breaking news," and conservatives and liberals appear to live in separate worlds that intentionally exclude mutual listening. But for several decades a countervailing trend has gained momentum: a persistent if slow-motion social movement in which everyday citizens speak and listen to each other across differences. Stimulated by groups that value diversity in cultural and political beliefs, ordinary conversation, and storytelling, the trend counterbalances cynicism about democracy's most effective values, including the escalating attacks on journalists and basic research, the hardened distrust of unfamiliar cultures and groups, and, for that matter, the silencing distrust among partisans toward fellow citizens holding conflicting opinions. Unfortunately, too many citizens remain unfamiliar with the historic foundation for sustaining engaged citizenship-journalism cooperation.

**FYI**

"A certain spirit—what John Dewey called 'democratic faith'—is essential to our system of self-rule. To put it simply: democracy works only if enough of us believe democracy works."[8]

—American Academy of Arts and Sciences, Commission on the Practice of Democratic Citizenship

A widely influential model for civic involvement forums—in a sense a grandparent of them—is the ongoing success of the Kettering Foundation's ambitiously titled National Issues Forums (NIF). Since 1982, and largely through the leadership of David Mathews, citizen groups and communities have taken advantage of NIF-convened forums, representing a spectrum of public life: churches, city and community planning committees, correctional facilities, leadership training, adult education, groups confronting local controversies, special interest organizations such as women's and seniors' groups, and a variety of professional associations (including journalism). All of them, write Mathews and his colleagues, have been guided by the principle that "democracy does not begin with elections; it begins with conversations."[9]

Nonpartisan moderators of NIF events encourage attendees to check certainties and prepackaged answers at the door. Participants discover they are not there to debate, convert, or persuade other participants or to learn a polite way to say, "Let's just agree to disagree." Because of Kettering's problem orientation, the groups engage in deliberative dialogue: what can be done about immigration, or taxation, or voting procedures, to improve democracy? In the NIF approach, opinions are valued because they become routes to discover the resources and goals of a variety of different people, all of whom have a stake in making the best decision. *Public judgment* is the task of NIF participants.

## Marginalia

Ideas from NIF groups:

"Deliberation doesn't necessarily change political positions, but it does change attitudes about personal points of view."

"Citizens were creating a distinctive kind of knowledge in the forums, a knowledge of the public produced *by* the public."

"Deliberation does more than *tolerate* differences, it *uses* them."[10]

—David Mathews, founder, Kettering Foundation

NIF participants return home with expanded vocabularies of public life and, by many accounts, the motivation to petition governmental leaders for useful change. They no longer just hold opinions but now have participated in decision-making that tests the practicality of the opinions. A popular NIF saying captures why this rings true for participants: "There's a space between agree/disagree waiting to be discussed."

## The Promise of Engagement

A prominent 1990s movement toward "public" or "civic" journalism resembles philosophies like those of the Kettering Foundation by expanding journalism's communication mission. The movement tested conventional wisdom among traditional twentieth-century practitioners, which held that the goal of news media should be to produce news as objectively as possible, package it, and deliver it to a public that would recognize its value and want to pay for it. Journalists simply content to define, write, and deliver facts to the public, the reformers argued, shunned a deeper responsibility to listen carefully to the concerns of their own communities. The movement encouraged veteran journalists to grow closer to the public for the sake of better journalism and stronger audience loyalty, which was already showing signs of slippage.[11]

Despite notable successes, the overall movement foundered for many reasons. Some prominent establishment journalists considered it a mere fad. Another critique came from news professionals who claimed the movement simply repackaged what solid journalists had always done but with more hoopla and glitz. Still others interpreted it as an attack on journalistic objectivity itself and argued that its cuddly philosophy elevated fickle public opinion over hard-won truths. Veteran journalists resented suggestions that they did not already know their communities well enough. Public journalism, and how it was touted, smelled to old-school practitioners like a targeted advertising and marketing ploy that the profession did not need—it was "fine" the way it was, independent and powerful. Until it was not so fine and until it became less independent and less powerful.

In 2016, career journalist Geneva Overholser found that journalism had evolved dramatically since the 1990s, and what was called civic or public journalism now seemed relevant to a goal of *engagement*—evidently a more palatable label. Within two decades, "the most basic principle of civic journalism has come into widespread usage," she said. "Virtually every newsroom has a richer conversation with its readers, viewers, listeners," and increasingly newsrooms are naming "engagement editors."[12] From Overholser's perspective, shared by others, journalists no longer enjoyed a monopoly on information. Members of the public were now their partners, which she said "could be a promising moment for a melding of legacy journalism's best strengths, civic journalism's commitment to community and the new culture of participation."[13]

Nieman Reports, a Harvard-based program with a mission to elevate the profession, described Overholser's "promising moment" in stronger terms, as "the 21st-century version" of 1990s civic journalism with a twist— "defining solutions, not problems." As noted in chapter 5, some journalists now use the term "solutions journalism" to indicate the shift.[14] Seong Jae Kim, author of *As Democracy Goes, So Does Journalism*, contends public journalism "laid a path on which citizen journalism practices can flourish today. It made journalism closer to the people it purported to serve."[15]

Other aspects of American society took cues from the spreading turn to a conversational style of public life. Spreading political polarization motivated a two-year research project of the prestigious American Academy of Arts and Sciences (AAAS). It should be no surprise that its primary findings became blueprints for improving public dialogue across communities and entrenched opinions. Indeed, it reached its conclusions through direct involvement with the communities themselves. The AAAS issued its bipartisan report in June 2020, including six strategies for "a more resilient democracy." Its sixth strategy (the one most difficult for the participants to articulate) was "Inspire a Culture of Commitment to American Constitutional Democracy and One Another." Despite its grandiose heading, it contains highly pragmatic recommendations for national citizen dialogues supported by "public media efforts that support grassroots engagement." A number of recommendations focus on encouraging public service, soliciting democratic narratives, and expanding opportunities by which to acknowledge the differences in citizens' experiences.[16]

Journalism's recent history with public listening and outreach has been impressive. A profession that once defined its primary communication role as objective *writing*[17] is rethinking its goals and expanding its focus on communicating. While the clarity, fairness, and accuracy of newswriting remains crucial, the profession increasingly recognizes its mission to build relationships with neglected audiences. And if those audiences shy away from their responsibilities to interact, journalists can and should assist their participation.

"Dialogue," "conversation," and "community" became terms floating in the new atmosphere that combined core news principles with innovative ways to serve citizens. In 2019, the Journalism Institute of the National Press Club hosted journalists and government officials in a two-day "intensive" set of face-to-face conversations about building "dialogue in a divided democracy." Journalists attending weighed in with suggestions. The editor of the *Capital Gazette*, for example, which lost five employees after a fatal attack by a deranged gunman, thought that the "key" to the journalism-community relationship is to "keep talking" and hear criticism. The head of the journalism consortium Your Voice Ohio argued that journalists should not just cover communities but define themselves as *fellow* community members, unafraid to say they want the world to be better—and offer solutions.[18]

About the same time, the American Press Institute (API) sponsored a series of programs for journalists aimed at improving mutual conversations within their communities, including the 2018 "Creating a Culture of Listening," a summit of editors, reporters, and leaders of nonprofits hoping to ensure that journalists stay in touch with how their communities define news. Within two years, aided by a grant from the Craig Newmark Graduate School for Journalism at the City University of New York, the API launched its Community Listening Fellowship project. The first group of fellows, mentored by advisers skilled in engaging the public, are now working in newsrooms to strengthen ties with underserved cultural and civic groups who do not always see their values and goals reflected in mainstream news.[19]

David Preston's group, then, was not an isolated one-off experiment. It was organized in part by Spaceship Media, probably the most representative and influential of many recent start-up organizations bridging journalism and community on a national scale. The first major endeavor of the oddly but memorably named initiative[20]—a facilitated national conversation of voters representing divergent sides in the 2016 presidential election—began to chart journalism's new role to create opportunities for discovering the concerns of real people and then cover the issues on people's minds. Cofounders Eve Pearlman and Jeremy Hay adopt a holistic look at the news by expanding the concept of the newsroom to include wider community concerns and the conversations that fuel them. One project called "Talking Across Borders" represented diversity beyond the usual parameters to include, for example, "a tea party lawyer, a young DACA (Deferred Action for Childhood Arrivals) recipient, a social worker, a businessman who crossed the U.S.-Mexico border illegally as a child and is now a U.S. citizen, teachers, a construction worker who attributes his unemployment to undocumented labor, an advertising professional, an academic, and a veterans' advocate."[21]

## Journalism Arising from Conversation, not Conflict

The face-off character of much contemporary news no longer serves democracy, if it ever did. Eve Pearlman describes a defining characteristic of the Spaceship Media approach when she says: "Instead of going, as journalists often have, to the hearts of divides and getting a spokesperson from each side that articulates the oppositional points, and sometimes serves to divide people further, we wanted to go to those gaps and see what we could do not to change minds or convert people but to find points of commonality and to restore civil civic dialogue."[22] Nonintrusive facilitation and an expectation of off-the-record privacy reassure participants. They learn that people sitting alongside them have names, interests, passionate commitments, blind spots, and active lives to live. Participants need not agree with someone in order to affirm or understand them. Storytelling, always a rich resource for journalists, allows different shades of belief to emerge, humanizing attendees while trust slowly builds. As with the NIF, dialogue journalism does not involve changing beliefs or crowning winners and dismissing losers. Rather, its methods elicit narrative accounts that participating journalists can follow up later with sensitive stories at the human core of conflict.

Media representatives and political consultants, among others, tap into various forms of citizen dialogue with mixed outcomes. For decades, news services, major newspapers and networks, and other organizations that measure public opinion have conducted polls that supposedly gauge the sentiment for or against a particular policy, political strategy, or candidate. The results get published and thereby ratify the poll findings as newsworthy and presumably helpful to readers and political decision-makers. Unfortunately, according to noted political scientist James Fishkin, whose research extends back decades, interviewees and survey respondents respond to opinion polls in problematic ways at best. Opinion polling often amounts to "snapshot events" that ask people who might never have given thought to the details or dynamics of, say, America's foreign policy with Israel to come up with an evaluation on the spot. Under pressure, they commonly invent responses, or their answer is rote—a nearly automatic reaction based on talking points advanced by a preferred candidate or special interest group.[23]

Besides being superficial, current polling often misleads readers and listeners who presume both its accuracy and its relevance to important civic decision-making. The process additionally can reinforce entrenched political attitudes. Its dominance in journalistic culture encourages "the permanent campaign," the phenomenon of elected politicians making governmental decisions by consulting poll numbers rather than prioritizing policy benefits.[24]

Fishkin proposed a different kind of polling that elicits opinions after people build a basic factual background for themselves and after they compare ideas in dialogue about different perspectives. Fishkin called the format "deliberative polling." He transformed the approach from theory to practical application and research. More than one hundred groups across the United States and other countries since 1994 have generated a mountain of evidence supporting the viability of various forms of deliberative polling. Fishkin urged journalists to report on the successes of a new method of measuring opinion.

Fishkin gatherings resemble Kettering projects by encouraging the realistic "coming to public judgment." Topics range from undocumented immigration to multiple policy issues, such as those covered in a megameeting called "America in One Room," which probed opinions on the five policy areas of immigration, health care, the economy, the environment, and foreign policy.[25] Fishkin selects participants through scientific sampling of registered voters who represent a range of personal positions on controversial issues. They all receive preliminary briefing books that contain factual details and context to read before attending. Meetings last from an intensive day to a full weekend or longer. Events might involve five hundred people or more, but participants get the chance to be heard and question a diverse group of experts about factual issues. Much of the interpersonal dialogue happens in small breakout groups.

In feedback surveys, Fishkin found evidence that everyday voters are willing to adjust attitudes after they digest solid information and diverse arguments. In the "America in One Room" event, "the percentage saying the system of American democracy was 'working well' doubled to 60 percent from 30 percent," and there were significant shifts of opinion after dialogue among Republicans (toward moderation on immigration policies) and Democrats (toward less support for federal minimum wage and other issues of government spending).[26]

Not everyone comes away enthused or impressed by dialogue-based programs. Some see them as havens for liberal pie-in-the-sky thinking. They sound good, the objection goes, but are impractical and typical of how out of touch political liberalism can be. Our take: The questioning person might be unaware that public conversation is the very constitutional basis for a democratic republic in which citizens are trusted to argue reasonably with each other while listening carefully to reasoned opposition. Despite any shortcomings of these arranged events, participants, we believe, develop into citizens who listen and assess as opposed to closing their ears and minds to others. They engage in dialogue and its near relative, deliberation.

People do not "do" dialogue to each other, rehearse for it, or plan exactly the proper type of dialogue a group should have. If we knew exactly what dialogue should be, we might be tempted to package it and deliver it like an entertaining Ted Talk. Dialogue is not an inoculation but a commitment. It depends on speaking and listening tentatively, each person relying on others to help collaborate and coauthor what happens. Participants find it beneficial to clear a space for dialogue to happen—a particular physical and emotional place in which considering ideas will be the primary activity.

No specific training in dialogue is necessary for the experience, although it often improves deliberations to have a skilled moderator or facilitator present to respond if a group veers off-topic or rhetoric gets offensive or objectionable. You only need to be willing to be surprised by ideas different from yours and, just as important, be aware of your own reactions. Realistically, dialogue flows, ebbs, and often peters out. Certainly, it is not the possession of a few enlightened souls.

Communication research shows that dialogue occurs between persons in moments—occasionally, tiny ones. The moments are often fleeting and unexpected. They can happen in the midst of arguments, misjudgments, or even trivial wordplay, provided participants stay alert. In the ideal, it occurs when people "turn toward" each other, recognizing differences and otherness. The dialogue moment depends primarily on human abilities to empathize, that is, to imagine the other's perspective. Little about dialogue is meant to persuade others to adopt one's beliefs. These moments of meeting, which could be considered the "we" points of interaction to distinguish them from self-oriented "I" points, are perhaps the most vivid and memorable from participants in public meetings and deliberations.[27]

## Journalism Reassesses Its Role, and Rightly So

The forty-fifth president of the United States tried to tweet the national news media into submission. Mainly he succeeded by turning millions of Americans against an institution that keeps them reliably informed and safeguards their rights. He made it seem easy. The Trump regime, however, challenged journalism to justify its roles and defend its legitimacy. Perhaps he did news organizations a favor by pushing them toward introspection. Journalists have long opened themselves to public criticism and responded with corrections, retractions, or apologies. Beyond mea culpas, though, the news profession should ask itself deeper questions, mainly regarding how well it maintains the republic. Does it connect with citizens or distance them? Does it listen well and pay heed to issues that most concern the broad range of people it serves? Is public affairs reporting—such as thorough coverage of law enforcement, education, government entities, and public health—a priority or an afterthought? Does the profession share blame for the widespread dislike and mistrust from which it suffers? In contemplating such questions, we find room for improvement. Trump fed negative public perceptions of the news media by tapping into an existing current of estrangement evidenced by how ordinary citizens—neighbors, coworkers, relatives, golf buddies, church friends—came to believe that the press was an enemy.

Without actively seeking the public's support and goodwill, journalism puts its survival in jeopardy. It cannot wait for the rescuers to arrive. As it should, the profession has launched its own initiatives.

## Reinforcing Sustainable Models

Hard news journalism—local public affairs reporting, investigations, and in-depth analyses—shows signs of renewed life, but it remains expensive and thinly spread. Assorted strategies—nonprofit IRS status, volunteerism, fundraising, and partnerships—are encouraging. What is so obviously unsustainable is journalism primarily dependent on strong audience numbers and robust advertising income. Only a handful of mainstream news organizations earn profits sufficient to meet the high costs of extensive statewide, national, and international news coverage. For nearly all other news outlets, the inescapable question is, Who pays for journalism absent a substantive advertising and subscriber base?

A nonprofit model promises hope for both national and local news. The success of ProPublica stands out. Founded in 2007, ProPublica produces investigative journalism that, as its website describes, "focuses on abuses of power and betrayals of public trust." In 2010, it became the first online news organization to win a Pulitzer Prize, winning four more as of 2020, including one for a comprehensive investigation of failures by police to investigate rape cases properly or to understand the trauma that victims experience. ProPublica excels primarily thanks to foundation grants and donations, and its reputation and mounting achievements keep a faucet of private funding flowing. ProPublica shares its resources and augments its coverage by partnering, by its own estimate, with ninety other news organizations ranging from big-city newspapers, such as the *Miami Herald*, to smaller regional nonprofit news sites, such as Pine Tree Watch in Hallowell, Maine, which, in turn, collaborates with a variety of news media throughout its state.[28] ProPublica practices pay-it-forward journalism.

The nonprofit model fits today's reemerging hometown news. It fosters a sense of togetherness, a United Way-type approach that reinvests local contributions for community betterment. Until the 1980s, large to midsize cities' local newspapers often dictated the terms of relationships with the community; they were accustomed to newsroom visitors as supplicants, including candidates for office seeking favorable coverage or editorial endorsements. We remember when the daily newspaper occupied prime real estate on Main Street or in multistory edifices like the one the management of the *St. Petersburg Times* (now the *Tampa Bay Times*) once called "The Tower of Power." The newspaper sold its headquarters for $40 million in 2018, allowing it to pay down long-standing debt.[29] A humbling fall from grace shakes sense into once flush and influential national and local news organizations. Today's nonprofits suffer no delusions of grandeur.

The nonprofit model spares reporters and editors from the economic pressure to put flashier lifestyle and celebrity content ahead of serious reporting. It also frees journalists to deal with sensitive subjects that corporate ownership might rather avoid, such as criticism of the National Rifle Association or coverage of LGBTQ issues. Finally, being a nonprofit helps reduce—but not eliminate—public suspicions that news organizations owe fealty to monied power brokers in politics and business.

That said, thousands of corporate- or privately owned for-profit news organizations deserve support by virtue of their commendable records of public service. The pandemic prompted a spike in local media popularity, but revenues stood stagnant, and many for-profit operations still struggle to make ends meet. Providing free access to coronavirus-related coverage gave news organizations an occasion to seek support publicly and with humility. According to Nancy Cawley Lane, CEO of the Local Media Association, "Journalists need to be having honest conversations with their communities about why they need to pay for news, whether that's a digital subscription, membership, or contributions."[30]

Nearly all news organizations—large, small, corporate, or nonprofit—realize they cannot keep going it alone. They need financial transfusions and caring people, like civic blood donors, to pitch in. Revenue-producing initiatives include government subsidies, grants, and corporate philanthropy. None of them are ideal, but a bundle of funding methods appears to be doing some good in preserving and perhaps expanding worthwhile hometown journalism.

Can government step in? Perhaps. Subsidies for public media are nothing new. In 1967, Congress created the Corporation for Public Broadcasting (CPB) to oversee and distribute federal subsidies that to this day partially support more than fifteen hundred radio and television stations in communities throughout the country, although the over-the-air signals fail to reach some remote areas. The $445 million that the CPB receives annually amounts to one-hundredth of 1 percent of the federal budget—$1.35 a year from each American. But every year he was in office, President Trump called for reducing the subsidy to $30 million, all but eliminating funding for public media. Congress stopped him, partly in reaction to a 2017 bipartisan research survey that found voters "across the political spectrum overwhelmingly oppose eliminating federal funding for public television and that more than seven in ten see public television as a good or excellent value for their tax dollars, on par with investments in highways, roads and bridges."[31]

The federal contribution to public media funding is minuscule compared to an average of $85 per capita spent by such Western nations as Norway, France, and Italy. The subject of increased government funding keeps coming up.[32] Postelection, Casey Kelly wrote in Current, a nonprofit website for public media, that an appeal to the Biden administration for enhanced government underwriting "should be considered low-hanging fruit that could help restore our broken information system."[33] Biden, however, inherited a full agenda of potentially life-and-death issues, so increased federal spending on media was not an immediate priority. The objectives and operation of the CPB, however, underscore the obvious importance of well-informed voters. Can the CPB model fit to bolster print and online media? Suggestions include reorganizing the CPB as the Corporation for Public Service Media to encompass nonprofit news initiatives that resemble in content and spirit the nation's fifteen hundred public radio stations with their loyal listeners. There are obstacles to overcome. State and federal Republican lawmakers generally oppose higher subsidies by portraying public broadcasting as a vehicle for liberal-leaning programming.

A glimmer of hope appeared late in Biden's first year when the White House and Democrats in Congress came up with a plan that perhaps enough Republicans might accept—the Local Journalism Sustainability Act. Proponents called it "a game-change for small-town USA."[34] An early draft of the bill included a series of advertiser and subscriber tax credits to boost income for news outlets. Only one survived the legislative gauntlet—a credit to local news organizations for paying a portion of reporter salaries. The provision ended up as part of the Build Back Better bill that underwent a prolonged period of compromise and revision, with some of its provisions reemerging in the Inflation Reduction Act that became law in August 2022. The plan for federal support of local journalism as of late 2022 remains in legislative limbo, but it would have established a modest precedent for other federal government-backed aid programs of a wider scope.

A more wishful plan, the Local Journalism Initiative (LJI), emerged in November 2021 from two noted media reformers, Robert W. McChesney and John Nichols. It calls ambitiously for the federal government to provide funding to every county in the country to underwrite nonprofit journalism. It set out other steps, including oversight by the United States Postal Service, and provisions on how and where money would be used. McChesney and Nichols admitted that "there remains much to flesh out to make the LJI practical," so the project started off as a plea for action rather than a piece of sponsored legislation, and maybe that is all that will become of it. McChesney and Nichols, though, did add their influential voices to a growing refrain of academics, journalists, and civil leaders who are at least willing to ask politicians for help.[35]

Another positive development comes from grassroots citizens, joined by state officials, who recognize that nonprofit news media offer vital resources that stimulate civic life. In New Jersey, most notably, thousands of residents organized and lobbied lawmakers to pass legislation that created the Civic Information Consortium (CIC), with a dual mission to strengthen local news coverage and boost civic engagement. The state allocated $2 million in public money in the first year, but the funds were frozen due to the pandemic. In March 2021, the CIC began accepting applications for its inaugural round of grant funding. The first recipient was the journalism program at Rowan University in Glassboro, New Jersey, whose students and faculty partner with local news outlets through joint reporting projects and training in journalism for community members. New Jersey's modest step toward public funding for journalism demonstrates the potential for the concept.[36]

Journalists themselves question if government funding—whether state or federal—is a long-term answer. "In a perfect world, I would like to see that happen," said John Stanton, who, along with Laura Bassett, cofounded the Save Journalism Project. "I find it difficult to imagine Congress passing any kind of legislation that actually gives money to the news industry that does not somehow come with a lot of weird, terrible strings."[37] The Save Journalism Project, he hopes, can at least persuade Congress to exert pressure on Facebook and Google to share a portion of profits to help general interest reporting survive.

A voluntary approach might be more practical. In March 2020, Facebook committed $25 million in emergency grant funding for local news through the Facebook Journalism Project and earmarked $75 million to buy advertising in newspapers.[38] In the midst of the coronavirus pandemic, Google Inc. announced its own $100 million project, the Journalism Emergency Relief Fund, "to deliver urgent aid to thousands of small, medium and local news publishers globally."[39] The revenues of Facebook and Google, of course, dwarf the contributions each has pledged.

Corporate giving and foundations feed another revenue-generating stream. The creators of a start-up organization called the American Journalism Project, journalist Elizabeth Green and technology investor John Thornton, hope to raise $500 million a year in national philanthropy for local news and match that amount with membership fees, advertising, and locally generated revenue. They estimate that the combined $1 billion for local publications would approach the donor support that keeps public radio going.[40] Several philanthropic foundations now embrace the survival of journalism as a worthy goal. A 2019 report concluded that journalism philanthropy had quadrupled in ten years, with $326 million going to investigative reporting as of 2019.[41] A working example of such intervention is the New York-based nonprofit the Marshall Project. In 2021, it received a George Gund Foundation grant to open a bureau in Cleveland, where it will expand its Pulitzer Prize-winning coverage of abuses in criminal justice systems.[42]

Efforts to reinforce the financial stability of journalism are becoming community priorities. Word is getting out that contributing in various ways to hometown journalism is like keeping the town library open and stocked, ensuring that the hospital auxiliary thrives, or fundraising for the Boys and Girls Club. Journalism in many places has done its share to improve and justify a stronger alliance with citizens. We highlight several successful ventures.

## Merging Resources and Promoting Historic Preservation

The death of so many daily newspapers, some with histories that date to the mid-nineteenth century, left more than news deserts. Those fatalities nearly erased public memories of the people and the institutions that significantly contributed to the character and influence of their cities. Civic preservationists and journalists born well after the great demise of newspapers understand the significance of their legacy as champions of public affairs journalism—and spared a few from extinction, as happened recently in Chicago. Once served by four high-circulation, profit-making dailies, by 1980, the nation's third largest city had only the struggling *Chicago Tribune* and *Chicago Sun-Times*. For decades, each mounted a cost-cutting rear-guard effort to fend off closure. But in 2022, the *Sun-Times*, on life support, found a savior—Chicago Public Media, the nonprofit owner of the flagship NPR station WBEZ, which raised $61 million from community organizations and foundations. WBEZ and the *Sun-Times* were to operate separate newsrooms but share content and platforms with a combined staff of three hundred. The Chicago project might be one-of-a-kind, perhaps only possible in a city with one of the nation's largest NPR local news operations. Nonetheless, it dramatizes that even the most ambitious of proposals can succeed, and the merger will likely be studied for its applicability in other cities and regions.

## Implementing Innovative Methods

*The Democrat and Chronicle* of Rochester, New York, in collaboration with community organizations, launched a mobile newsroom in neighborhoods traditionally underrepresented in coverage. Covid-19 forced the newspaper to put the project on hold. But while active, a team of reporters frequented such gathering places and community centers as the Ibero-American Action League, which provides a variety of human services. Residents who visited its office interacted with journalists eager to collect story ideas and make connections with respected neighborhood residents.[43] The mobile newsroom exemplifies collaborative, public-grounded journalism.

As news organizations move from centralized newsrooms into compact, less expensive spaces, more journalists will resettle in street-view settings and gain closer proximity to community ebb and flow. We can vouch for the concept through the experience of starting the Neighborhood News Bureau (NNB) in St. Petersburg, Florida, in 2001. It still operates from a working newsroom in Midtown with its rich history as a community of arts, Black-owned businesses, and professional services. Hosted by the University of South Florida Department of Journalism and Digital Communication, the NNB provides training for journalism students, functions as a community connection for collecting and disseminating information and news, and produces stories, features, and announcements for free use by local and regional news media and community organizations, including the *Weekly Challenger*, an African American newspaper founded in the 1960s.[44]

We see the NNB concept as a career catalyst for students interested in public service. The "Woodstein" era—Bob Woodard and Carl Bernstein of Watergate fame—along with the civil rights movements of the 1960s brought justice-minded young men and women into the profession, changing the dynamics of what constituted news and newsgathering. We expect that politicians' disregard for truth and calls for political and social reform will do the same. Newcomers will regenerate a profession worn down by layoffs and political bashing. Despite fewer traditional news jobs, the rise of nonprofit journalism offers fresh opportunities, including the satisfaction of supporting community life, to offset sometimes meager salaries. A major outreach program called Report for America (RFA) announced in late 2021 that it was placing three hundred journalists in more than two hundred local newsrooms.[45] Its cofounder Steve Waldman explained why he helped create RFA in 2017:

> The problems with local news are business model problems. There is no shortage of great journalists who want to do the work. There's no shortage of news organizations who want to serve their communities, and my God, there's certainly no shortage of need for really trusted, accurate information.[46]

RFA pays half a reporter's salary, the news organization covers 25 percent, and the community raises the remaining 25 percent. It recruits "emerging journalists," particularly minorities and career changers who believe in journalism's mission.

## Stressing Local Coverage

The Washington, DC, Beltway refers to Interstate 495, a highway encircling the city since the mid-1960s. When journalists say "inside the Beltway," they usually mean the workings of a relatively small enclave of federal government offices and an extended support system of lawyers, lobbyists, media, and fundraisers. Beltway journalists often report from the lawn of the White House or the rotunda of the Capital, serving up stories that skirt the concerns of ordinary Americans. The disproportionate attention paid to officialdom occurs in news coverage far from the Beltway, as state and regional journalists focus on local government offices and established community groups and spend less time covering issues and conditions that impact the larger community. Localized journalism requires an understanding of a community in its fullest, not just as defined by downtown or middle-class suburbs. Journalists gain credibility and news acquires authenticity when stories provide a sense of place inhabited by relatable people who could be neighbors or family—a place where at least a modicum of personal control exists. Journalism should never perpetuate "othering," in which society excludes people of presumably lesser status or unfamiliar cultural traditions. Through community-attuned local news, voices get heard, issues become known, and, when possible, they get resolved.

The managing editor for Oaklandside, a start-up nonprofit news site in Oakland, California, said it is especially important that citizens, particularly "our most vulnerable neighbors, be clearly heard and understood, and that far more Oaklanders are empowered to share their lived experiences with their neighbors in their own words." Listening improves journalism as it proactively stimulates citizen response to questions like these: "Tell me about life in your neighborhood. Tell me about what's working in your neighborhood school. What keeps you up at night? What would make life better around you?"[47]

## Laying Out Welcome Mats

Before security guards and body scanners began to isolate journalists, all sorts of gadflies, cabbies, cranks, and politicians used to wander unchallenged around the newsroom to engage the staff in banter, some purposeful, like pitching a story idea. Today some nonprofit newsrooms invite the public in for sit-down meetings, listening sessions, and story conferences.

Journalism, however, could do even more. Hospitals, schools, libraries, and a range of service centers encourage volunteerism. News organizations, not so much, in part because editors often view journalism as a profession based on experience and expertise—no amateurs, please. Good journalism needs talented writers and editors; it also needs people to fact-check, return phone calls, collect details for paid obituaries, and sort through emailed announcements of public gatherings. Volunteers become boosters for the organizations they support and spread enthusiasm internally because they truly want to help. Given training, part-time volunteers can assume even larger roles that include newsgathering. Local journalism requires community awareness and social sensitivity as credentials; they complement academic degrees and professional training.

## Addressing Trust Issues

Trust often starts close to home, which explains why a Knight-Gallup study in 2019 found that six in ten respondents trusted hometown newspapers or radio news.[48] In some cases, longtime residents grew up with news produced in storefront offices they passed by frequently and got a glimpse of journalism in action. Hometown journalism earns no bragging rights for a 60 percent level of trust, but national media fare far worse. Simmons Research, which tracks consumer behavior, surveyed 2,009 Americans in August 2018, asking whether or not they trusted thirty-eight different news organizations. At the top was the *Wall Street Journal* (58 percent); in the middle (47-44 percent) were MSNBC, CNN, and Fox News. The six at the bottom—Breitbart, DailyKos, Palmer Report, Occupy Democrats, InfoWars, and the Daily Caller—were identified as explicitly partisan, three liberal and three conservative, with trust levels ranging from 28 to 22 percent.[49] In a news report about the study, Joshua Benton referred to the "depressing finding" that 13 percent of the respondents said they found none of these news outlets trustworthy; the study termed this group "the Doubters," marked by less education, income, and political knowledge than other participants in the survey.[50] Clearly, some Americans have placed themselves outside the reach of trust-building efforts, but their indifference and suspicions can spread within the broader community.

Trust grows best where journalists and citizens mingle, where both maintain mutual respect and cooperation, like tending a community garden. Trust declines as physical and emotional distance grow. Little things matter, like answering an email from a disgruntled reader with a dose of

## Quotables

"Real news is news reported by those whose aspiration it is to be faithful to fact; not success in that aspiration but *having* that aspiration is what distinguishes the real from the fake."[51]

—Stanley Fish, legal scholar and author

caring or writing a thank-you note to those who patiently answered questions put to them by a reporter.

## Confessing Past Sins

On April 26, 2018, the opening day of the National Memorial for Peace and Justice dedicated to thousands of lynching victims, the *Montgomery Advertiser* apologized for its "shameful" coverage of mob violence against African Americans. Its editorial, "A Time to Face the Past," acknowledged that "we propagated a world view rooted in racism and the sickening myth of racial superiority."[52] In the 1960s the *Advertiser*, along with hundreds of other southern newspapers, took offense when "sanctimonious" reporters from northern newspapers reported on civil rights injustices. In fact, the *Advertiser* convinced the city's police commissioner, L. B. Sullivan, to sue the *New York Times*, leading to the landmark libel case *Times v. Sullivan* (1964). Other publications have followed the *Advertiser*'s lead. In 2020, the *Los Angeles Times*, which admitted to an "institutional bias" early in its history "deeply rooted in white supremacy,"[53] and, similarly, the *Kansas City Star* apologized for its decades of racist coverage, calling the apology long overdue.[54]

We expect additional expressions of remorse for lapses in coverage, for instance, of Indigenous people, Asian Americans, Hispanics, and the LGBTQ community. Phillip Luke Sinitiere, professor of history at the College of Biblical Studies in Houston, asks a pertinent question: "But beyond an apology, how are these newspapers and contemporary journalistic institutions working to repair society in the present day? In other words, how are they working to reverse structural disadvantage in a society to which their previous reporting contributed? And are they commenting on current media organizations whose current reporting imperils the lives of black people in very real ways?"[55] A shortage of penetrating news coverage of racial issues remains a problem that professional journalism generally acknowledges and attempts to address, with varying degrees of success.

Reporting on race often exposes a community to a heritage it would rather forget or ignore. It can be a delicate but necessary endeavor. These stories are not told to assign guilt; the predominant purpose is to acknowledge a truthful past—a history of the wretched treatment of minorities that spills over to impact the lives of later generations. Citizens should not cringe or feel insulted when a city removes its Confederate statues or protestors turn out to shout "No justice. No peace." Nor should they damn journalists for reporting on sensitive racial issues or excavating the past to reveal its lessons.

## Citizens Taking on More Civic Responsibility

Midway through the twentieth century, teacher and activist Myles Horton got himself arrested by the National Guard following his meeting with striking coal miners in Wilder, Tennessee. Horton was not even striking, much less breaking the law. He had talked with workers about the importance of learning to read and write. To be precise, he was arrested for "coming here, gathering information, going back and teaching it."[56] The words on the arrest citation amount to a brief but pretty good prescription for engaging citizens in a democratic republic. The arrest? Not a bad metaphor for obstructing citizenship. Quite a few people back then were not thrilled at the prospect of an educated and active citizenry. "Coming here, gathering information, going back and teaching it." Horton's "crime" also sounds like a working definition for professional journalists: go where the action is, gather what citizens need to know, and share information with them by teaching its relevance. Who would want to arrest *this*?

To understand Myles Horton's experience on his own terms, try to imagine the historical context. Those were days in the South when working folks, exploited and denied rights by wealthy companies, sought to unionize and claim a voice for themselves. Horton, who helped found Tennessee's Highlander Folk School in 1932 and dedicated himself to the cause of adult education, searched for practical ways to help workers in the trades. Throughout the 1940s and early 1950s, the Highlander school worked with unions and nascent civic rights groups.[57]

Horton also confronted a parallel problem of social injustice. State and local officials used literacy tests to discourage Black voter registration. As a result, thousands of citizens were denied use of the ballot to express their hopes and preferences for themselves and their children. A Black community leader from Johns Island, South Carolina, Esau Jenkins, suggested a partnership with Horton to build a culture of literacy in his community. Jenkins himself exemplified committed citizenship—driving a bus forty miles a day to transport factory workers from his island to their jobs in the city. He preached the gospel of education *while driving the bus.* Jenkins understood that the workers he shepherded back and forth could never expect full citizenship and civil rights without knowledge based on current events and history. Civic education had to happen somehow. Common citizens, in some cases solitary activists, did what they needed to do, perhaps inspired by the examples of Horton and Jenkins.[58]

The cooperative "Citizenship School" project spread rapidly, eventually becoming one of the touchstones of the civil rights movement. It addressed the need for respect through the fluid conversation between teachers and students by recruiting volunteers from the community—not conventionally certified "teachers" from white colleges—to teach reading, writing, and problem solving. There was no "talking down" and none of the attitude of superiority that can dominate many types of instruction. People had to want to be there, and teachers had to want to respect the lives of students. It worked. By the early 1970s, the Southern Christian Leadership Conference estimated that Citizenship Schools throughout the South had taught about one hundred thousand Black adults to read and write.

The story of Myles Horton offers an object lesson for any American disturbed by strained relationships at home, in the community, and around the country. His life was an ongoing self-examination of how individual vision contributes to civic life. He made a *commitment.* A drop in political temperature might enable us to pop our heads out of trenches and discuss openly, as Horton did, an ethic of citizenship. Of all the damage done to our social fabric, none is so pronounced as how we have taken sides. It is a condition that can be described in various ways—blue versus red states;

## Quotables

"When I couldn't think of a good way to do something, I would involve the first person I saw in a conversation about it or get some people to talking about it because I found I could learn things from other people that up to that time I thought I had to work out for myself. I didn't make much of it at the time, but it started a new kind of practice for me, an appreciation of having the group make a contribution instead of me as an individual."[59]

—Myles Horton, educator and civil rights activist

far-right in one corner, radical left in another; Black Lives Matter or All Lives Matter; homeless encampments or gated neighborhoods. Our boiling pot of perceived differences threatens the stability of distinct communities and perhaps the nation itself.

The issues that divide us persist, but today people who have never heard of Myles Horton follow paths he pioneered. A Vermont-based online site, Front Porch Forum, started as a seedling in 2006 when Michael Wood-Lewis and his wife, Valerie, sought a way to know their neighbors. Fifteen years later, a majority of the state's residents belong to Front Porch, sharing millions of postings, according to Wood-Lewis. "People often report feeling more connected to neighbors, more tuned in to local goings on, and more a part of their community," he said. "And in many cases, people then become more active . . . organizing a group yard sale, mentoring a local kid, volunteering for a park clean-up, voting on election day, etc."[60] Sometimes, people congregating on a front porch or in a church basement accomplish greater good for the community than planning done in boardrooms.

## Relying Less on Social Media for News

If people can be convinced that consumption of so-called liberal or conservative media will not cause lasting harm, they might begin to discover credible information that broadens their outlooks and expands opportunities for comparing ideas—food for thought and sounder grounds for decision-making. Smart phones and mobile devices tempt us with drive-through "headlines to go" instead of substantive stories relevant for explaining community issues.

Despite their advantages for immediate human connection, social media also take a toll on the psyche, according to research based on a sample of 2,700 users who voluntarily deactivated their Facebook accounts for four weeks ending just after the 2020 vote. The researchers concluded that "four weeks without Facebook improves subjective well-being" and reduces polarization "by at least some measures, consistent with the concern that social media have played some role in the recent rise of polarization in the United States."[61] Addictive social media users probably could never go cold turkey, but those willing to rely less on fragmented news from social media and try sampling alternative but respectable sources might discover a richer array of fair-minded journalism and less reason to suspect bias.

## Practicing Skepticism

The writer Salman Rushdie understands the power of words. Iran's ayatollah condemned Rushdie to death in 1989 for his allegedly blasphemous novel *The Satanic Verses*. Despite several failed assassination attempts, Rushdie never shied away from controversial topics, and in August 2022, he survived a vicious knife attack during a public talk in Chautauqua, New York. A lifelong advocate of truth in political discourse, in a 2015 commencement address he warned of a "very credulous age" in which "people seem ready to believe almost anything." He proposed a "tool to avoid such a fate," one that is especially useful for younger audiences:

> You need to have, and refine, and hone, what Ernest Hemingway said every writer needs: a really good shit detector. He said it. (Once again, good advice for writers turns out to be excellent advice for life.) The world in which you have grown up is unusually full of crap. In the information age, the quantity of disinformation has grown exponentially. If you seek the truth, beware of what Stephen Colbert unforgettably named "truthiness" or, for those with a bit of Latin, "veritasiness."[62]

Rushdie's warning applies as well to BS, an insidious form of self-serving, manipulative talk. Yale philosophy professor Harry Frankfurt found the subject so salient that he published a 2005 book about it. The bullshitter, Frankfurt explained, "does not reject the authority of truth, as a liar does, and oppose himself to it. He pays no attention to it at all."[63] In a post-truth world, the bullshitter usually gets a free pass and enlists another style of misrepresentation by which to corrupt democracy. Skeptical citizens stay alert for BS, knowing its prevalence and its sneaky nature. Of course, organized lie-detection efforts remain a priority if citizens want to minimize exposure to ideological scam artists.

## Advocating for Truth

How many people have you heard say—or perhaps you have said it yourself—"You can't expect the truth from the news" and the variant "Don't believe what a politician says"? Such a viewpoint conveniently enables citizens to shirk personal responsibility for ascertaining the truth, as if it were a fruitless cause not worth the trouble. It is worth it. Anyone who accepts unquestionably someone's claim that, for example, the Democratic Party and Hollywood celebrities operate a child sex trafficking ring out of pizza parlors or a liberal deep state "owns" CNN and the *New York Times* becomes an accessory to the harmful spread of disinformation. There is a parallel in everyday life when citizens remain silent as someone utters a vile remark about, say, an Asian woman or a same-sex married couple. At times, the failure to object constitutes complicity with the speaker. Moreover, giving credence to falsehoods, even implicitly, undermines the efforts of others dedicated to respecting the truth.

Advocates for truthful speech include those involved in media literacy initiatives that unite journalists, educators, and citizens in teaching people, particularly the next generation of voters, how to be discerning, responsible consumers of social media information. Participants in media literacy programs often find their personal "truths" challenged and sometimes discover flaws in their long-held positions on sensitive social issues. The News Literacy Project and the E. W. Scripps Company partnered to launch an annual National News Literacy Week (NNLW), from January 27 to 31. Calling news literacy a "fundamental life skill," NNLW also promotes, through advertising and activities, the role of the free press in America.[64] One of its programs, "Viral Rumor Rundown," uncovers and debunks online videos and messages, such as the recent montage that falsely shows athletes collapsing after receiving a Covid-19 vaccine shot.

## Quotables

"We have a huge segment of the population that believes in outright falsehoods, lies, and conspiracy theories that are bizarre. How is that possible? How do we operate a democracy when we can't agree on a common set of facts? How does the press operate in an environment where we can't agree on what happened yesterday?"[65]

—**Marty Baron, former executive editor,** *Washington Post*

## Supporting Local News

An expression of support can be as easy as placing an Amazon order. A $25 donation via PayPal represents a small investment with larger symbolic value. Think of the Green Bay Packers when you weigh the condition of your local news and why it is worth supporting. MVP Aaron Rodgers, the face of the Packers, knows that the team's owners—thousands of them—fill the stands of Lambeau Field on Sundays. The Packers have been a publicly owned, nonprofit corporation since 1923, with more than 360,760 stockholders, not one of whom expects or receives dividend checks or stock splits. Its status as a jointly held community asset protects the team from hostile takeovers or forced relocation to a market far larger than Green Bay (population 105,000) and its environs.

Green Bay illustrates another form of community involvement—venture philanthropy. It differs from philanthropy that doles out million-dollar-plus gifts earmarked for social causes. In simple terms, venture philanthropy represents an investment of both capital and expertise to bolster a struggling civic-minded business or organization, among them news outlets. Henry Blodget, editor of the website Business Insider, explained: "You had to attack social problems the way venture capitalists and entrepreneurs attacked business problems—with hands-on, we're-in-this-together, failure-isn't-an-option partnerships between *investors* and *investees*."[66] The concept combines community service goals with the practical fiscal goal of earning on investments. Applied to larger newspapers, venture philanthropy looks risky. Investment mogul Warren Buffett announced in January 2020 the sale of more than seventy-five weekly and daily newspapers he tried to save and make profitable.[67] Venture philanthropy seems better suited for helping smaller-scale news outlets, with local investors and entrepreneurs leading the way.

By imagining news as a community endeavor, journalists and citizens together can make a big difference. A group called the Tiny News Collective recently proposed the following opportunity:

> Whether you're a lifetime journalist, a committed organizer or an individual looking to support your area, we believe that the next generation of news looks like you. . . . We hope for its success in putting journalists and citizens together in a joint enterprise. We envision a newsroom occupied by retired teachers, teenagers, journalism school graduates, a collection of ages and backgrounds all drawn by doing journalism.[68]

Belying its name, the organization's ambitions appear massive. A few months after its founding in December 2020, the Tiny News Collective announced it would launch five hundred new local news organizations in three years, primarily in areas unserved or underserved by for-profit media. Kara Meyberg Guzman, a Tiny News board member, explained part of its mission: "We want to support people who are part of and are deeply invested in their communities, and give them the training, financial and backroom support to make it easier to own and operate a local newsroom." Nonetheless, she anticipates a daunting task: "I know for many prospective founders of color, a huge barrier is financial security. It's scary to leave a steady job, go without health insurance, etc." Meyberg Guzman speaks from the experience of starting her own news site, the Santa Cruz Local, going without pay for a year and depending on her husband's steady job and health insurance. As of early 2021, her news site had seven hundred paying subscribers.[69] She hopes its modest success will be replicated "hundreds of times" elsewhere.

To succeed as a news start-up takes perseverance and ingenuity. Berkeleyside, a seven-year-old Bay Area digital news site, solidified its connections with a direct public offering (DPO)—a type of crowdfunding—so people who appreciated its journalism could invest in its future and that of the community as well. When it announced plans for the DPO, Berkeleyside's website posted the slogan, "You invest in Main Street not Wall Street." By the time the DPO period ended in 2018, Berkeleyside had raised $1 million in capital from 355 readers.[70] Realistically, investments on Main Street usually pay fewer dividends. But for local investors, the real payout comes with the satisfaction of community collaboration.

## Tuning In, Turning Out

Signs of renewed civic responsibility include hometown organizations that sponsor forums where people with opposing viewpoints can interact in safe, moderated settings. As David Preston discovered when he said "yes" to joining a dialogue group, hundreds of civic renewal and education projects begun around the country suggest that people care about civic life and would rather discuss than argue, would rather get involved than bellyache. Through such approaches as beautification projects, roundtables, and shared meals, participants learn that to be heard you need to engage. In Amherst, Massachusetts, the town manager held casual conversations with residents at bakeries and coffee shops. He wanted to promote casual exchanges among residents and build rapport between the community and its government leaders.[71] Online offerings, too, provide alternatives for deliberative discourse outside the verbal fights of Twitter and Facebook. The website Kialo, for one, hosts thoughtful explorations of trending issues, among them a proposal to counter hate speech. Appropriately, the word *kialo* in Esperanto means "reason." Its mission: "Making the world more thoughtful."[72]

Another relatively painless step: Go to a scheduled civic or government meeting that fits your interests or your schedule. Someone you know likely will be attending too, and perhaps you will speak up during public comments. The experience might confirm your impression that civic life can be on the tedious side, but it might also illuminate how decisions, substantive and mundane, get made and how agreements are forged. Citizens witnessing democracy firsthand boost the morale of public servants just by attending. The same can be said of going to a public lecture, or a rezoning hearing, or a meeting of the school board. Your presence matters. Most civic and governing entities welcome an audience to keep them on their toes, alert, and aware of their public duties.

## Expanding Sociocultural Awareness

People bowl in teams, belong to a church of choice, and visit the closest neighborhood park—all good for promoting togetherness. But the ruts of our daily existence can lead to inadvertent isolation from the greater community. Journalists and citizens can expand their worlds by checking out a library across town or going to a festival in a Latino neighborhood. Venturing out opens senses and sensibilities. It generates appreciation and awareness of others. We found it inspiring to witness a tree gathering in Bradenton, Florida, a tradition with deep roots in African life. In Malawi, for example, villagers gather under the shade of a large mango tree to discuss problems, get advice from elders, and share music and food.[73] If you saw a midday congregation of Black men, women, and children in a public park, would you be interested in its cultural roots? Sampling experiences and traditions outside of your own helps build community and counter stereotypes.

## *Our Hopeful Conclusion*

*Democracy's News* responds to a disturbing and persistent cynicism in how American citizens now imagine politics. Especially in the past decade, public life seemingly has involved a rhetoric of accusations, palpable falsehoods, put-downs, and strategic exaggerations of the distance separating camps of citizen commitment. We understand the cynicism, but we do not wish to contribute to it. Throughout this book, we examine symptoms of and causes for such divisiveness that, if not completely new, are of a sort surprisingly ugly and counterproductive in a democracy. Alongside the well-documented fact of division, we try to pose journalism's persistent defense of inquisitiveness, accuracy, context, and responsibility—even when fallible humans enact them poorly. We blend these ideas with the committed citizen's desire for social collaboration and understanding. That is why we chose to make clear through our subtitle that we are writing *about* and *to* citizens who care about democracy.

We mainly limit our scope to the basic elements that connect journalism, citizenship, and political discourse necessary for a healthy public life. We hope our guide proves useful as it answers questions, provides background, dispels misrepresentations, and makes the case for citizens' partnership with journalism. News should not be something to dread, mistrust, or shun. By their faith in reliable journalism, citizens develop a community-based ethic and acquire the knowledge to cope with social issues great and small. They discover fellow community members as more than stereotypes or opponents. They become collaborators with whom to identify and somehow sustain a working republic. When local news wastes away, so does community self-awareness, and citizens become less likely to step outside themselves or link arms with one another. In March 2021, as the impact of Covid-19 was still being felt, the *Northeast News*, an eighty-nine-year-old newspaper that covers northeast Kansas City for 8,500 subscribers, printed a blank front page to dramatize its precarious financial situation and outlook. Publisher and co-owner Michael Bushnell said, "If we print a blank front page with no news, people are going to see what it's like if we're gone."[74] The good news is that more citizens want to make sure that does not happen.

Citizens are right to question whether dialogue journalism and its innovative partner initiatives can "work" effectively in achieving their goals. Will we see reductions in political and cultural division and increased public trust in government and news media? Part of the answer, obviously, depends on how aggressively opponents will work to subvert or undermine the initiatives. A better outlook is found in the current groundswell of public and professional projects and their community acceptance. The evidence points in the right direction, according to the editors of *Democracy in Motion: Evaluating the Practice and Impact of Deliberative Civic Engagement*. In the main findings of their research, they report that deliberative civic engagement is becoming more popular and effective as an adjunct to public life—that it can produce high-quality outcomes even with diverse participants, help alleviate such social problems as "exclusion, marginalization, and inequality," and improve the quality of opinions raised in civic encounters. Many citizens, they conclude, "are eager" to participate in deliberative events, "capable of doing so, and routinely benefit from them."[75]

It would be encouraging to assume that the fans of democracy make up a large and expansive network, but daily experience indicates that responsible citizenship has a long way to go. There are people who simply do not want to hear about the death of democracy or the rise of fascism. They figure there is already too much to worry about. How do you convince people things are truly bad and getting worse? Can it be that many Americans still think Trump and his ideology will disappear? Or that the warnings are exaggerated? Or that even if the big storm hits, they can just ride it out?

It is especially hard to generate optimism when close observers, national and international, notice a disturbing American tolerance, even enthusiasm, for autocratic leadership.[76] How many citizens and their government representatives would rather see civic commitments shrink and trust in democratic institutions shrink with them? Some civil norms already veer toward either an unswerving loyalty to a potentially violent cause, party, or strong leader, on the one hand, or a willful disengagement from deliberation, accompanied by a scornful attitude of not caring, on the other. They represent a minority that, however, sometimes seems to hold the upper hand.

Citizenship must mean more—more discerning, more thoughtful, and more determined—because the community, broadly or narrowly construed, depends on it. Journalist David Ryfe reinforces our conviction that we should talk about good journalism and good models of public citizenship at the same time: A "cohesive, broad story of journalism, its history, current practices, and likely futures . . . centers on journalism's relation to public life."[77] Citizens and journalists team up, helping to build the social formula that keeps government—and democracy—evolving. George Packer of *The Atlantic*, punctuates Ryfe's point. "Citizens will have to do boring things—run for obscure local election offices and volunteer as poll watchers—with the same unflagging energy as the enemies of democracy," he says. "Decent Republicans will have to work and vote for Democrats, and Democrats will have to work and vote for anti-Trump Republicans or independents in races where no Democrat has a chance to win." The "overriding concern" for citizens, Packer contends, is that they break the "cycle of mutual antagonism" and rebuild an alliance of Americans willing to keep democracy alive and healthy.[78]

Democracy can seem harder to maintain than to build in the first place. The American experience has included periods of bigotry, intolerance, tyranny, and alternative realities; each has torn at the republic and threatened its existence, but the nation has survived. When we began our careers in journalism, communication, and higher education—as we served in the military, started families, and settled into the rhythms of everyday life—we never expected to witness a nation as divided, coarse, and apparently rudderless as ours. By writing *Democracy's News*, we hope to join the ranks of the latest generation of Americans unwilling to let the republic fall to inertia, disinformation, demagoguery, or authoritarianism.

# *Notes*

## Introduction

1. Brian Naylor, "Read Trump's Jan. 6 Speech, a Key Part of Impeachment Trial," NPR, February 10, 2021, https://www.npr.org/2021/02/10/966396848/read -trumps-jan-6-speech-a-key-part-of-impeachment-trial

2. Alia Shoaib, "Donald Trump Was 'Almost Giddy' Watching the Capitol Riot on TV, Author Says," Insider, July 24, 2021, https://www.businessinsider.com/dona ld-trump-was-almost-giddy-during-the-capitol-riot-author-says-2021-7

3. "Trump's Son Urged Father to Intervene in 6 January Capitol Riot," BBC News, December 14, 2021, https://www.bbc.com/news/world-us-canada-5965 0800; and Maggie Haberman and Jonathan Martin, "After the Speech: What Trump Did as the Capitol Was Attacked," *New York Times*, February 13, 2021, https://www .nytimes.com/2021/02/13/us/politics/trump-capitol-riot.html

4. Ryan Bort, "Capitol Rioters 'Surged' Immediately After Trump Bashed Pence on Twitter: January 6 Hearing," *Rolling Stone*, June 16, 2022, https://www.ro llingstone.com/politics/politics-news/capitol-rioters-surged-after-trump-pence -tweet-1369633/

5. "'I Know Your Pain. I Know Your Hurt': Donald Trump Tells Rioters to Go Home," *Florida Politics*, January 6, 2021, https://floridapolitics.com/archives/3926 09-police-order-evacuation-of-buildings-on-capitol-hill/

6. Tara Dublin, "Shocking Revelations at Tuesday's January 6 Hearing Portrays Trump As 'Indecent, Vile and Uncivil Man' Says Chuck Rosenberg," Hill-Reporter.com, June 27, 2022, https://hillreporter.com/watch-shocking-revelations -at-tuesdays-january-6th-hearing-portrays-trump-as-indecent-vile-and-uncivil -man-says-chuck-rosenberg-134371

7. Jonathan Rauch, *The Constitution of Knowledge: A Defense of Truth* (Washington, DC: Brookings Institute Press, 2021), 116.

8. Rob Anderson, Robert Dardenne, and George M. Killenberg, *The Conversation of Journalism: Communication, Community, and News* (Westport, CT: Praeger, 1994), xxi.

9. See David Byrne, *How Music Works* (San Francisco: McSweeny's, 2012), 189-91. Music lovers with different preferences will find similar support for collaborative dialogue in the classical pianist and conductor Daniel Barenboim's book

about music and human connection, *Music Quickens Time* (New York: Verso, 2008). "'The power of music lies in its ability to speak to all aspects of the human being. . . . How often we think that personal, social and political issues are independent, without influencing each other. From music we learn that this is an objective impossibility; there simply are no independent elements. . . . Music teaches us, in short, that everything is connected" (108).

## Chapter 1

1. The description of the June 1, 2020, clash is a composite of broadcast video, news reports, and follow-up investigations. Sources include Matt Cohen, "The Park Police's Account of Lafayette Square Attack Doesn't Add Up," *Mother Jones*, July 28, 2020, https://www.motherjones.com/anti-racism-police-protest/2020/07/the-park-polices-account-of-lafayette-square-attack-doesnt-add-up/; and Catie Edmondson, "Despite Evidence, Park Police Chief Says 'Tremendous Restraint' Was Used in Lafayette Clash," *New York Times*, July 28, 2020, https://www.nytimes.com/2020/07/28/us/politics/lafayette-square-park-police-protests.html

2. Ted Johnson, "Park Police Claim That Protesters Threw Projectiles at Lafayette Square Park, but Reporters Say They Saw Peaceful Demonstration," Deadline, June 2, 2020, https://deadline.com/2020/06/donald-trump-george-floyd-demonstrators-lafayette-square-park-1202949717/; and Alex Emmons, "National Guard Major Calls Assault on D.C. Protesters 'Deeply Disturbing,'" *The Intercept*, July 28, 2020, https://theintercept.com/2020/07/28/dc-lafayette-square-protesters-congress-hearing/

3. Ruth Marcus, "First, Exhale. Then Pray for Biden. He's Going to Need It," *Washington Post*, January 22, 2021, https://www.washingtonpost.com/opinions/first-exhale-then-pray-for-biden-hes-going-to-need-it/2001/01/22/ff5457a2-5cea-11ed-8bcf-3877871c819_story.html/

4. Zeynep Tufekci, "America's Next Authoritarian Will Be Much More Competent," *The Atlantic*, November 6, 2020, https://www.theatlantic.com/ideas/archive/2020/11/trump-proved-authoritarians-can-get-elected-america/617023/

5. Jamelle Bouie, "This Is Why Republicans Fear Change," *New York Times*, October 23, 2020, https://www.nytimes.com/2020/10/23/opinion/lindsey-graham-senate-statehood.html; and Fintan O'Toole, "Democracy's Afterlife: Trump, the GOP, and the Rise of Zombie Politics," *New York Review*, December 3, 2020, https://www.nybooks.com/articles/2020/12/03/democracys-afterlife/

6. John Haltiwanger, "Republicans Are Putting America's Democracy in Mortal Danger, 100 Scholars Warn," Insider, June 1, 2021, https://www.businessinsider.com/us-democracy-danger-gop-voting-restrictions-over-100-scholars-warn-2021-6; and Thomas L. Friedman, "Trump's Big Lie Devoured the G.O.P. and Now Eyes Our Democracy," *New York Times*, May 4, 2021, https://www.nytimes.com/2021/05/04/opinion/gop-trump-2020-election.html

7. Matthew C. MacWilliams, "Trump Is an Authoritarian. So Are Millions of

Americans," Politico, September 23, 2020, https://www.politico.com/news/magazi
ne/2020/09/23/trump-america-authoritarianism-420681

8. Matt Ford, "The Trump Lawyer Plotting the Next American Coup," *New Republic*, September 24, 2021, https://newrepublic.com/article/163764/john-east man-coup-memo-pence; and Bob Woodward and Robert Costa, *Peril* (New York: Simon & Schuster, 2021).

9. Paul Farhi, "The Washington Post's New Slogan Turns Out to Be an Old Saying," *Washington Post*, February 24, 2017, https://www.washingtonpost.com /lifestyle/style/the-washington-posts-new-slogan-turns-out-to-be-an-old-sayi ng/2017/02/23/cb199cda-fa02-11e6-be05-1a3817ac21a5_story.html

10. Becky Yerak, "Charleston Gazette-Mail Owner Files for Bankruptcy," *Wall Street Journal*, January 31, 2018, https://www.wsj.com/articles/charleston-gazette -mail-owner-files-for-bankruptcy-1517420451

11. Kristen Hare, "The Charleston Gazette-Mail Just Let Go of Its Second Editor in Less Than 2 Years," Poynter, February 20, 2020, https://www.poynter.org/bu siness-work/2020/the-charleston-gazette-mail-just-let-go-of-its-second-editor -in-less-than-2-years/

12. Bridget O'Brian, "Pulitzer Prizes Celebrate 100 Newsworthy Years," *Columbia News*, February 16, 2016, https://news.columbia.edu/news/pulitzer-prizes-cele brate-100-newsworthy-years

13. Erin Keane, "The U.S. Newspaper Crisis Is Growing: More Than 1 in 5 Local Papers Have Closed since 2004," *Salon*, October 16, 2018, https://www.salon.com /2018/10/16/the-u-s-newspaper-crisis-is-growing-more-than-1-in-5-local-pape rs-have-closed-since-2004/. See Penelope Muse Abernathy, "News Deserts and Ghost Newspapers: Will Local News Survive?," *The Expanding News Desert*, University of North Carolina, Hussman School of Journalism and Media, 2019, https:// www.usnewsdeserts.com/reports/news-deserts-and-ghost-newspapers-will-loc al-news-survive/

14. Richard Fausset, "The Last Edition: Dying Gasp of One Local Newspaper," *New York Times*, August 1, 2019, https://www.nytimes.com/2019/08/01/us/warroad -pioneer-news-desert.html

15. Nu Yang, "Can News Publishers Survive the Coronavirus?" *Editor & Publisher*, March 23, 2020, https://www.editorandpublisher.com/stories/can-news-pu blishers-survive-the-coronavirus,1415

16. Quoted in Harold Evans, "The Daily Show," *New York Times*, August 20 2009, https://www.nytimes.com/2009/08/23/books/review/Evans-t.html. See Alex S. Jones, *Losing the News: The Future of the News That Feeds Democracy* (New York: Oxford University Press, 2009).

17. Associated Press, "GateHouse, Gannett Merger Is Official, Creating Largest U.S. Newspaper Chain," Marketwatch, November 19, 2019, https://www.marketwat ch.com/story/gatehouse-gannett-merger-is-official-creating-largest-us-newspap er-chain-2019-11-19

18. Nathan Bomey, "GateHouse Media Owner to Acquire USA TODAY Owner

Gannett," *USA Today*, August 5, 2019, https://www.usatoday.com/story/money/20 19/08/05/gannett-gatehouse-media-new-media-investment-group/1902550001/

19. "Most Americans Think Their Local News Media Are Doing Well Financially; Few Help to Support It," in *For Local News, Americans Embrace Digital but Still Want Strong Community Connection*, Pew Research Center, March 26, 2019, https://www.journalism.org/2019/03/26/most-americans-think-their-local-news -media-are-doing-well-financially-few-help-to-support-it/

20. Rob Garver, "The Strip Mining of the U.S. News Industry," VOA News, September 18, 2019, https://www.voanews.com/usa/strip-mining-us-news-industry

21. Dan Barry, "The Last Reporter in Town Had One Big Question for His Rich Boss," *New York Times*, July 10, 2020, https://www.nytimes.com/2020/07/10/us/al den-global-capital-pottstown-mercury.html?smid=em-share

22. See Margaret Sullivan, *Ghosting the News: Local Journalism and Crisis of American Democracy* (New York: Columbia Global Reports, 2020).

23. Marc Tracy, "McClatchy, Family-Run News Chain, Goes to Hedge Fund in Bankruptcy Sale," *New York Times*, August 4, 2020, https://www.nytimes.com/20 20/08/04/business/media/mcclatchy-newspapers-bankrutpcy-chatham.html

24. Alana Levinson, "Brand-Backed Media Gets Another Look," *Predictions for Journalism 2020*, Nieman Lab, 2020, https://www.niemanlab.org/2019/12/brand-ba cked-media-gets-another-look/

25. Elizabeth Grieco, "U.S. Newspapers Have Shed Half of Their Newsroom Employees since 2008," Pew Research Center, April 20, 2020, https://www.pewrese arch.org/fact-tank/2020/04/20/u-s-newsroom-employment-has-dropped-by-a-q uarter-since-2008/

26. Amy Mitchell, Mark Jurkowitz, J. Baxter Oliphant, and Elisa Shearer, "Americans Who Mainly Get Their News on Social Media Are Less Engaged, Less Knowledgeable," Pew Research Center, July 30, 2020, https://www.journalism.org /2020/07/30/americans-who-mainly-get-their-news-on-social-media-are-less -engaged-less-knowledgeable/

27. Greg Jackson, "Vicious Cycles: Theses on a Philosophy of News," *Harpers*, February 19, 2020, https://harpers.org/archive/2020/01/vicious-cycles-theses-on -a-philosophy-of-news/

28. Chloe Reichel, "Civic Engagement Declines When Local Newspapers Shut Down," Journalist's Resource, Shorenstein Center on Media, Politics and Public Policy, Harvard Kennedy School, June 22, 2018, https://journalistsresource.org/st udies/society/news-media/local-newspapers-civic-engagement/; and Jonas Heese, Gerardo Perez Cavazos, and Caspar David Peter, "When the Local Newspaper Leaves Town: The Effects of Local Newspaper Closures on Corporate Misconduct," *Journal of Financial Economics*, July 21, 2021, https://papers.ssrn.com/sol3/papers.cfm?abst ract_id=3889039

29. Lara Takenaga, "More Than 1 in 5 U.S. Papers Has Closed. This Is the Result," *New York Times*, December 21, 2019, https://www.nytimes.com/2019/12/21 /reader-center/local-news-deserts.html?smid=em-share

30. Elaine Godfrey, "What We Lost When Gannett Came to Town," *The Atlantic*, October 5, 2021, https://www.theatlantic.com/politics/archive/2021/10/ganne tt-local-newspaper-hawk-eye-iowa/619847/?utm_source=newsletter&utm_medi um=email&utm_campaign=masthead-newsletter&utm_content=20211009&silve rid=%%RECIPIENT_ID%%&utm_term=Subscriber

31. Phil Di Vece, "We Need Newspapers: Here's Why," *Boothbay Register*, February 26, 2020, https://www.boothbayregister.com/article/we-need-newspapers -here-s-why/130817

32. Charles Angelucci, Julia Cage, and Michael Sinkinson, "Competition and News Diets, " SSRN, September 4, 2021, https://dx.doi.org/10.2139/ssrn.3537040

33. Barbara Ehrenreich, *Nickel and Dimed: On (Not) Getting By in America* (New York: Metropolitan Books, 2001).

34. Barbara Ehrenreich, "In American, Only the Rich Can Afford to Write about Poverty," *The Guardian*, August 6, 2015, https://www.theguardian.com/commentis free/2015/aug/06/america-rich-write-about-poverty

35. David Winston, "When We Stop Talking to Each Other, Democracy Dies in Silence," Rollcall, August 14, 2019, https://www.rollcall.com/2019/08/14/when-we -stop-talking-to-each-other-democracy-dies-in-silence/

36. *Disinformation: A Primer in Russian Active Measures and Influence Campaigns.* Hearing before the Select Committee on Intelligence, Senate, 150th Cong. (March 30, 2017), https://www.intelligence.senate.gov/sites/default/files/hearin gs/S Hrg 115-40 Pt 1.pdf

37. See, in general, *Report on the Investigation into Russian Interference in the 2016 Presidential Election, Volume I of II.* Washington, DC: U.S. Department of Justice, March 2019, https://www.justice.gov/storage/report.pdf

38. Mark Mazzetti, "G.O.P.-Led Senate Panel Details Ties between 2016 Trump Campaign and Russia," *New York Times*, August 18, 2020, https://www.nytimes .com/2020/08/18/us/politics/senate-intelligence-russian-interference-report .html

39. Salvador Rodriguez, "Here Are the Scandals and Other Incidents That Have Sent Facebook's Share Price Tanking in 2018," CNBC, November 20, 2018, https:// www.cnbc.com/2018/11/20/facebooks-scandals-in-2018-effect-on-stock.html

40. Claire Allbright, "A Russian Facebook Page Organized a Protest in Texas. A Different Russian Page Launched the Counterprotest," *Texas Tribune*, November 1, 2017, https://www.texastribune.org/2017/11/01/russian-facebook-page-organized -protest-texas-different-russian-page-l/

41. Craig Timberg and Tony Romm, "It's Not Just the Russians Anymore as Iranians and Others Turn Up Disinformation Efforts Ahead of 2020 Vote," *Washington Post*, July 25, 2019, https://www.washingtonpost.com/technology/2019/07 /25/its-not-just-russians-anymore-iranians-others-turn-up-disinformation-effo rts-ahead-vote/

42. Matt Field, "Congressional Testimony: How the Pentagon Can Fight Information Warfare," Bulletin of the Atomic Scientists, May 4, 2021, https://thebullet

in.org/2021/05/congressional-testimony-how-the-pentagon-can-fight-informati on-warfare/

43. Mike McIntire and Nicholas Confessore, "Trump's Twitter Presidency: 9 Key Takeaways," *New York Times,* November 2, 2019, https://www.nytimes.com/20 19/11/02/us/trump-twitter-takeaways.html

44. Lauren Aratani, "'Tsunami of Untruths': Trump Has Made 20,000 False or Misleading Claims—Report," *The Guardian,* July 13, 2020, https://www.theguardi an.com/us-news/2020/jul/13/donald-trump-20000-false-or-misleading-claims

45. Glenn Kessler, Salvador Rizzo, and Meg Kelly, "Trump Made 30,573 False or Misleading Claims as President. Nearly Half Came in His Final Year," *Washington Post,* January 24, 2021, https://www.washingtonpost.com/politics/2021/01/24/tru mps-false-or-misleading-claims-total-30573-over-four-years/

46. Aaron Kessler, "Who Is @TEN_GOP from the Russia Indictment? Here's What We Found Reading 2,000 of Its Tweets," CNN, February 17, 2018, https:// www.cnn.com/2018/02/16/politics/who-is-ten-gop/index.html

47. S. V. Dáte, "The Ministry of Untruth," HuffPost, January 15, 2020, https:// www.huffpost.com/entry/trump-untruth-lies-false_n_5e0bac46e4b0843d360c 94ea

48. "An American Original," *Vanity Fair,* October 6, 2010, https://www.vanityfa ir.com/news/2010/11/moynihan-letters-201011

49. Bandy X. Lee, ed., *The Dangerous Case of Donald Trump: 27 Psychiatrists and Mental Health Experts Assess a President* (New York: Thomas Dunne, 2017).

50. Amanda Carpenter, *Gaslighting America: Why We Love It When Trump Lies to Us* (New York: HarperCollins, 2018).

51. Bob Woodward, *Rage* (New York: Simon & Schuster, 2020), xix.

52. "Immunizing the Public against Misinformation," World Health Organization, August 25, 2020, https://www.who.int/news-room/feature-stories/detail/im munizing-the-public-against-misinformation

53. Angelo Fichera, "Post on Floyd Protests Uses Old Vandalism Photos," FactCheck, June 3, 2020, https://www.factcheck.org/2020/06/post-on-floyd-protests -uses-old-vandalism-photos/

54. Paul Krugman, *Arguing with Zombies: Economics, Politics, and the Fight for a Better Future* (New York: W. W. Norton, 2020), 3.

55. Steven Levitsky and Daniel Ziblatt, *How Democracies Die* (New York: Crown, 2018), 9.

56. Brian Niemietz, "Racist Dallas Woman Threatens to Call ICE on Latina Workers Operating a Taco Truck," *New York Daily News,* April 8, 2019, https://www .nydailynews.com/news/national/ny-racist-white-woman-call-ice-taco-truck-wo rkers-20190408-rzupx4ym5fdpvpb6en3iyw5zna-story.html; and Sebastian Herrera, "'Taco Truck Tammy' Viral Video Was Amplified by Russian Trolls, Researchers Say," *Austin American-Statesman,* April 23, 2019, https://www.statesman.com /news/20190423/taco-truck-tammy-viral-video-was-amplified-by-russian-trol ls-researchers-say

57. Barbara Sprunt, "Trump Questions Election Again after White House Walked Back His Earlier Remarks," NPR, September 24, 2020, https://www.npr.org /2020/09/24/916440816/republican-leaders-reject-trump-hedging-on-transfer -of-power-amid-war-over-confi

58. Eric Burns, *Infamous Scribbler: The Founding Fathers and the Rowdy Beginnings of American Journalism* (New York: Public Affairs, 2006).

59. "Letter from Thomas Jefferson to John Tyler, 28 June 1804," Founders Online, National Archives, https://founders.archives.gov/documents/Jefferson/01 -43-02-0557

60. James Madison, Federalist Paper No. 10 (1787), Bill of Rights Institute, https://billofrightsinstitute.org/founding-documents/primary-source-documents /the-federalist-papers/federalist-papers-no-10/

61. *Areopagitica*; A Speech of Mr. John Milton, For the Liberty of Unlicenc'd Printing, To the Parlament of England, 1644, Dartmouth University, 2020, https:// www.dartmouth.edu/~milton/reading_room/areopagitica/text.html

62. Timothy Snyder, *On Tyranny: Twenty Lessons from the Twentieth Century* (New York: Tim Duggan Books, 2017), 71.

63. Kevin Roose, "Following Falsehoods: A Reporter's Approach on QAnon," *New York Times*, October 3, 2020, https://www.nytimes.com/2020/10/03/insider /qanon-reporter.html

64. Amanda Seitz and Barbara Ortutay, "Facebook, Twitter Flounder in QAnon Crackdown," ABC News, October 1, 2020, https://abcnews.go.com/Politics/wireSto ry/facebook-twitter-flounder-qanon-crackdown-73370661

65. *Reno v. American Civil Liberties Union*, 521 U.S. 844 (1997).

66. Masha Gessen, *Surviving Autocracy* (New York: Riverhead Books, 2020), 112.

67. Michael D. Shear, Maggie Haberman, Nicholas Confessore, Karen Yourish, Larry Buchanan, and Keith Collins, "How Trump Reshaped the Presidency in over 11,000 Tweets," *New York Times*, November 2, 2019, https://www.nytimes.com/int eractive/2019/11/02/us/politics/trump-twitter-presidency.html

68. David E. McCraw, *Truth in Our Times* (New York: St. Martin's Press, 2019), 161.

69. A. G. Sulzberger, "The Growing Threat to Journalism around the World," *New York Times*, September 23, 2019, https://www.nytimes.com/2019/09/23/opini on/press-freedom-arthur-sulzberger.html

70. See U.S. Press Freedom Tracker, pressfreedomtracker.us

71. "Nobel Peace Prize Awarded to 2 Journalists, Highlighting Fight for Press Freedom," *New York Times*, October 8, 2021, https://www.nytimes.com/live/2021 /10/08/world/nobel-prize

72. Ben Westcott, "Nobel Winner Maria Ressa Vows to Fight for Facts and the Rule of Law," CNN, October 8, 2021, https://www.cnn.com/2021/10/08/media/mar ia-ressa-nobel-peace-prize-interview-intl/index.html

73. See Brian Stelter, *Hoax: Donald Trump, Fox News, and the Dangerous Distortion of Truth* (New York: Atria/One Signal, 2020).

74. Jim Windolf and John Koblin, "Fox News Hosts Take the Offensive about Texts to Meadows," *New York Times*, December 16, 2021, https://popnews247.com/2021/12/16/fox-news-hosts-take-the-offensive-about-texts-to-meadows/

75. "Interview: Jeanine Pirro Interviews Donald Trump at the White House," Factbase, September 12, 2020, https://factba.se/transcript/donald-trump-interview-jeanine-pirro-fox-news-september-12-2020

76. "Occupational Employment and Wages: Reporters and Correspondents." U.S. Bureau of Labor Statistics, May 2018, https://www.bls.gov/oes/2018/may/oes273022.htm

77. Woodward, *Rage*, 256.

78. Liam Moriarty, "'Both-Sides Journalism' vs. 'A Place of Moral Clarity,'" Jefferson Public Radio, July 6, 2020, https://www.ijpr.org/media-society/2020-07-06/both-sides-journalism-vs-a-place-of-moral-clarity. For an extended discussion of objectivity in journalism, see Lewis Raven Wallace, *The View from Somewhere: Undoing the Myth of Journalistic Objectivity* (Chicago: University of Chicago Press, 2019).

79. Zack Beauchamp, "The New York Times Staff Revolt over Tom Cotton's Op-ed, Explained," Vox, June 7, 2020, https://www.vox.com/2020/6/5/21280425/new-york-times-tom-cotton-send-troops-staff-revolt

80. Astra Taylor, *Democracy May Not Exist, but We'll Miss It When It's Gone* (New York: Metropolitan Books, 2019), 14.

Chapter 2

1. Sharon V. Salinger, *Taverns and Drinking in Early America* (Baltimore: Johns Hopkins University Press, 2002), 1–6.

2. David W. Conroy, *In Public Houses: Drink and the Revolution of Authority in Colonial Massachusetts* (Chapel Hill: University of North Carolina Press, 1995), 11.

3. Conroy, *In Public Houses*, 302.

4. Harry S. Stout, *The New England Soul: Preaching and Religious Culture in Colonia New England* (New York: Oxford University Press, 1986), 3.

5. John Wagner and Julie Zauzmer, "Trump Vows to 'Totally Destroy' Restrictions on Churches' Support of Candidates," *Washington Post*, February 2, 2017, https://www.washingtonpost.com/politics/trump-vows-to-totally-destroy-restrictions-on-churches-support-of-candidates/2017/02/02/fed9bad2-e981-11e6-bf6f-301b6b443624_story.html

6. Konstantin Dierks, *In My Power: Letter Writing and Communications in Early America* (Philadelphia: University of Pennsylvania Press, 2009).

7. Stephen D. Solomon, "Cato's Letters, 1720-1723," First Amendment Watch, September 19, 2019, https://firstamendmentwatch.org/history-speaks-catos-letters-1720-1723/

8. Our summary is based on several detailed accounts that describe the life, prosecution, and trial of John Peter Zenger. They include Eric Burns, *Infamous*

*Scribblers: The Founding Fathers and the Rowdy Beginnings of American Journalism* (New York: Public Affairs, 2006), 98-111; Christopher B. Daly, *Covering America: A Narrative History of a Nation's Journalism* (Amherst: University of Massachusetts Press, 2012), 26-30; Stephen D. Solomon, *Revolutionary Dissent: How the Founding Generation Created the Freedom of Speech* (New York: St. Martin's, 2016), 27-28, 45-51, 53-55; and John Tebbel, *The Compact History of the American Newspaper* (New York: Hawthorn Books, 1963), 26-31.

9. Solomon, *Revolutionary Dissent*, 42.

10. Burns, *Infamous Scribblers*, 109.

11. Leonard W. Levy, *Legacy of Suppression: Freedom of Speech and Press in Early American History* (Cambridge: Belknap Press of Harvard University Press, 1960).

12. See Leonard W. Levy, *Emergence of a Free Press* (Chicago: Ivan R. Dee, 1985).

13. Daly, *Covering America*, 33.

14. Pauline Maier, *From Resistance to Revolution* (New York: W. W. Norton, paperback ed., 1991).

15. Benjamin L. Carp, *Defiance of the Patriots: The Boston Tea Party and the Making of America* (New Haven: Yale University Press, 2010).

16. J. Dennis Robinson, "History Matters: Portsmouth Tea Party Narrowly Avoided," Seacoastonline, September 21, 2020, https://www.seacoastonline.com/st ory/news/local/2020/09/21/history-matters-portsmouth-tea-party-narrowly-avo ided/42673275/

17. Jon Katz, "The Age of Paine," *Wired*, May 1, 1995, https://www.wired.com/19 95/05/paine/. A number of reputable sources accept the numbers cited by Katz, but those figures seem high for a time when books were printed one sheet at a time. Paine self-reported sales of *Common Sense*, so perhaps he exaggerated for publicity's sake.

18. Katz, "The Age of Paine."

19. Several major works guided our account of the Constitutional Convention: Catherine Drinker Bower, *Miracle at Philadelphia: The Story of the Constitutional Convention May to September 1787* (Boston: Little, Brown, 1966, reissued in paperback, 1986); Joseph J. Ellis, *Founding Brothers: The Revolutionary Generation* (New York: Alfred A. Knopf, 2000); David O. Stewart, *The Summer of 1787: The Men Who Invented the Constitution* (New York: Simon & Schuster, 2007); and Gordon S. Wood, *Empire of Liberty: A History of the Early Republic, 1789-1815* (New York: Oxford University Press, 2009).

20. "Constitution of the United States—A History," American's Founding Documents, National Archives, https://www.archives.gov/founding-docs/more-perfe ct-union

21. Sam Roberts, "Forrest McDonald, Historian Who Punctured Liberal Notions, Dies at 89," *New York Times*, January 22, 2016, https://www.nytimes.com /2016/01/22/us/politics/forrest-mcdonald-historian-who-punctured-liberal-notio ns-dies-at-89.html

22. Danielle Allen, *Our Declaration: A Reading of the Declaration of Independence in Defense of Equality* (New York: Liveright, 2014), 103.

23. Jesse Wegman, "Why We Should Abolish the Electoral College," *Washington Post*, March 17, 2020, https://www.nytimes.com/2020/03/17/books/review/let-the-people-pick-the-president-jesse-wegman.html; and see Ellis Cose, *The Short Life and Curious Death of Free Speech in America* (New York: HarperCollins, 2020), chap. 5, "What the Founders Never Imagined."

24. Wood, *Empire of Liberty,* 7.

25. Jill Lepore, *These Truths: A History of the United States* (New York: W. W. Norton, 2018), 126–28.

26. Quoted in John P. Kaminski, Gaspare J. Saladino, Richard Leffler, Charles H. Schoenleber, and Margaret A. Hogan, eds., *The Documentary History of the Ratification of the Constitution* (Charlottesville: University of Virginia Press, 2009), http://digital.library.wisc.edu/1711.dl/History.DHRCv1

27. "The Constitution of the United States: A Transcription," America's Founding Documents, National Archives, retrieved October 1, 2021, https://www.archives.gov/founding-docs/constitution-transcript

28. Akhil Reed Amar, *The Words That Made Us: America's Constitutional Conversation, 1760–1840* (New York: Basic Books, 2021), xiii.

29. Linda Colley, *The Gun, the Ship, and the Pen: Warfare, Constitutions, and the Making of the Modern World* (New York: Liveright, 2021), 122.

30. "To James Madison from Thomas Jefferson, 20 December 1787," Founders Online, National Archives, https://founders.archives.gov/documents/Madison/01-10-02-0210

31. Robert Allen Rutland, "The First Great Newspaper Debate: The Constitutional Crisis of 1787-88," *Proceedings of the American Antiquarian Society* 97 (1987): 43–58, https://www.americanantiquarian.org/proceedings/44539394.pdf

32. Tony Rosado, "What Is the Meaning of the Term 'Founding Fathers'?" *Professional Interpreter* (blog), July 4, 2017, https://rpstranslations.wordpress.com/2017/07/04/what-is-the-meaning-of-the-term-founding-fathers/

33. Danielle Susan Allen, "The Flawed Genius of the Constitution," *The Atlantic*, October 5, 2020, https://www.theatlantic.com/magazine/archive/2020/10/danielle-allen-constitution/615481/

34. "From Thomas Jefferson to Barnabas Bidwell, 5 July 1806," Founders Online, National Archives, https://founders.archives.gov/documents/Jefferson/99-01-02-3958

35. "From Thomas Jefferson to Marc Auguste Pictet, 5 February 1803," Founders Online, National Archives, https://founders.archives.gov/documents/Jefferson/01-39-02-0391

36. Michael Schudson, *The Good Citizen: A History of American Civic Life* (New York: The Free Press, 1998).

37. "From Thomas Jefferson to James Madison, 31 July 1788," Founders Online, National Archives, https://founders.archives.gov/documents/Jefferson/01-13-02-0335

38. Quoted in *Near v. Minnesota*, 283 U.S. 697 (1931).

39. Brad Sylvester, "Fact Check: Did Voltaire Say, 'I May Disapprove of What You Say, but I Will Defend Your Right to Say It'?" Check Your Fact, September 17, 2019, https://checkyourfact.com/2019/09/17/fact-check-voltaire-disapprove-defend-death-right-freedom-speech/

40. "From Thomas Jefferson to John Tyler, 28 June 1804," Founders Online, National Archives, https://founders.archives.gov/documents/Jefferson/01-43-02-0557

41. Zechariah Chafee, *Freedom of Speech* (New York: Harcourt, Brace, and Howe, 1920), 366.

42. See Alexander Meiklejohn, *Free Speech and Its Relation to Self-Government* (New York: Harper Brothers, 1948).

43. Rodney A. Smolla, *Free Speech in an Open Society* (New York: Vintage, 1992), 16.

44. See Thomas I. Emerson, *The System of Freedom of Expression* (New York: Random House, 1970).

45. See Frederick Schauer, *Free Speech: A Philosophical Enquiry* (Cambridge: Cambridge University Press, 1982).

46. See Catharine A. MacKinnon, *Only Words* (Cambridge, MA: Harvard University Press, 1993). See also a body of work in "critical race theory," which balances expressive rights with the status of vulnerable targeted victims of assaultive hate speech in such contexts as universities and workplaces.

47. See, e.g., Mari J. Matsuda et al., *Words That Wound: Critical Race Theory, Assaultive Speech, and the First Amendment* (Boulder: Westview, 1993).

48. Wendell Berry, *What Are People For?* (San Francisco: North Point, 1990), 81.

49. Irving Kristol, "Republican Virtue vs. Servile Institutions," *The Alternative*, February 1975, https://contemporarythinkers.org/irving-kristol/essay/republican-virtue-vs-servile-institutions/

50. Adam J. White, "A Republic, if We Can Keep It," *The Atlantic*, February 4, 2020, https://www.theatlantic.com/ideas/archive/2020/02/a-republic-if-we-can-keep-it/605887/

51. Kevin C. O'Leary, *Madison's Sorrow: Today's War on the Founders and America's Liberal Ideal* (New York: Pegasus Books, 2020), 219, 237-38.

52. Schudson, *The Good Citizen*, 9.

53. Adam Garfinkle, "The Erosion of Deep Literacy," *National Affairs*, Spring 2020, https://www.nationalaffairs.com/publications/detail/the-erosion-of-deep-literacy

54. Annette Gordon-Reed, "Hopes for the American Experiment," *New York Review of Books*, November 19, 2020, https://www.nybooks.com/articles/2020/11/19/election-hopes-american-experiment/

55. Matthew Shaer, "What Emotion Goes Viral the Fastest?" *Smithsonian* magazine, April 2014, https://www.smithsonianmag.com/science-nature/what-emotion-goes-viral-fastest-180950182/

56. Colby Itkowitz, "Wisconsin State Supreme Court Hears GOP Lawmakers' Challenge to Stay-at-Home Order," *Washington Post*, May 5, 2020, https://www.wa shingtonpost.com/nation/2020/05/05/wisconsin-state-supreme-court-hears-gop -lawmakers-challenge-stay-at-home-order/

## Chapter 3

1. Comments of Margaret Gilleo, C-SPAN, February 23, 1994, Washington, DC, https://www.c-span.org/person/?margaretgilleo

2. *City of Ladue v. Gilleo*, 512 U.S. 43 (1994).

3. Anthony D. Romero, "Equality, Justice and the First Amendment," ACLU, August 15, 2017, https://www.aclu.org/blog/free-speech/equality-justice-and-first -amendment

4. Nora Benavidez, "First Amendment Rights—If You Agree with the President," *The Atlantic*, June 1, 2020, https://www.theatlantic.com/ideas/archive/2020 /06/first-amendment-rightsif-you-agree-with-the-president/612211/

5. Associated Press, "Floridians Mark Trump's Birthday with Flotillas, Caravans," *Los Angeles Times*, June 14, 2020, https://www.latimes.com/world-nation/st ory/2020-06-14/floridians-mark-trumps-birthday-with-flotillas-caravans

6. "John Adams Letter to Abigail Adams, April 26, 1777," Founders Online, National Archives, https://founders.archives.gov/documents/Adams/04-02-02 -0169

7. Owen M. Fiss, *The Irony of Free Speech* (Cambridge, MA: Harvard University Press, 1996), 4.

8. *Cox v. New Hampshire*, 312 U.S. 569 (1941).

9. Perry Stein, "Disability Advocates Arrested during Health Care Protest at McConnell's Office," *Washington Post*, June 22, 2017, https://www.washingtonpost .com/local/public-safety/disability-advocates-arrested-during-health-care-prote st-at-mcconnells-office/2017/06/22/f5dd9992-576f-11e7-ba90-f5875b7d1876_st ory.html

10. Charles Curtis, "Colin Kaepernick: I Won't Stand 'to Show Pride in a Flag for a Country That Oppresses Black People,'" *USA Today*, August 27, 2016, https:// ftw.usatoday.com/2016/08/colin-kaepernick-49ers-national-anthem-sit-explains

11. Allen Lynch, "Woodrow Wilson and the Principle of 'National Self-Determination': A Reconsideration," *Review of International Studies* 28, no. 2 (2002): 419-36, retrieved December 11, 2020, http://www.jstor.org/stable/2009 7800

12. *Kleindienst v. Mandel*, 408 U.S. 753 (1972).

13. Darren Walker, "With Four Freedoms, Four Responsibilities," Ford Foundation, https://www.fordfoundation.org/ideas/ford-forum/with-four-freedoms-four -responsibilities/

14. *Brandenburg v. Ohio*, 395 U.S. 444 (1969).

15. *Virginia v. Black*, 538 U.S. 343 (2003).

16. Geoffrey R. Stone, *Sex, Religion, and Law from America's Origins to the Twenty-First* (New York: Century Liveright, 2017).

17. *Miller v. California*, 413 U.S. 15 (1973). The *Miller* test for obscenity is based on three determinations: Would the average person, based on prevailing community standards, find the work appealing to prurient interest? Does the work depict or describe sexual conduct that is defined by state law as patently offensive? Does the work, as a whole, lack serious literary, artistic, political, or scientific value? *Miller* replaced the Court's earlier, broader standard, "utterly without redeeming social value," established in *Roth v. United States*, 354 U.S. 476 (1957).

18. Stone, *Sex, Religion, and Law*, x.

19. Thomas L. Friedman, "If Our Masks Could Speak," *New York Times*, July 23, 2020, https://www.nytimes.com/2020/07/28/opinion/coronavirus-masks.html

20. See Shirley Ardener, ed., *Perceiving Women* (New York: John Wiley & Sons, 1975); and Cheris Kramerae, "Muted Group Theory," in Stephen W. Littlejohn and Karen A. Foss, eds., *Encyclopedia of Communication Theory* (Thousand Oaks, CA: Sage, 2009).

21. *United States v. Alvarez*, 567 U.S. 709 (2012).

22. *Gertz v. Robert Welch, Inc.* 418 U.S. 323 (1974).

23. *Schenck v. United States*, 249 U.S. 47 (1919).

24. *Abrams v. United States*, 250 U.S. 616 (1919).

25. For details, see *Gitlow v. New York*, 268 U.S. 652 (1925).

26. *West Virginia State Board of Education v. Barnette*, 319 U.S. 624 (1943).

27. *National Association for the Advancement of Colored People v. Alabama*, 357 U.S. 449 (1958).

28. *Talley v. California*, 362 U.S. 60 (1960).

29. *United States v. O'Brien*, 391 U.S. 367 (1968).

30. *Cohen v. California*, 403 U.S. 15 (1971).

31. *Tinker v. Des Moines Independent Community School District*, 393 U.S. 503 (1969).

32. See *Texas v. Johnson*, 491 U.S. 397 (1989) and *United States v. Eichman*, 496 U.S. 310 (1990).

33. *Red Lion Broadcasting Co. v. Federal Communications Commission*, 395 U.S. 367 (1969).

34. *Miami Herald Publishing Co. v. Tornillo*, 418 U.S. 241 (1974).

35. Neil Postman, *Amusing Ourselves to Death: Public Discourse in the Age of Show Business* (New York: Viking Penguin, 1985).

36. *Reno v. American Civil Liberties Union*, 521 U.S. 844 (1997).

37. *Zeran v. America Online, Inc.*, 129 F.3d 327 (4th Cir. 1997), cert. denied, 524 U.S. 937 (1998).

38. *Valentine v. Chrestensen*, 316 U.S. 52 (1942).

39. Joe McGinniss, *The Selling of the President 1968* (New York: Trident Press, 1969).

40. *Citizens United v. Federal Election Commission*, 558 U.S. 310 (2010) at 354.

41. 558 U.S. 310 at 394.

42. Philip Elliott, "The Koch Brothers Plan to Spend a Record-Setting $400 Million," *Time*, January 27, 2018, https://time.com/5121930/koch-brothers-fall-elections/

43. 588 U.S. 310 at 479.

44. *Wooley v. Maynard*, 430 U.S. 705 (1977).

45. Petula Dvorak, "The Woman Who Got Fired for Flipping Off President Trump Just Sued Her Former Employer," *Washington Post*, April 4, 2018, https://www.washingtonpost.com/local/the-woman-who-got-fired-for-flipping-off-pres ident-trump-just-sued-her-former-employer/2018/04/04/64c7376c-3840-11e8 -acd5-35eac230e514_story.html

46. Associated Press, "Judge: Panhandling Protected by the First Amendment," *New Orleans City Business*, June 21, 2017, https://neworleanscitybusiness.com/bl og/2017/06/21/judge-panhandling-protected-by-the-first-amendment/

47. See *Matter of Gordon v. Marrone*, 202 A.D.2d 104 (1992).

48. "Anti-SLAPP Statutes and Commentary," Media Law Resource Center, retrieved December 11, 2020, http://www.medialaw.org/component/k2/item/3494

49. Andrew Albanese, "ALA Strips 'Laura Ingalls Wilder' Name from Children's Book Award," *Publishers Weekly*, June 26, 2018, https://www.publishersweekly.com /pw/by-topic/industry-news/libraries/article/77362-ala-2018-ala-strips-laura-in galls-wilder-name-from-children-s-book-award.html

50. Itzkoff, "Shane Gillis Dropped from 'S.N.L.' Cast amid Criticism of Racist Slurs," *New York Times*, September 16, 2019, https://www.nytimes.com/2019/09/16 /arts/television/shane-gillis-snl.html

51. Sarah Hagi, "Cancel Culture Is Not Real—At Least Not in the Way People Think," *Time*, November 21, 2019, https://time.com/5735403/cancel-culture-is -not-real/

52. "Only in America," October 22, 2021, *The Week* (TheWeek.com), 6.

53. See Nick Estes, *Our History Is the Future: Standing Rock versus the Dakota Access Pipeline, and the Long Tradition of Indigenous Resistance* (Brooklyn: Verso, 2019).

54. Lisa Friedman, "Standing Rock Sioux Tribe Wins a Victory in Dakota Access Pipeline Case," *New York Times*, March 25, 2020, https://www.nytimes.com /2020/03/25/climate/dakota-access-pipeline-sioux.html

55. Stanley Fish, *The First: How to Think about Hate Speech, Campus Speech, Religious Speech, Fake News, Post-Truth, and Donald Trump* (New York: One Signal, 2019), 1.

56. Kirby Wilson, "Ron DeSantis: Any Municipality That 'Defunds' Police Will Lose State Funding," *Tampa Bay Times*, September 21, 2020, https://www.tampabay .com/news/florida-politics/2020/09/21/ron-desantis-any-municipality-that-defu nds-police-will-lose-state-funding/

57. Tadhg A. J. Dooley and David Roth, "Supreme Court Update," *National Law Review*, November 5, 2020, https://www.natlawreview.com/article/supreme-court -update-taylor-v-riojas-no-19-1261-mckesson-v-doeno-19-1108-merrill-v

58. Sophia Cope and Adam Schwartz, "You Have a First Amendment Right to Record the Police," Electronic Freedom Foundation, June 8, 2020, https://www.eff .org/deeplinks/2020/06/you-have-first-amendment-right-record-police

59. Kermit L. Hall, "The Bill of Rights, Liberty, and Original Intent," in Ray-

mond Arsenault, ed., *Crucible of Liberty: 200 Years of the Bill of Rights* (New York: Free Press, 1991), 20.

60. *Whitney v. California*, 352 U.S. 357 (1927) at 375.

61. Vincent Blasi, "The First Amendment and the Ideal of Civic Courage: The Brandeis Opinion in *Whitney v. California*," *William & Mary Law Review* 29, no. 4 (May 1988), https://scholarship.law.wm.edu/wmlr/ vol29/iss4/2

62. *Roe v. Wade*, 410 U.S. 113.

63. *Dobbs v. Jackson Women's Health Organization*, 597 U.S, ___ (2022) at 5, No. 19-1392, slip op. at 1 (U.S. June 24, 2022), https://www.supremecourt.gov/opinions /21pdf/19-1392_6j37.pdf

64. David Cole, "'Egregiously Wrong': The Supreme Court's Unprecedented Turn," *New York Review*, July 8, 2022, https://www.nybooks.com/articles/2022/08 /18/egregiously-wrong-the-supreme-courts-unprecedented-turn-david-cole/

65. Olivia Eubanks, "The History of the Phrase 'When the Looting Starts, the Shooting Starts' Used by Trump," ABC News, May 29, 2020, https://abcnews.go .com/Politics/history-phrase-looting-starts-shooting-starts-trump/story?id=709 50935

## Chapter 4

1. The massive peace protests of early 1971 included a bombing at a restroom in the Capitol and the mass arrest on May Day—May 3—of more than twelve thousand people caught up in clashes in Washington, DC. Thousands of others stumbled away after being tear-gassed by police. Among them was Daniel Ellsberg. Those events, according to journalist Lawrence Roberts, were "rendered obscure by the momentous scandals that immediately followed." See Lawrence Roberts, *Mayday 1971: A White House at War, a Revolt in the Streets, and the Untold History of America's Biggest Mass Arrest* (Boston: Houghton Mifflin Harcourt, 2020).

2. Compiled from multiple sources, including David Rudenstine, *The Day the Presses Stopped: A History of the Pentagon Papers Case* (Berkeley: University of California Press, 1996); Sanford J. Unger, *The Papers & the Papers: An Account of the Legal and Political Battle over the Pentagon Papers* (New York: Columbia University Press, 1989); and Floyd Abrams, *Speaking Freely: Trials of the First Amendment* (New York: Viking, 2005).

3. Janny Scott, "Now It Can Be Told: How Neil Sheehan Got the Pentagon Papers," *New York Times*, January 7, 2021, https://www.nytimes.com/2021/01/07/us /pentagon-papers-neil-sheehan.html

4. Arthur Gelb, *City Room* (New York: G. P. Putnam's Sons, 2003), 559-66.

5. *New York Times Co. v. United States*, 403 U.S. 713 (1971) at 715.

6. 403 U.S. 713 at 763.

7. Laura K. Ray, "The Road to Bush v. Gore: The History of the Supreme Court's Use of the Per Curiam Opinion," *Nebraska Law Review* 79, no. 3 (2000): 551-54, https://digitalcommons.unl.edu/nlr/vol79/iss3/2

8. Scott, "Now It Can Be Told."

9. Dana Priest, "Did the Pentagon Papers Matter?" *Columbia Journalism Review*, Spring 2016, https://www.cjr.org/the_feature/did_the_pentagon_papers _matter.php

10. Rudenstine, *The Day the Presses Stopped*, 355–56.

11. Andrew Pearson, "How Vietnam Changed Journalism," *New York Times*, March 29, 2018, https://www.nytimes.com/2018/03/29/opinion/vietnam-war-jou rnalism.html

12. "The Freedom of the Press Is Yours," *The Atlantic*, August 15, 2018, https:// www.theatlantic.com/ideas/archive/2018/08/the-freedom-of-the-press-is-yours /567655/

13. "From Thomas Jefferson to Edward Carrington, 16 January 1787," Founders Online, National Archives, https://founders.archives.gov/documents/Jefferson/01 -11-02-0047

14. Potter Stewart, "Or of the Press," *Hastings Law Journal* 26 (1975): 631–38, https://repository.uchastings.edu/hastings_law_journal/vol26/iss3/1

15. Robert N. Pierce, *A Sacred Trust: Nelson Poynter and the St. Petersburg Times* (Gainesville: University Press of Florida, 1993).

16. See Anthony Lewis, *Make No Law: The Sullivan Case and the First Amendment* (New York: Random House, 1991). See also Thomas B. Littlewood, *Coals of Fire: The Alton Telegraph Libel Case* (Carbondale: Southern Illinois University Press, 1988).

17. *New York Times Co. v. Sullivan*, 376 U.S. 254 (1964) at 279–80.

18. *Curtis Publishing Co. v. Butts*, 388 U.S. 130 (1967) at 158.

19. *Griswold v. Connecticut*, 381 U.S. 479 (1965) at 485.

20. See *Galella v. Onassis*, 533 F. Supp. 1076 (S.D.N.Y. 1982); and Andrew Goldman, "Barbarian at the Lens: Ron Galella and the Dawn of the Age of Paparazzi," *Town & Country*, May 10, 2020, https://www.townandcountrymag.com/society/mo ney-and-power/a30171412/ron-galella-paparazzi-photographer-jackie-kennedy/

21. *Florida Star v. BJF*, 491 U.S. 524 (1989) at 533.

22. *Gannett Co., Inc. v. DePasquale*, 443 U.S. 368 (1979).

23. *Richmond Newspapers Inc. v. Virginia*, 448 U.S. 555 (1980) at 576, 578.

24. 488 U.S. 555 at 583.

25. Quoted in Jeff Jarvis, "Journalism Is the Conversation. The Conversation Is Journalism," Buzz Machine, January 27, 2019, https://buzzmachine.com/2019/01 /27/journalism-is-the-conversation-the-conversation-is-journalism/

26. *Snyder v. Phelps, et al.*, 562 U.S. 443 (2011) at 460–61.

27. 562 U.S. 443 at 475.

28. Ronald J. Krotoszynski Jr., *The Disappearing First Amendment* (Cambridge: Cambridge University Press, 2019), 162.

29. Nicole Bergstrom, "Supreme Court Justice Clarence Thomas Speaks Up about New York Times v. Sullivan," IP & Media Law, Frankfurt Kurnit Klein and Selz, PC, July 13, 2021, https://ipandmedialaw.fkks.com/post/102h2os/supreme-court-justice-clarence-thomas-speaks-up-about-new-york-times-v-sullivan?utm _source=Mondaq&utm_medium=syndication&utm_campaign=LinkedIn-integration

30. Natasha Cooper, "Reevaluating *New York Times v. Sullivan* in the Wake of Modern Day Journalism," American Bar Association, February 27, 2019, https://www.americanbar.org/groups/litigation/committees/woman-advocate/practice/2019/reevaluating-new-york-times-v-sullivan-in-the-wake-of-modern-day-journalism/

31. Andrew Chung, "U.S. Justices Thomas, Gorsuch Question Libel Protections for Media," Reuters, July 2, 2021, https://www.reuters.com/world/us/us-justices-thomas-gorsuch-question-libel-protections-media-2021-07-02/; and *Berisha v. Lawson*, No. 17-1542, slip op. at 8,—S. Ct.—(July 2, 2021) (Gorsuch, J., dissenting from denial of certiorari).

32. Floyd Abrams, "The Supreme Court Faces a Huge Test on Libel Law," *New York Times*, October 22, 2021, https://www.nytimes.com/2021/10/22/opinion/supreme-court-libel-news-media.html

33. Callum Borcers, "Donald Trump Vowed to 'Open Up' Libel Laws to Make Suing the Media Easier. Can He Do That?" *Washington Post*, February 26, 2016, https://www.washingtonpost.com/news/the-fix/wp/2016/02/26/donald-trump-vows-to-open-up-libel-laws-to-make-suing-the-media-easier-heres-how-he-could-do-it/

34. Jonathan Miller, "It's Devin Nunes v. World When It Comes to Lawsuits," Roll Call, December 3, 2019, https://www.rollcall.com/2019/12/03/its-devin-nunes-v-world-when-it-comes-to-lawsuits/

35. Aaron Blake, "An Embarrassing Moment for Trump's Legal Team," *Washington Post*, January 21, 2020, https://www.washingtonpost.com/politics/2020/01/21/an-embarrassing-moment-trumps-legal-team/

36. "Statement by the President upon Signing S. 1160," Nation Security Archive, July 4, 1966, nsarchive2.gwu.edu

37. Jeffrey Schweers, "'A Little Darker Than We Were Before': Florida Public Records Exemptions Further Limit Access," *Tallahassee Democrat*, May 13, 2019, https://www.tallahassee.com/story/news/local/state/2019/05/13/florida-public-records-exemptions-further-limit-access-session-legislature-bills-sunshine/1164014001/

38. Kenny Jacoby and Ryan Gabrielson, "Marsy's Law Was Meant to Protect Crime Victims. It Now Hides the Identities of Cops Who Use Force," *USA Today* and ProPublica, October 29, 2020, https://www.usatoday.com/in-depth/news/investigations/2020/10/29/police-hide-their-identities-using-victims-rights-bill-marsys-law/3734042001/

39. Micah Morrison, "How They Uncovered the Truth," *Parade*, January 25, 2004, 4.

40. Jack Jones, "Reporter Farr Dies; Went to Jail to Protect Sources," *Los Angeles Times*, March 6, 1987, https://www.latimes.com/archives/la-xpm-1987-03-06-me-5024-story.html

41. *Branzburg v. Hayes*, 408 U.S. 665 (1972).

42. Erick Wemple, "Enough about 'Sources,' Mr. President," *Washington Post*,

April 20, 2020, https://www.washingtonpost.com/opinions/2020/04/20/enough
-about-sources-mr-president

43. Mike Royko, "Gossip's Credibility Is Only a Bad Rumor," *Chicago Tribune*, May 22, 1989.

44. *Zurcher v. Stanford Daily* (1978).

45. Privacy Protection Act of 1980, (PPA), Pub. L. No. 96-440, 94 Stat. 1879 (Oct. 13, 1980), codified at 42 U.S.C. §2000aa et seq.

46. Heather Cox Richardson, "Letters from an American," Substack, June 10, 2021, https://heathercoxrichardson.substack.com/p/june-10-2021; and Stephen J. Adler and Bruce D. Brown, "The Press Just Got a Big Win. Let's Make It Permanent, *New York Times*, July 20, 2021, https://www.nytimes.com/2021/07/20/opinion/pre ss-freedom-justice-department.html

47. Pema Levy, "Trump on Ukraine Whistleblower: 'Somebody Oughta Sue His Ass Off,'" *Mother Jones*, April 4, 2020, https://www.motherjones.com/politics/20 20/04/trump-on-ukraine-whistleblower-somebody-oughta-sue-his-ass-off/

48. See National Whistleblowers Center, whistleblowers.org

49. John Romano, "You Have a Right to Be Angry, Gov. DeSantis. But Not Petty and Petulant," *Tampa Bay Times*, March 29, 2020, https://www.tampabay.com/opin ion/2020/03/29/you-have-a-right-to-be-angry-gov-desantis-but-not-petty-and -petulant/

50. "U.S. 2020: Another Facebook Disinformation Election?," Avaaz, November 5, 2019, https://secure.avaaz.org/campaign/en/disinfo_report_us_2020/

51. David E. McCraw, *Truth in Our Times: Inside the Fight for Press Freedom in the Age of Alternative Facts* (New York: All Points Books, 2019), 275.

52. Tamara Lush and Michael Liedtke, "Tech Billionaire Is Unlikely Hulk Hogan Ally in Gawker Fight," *Christian Science Monitor*, May 26, 2016, https://www.csmo nitor.com/Technology/2016/0526/Tech-billionaire-is-unlikely-Hulk-Hogan-ally -in-Gawker-fight

## Chapter 5

1. Chris Arnade, *Dignity: Seeking Respect in Back Row America* (New York: Sentinel, 2019), 17.

2. Arnade, *Dignity*, 7.

3. Eric Eyre, *Death in Mud Lick: A Coal Country Fight against the Drug Companies That Delivered the Opioid Epidemic* (New York: Scribner, 2020).

4. See, e.g., Katharine Graham, *Personal History* (New York: Alfred A. Knopf, 1997); and Jay Rosen, *What Are Journalists For?* (New Haven: Yale University Press, 1999).

5. "Those We've Lost: The Coronavirus Pandemic Has Taken an Incalculable Death Toll. This Series Is Designed to Put Names and Faces to the Numbers," *New York Times*, January 30, 2021, https://www.nytimes.com/interactive/2020/obituari es/people-died-coronavirus-obituaries.html

6. Joseph P. Ritz, *I Never Looked for My Mother and Other Regrets of a Journalist* (Bangor, ME: Booklocker.com, 2006), 105, 106.

7. Hadas Gold, "Survey: 7 Percent of Reporters Identify as Republican," Politico, May 6, 2014, https://politico.com/blogs/media/2014/05/survey-7-percent-of-reporters-identify-as-republican-188053

8. Caitlin Dickerson, "1862–1931, Ida B. Wells: Took on Racism in the Deep South with Powerful Reporting on Lynchings," *New York Times*, March 8, 2018, https://www.nytimes.com/interactive/2018/obituaries/overlooked-ida-b-wells.html

9. Donald M. Murray, "Writing on Writing," no. 3, *Boston Globe*, January 1988, 2.

10. Sam Sanders, "All of It Matters: On Hard and Soft News," *Columbia Journalism Review* (Fall 2021), https://www.cjr.org/special_report/all_news_matters_hard_soft.php

11. Quoted in G. Michael Killenberg, *Public Affairs Reporting Now: News of, by and for the People* (Burlington, ME: Focal Press, 2008), 12.

12. Elizabeth Grieco, "Newsroom Employees Are Less Diverse than U.S. Workers Overall," Pew Research Center, November 2, 2018, https://www.pewresearch.org/fact-tank/2018/11/02/newsroom-employees-are-less-diverse-than-u-s-workers-overall/

13. "Donald Trump to CNN Reporter: You Are Fake News," YouTube, January 11, 2017, https://youtu.be/VIx_nMysTUY

14. Claire Wardle, "Fake News. It's Complicated," First Draft, February 16, 2017, https://firstdraftnews.org:443/fake-news-complicated/

15. Michelle Ruiz, "Becoming AOC," *Vanity Fair,* December 2020, https://archive.vanityfair.com/article/2020/12/1/becoming-aoc.

16. Michael Bamberger, "Golf's Ultimate Secret Legend, Ann Gregory, Lived a Life of Firsts," *Golf*, November 18, 2020, https://golf.com/news/features/golfs-ultimate-secret-legend-ann-gregory/

17. Patrice Peck, "The Messenger," *Wired*, December/January 2020, https://www.questia.com/magazine/1P4-2460988517/the-messenger

18. Rob Anderson, Robert Dardenne, and George M. Killenberg, *The Conversation of News: Communications, Community, and News* (Westport, CT: Praeger, 1994), 5.

19. John J. Pauly, "Journalism and the Sociology of Public Life," in Theodore L. Glasser, eds., *The Idea of Public Journalism* (New York: Guilford Press, 1999), 135.

20. Quoted in Jeff Jarvis, "Journalism Is the Conversation. The Conversation Is Journalism," Medium, January 27, 2019, https://medium.com/whither-news/journalism-is-the-conversation-the-conversation-is-journalism-22a8c631e952

21. Darryl Holliday, "Journalism Is a Public Good. Let the Public Make It," *Columbia Journalism Review,* December 15, 2021, https://www.cjr.org/special_report/journalism-power-public-good-community-infrastructure.php

22. Paul Swider, "Sembler, Neighbors Spar over Tyrone Proposal," *St. Petersburg*

*Times*, February 26, 2006, https://www.tampabay.com/archive/2006/02/26/sembl er-neighbors-spar-over-tyrone-proposal/; and Howard Troxler, "18 Mostly Vacant Acres Put City Council in Tight Spot," *St. Petersburg Times*, March 2, 2006, https:// www.tampabay.com/archive/2006/03/02/18-mostly-vacant-acres-put-city-counc il-in-tight-spot/

23. See Andrea Wenzel, *Community-Centered Journalism: Engaging People, Exploring Solutions, and Building Trust* (Champaign: University of Illinois Press, 2020).

24. See Jacob L. Nelson, *Imagined Audiences: How Journalists Perceive and Pursue the Public* (New York: Oxford University Press, 2021).

25. "Mission and Philosophy," Department of Journalism and Digital Communication, University of South Florida, https://www.usf.edu/arts-sciences/departme nts/journalism/about/index.aspx

26. See Maxwell McCombs, *Setting the Agenda: Mass Media and Public Opinion* (Malden, MA: Polity Press, 2004).

27. Edmund Lee, "The New York Times Tops 7.8 Million Subscribers as Growth Slows," May 5, 2021, https://www.nytimes.com/2021/05/05/business/media/nyt -new-york-times-earnings-q1-2021.html

28. Ben Smith, "Why the Success of The New York Times May Be Bad News for Journalism," *New York Times*, March 1, 2020, https://www.nytimes.com/2020 /03/01/business/media/ben-smith-journalism-news-publishers-local.html?smid =em-share

29. Max Cohen, "New York Times Opinion Writer Bari Weiss Resigns, Citing Hostile Culture and Lack of Ideological Diversity," Politico, July 7, 2020, https:// www.politico.com/news/2020/07/14/new-york-times-bari-weiss-resigns-360730

30. Chang Che, "Is the New York Times Bad for Democracy?" *Quillette*, March 20, 2020, https://quillette.com/2020/03/20/is-the-new-york-times-bad-for-dem ocracy/

31. Olivier Sorgho, "Apple's 'Netflix for News,'" Medium, November 27, 2020, https://medium.com/swlh/apples-netflix-for-news-1872b2b00c9c

32. "About Axios," Axios, February 19, 2021, https://www.axios.com/about/

33. "About," Storyful, February 12, 2021, https://storyful.com/about/

34. "About Us: Building a Better Future for Writing," Substack, retrieved February 19, 2021, https://substack.com/about

35. Ben Smith, "Heather Cox Richardson Offers a Break from the Media Maelstrom. It's Working," *New York Times*, December 27, 2020, https://www.nytimes .com/2020/12/27/business/media/heather-cox-richardson-substack-boston-colle ge.html

36. "About Us," Mountain State Spotlight, retrieved February 12, 2021, https:// mountainstatespotlight.org/about/

37. See "About," Association of Alternative Newsmedia, retrieved February 12, 2021, https://aan.org/about/

38. "Harvest of Shame," Wikipedia, retrieved November 11, 2021, https://en.wikipedia.org/wiki/Harvest_of_Shame

39. Reporters of the Associated Press, *Breaking News: How the Associated Press Has Covered War, Peace, and Everything Else* (New York: Princeton Architectural Press, 2007); and "About Us," AP, retrieved November 11, 2021, https://www.ap.org/about/

40. See Michael Schudson, *Discovering the News: A Social History of American Newspapers* (New York: Basic Books, 2001).

41. Jelle Boumans, Damian Trilling, Rens Vliegenhart, and Hajo Boomgaarden, "The Agency Makes the (Online) News World Go Round: The Impact of News Agency Content on Print and Online News," *International Journal of Communication* 12 (2018): 1768-89.

42. Joyce Sohyun Lee, Robert O'Harrow Jr., and Elyse Samuels, "Kenosha: How Two Men's Paths Crossed in an Encounter That Has Divided the Nation," *Washington Post,* November 19, 2020, https://www.washingtonpost.com/investigations/2020/11/19/kenosha-shooting-kyle-rittenhouse-interview/?arc404=true

43. "The Race to Make Ventilators," *NPR Planet Money* (blogcast), March 31, 2020, https://www.npr.org/transcripts/82488628644

44. Anderson, Dardenne, and Killenberg, *The Conversation of Journalism,* 113-14.

45. "About Us," Solutions Journalism Network, retrieved February 19, 2021, http://www.solutionsjournalism.org

46. Steve Hartman, "The Little Patriot," CBS News, September 15, 2019, https://www.cbsnews.com/video/the-little-patriot/

47. Greg Jaffe, "A Pandemic, a Motel without Power and a Potentially Terrifying Glimpse of Orlando's Future, *Washington Post*, September 10, 2020, https://www.washingtonpost.com/graphics/2020/national/kissimmee-star-motel/

48. Quoted in Michael Ricciardelli, "Historian and Philosopher Will Durant," Seton Hall University, July 27, 2018, https://www.shu.edu/news/historian-and-philosopher-will-durant.cfm

49. Kali Holloway, "'Feel-Good News' Story or Poverty Propaganda?" *The Nation*, October 1, 2021, https://www.thenation.com/article/society/safety-net-democrats/

50. "Muckrake," Theodore Roosevelt Center, retrieved December 8, 2020, https://www.theodorerooseveltcenter.org/Learn-About-TR/TR-Encyclopedia/Culture and Society/Muckraker

51. Mike Mago, "Public Health, the Media, and the Performance of Deborah Birx," Health Community, April 28, 2020, http://www.healthcommentary.org/2020/04/28/public-health-the-media-and-the-performance-of-deborah-birx/

52. Lucia Graves, "Five Years On, the Lessons from the Rolling Stone Rape Story," *The Guardian*, December 29, 2019, https://www.theguardian.com/society/2019/dec/29/rolling-stone-rape-story-uva-five-years

53. See *Local Matters* (newsletter), Investigative Reporters & Editors, ire.org

54. Mark Coddington and Seth Lewis, "'Engaged Journalism' Is Taking Us Back to the 'Public Journalism' Debates of the 1990s," Nieman Lab, April 3, 2020, https://www.niemanlab.org/2020/04/engaged-journalism-is-taking-us-back-to-the-pub lic-journalism-debates-of-the-1990s/

55. Samuel G. Freedom, *Letters to a Young Journalist* (New York: Basic Books, 2006).

56. Tom Smith, *To Absent Friends from Red Smith* (New York: Scribner, 1982).

57. Roy Peter Clark, "Beware of Buzzwords and 9 Other Tips for Cutting Clichés," Poynter, February 9, 2016, https://www.poynter.org/educators-students/20 16/beware-of-buzzwords-and-9-other-ideas-for-cutting-cliches/; and Paul Bradshaw, "How to Prevent Confirmation Bias Affecting Your Journalism," Online Journalism Blog, April 7, 2020, https://onlinejournalismblog.com/2020/04/07/how-to -prevent-confirmation-bias-affecting-your-journalism/

58. See Edna Buchanan, *The Corpse Had a Familiar Face: Covering Miami, America's Hottest Beat* (New York: Pocket Books, 1987).

59. Bill Sanderson, "Merriman Smith's Account of JFK's Assassination," Pulitzer Prizes, retrieved December 8, 2020, https://www.pulitzer.org/article/merriman -smiths-account-jfks-assassination

60. Mitchell Stephens, *The History of News: From the Drum to the Satellite* (New York: Penguin Books, 1988), 252.

61. Farah Stockman, "What I Learned from a List of Trump Accomplishments," *New York Times*, September 11, 2020, https://www.nytimes.com/2020/09/11/opini on/trump-fact-check.html?smid=em-share

62. Alex Traub, "Times Insider: Reporting on the Issues That Set Our Brains on Fire," *New York Times*, September 24, 2021, https://www.nytimes.com/2021/09/24 /insider/michael-powell-free-speech.html

63. Dan Froomkin, "Let Me Rewrite That for You!" Press Watch, October 1, 2021, https://presswatchers.org/2021/10/let-me-rewrite-that-for-you/

64. Alex Traub, "Times Insider: Leading the News Coverage of 'This Big, Messy Country of Ours,'" October 28, 2021, *New York Times*, https://www.nytimes.com/20 21/10/28/insider/jia-lynn-yang-national-editor.html

65. Roger Sollenberger, "The 17 Worst *New York Times* Headlines of 2018," Paste magazine, December 27, 2018, https://www.pastemagazine.com/politics/new-york -times/the-20-worst-new-york-times-headlines-of-2018/

66. "Surfside Official, Despite Report, Told Board That Condo Was in 'Good Shape,'" *Tampa Bay Times,* June 28, 2021, https://www.tampabay.com/news/flori da/2021/06/28/surfside-official-despite-report-told-board-that-condo-was-in-go od-shape/

67. ACEJMC: Accrediting Council on Education in Journalism and Mass Communications, https://www.acejmc.org/

68. "NPR Ethics Handbook: These Are the Standards of Our Journalism," NPR, https://www.npr.org/ethics/

69. Killenberg, *Public Affairs Reporting Now*, xvi.

Chapter 6

1. S. Robert Lichter, "Theories of Media Bias," in Kate Kenski and Kathleen Hall Jamieson, eds., *The Oxford Handbook of Political Communication* (New York: Oxford University Press, 2017), https://doi.org/10.1093/oxfordhb/9780199793471 .013.44. Lichter reports that "the lack of evidence of consistently liberal media bias had led to efforts to understand *the widespread and growing public perception to the contrary*" (409) and that "the *increasing public perception* of liberal media bias has been linked to audience biases and strategic efforts by conservative elites" (412). Emphasis added.

2. Tom Wicker, *On the Record: An Insider's Guide to Journalism* (New York: Bedford/St. Martin's, 2002), 89-90.

3. Nicole Hemmer, "Attacking the Press for Liberal Bias Is a Staple of Republican Campaigns—and It All Began in 1964." CNN, February 29, 2020, https://www .cnn.com/2020/02/29/opinions/lyndon-johnson-barry-goldwater-liberal-media -bias-hemmer/index.html

4. Quotes are from L. Brent Bozell and Tim Graham, "Deniers of the Reality of Media Bias," *The Ledger*, November 30, 2017, https://www.theledger.com/story /opinion/columns/2017/11/30/bozell-graham-deniers-of-reality-of-liberal-media -bias/16939085007/; and Clyde Wayne Crews Jr., "We're Not Biased, We're Liberals: How Cultural Leftism Will Slant Social Media Regulation," *Forbes*, February 17, 2020, https://www.forbes.com/sites/waynecrews/2020/02/17/were-not-biased -were-liberals-how-cultural-leftism-will-slant-social-media-regulation/?sh=3a3 431fc503c

5. Quoted in Thomas Gilovich, *How We Know What Isn't So: The Fallibility of Human Reason in Everyday Life* (New York: Free Press, 1991), 1.

6. Corky Becker, Laura Chasin, Maggie Herzog, and Sallyann Roth, *Fostering Dialogue on Abortion: A Report from the Public Conversations Project*, 1992, 1. This is a brief, occasional report that is not archived.

7. Nicole Hemmer, *Messengers of the Right: Conservative Media and the Transformation of American Politics* (Philadelphia: University of Pennsylvania Press, 2016), xii-xiii.

8. Art Swift, "Six in 10 in U.S. See Partisan Bias in News Media," Gallup News, April 5, 2017, https://news.gallup.com/poll/207794/six-partisan-bias-media.aspx

9. David M. Ryfe, *Journalism and the Public* (Malden, MA: Polity, 2017); Barbie Zelizer, *What Journalism Could Be* (Malden, MA: Polity, 2017).

10. David E. McCraw, *Truth in Our Times: Inside the Fight for Press Freedom in the Age of Alternative Facts* (New York: All Points, 2019), 152-58.

11. Media Research Center (mrc.org). This organization was founded by Brent Bozell, whose rhetoric we sample above.

12. Quoted in Howard Polskin, "The Sentinel of the Liberal Media," *Columbia Journalism Review*, January 13, 2020, https://www.cjr.org/politics/newsbustersphp

13. Thomas Frank, *Pity the Poor Billionaire: The Hard-Times Swindle and the*

*Unlikely Comeback of the Right,* fully updated and expanded ed. (New York: Picador, 2012), 159.

14. Mark D. Watts et al., "Elite Cues and Media Bias in Presidential Campaigns: Explaining Public Perceptions of a Liberal Press," *Communication Research* 26 (1999): 144-75.

15. See the website for Fairness and Accuracy in Reporting: fair.org

16. See William Falk, "Why Fox News Was Created," *The Week,* November 22, 2019, https//theweek.com/articles/880107/why-fox-news-created. Naturally, this strategy did not sit well with the executive editor of the *New York Times,* Abe Rosenthal, who in a 1976 speech argued that President Nixon was also trying to "break the press—or rather those journals and broadcasters that Nixon-Agnew felt threatened the control of the American mind that the administration believed was its prerogative." Quoted from the Rosenthal Papers in the New York Public Library by Matthew Pressman, *On Press: The Liberal Values That Shaped the News* (Cambridge, MA: Harvard University Press, 2018), 252.

17. Tim O'Sullivan et al., *Key Concepts in Communication and Cultural Studies,* 2nd ed. (London: Routledge, 1994), 29. Emphasis added.

18. Quoted in Manuel Roig-Franzia and Sarah Nelson, "A History of the Trump War on Media—the Obsession Not Even Coronavirus Could Stop," *Washington Post,* March 29, 2020, https://www.washingtonpost.com/lifestyle/media/a-history-of -the-trump-war-on-media--the-obsession-not-even-coronavirus-could- stop/2020/03/28/71bb21d0-f433-11e9-8cf0-4cc99f74d127_story.html

19. Rob Faris et al., "Partisanship, Propaganda, and Disinformation: Online Media and the 2016 US Presidential Election," Berkman Klein Center, Harvard University, August 16, 2017, https://cyber.harvard.edu/publications/2017/08/medi acloud

20. Duncan J. Watts and David M. Rothchild, "Don't Blame the Election on Fake News. Blame It on the Media," *Columbia Journalism Review,* December 5, 2017, https://www.cjr.org/analysis/fake-news-media-election-trump.php

21. John Prados, *Hoodwinked: The Documents That Reveal How Bush Sold Us a War* (New York: New Press, 2006).

22. See, e.g., Franklin Foer, "The Source of the Trouble," *New York,* May 28, 2004, https://nymag.com/nymetro/news/media/features/9226/

23. Summarized in Dominik Stecula, "More Republicans in the News? That's Not Media Bias," *The Conversation,* July 31, 2018, https://theconversation.com./mo re-republicans-in-the-news-thats-not-media-bias-100632

24. David Craig, *The Ethics of the Story: Using Narrative Methods Responsibly in Journalism* (Lanham, MD: Rowman & Littlefield, 2006), 20.

25. Cited in Erik Wemple, "Dear Mainstream Media: Why so Liberal?," *Washington Post,* January 27, 2017, https://www.washingtonpost.com/blogs/erik-wemple /wp/2017/01/2017/dear-mainstream-media-why-so-liberal/?arc404=true

26. Michael Schudson, *The Sociology of News* (New York: Norton, 2003), 41, 42-43. In a recent book, *Journalism: Why It Matters* (Medford, MA: Polity, 2020),

Schudson adds that, although no human can be totally unbiased, "it seems to me wildly naïve to assume that 'bias' inevitably overwhelms self-restraining efforts of this sort. . . . There is such a thing as trying to get outside oneself. There is such a thing as empathy. There is such a thing as wanting to give others a fair shake" (54). Critics who presume a liberal media bias in all traditional American journalism should know, too, that these same institutions are also routinely attacked from the far left for propping up *conservative* ideology. These cross-pressures felt by institutional journalism hardly amount to co-conspiracy, coming from such well-known liberals as Noam Chomsky, Douglas Kellner, and Robert McChesney.

27. McCraw, *Truth in Our Times*, 59–60.

28. Tien-Tsung Lee, "The Liberal Media Myth Revisited: An Examination of Factors Influencing Perceptions of Media Bias," *Journal of Broadcasting & Electronic Media* 49, no. 1 (2005): 43–64, https://www.tandfonline.com/doi/abs/10.1207/s155 06878jobem4901_?journalCode=hbem20

29. Lichter, "Theories of Media Bias," 403.

30. Lichter, "Theories of Media Bias," 409. Emphasis added. See also David Domke et al., "The Politics of Conservative Elites and the Liberal Media Argument," *Journal of Communication* 49, no. 4 (1999): 35–58, https://doi.org/10.1111 /j.1460-2466.1999.tb02816.x

31. Examples are Matthew A. Baum and Phil Gussin, "In the Eye of the Beholder: How Information Shortcuts Shape Individual Perceptions of Bias in the Media," *Quarterly Journal of Political Science* 3, no. 1 (2008): 1–31; Carroll J. Glynn and Michael E. Huge, "How Persuasive Are Perceptions of Bias? Exploring Judgments of Media Bias in Financial News," *International Journal of Public Opinion Research* 26, no. 4 (2014): 543–53; William P. Eveland Jr. and Dhavan V. Shah, "The Impact of Individual and Interpersonal Factors on Perceived News Media Bias," *Political Psychology* 24, no. 1 (2003): 101–17; and Natalie Jomini Stroud, Ashley Muddiman, and Jae Kook Lee, "Seeing Media as Group Members: An Evaluation of Partisan Bias Perceptions," *Journal of Communication* 64, no. 5 (2014): 874–94.

32. Lichter, "Theories of Media Bias," 412.

33. Faris et al., "Partisanship, Propaganda, and Disinformation."

34. Glynn and Huge, "How Persuasive Are Perceptions of Bias?"

35. "Political Polarization in the American Public: Section 1: Growing Ideological Consistency," Pew Research Center, June 12, 2014, https://www.people-press.org /2014/06/12/section-1-growing-ideological-consistency/

35. Amy Mitchell et al., "Political Polarization & Media Habits," Pew Research Center, October 21, 2014, https://www.journalism.org/2014/10/21/political-polariz ation-media-habits/

37. Faris et al., "Partisanship, Propaganda, and Disinformation."

38. Hans J. G. Hassell, John Holbein, and Matthew R. Miles, "There Is No Liberal Media Bias in Which News Stories Political Journalists Choose to Cover," *Science Advances* 6, no. 14 (April 1, 2020). https://doi.org/10.1126/sciadv.aay9344 (emphasis added).

39. Hassell, Holbein, and Miles, "There Is No Liberal Media Bias."

40. Hans J. G. Hassell et al., "Claims of Ideological Bias among the Media May Be Overblown," *The Conversation*, May 18, 2020, https://theconversation.com/clai ms-of-ideological-bias-may-be-overblown-135617

41. Peter H. Ditto et al., "At Least Bias Is Bipartisan: A Meta-Analytic Comparison of Partisan Bias in Liberals and Conservatives," *Perspectives on Psychological Science* 14, no. 2 (2019): 273-91, https://doi.org/10.1177/1745691617746796

42. Jonathan Baron and John T. Jost, "False Equivalence: Are Liberals and Conservatives in the United States Equally Biased?," *Perspectives on Psychological Science*, 2019, 14, no. 2 (2019): 292-303, https://doi.org/10.1177/1745691618788876

43. Baron and Jost, "False Equivalence," 293.

44. Soroush Vosoughi, Deb Roy, and Sinan Aral, "The Spread of True and False News Online," *Science* 359 (2018): 1146-51.

45. Baron and Jost, "False Equivalence," 294.

46. Baron and Jost, "False Equivalence," 299-300.

47. Douglas Kellner, *Media Spectacle and the Crisis of Democracy* (Boulder, CO: Paradigm, 2005), xv.

48. Robert M. Hutchins et al., *A Free and Responsible Press* (Chicago: University of Chicago Press, 1947), 57.

49. Kathleen Hall Jamieson and Paul Waldman, *The Press Effect: Politicians, Journalists, and the Stories That Shape the Political World* (New York: Oxford University Press, 2003), 171.

50. Zelizer, *What Journalism Could Be*, 258-59.

51. Deborah Tannen, *The Argument Culture: Moving from Debate to Dialogue* (New York: Random House, 1998), 284-85.

52. Quoted in Tannen, *The Argument Culture*, 285.

53. Eric Alterman, *What Liberal Media? The Truth about Bias and the News* (New York: Basic Books, 2003), 24.

54. Jill Lepore, "Hard News: The State of Journalism," *New Yorker*, January 28, 2019, 18.

55. Tracy Grant interview in Erik Wemple, "Dear Mainstream Media: Why so Liberal?" *Washington Post*, January 27, 2017, https://www.washingtonpost.com/blo gs/erik-wemple/wp/2017/01/27/dear-mainstream-media-why-so-liberal/?arc404 =true

56. McCraw, *Truth in Our Times*, 97.

57. Clifford G. Christians, John P. Ferre, and P. Mark Fackler, *Good News: Social Ethics and the Press* (New York: Oxford University Press, 1993).

58. Craig, *The Ethics of the Story*, 22.

59. "SPJ Code of Ethics," Society of Professional Journalists, https://www.spj .org/ethicscode.asp

60. Cass Sunstein, *republic.com* (Princeton: Princeton University Press, 2002), 30-37.

61. Sara M. Evans and Harry C. Boyte, *Free Spaces: The Sources of Democratic*

*Change in America* (Chicago: University of Chicago Press, 1992), 1-26. Also see Rob Anderson, Robert Dardenne, and George M. Killenberg, *The Conversation of Journalism: Communication, Community, and News* (Westport, CT: Praeger, 1994), 129-36.

62. Katherine Cross, "The Art of the Real: Disinformation vs. Democracy," *The Baffler*, Summer 2017, 23-24, https://thebaffler.com/salvos/art-of-the-real-cross

## Chapter 7

1. Seyla Benhabib, interview with Karin Wahl-Jorgensen, "On the Public Sphere, Journalism and Dignity," *Journalism Studies* 9, no. 6 (December 2008): 962-70, https://doi.org/10.1080/14616700802373870

2. See Hannah Arendt, *Between Past and Future* (New York: Viking Press, 1961). See especially her essay "The Crisis in Culture."

3. James Carey, "'A Republic, if You Can Keep It': Liberty and Public Life in the Age of Glasnost," in Raymond Arsenault, ed., *Crucible of Liberty: 200 Years of the Bill of Rights* (New York: Free Press, 1991), 118.

4. Robert J. Wagman, *The First Amendment Book* (New York: World Almanac, 1991), 239. Wagman was an investigative reporter and Supreme Court historian.

5. William Caspary, *Dewey on Democracy* (Ithaca: Cornell University Press), 140-41.

6. Alasdair MacIntyre, *After Virtue*, 2nd ed. (Notre Dame: University of Notre Dame Press, 1984), 210-11.

7. Czeslaw Milosz, *The Captive Mind*, trans. Jane Zielonko (New York: Knopf, 1951), 215.

8. Hannah Arendt, "Truth and Politics," in *Between Past and Future*, 241.

9. W. Barnett Pearce, "Achieving Dialogue with the Other in the Postmodern World," in Philip Gaunt, ed., *Beyond Agendas: New Directions in Communication Research* (Westport, CT: Greenwood, 1993), 67.

10. Parker Palmer, *The Company of Strangers: Christians and the Renewal of America's Public Life* (New York: Crossroad, 1985), 56.

11. Palmer, *The Company of Strangers*, 57.

12. Palmer, *The Company of Strangers*, 58-59.

13. See Eli Saslow, *Rising Out of Hatred: The Awakening of a Former White Nationalist* (New York: Doubleday, 2018).

14. See Corey Brettschneider, *The Oath and the Office: A Guide to the Constitution for Future Presidents* (New York: W. W. Norton, 2018), xi, xii. The author's wise reminders are addressed to a hypothetical newly elected president, including the central fact that an oath of office "requires that the president uphold the Constitution—even parts with which he or she disagrees." A newly elected president performs a constitutional act composed of words, "literally dictating your first instant in office, signal[ing] clearly that you are not free to act however you wish." In other words, even the power of the most powerful person on earth must answer to ordinary citizens. This relationship is inherent in the American DNA.

The oath contradicts a president who believes she or he can do whatever she or he wants. "You are promising to 'preserve, protect and defend' the Constitution," Brettschneider writes, "not just to avoid violating it," and "you promise to put aside your private interests to occupy a limited role on behalf of the American people."

15. Edward Schiappa, *Defining Reality: Definitions and the Politics of Meaning* (Carbondale: Southern Illinois University Press, 2003), 151.

16. Kathleen Hall Jamieson and Paul Waldman, *The Press Effect: Politicians, Journalists, and the Stories That Shape the Political World* (New York: Oxford University Press, 2003).

17. Jamieson and Waldman, *The Press Effect*, xv.

18. Jamieson and Waldman, *The Press Effect*, xv.

19. Erving Goffman, *Frame Analysis: An Essay on the Organization of Experience* (Cambridge, MA: Harvard University Press, 1974).

20. Cass Sunstein, *republic.com* (Princeton: Princeton University Press, 2002).

21. Allyson Chiu, "Shepard Smith, a Trump Target, Blasts Vilification of Journalists in His First Post-Fox Speech," *Washington Post*, November 22, 2019, https://www.washingtonpost.com/nation/2019/11/22/shepard-smith-trump-blasts-vilification-media-first-speech-post-fox-news/

22. Quoted in Daniel Kemmis, *Community and the Politics of Place* (Norman: University of Oklahoma Press, 1990), 18.

23. David A. Strauss, "Law and the Slow-Motion Emergency," in Cass R. Sunstein, ed., *Can It Happen Here?: Authoritarianism in America* (New York: Dey Street, 2018), 365–85.

24. William Julius Wilson, "Multiracial Cooperation," in Eric Klinenberg, Caitlin Zaloom, and Sharon Marcus, eds., *Antidemocracy in America: Truth, Power, and the Republic at Risk* (New York: Columbia University Press, 2019), 268–69.

25. Rob Anderson, Robert Dardenne, and George M. Killenberg, *The Conversation of Journalism: Communication, Community, and News* (Westport, CT: Praeger, 1994).

26. James Carey, *Communication as Culture: Essays on Media and Society* (Winchester, MA: Unwin Hyman, 1989), 4.

27. Kenneth N. Cissna and Rob Anderson, "Communication and the Ground of Dialogue," in Rob Anderson, Kenneth N. Cissna, and Ronald C. Arnett, eds., *The Reach of Dialogue: Confirmation, Voice, and Community* (Cresskill, NJ: Hampton, 1994), 10.

28. Quoted in Kemmis, *Community and the Politics of Place*, 12.

29. David Ryfe, *Journalism and the Public* (Cambridge, MA: Polity, 2017), 9.

30. Anderson, Dardenne, and Killenberg, *The Conversation of Journalism*, 73.

31. Sara M. Evans and Harry C. Boyte, *Free Spaces: The Sources of Democratic Change in America* (Chicago: University of Chicago Press, 1992).

32. Sunstein, *republic.com*, 68.

33. Sunstein, *republic.com*, 67.

34. Angel Parham and Danielle Allen, "Achieving Rooted Cosmopolitanism in

a Digital Age," in Danielle Allen and Jennifer S. Light, eds., *From Voice to Influence: Understanding Citizenship in a Digital Age* (Chicago: University of Chicago Press, 2015), 254–72. For the research on how blogging and social media use correlates with increased citizen involvement, see 311 and 356.

35. Kwame Anthony Appiah, *Cosmopolitanism: Ethics in a World of Strangers* (New York: W. W. Norton, 2006); Kwame Anthony Appiah, *The Ethics of Identity* (Princeton: Princeton University Press, 2005), especially chapter 6, "Rooted Cosmopolitanism," 213–72.

36. Appiah, *Cosmopolitanism*, 85.

37. Michael Schudson, *Journalism: Why It Matters* (Medford, MA: Polity, 2020), 51–52.

38. Media Insight Project, "What Americans Know, and Don't, about How Journalism Works," American Press Institute, June 11, 2018, https://www.americanpres sinstitute.org/publications/reports/survey-research/what-americans-know-about -journalism/

39. Bill Kovach and Tom Rosenstiel, *Blur: How to Know What's True in the Age of Information Overload* (New York: Bloomsbury, 2010). See also Bill Kovach and Tom Rosenstiel, *The Elements of Journalism*, revised and updated 4th ed. (New York: Crown, 2021), especially chapter 1, "What Is Journalism For?"; chapter 7, "Journalism as a Public Forum"; chapter 8, "Engagement and Relevance"; and chapter 11, "The Rights and Responsibilities of Citizens."

40. Kovach and Rosenstiel, *Blur*, 175–81.

41. Quoted in Stefanie Murray, "Collective Impact Models Will Strengthen and Redefine Local News," Nieman Lab, December 2021, https://www.niemanlab.org /2021/12/collective-impact-models-will-strengthen-and-redefine-local-news/

## Chapter 8

1. Eleanor Roosevelt with Michelle Markel, *When You Grow Up to Vote: How Our Government Works for You* (New York: Roaring Brook Press, 2018), 82; first published 1932 by Houghton Mifflin (Boston). This excerpt was originally published in Roosevelt's *Tomorrow Is Now* (New York: Harper & Row, 1963).

2. Eleanor Roosevelt, *The Moral Basis of Democracy* (New York: Howell, Soskin, 1940).

3. Roosevelt with Markel, *When You Grow Up to Vote*, 83.

4. Danielle Allen and Jennifer S. Light, eds., *From Voice to Influence: Understanding Citizenship in a Digital Age* (Chicago: University of Chicago Press, 2015), 5.

5. John Hope Franklin, "African-Americans and the Bill of Rights," in Raymond Arsenault, ed., *Crucible of Liberty: 200 Years of the Bill of Rights* (New York: Free Press, 1991), 24–35.

6. Michael Schudson, *The Good Citizen: A History of American Civic Life* (New York: Free Press, 1998), 11–31.

7. Schudson, *The Good Citizen*.

8. Schudson, *The Good Citizen*, 16.

9. Schudson, *The Good Citizen*, 20.

10. Iris Marion Young, *Justice and the Politics of Difference* (1990; repr., Princeton: Princeton University Press, 2011), 119.

11. Eric Liu and Nick Hanauer, *Gardens of Democracy: A New American Story of Citizenship, the Economy, and the Role of Government* (Seattle: Sasquatch, 2011), 51.

12. Robert Coles, *Handing One Another Along: Literature and Social Reflection* (New York: Random House, 2010). The examples discussed are George Orwell, William Carlos Williams, Flannery O'Connor, and Billie Holiday.

13. Schudson, *The Good Citizen*, 310–12.

14. John Keane, "Democracy and the Media—Without Foundations," *Political Studies*, Special Issue, 40 (1992): 124.

15. W. Barnett Pearce and Stephen W. Littlejohn, *Moral Conflict: When Social Worlds Collide* (Thousand Oaks, CA: Sage, 1997).

16. Bill Kovach and Tom Rosenstiel, *Blur: How to Know What's True in the Age of Information Overload* (New York: Bloomsbury, 2010), 199.

17. Stephen J. A. Ward, *Ethical Journalism in a Populist Age: The Democratically Engaged Journalist* (Lanham, MD: Rowman & Littlefield, 2019), 121.

18. Lincoln Steffens, quoted in Bill Moyers, *Moyers on America: A Journalist and His Times* (New York: Anchor, 2005), 38.

19. Clifford Christians, "Universal Values and the Common Good." Transcript of lecture at "Mixed News" conference, University of South Florida St. Petersburg, October 4, 1994.

20. John Rawls, *Political Liberalism* (New York: Columbia University Press, 1996), 217–18. Emphasis added.

21. Czeslaw Milosz, *The Captive Mind*, trans. Jane Zielonko (New York: Knopf, 1951).

22. Rawls, *Political Liberalism*, 49.

23. Wayne Booth, *The Company We Keep: An Ethics of Fiction* (Berkeley: University of California Press, 1988), 73; see also chapter 3, "The Peculiar 'Logic' of Evaluative Criticism."

24. Benjamin Barber, *A Place for Us: How to Make Society Civil and Democracy Strong* (New York: Hill and Wang, 1998), 117–18.

25. Danielle Allen, *Talking to Strangers: Anxieties of Citizenship Since Brown v. Board of Education* (Chicago: University of Chicago Press, 2004), xix. Aristotle's idea of "political friendship" is described, although often indirectly, in *Nicomachean Ethics*, trans. Martin Ostwald (New York: Macmillan, 1962); see especially book 8, 214–44.

26. Mario Cuomo, "Religious Belief and Public Morality: A Catholic Governor's Perspective," lecture presented at the University of Notre Dame, September 13, 1984. Quoted in Amy Gutmann and Dennis Thompson, *Democracy and Disagreement* (Cambridge, MA: Harvard University Press, 1996), 84. For more on the search for "mutually acceptable values" in dialogue, see 83–91.

27. Martha Nussbaum, "Compassion: The Basic Social Emotion," in E. F. Pau, F. D. Miller Jr., and J. Paul, eds., *The Communitarian Challenge to Liberalism* (Cambridge: Cambridge University Press, 1996), 50–51. Nussbaum's concern with inclusive conversations complements the work of well-known American ethicist Kwame Anthony Appiah, who reminds citizens not to expect cross-identity dialogue to be a magical shortcut to persuasion or even to broad agreement about issues or values. The most realistic goals of dialogue are engagement and learning. See Appiah's *Cosmopolitanism: Ethics in a World of Strangers* (New York: W. W. Norton, 2006), 85.

28. Shawn Spano, *Public Dialogue and Participatory Democracy: The Cupertino Community Project* (Cresskill, NJ: Hampton Press, 2001), xi–xii. For a more comprehensive overview of the Public Dialogue Consortium, including other community clients, see Kimberly Pearce, Shawn Spano, and W. Barnett Pearce, "The Multiple Faces of the Public Dialogue Consortium: Scholars, Practitioners, and Dreamers of Better Social Worlds," in Lawrence R. Frey and Kenneth N. Cissna, eds., *Routledge Handbook of Applied Communication Research* (New York: Routledge, 2009), 611–32.

29. David L. Eason, "On Journalistic Authority: The Janet Cooke Scandal," *Critical Studies in Mass Communication* 3 (1986), 429–47; Elizabeth Blanks Hindman, "Jayson Blair, *The New York Times*, and Paradigm Repair," *Journal of Communication* 55, no. 2 (2005): 225–41.

30. Edmund B. Lambeth, *Committed Journalism: An Ethic for the Profession* (Bloomington: University of Indiana Press, 1986); Judith Sylvester, "The Continuing Relevance of Edmund Lambeth's *Committed Journalism: An Ethic for the Profession*," *Media Ethics*, 29, no. 2, (2018), https://www.mediaethicsmagazine.com/index.php/browse-back-issues/209-spring-2017-vol-29-no-2/3999194-the-continuing-relevance-of-edmund-lambeth-s-committed-journalism-an-ethic-for-the-profession. For additional context on journalists' representations to news sources, see Joe McGinniss, *The Selling of the President 1968; Fatal Vision* (New York: Putnam 1983); Janet Malcolm, *The Journalist and the Murderer* (New York: Vintage, 1990); and Michael Wolff, *Fire and Fury: Inside the Trump White House* (New York: Henry Holt, 2018).

31. For additional context on communication ethics, see David Craig, *The Ethics of the Story: Using Narrative Techniques Responsibly* (Lanham, MD: Rowman and Littlefield, 2006); and Rob Anderson and Veronica Ross, "When Is the Effective Choice the Ethical Choice?," in *Questions of Communication: A Practical Introduction to Theory*, 3rd ed. (New York: Bedford/St. Martins, 2002), 299–327.

32. Amy Kovac-Ashley and Kevin Loker, "Ten Engagement Leaders Share Insights through API Community Listening Fellowship," American Press Institute, February 25, 2020, https://www.americanpressinstitute.org/publications/api-updates/ten-engagement-leaders-share-insights-through-api-community-listening-fellowship/. See also "API Summit: Creating a Culture of Listening," American Press Institute, https://www.americanpressinstitute.org/training-tools/summits/api-summit-creating-culture-listening/

33. John Dewey, *The Public and Its Problems* (New York: Henry Holt, 1927), 218–19.

34. Rob Anderson, Robert Dardenne, and George M. Killenberg, *The Conversation of Journalism: Communication, Community, and News* (Westport, CT: Praeger, 1994), 135.

35. Yochai Benkler, Robert Faris, Hal Roberts, and Ethan Zuckerman, "Study: Breitbart-Led Right-Wing Media Ecosystem Altered Broader Media Agenda," *Columbia Journalism Review*, March 3, 2017, https://www.cjr.org/analysis/breitbart -media-trump-harvard-study.php

36. Nussbaum, "Compassion," 51.

37. Federal Register, vol. 67, no. 36, Friday, February 22, 2002/Notices. "Guidelines for Ensuring and Maximizing the Quality, Objectivity, Utility, and Integrity of Information (8452-8460)." Citizens should know that in November 2021, the House Coronavirus Subcommittee released transcripts of interviews with Centers for Disease Control and Prevention officials, who disclosed that the Trump administration prevented them from speaking in public of dangers from the virus and then "altered their scientific guidance about the coronavirus" because it feared this information would "harm" the president. See Heather Cox Richardson, "Letters from an American," Substack, November 14, 2021. Richardson, a history professor at Boston College, has published six books of American political history, including a history of the Republican Party.

38. Peter Gwynne, "U.S. Government Websites Cull References to Climate Change," *Physics World*, August 1, 2019, https://physicsworld.com/a/us-governme nt-websites-cull-references-to-climate-change/

39. Bob Woodward, *Fear: Trump in the White House* (New York: Simon & Schuster, 2018).

40. Sarah Harrison Smith, *The Fact Checker's Bible: A Guide to Getting It Right* (New York: Anchor, 2004). See also the Poynter Institute International Fact-Checking Network's "Fact-Checkers' Code of Principles," poynter.org

41. Quoted in Sissela Bok, *Lying: Moral Choice in Public and Private Life* (New York: Vintage, 1979), 302. Emphasis added. Bok mirrors some aspects of Bonhoeffer's criterion of serious reflection in chapter 2, "Truthfulness, Deceit, and Trust."

42. Hannah Arendt, "Truth and Politics," *New Yorker*, February 25, 1967.

43. Martin Buber, *The Knowledge of Man* (New York: Harper & Row, 1965), 70.

44. Adrienne Rich, "Women and Honor: Some Notes on Lying," in *On Lies, Secrets, and Silences: Selected Prose 1966-1978* (New York: Norton, 1979), 187-88.

45. Quoted in John Shotter, *Conversational Realities: Constructing Life through Language* (Thousand Oaks, CA: Sage, 1993), 175.

46. Erin C. Carroll, "How We Talk about the Press," *Georgetown Law Technology Review*, July 2020, https://georgetownlawtechreview.org/how-we-talk-about-the -press/GLTR-07-2020/

47. David Welna, "After Contentious Interview, Pompeo Publicly Accuses NPR Journalist of Lying to Him," *NPR*, January 25, 2020, www.npr.org/2020/ 01/25/799562818/after-contentious-interview-pompeo-publicly-accuses-npr; Oliver Laughland, "Emails Cast Further Doubt on Pompeo's Claim NPR Reporter

Lied to Him," *The Guardian*, January 27, 2020, www.theguardian.com/us-news/20 20/jan/mike-pompeo-npr-mary-louise-kelly-ukraine. In 2020, less than 1 percent of the NPR budget came from the federal government. See Jenn Fink, "Where Does NPR Get Its Funding From? Calls to Defund Outlet Met with Calls to Donate," *Newsweek*, September 1, 2020, https://newsweek.com/where-does-npr-get-its-fun ding-calls-defund-met-calls-donate-1529009

48. U.S. Department of State, "Statement by Secretary Michael R. Pompeo," press release, January 25, 2020.

49. "CPJ Calls on Trump to Improve Press Freedom in US," Committee to Protect Journalists, April 16, 2020, https://cpj.org/2020/04/cpj-calls-on-trump-to-im prove-press-freedom-in-us.php

50. Dewey, *The Public and Its Problems*; Louis Menand, ed., *Pragmatism: A Reader* (New York: Vintage, 1997); William R. Caspary, *Dewey on Democracy* (Ithaca: Cornell University Press, 2000).

51. Daisy Grewal, "Do Trump Tweets Spur Hate Crimes?" *Scientific American*, June 26, 2018. The study was Karsten Muller and Carlo Schwarz, "From Hashtag to Hate Crime: Twitter and Anti-Minority Sentiment," SSRN, October 31, 2019, http://dx.doi.org/10.2139/ssrn.3149103. See also "Poll: Nearly 4 in 5 Voters Concerned Incivility Will Lead to Violence," NPR, November 1, 2018, https//www.npr .org/2018/11/01/662730647/poll-nearly-4-in-5-voters-concerned-incivility-will -lead-to-violence

52. Gutmann and Thompson, *Democracy and Disagreement*, 174.

53. Liu and Hanauer, *Gardens of Democracy*, 27.

54. Hannah Arendt, *Between Past and Future* (New York: Viking, 1961), 221.

55. Commission on Freedom of the Press, *A Free and Responsible Press* (Chicago: University of Chicago Press, 1947), 20–29.

## Chapter 9

1. See Dan Kennedy, *The Wired City: Reimagining Journalism and Civic Life in the Post-Newspaper Age* (Amherst: University of Massachusetts Press, 2013).

2. Richard R. Beeman, "Perspectives on the Constitution: 'A Republic, If You Can Keep It,'" National Constitution Center, retrieved April 5, 2021, https://const itutioncenter.org/learn/educational-resources/historical-documents/perspectives -on-the-constitution-a-republic-if-you-can-keep-it

3. David Preston, "Lessons from a Year-Long Community Dialogue on Guns," Advance Local, March 27, 2019, https://al.com/opinion/2019/03/lessons-from-a-ye ar-long-community-dialogue-on-guns.html

4. John J. Pauly, "Recovering Journalism as a Democratic Art," in Joseph Harper and Thom Yantek, eds., *Competing Priorities in an Open Society* (Kent, OH: Kent State University Press, 2003), 28.

5. After years of mounting financial losses, the Newseum, known for its interactive displays and artifacts about freedom of the press, closed its doors to the pub-

lic in December 2019. Johns Hopkins University bought the impressive multistory building that once welcomed more than 800,000 visitors yearly.

6. See Preston, "Lessons from a Year-Long Community Dialogue."

7. Jeff Jarvis, "The Trouble with Going It Alone," *The Atlantic,* May 25, 2017, https://www.theatlantic.com/technology/archive/2017/05/the-trouble-with-goi ng-it-alone/524016/

8. Commission on the Practice of Democratic Citizenship, "Our Common Purpose," American Academy of Arts and Science, June 2020, https://www.amacad .org/ourcommonpurpose/report/section/11

9. David Mathews, Noelle McAfee, and Robert McKenzie, *Hard Choices* (Dayton, OH: Kettering Foundation, 1990), 4. For a complementary perspective, see Daniel Yankelovich, *Coming to Public Judgment* (Syracuse: Syracuse University Press, 1991).

10. David Mathews, *Politics for People*, 2nd ed. (Urbana: University of Illinois Press, 1999), 235, 236-37.

11. For summaries, see Jay Black, ed., *Mixed News: The Public/Civic/Communitarian Journalism Debate* (New York: Routledge, 1997); and Theodore L. Glasser, ed., *The Idea of Public Journalism* (New York: Guilford, 1999). Our own book, *The Conversation of Journalism*, is thought by some to have contributed to this movement's project to redefine journalistic goals: see Rob Anderson, Robert Dardenne, and George M. Killenberg, *The Conversation of Journalism: Communication, Community, and News* (Westport, CT: Praeger, 1994).

12. Geneva Overholser, "Civic Journalism, Engaged Journalism: Tracing the Connections," Democracy Fund, August 3, 2016, https://democracyfund.org/blog /entry/civic-journalism-engaged-journalism-tracing-the-connections

13. Overholser, "Civic Journalism, Engaged Journalism."

14. Ricki Morell, "Can Dialogue Journalism Engage Audiences, Foster Civil Discourse, and Increase Trust in the Media?," Nieman Reports, October 23, 2018, https://niemanreports.org/articles/can-dialogue-journalism-engage-audiences-fo ster-civil-discourse-and-increast-trust-in-the-media/

15. Seong Jae Kim, *As Democracy Goes, So Goes Journalism: Evolution of Journalism in Liberal, Deliberative, and Participatory Democracy* (Lanham, MD: Lexington Books, 2018), 35-36.

16. "Commission on the Practice of Democratic Citizenship," American Academy of Arts and Sciences, June 2020, https://amacad.org/project/practice-democra tic-citizenship

17. Pauly, "Recovering Journalism as a Democratic Art," 28.

18. "Dialogue in a Divided Democracy Summit," National Press Club Journalism Institute, 2019, https://www.pressclubinstitute.org/event/dialogue-in-a-divid ed-democracy-summit/. See, in addition to previous examples of locally engaged journalism, information about the recent "solutions journalism" work of Andrea Wenzel: *Community-Centered Journalism: Engaging People, Exploring Solutions, and Building Trust* (Urbana: University of Illinois Press, 2020).

19. See "API Summit: Creating a Culture of Listening," American Press Institute, 2019, https://www.americanpressinstitute.org/training-tools/summits/api -summit-creating-culture-listening/; and Amy Kovac-Ashley and Kevin Loker, "Ten Engagement Leaders Share Insights through API Community Listening Fellowship," American Press Institute, February 25, 2020, https://www.americanpre ssinstitute.org/publications/api-updates/ten-engagement-leaders-share-insights -through-api-community-listening-fellowship/

20. Older readers familiar with a systems approach to environment and society might be reminded of the famous Buckminster Fuller book from a previous era, *Operating Manual for Spaceship Earth* (Carbondale: Southern Illinois University Press, 1969). Fuller used the spaceship metaphor to suggest that human life is interdependent and ecological, with the whole, as the saying goes, always greater than the sum of its parts. The same concept could apply to dialogic citizenship.

21. Jeremy Hay and Eve Pearlman, "Can People Be Civil about Polarizing Topics? 'Dialogue Journalism' Could Serve as a Roadmap," Poynter, March 1, 2018, https:// www.poynter.org/tech-tools/2018/can-people-be-civil-about-polarizing-topics-di alogue-journalism-could-serve-as-a-roadmap/

22. Quoted in Madalina Clobanu, "Spaceship Media Is Using 'Dialogue Journalism' to Enable Productive Conversations between Communities at Odds," January 9, 2018, https://www.journalism.co.uk/news/spaceship-media-is-using-dialogue-journalism- to-enable-productive-conversations-between-communities-at-odds/s2/a715850/

23. James S. Fishkin, *Democracy and Deliberation: New Directions for Democratic Reform* (New Haven: Yale University Press, 1991), 1–20, 81ff.

24. Fishkin, *Democracy and Deliberation*, 47–49.

25. James Fishkin and Larry Diamond, "This Experiment Has Some Great News for Our Democracy," *New York Times*, October 2, 2019, https://www.nytimes .com/2019/10/02/opinion/america-one-room-experiment.html

26. Fishkin and Diamond, "This Experiment Has Some Great News."

27. The contemporary interest in dialogic moments and the metaphor of "turning toward" is indebted to the prolific work of twentieth-century philosopher Martin Buber. A summary and analysis appear in Kenneth N. Cissna and Rob Anderson, *Moments of Meeting: Buber, Rogers, and the Potential for Public Dialogue* (Albany: State University of New York Press, 2002), 173–207. For details, see Laura W. Black, "Deliberation, Storytelling, and Dialogic Moments," *Communication Theory* 18, no. 1 (February 2008): 93–116; Lea Sprain and Laura W. Black, "Deliberative Moments: Understanding Deliberation as an Interactional Accomplishment," *Western Journal of Communication* 82, no. 1 (July 2017): 1–20; Joohan Kim and Eun Joo Kim, "Theorizing Dialogic Deliberation: Everyday Political Talk as Communicative Action and Dialogue," *Communication Theory* 18, no. 1 (February 2008): 51–70; P. J. Conover and D. D. Searing, "Studying 'Everyday Talk' in the Deliberative System, *Acta Politica* 40 (2005): 269–83; P. J. Conover, D. D. Searing, and I. M. Crewe, "The Deliberative Potential of Political Discussion," *British Journal of Political Science* 32 (2002): 21–62.

28. See "About Us," ProPublica, https://www.propublica.org/about/

29. "Tampa Bay Times Sells St. Petersburg Headquarters, Will Remain as Tenant," *Tampa Bay Times*, April 22, 2016, https://www.tampabay.com/news/busi ness/realestate/tampa-bay-times-sells-st-petersburg-headquarters-will-remain -as-tenant/2274363/

30. Quoted in Catherine Buni, "4 Ways to Fund—and Save—Local Journalism," *Nieman Reports*, retrieved April 8, 2021, https://niemanreports.org/articles/4-ways -to-fund-and-save-journalism/

31. "New National Survey Shows 73% of Voters—Including Most Republicans— Oppose Eliminating Federal Funding for Public Television," Business Wire, February 16, 2017, https://www.businesswire.com/news/home/20170216006130/en /New-National-Survey-Shows-73-of-Voters-%E2%80%93-Including-Most-Rep ublicans-%E2%80%93-Oppose-Eliminating-Federal-Funding-for-Public-Televi sion

32. "International Comparison of Public Funding for Public Service Broadcasting, 2016 Final Report," prepared for CBC/Radio-Canada, May 25, 2018, https://site -cbc.radio-canada.ca/documents/vision/strategy/latest-studies/cbc-psb-governm ent-spending-comparison-en.pdf

33. Casey Kelly, "Why Biden's Presidency Is the Time for a Funding Boost for Pubmedia," Current, December 1, 2020, https://current.org/2020/12/why-bidens -presidency-is-the-time-for-a-funding-boost-for-pubmedia/?iMonezaUT=d9f8b ce4-d55e-4613-910f-42d80572082f%7c637438334082021562%7c63775369408 2021562%7cKwFejUa65eWInMGlKTq7J2E1RiKfHw5FTFwNkXEdJG4&iMoneza LT=JNYzsbV2bhm6dlp8oxnMytrPoYCNZ5Lw

34. Sarah Scire, "Some Questions (and Answers) about the Local Journalism Sustainability Act," Nieman Lab, September 14, 2021, https://www.niemanlab.org /2021/09/some-questions-and-answers-about-the-local-journalism-sustainab ility-act/; Ted Johnson, "Build Back Better Act Includes Tax Credit for Employing Local News Journalists, Incentive for Producing Sound Recordings," Deadline, November 3, 2021, https://deadline.com/2021/11/build-back-better-act-local-ne ws-sound-recordings-1234867570/

35. Robert W. McChesney and John Nichols, "The Local Journalism Initiative: A Proposal to Protect and Extend Democracy," *Columbia Journalism Review,* November 30, 2021, https://www.cjr.org/business_of_news/the-local-journalism-initiati ve.php

36. Joe Amditis, "NJ Civic Information Consortium Now Accepting Grant Applications for First Round of Funding," Center for Cooperative Media, March 3, 2021, https://medium.com/centerforcooperativemedia/nj-civic-information-con sortium-now-accepting-grant-applications-for-first-round-of-funding-f1bcee4b 3f45

37. Quoted in Travis Waldron, "The Pandemic Is Crushing the Journalism Industry. The Government Could Save It," HuffPost, April 12, 2020, https://www .huffpost.com/entry/journalism-coronavirus-bailout-stimulus_n_5e8de43ac5b6e 59ccbfb9381?ncid=engmodushpmg00000004

38. Marc Tracy, "Facebook Aims $100 Million at Media Hit by the Coronavirus," *New York Times*, March 30, 2020, https://www.nytimes.com/2020/03/30/bus iness/facebook-media-coronavirus.html

39. Richard Gingras, "A Global Journalism Emergency Relief Fund for Local News," Google, April 15, 2020, https://blog.google/outreach-initiatives/google-ne ws-initiative/global-journalism-emergency-relief-fund-local-news/

40. "American Journalism Project Launches Major Effort to Reinvigorate Local News with $42 Million in Founding Commitments," American Journalism Project, February 26, 2019, http://www.theajp.org/american-journalism-project-launc hes-major-effort-to-reinvigorate-local-news-with-42-million-in-founding-com mitments/; Gonzalo del Peon, "Stop Trying to Make a Profit from Local News," Medium, April 6, 2020, https://medium.com/american-journalism-project/stop-tr ying-to-make-a-profit-from-local-news-bda8257e99ee

41. Buni, "4 Ways to Fund."

42. Scott Suttell, "Criminal Justice-Focused Marshall Project Will Launch a Nonprofit News Operation in Cleveland," *Crain's Cleveland Business*, November 17, 2021, https://www.crainscleveland.com/media/criminal-justice-focused-marshall -project-will-launch-nonprofit-news-operation-cleveland

43. Michael Kilian, Cynthia Benjamin, and Len LaCara, "How the Rochester Democrat and Chronicle Forged Relationships with Communities of Color," Better News, https://betternews.org/rochester-democrat-and-chronicle-forged-relations hips-communities-of-color-table-stakes-knight-lenfest-newsroom-initiative/

44. "About," Neighborhood News Bureau, https://www.nnbnews.com/about-2/

45. Rick Edmonds, "In Its Fifth Year, Report for America Will Attack News Deserts in Rural Areas and Support a Broadened Group of Beats," Poynter, July 14, 2021, https://www.poynter.org/locally/2021/in-its-fifth-year-report-for-america -will-attack-news-deserts-in-rural-areas-and-support-a-broadened-group-of-be ats/

46. Quoted in Kristen Hare, "Report for America Is Sending 225 Journalists into Local Newsrooms around the Country," Poynter, April 23, 2020, https://www .poynter.org/reporting-editing/2020/report-for-america-is-sending-225-journali sts-into-local-newsrooms-around-the-country/

47. Jacob Simas, "Work with Us to 'Amplify Oakland' through First-Person Storytelling," Oaklandside, October 12, 2020, https://oaklandside.org/2020/10/12/wo rk-with-us-to-amplify-oakland-through-first-person-storytelling/

48. John Sands, "Local News Is More Trusted than National News—But That Could Change," Knight Foundation, October 29, 2019, https://knightfoundation.org /articles/local-news-is-more-trusted-than-national-news-but-that-could-cha nge/

49. "New Ranking Sheds Light on Consumers' Trust of Various News Outlets," Simmons Research, October 3, 2018, https://www.mrisimmons.com/press/simmo ns-research-releases-news-media-trust-index/

50. Joshua Benton, "Here's How Much Americans Trust 38 Major News Organizations (Hint: Not All That Much!)," Nieman Lab, October 5, 2018, https://www

.niemanlab.org/2018/10/heres-how-much-americans-trust-38-major-news-organizations-hint-not-all-that-much/

51. Stanley Fish, *The First: How to Think about Hate Speech, Campus Speech, Religious Speech, Fake News, Post-Truth, and Donald Trump* (New York: One Signal Publishers, 2019), 195.

52. Mark I. Pinsky, "Southern Newspapers Played a Major Role in Racial Violence. Do They Owe Their Communities an Apology?" Poynter, retrieved April 8, 2021, https://www.poynter.org/maligned-in-black-white/

53. Times Editorial Board, "Editorial: An Examination of The Times' Failures on Race, Our Apology and a Path Forward," *Los Angeles Times,* September 27, 2020, https://www.latimes.com/opinion/story/2020-09-27/los-angeles-times-apology-racism

54. Mike Fannin, "The Truth in Black and White: An apology from The Kansas City Star," *Kansas City Star*, December 20, 2020, https://www.kansascity.com/news/local/article247928045.html

55. Quoted in Pinsky, "Southern Newspapers."

56. Brenda Bell, John Gaventa, and John Peters, "Editors' Introduction," in Myles Horton and Paulo Freire, *We Make the Road by Walking: Conversations on Education and Social Change*, ed. Brenda Bell, John Gaventa, and John Peters (Philadelphia: Temple University Press), xxiv. For more background on Horton's contributions to active citizenship, see Frank Adams, "Highlander Folk School: Getting Information, Going Back and Teaching It," *Harvard Educational Review* 42, no. 4 (1972): 497-520; and Stephen Preskill's recent and powerful *Education in Black and White: Myles Horton and the Highlander Center's Vision for Social Justice* (Oakland: University of California Press, 2021).

57. Horton and Freire, *We Make the Road by Walking*, 67-68.

58. Bell, Gaventa, and Peters, "Editors' Introduction," xxv.

59. Horton and Freire, *We Make the Road by Walking*, 46-47.

60. "About Us," Front Porch Forum, retrieved April 8, 2021, https://frontporchforum.com/about-us

61. Adam Hermann, "A Month without Facebook Impacts Your Well-being, According to New Study," *Philly Voice*, January 31, 2019, https://www.phillyvoice.com/month-without-facebook-impacts-your-well-being-according-new-study/

62. "Salman Rushdie to Grads: Try to Be Larger Than Life," *Time*, May 19, 2015, https://time.com/collection-post/3889267/salman-rushdie-graduation-speech-emory/

63. Harry G. Frankfurt, *On Bullshit* (Princeton: Princeton University Press, 2005), 61, 63-64.

64. "About," News Literacy Project, retrieved April 8, 2021, https://newslit.org/about/

65. Joe Pompeo, "'You've Made the *Post* Swashbuckling Once Again': Marty Baron Receives a Star-Studded Farewell and Dishes in a Wide-Ranging Exit Inter-

view," *Vanity Fair*, February 25, 2021, https://www.vanityfair.com/news/2021/02/marty-baron-dishes-in-a-wide-ranging-exit-interview

66. Henry Blodget, "Grant Away: Why Venture Philanthropy Is Important, Even if It Sounds Ridiculous," *Slate*, November 13, 2006, https://slate.com/human-interest/2006/11/venture-philanthropy-what-is-it.html; and Michelle Celarier, "Henry Blodget Was Banned from the Financial Industry. So He Built a Financial Media Empire," *Institutional Investor*, July 28, 2020, https://www.institutionalinvestor.com/article/b1mpnkdvcmpcp9/Henry-Blodget-Was-Banned-From-the-Financial-Industry-So-He-Built-a-Financial-Media-Empire

67. Mike Snider, "Warren Buffett and Berkshire Hathaway to Sell Its Newspapers to Lee Enterprises for $140 Million," *USA Today*, January 29, 2020, https://www.usatoday.com/story/money/2020/01/29/warren-buffett-newspapers-berkshire-hathaway-lee-enterprises-newspapers/4607530002/

68. Sarah Scire, "Tiny News Collective Aims to Launch 500 New Local News Organizations in Three Years," Nieman Lab, January 12, 2021, https://www.niemanlab.org/2021/01/tiny-news-collective-aims-to-launch-500-new-local-news-organizations-in-three-years/

69. Scire, "Tiny News Collective."

70. See Berkleyside, https://invest.berkeleyside.com/

71. Office of the Town Manager, "Cuppa Joe with Paul," Town of Amherst, Massachusetts, https://www.amherstma.gov/DocumentCenter/View/47116/11-Town-Manager-Report-04-01-201972

72. "About," Kialo, retrieved April 9, 2021, https://www.kialo.com/about

73. "Under the Mango Tree," Nkwichi Lake Malawi, retrieved April 9, 2021, https://www.nkwichi.com/blog/under-the-mango-tree/

74. Meryl Kornfield, "Kansas City Newspaper Sends a Warning with a Blank Front Page," *Washington Post*, March 25, 2021, https://www.washingtonpost.com/media/2021/03/25/blank-front-page-local-newspaper/

75. Joshua L. Kalla and David E. Broockman, "Reducing Exclusionary Attitudes through Interpersonal Conversation: Evidence from Three Field Experiments," *American Political Science Review* 114, no. 2 (2020): 410. See also comparative evaluations of evidence in Tina Nabatchi, John Gastil, G. Michael Weiksner, and Matt Leighninger, eds., *Democracy in Motion: Evaluating the Practice and Impact of Deliberative Civic Engagement* (New York: Oxford University Press, 2012).

76. See, e.g., Anne Applebaum, *Twilight of Democracy: The Seductive Lure of Authoritarianism* (New York: Doubleday, 2020); and Masha Gessen, *Surviving Autocracy* (New York: Riverhead, 2020).

77. David Ryfe, *Journalism and the Public* (Malden, MA: Polity, 2017).

78. George Packer, "Are We Doomed? To Head Off the Next Insurrection, We'll Need to Practice Envisioning the Worst," *The Atlantic*, December 6, 2021, https://www.theatlantic.com/magazine/archive/2022/01/imagine-death-american-democracy-trump-insurrection/620841/

# Index

access model of news, 28

Accrediting Council on Education in Journalism and Mass Communications, 196

actual events criterion for evaluating media bias, 214, 224, 261

actual malice rule, 127-30, 135-37

Adams, John, 52-53, 57-58, 62, 83

Adams, Samuel, 52-53

advocacy orientation of journalism, 180

agenda setting, 169

Ailes, Roger, 38, 206

Alden Global Capital, 20

Alien and Sedition Acts, 93. *See also* Sedition Acts (1798, 1918)

Alito, Justice Samuel A., 115, 135

Allen, Danielle: on Constitution, 64; digital citizenship, 259-60, 271; inclusion and political friendship, 285-87; nation based on talk, 56

Alterman, Eric, 230

alternative facts, 31

Amar, Akhil Reed, 61

Amberg, Richard H., 180

American Civil Liberties Union, 34, 78

American pragmatic tradition, 306. *See also* William Caspary, John Dewey

American Press Institute, 265, 291, 309. *See also* listening

American Society of News Editors, 162

anonymous sources, 141-42, 145, 149, 189

anonymous speech, 97, 99

anticipatory orientation of journalism, 178

anti-Federalists, 61

anti-protest laws, 110

*apologia*, 203

Appiah, Kwame Anthony: cosmopolitan ethics, 373; dialogue, 375; rooted cosmopolitanism, 260

Arendt, Hannah: conversation and thinking-in-context, 241-42; enlarged mentality, 237, 309; lying, 300-301, 309; totalitarianism, 251-52

Aristotle: 257, 374n25. *See also* Danielle Allen

Arnade, Chris, 154-55, 157

Articles of Confederation, 55, 64

assaultive speech, 70-71

Associated Press, 173, 176, 195

attribution, 189, 219,

authoritarianism, 12-13, 199, 242, 251-52, 282, 300

Avaaz, 150

*Axios*, 37, 172

balance in journalism: and bias, 211-14; and citizens' cynicism about democracy, 315-16; "ethos of ideological balance," 221-22; "fair and balanced," 38, 206; and humane reporting, 181

Barber, Benjamin, 285

Barenboim, Daniel, 345-46n9

Baron, Jonathan, 223-24

Baron, Marty, 337

Bateson, Mary Catherine: importance of a "third," 229-30

beats, 16, 40, 142, 161, 216, 227, 306

Beauchamp, Zack, 41

Benavidez, Nora, 81

Benhabib, Seyla: citizenship and democratic stories, 236-37; "enlarged mentality," 237; journalism, 244, 269

Benton, Joshua, 331

Berkman Klein Center, 209-10

Bernstein, Carl, 124, 142, 182, 329

Berry, Wendell, 72

"between," the, 242, 322

Bezos, Jeffrey P., 14

bias: attacks on journalism, 152; confirmation bias, 188; evidence, 217-25; interpretation and accusation, 198-207; journalism's role, 236-37; liberal media, 8; media plural and diverse, 202; misconceptions, 207-15; newsrooms, 162; practical biases, 225-33; Supreme Court, 90

Biden, Joseph R., 2, 12, 13, 29, 148, 159, 325-26

"big lie," 12, 298

Bill of Rights: American identity, 50, 62; citizen awareness, 42, 76; communication and conversation, 73, 238; flexible, 112; influences, 67; journalism, 237; morally flawed, 64; privacy, 130; public forum, 234; race and rights, 68, 71-72, 125, 273; ratification, 54, 63, 68

Black Lives Matter, 25, 30, 33, 34, 78, 81, 129, 333, 335

Blackstone, William, 67

Blasi, Vincent, 114

Blodget, Henry, 338

Bonhoeffer, Dietrich. See serious reflection and real situations as ethical criteria

Booth, Wayne, 283

Boston massacre, 53

Boston tea party, 53

Bradley, Rebecca, 76-77

Brandeis, Justice Louis D., 94-95, 113-14, 130-31

Brandel, Jennifer, 167

Brandt, Evan, 19, 20, 40

*Branzburg v. Hayes*, 143-44, 147

breaking news, 21, 122, 173, 177, 186, 192, 228, 232, 315

*Breitbart*, 206, 303, 331

Brennan, Justice William J. Jr., 127

Briskman, Juli, 106

broadcasting, 99-100, 223, 262, 326

broadsides, 52

Buber, Martin, 300

Buchanan, Edna, 168

Burger, Chief Justice Warren, 105, 133-35

Burns, Eric, 151

Bush, George W., 58, 210

Bushnell, Michael, 341

Butler, Brent, 203

*BuzzFeed*, 23, 164, 172

Byrne, David, 9-10

cable and new media: coverage, 11, 21, 25, 47, 153, 173-75, 177, 230; political climate, 5, 23, 37-40, 199, 206, 251, 284, 292, 300; regulation, 100

Cambridge Analytica, 26

cancel culture, 108-9

*Capital Gazette*, 319

Carey, James: First Amendment, 238-39; journalism as conversation, 165, 254; public life and the press, 143

Carlson, Tucker, 13, 38

Carp, Benjamin, 53

Carpenter, Amanda, 29

Carroll, Erin, 304

Caspary, William, 240. *See also* American pragmatism; John Dewey

"Cato" (John Trenchard and Thomas Gordon), 48, 252

CBS, 168, 175, 181, 184, 209

certainty: in accusations of bias, 28, 200, 209, 214, 218-19, 222; and Iraq war, 216; and political lies, 301, 304

Chafee, Zechariah, Jr., 69

*Charleston Gazette-Mail*, 15, 156

Che, Chang, 171

check-backs in listening, 284-85

Cheney, Dick, 211

child pornography, 90

chilling effect, 37

Christians, Clifford G., 233, 281, 370

Cipollone, Pat, 4

citizenship ethic: citizen complicity, 299-304; early problems of American citizenship, 272-75; engaged citizenship, 279-81; inclusive citizenship, 285-89; informed citizenship, 278-79; monitorial citizenship, 276-77; political lying and the ethic, 291-99; reasonable citizenship, 281-85; responsibility, 276; roles of journalism, 271-72, 289-91

*Citizens United v. Federal Election Commission*: corporate speech, 103-4

civic agency, 271

Civic Information Consortium grants, 326-27

civility, 6, 242, 281, 307

civil rights, 70; ACLU, 80; activism, 89, 333-35; First Amendment, 82-83; Jim Crow laws, 97, 125-26; journalism, 125-27, 156, 160, 162, 211, 271, 329, 332-33; NAACP, 97

City Bureau, 165

*City of Ladue v. Gilleo*, 79-80

clear and present danger standard, 69, 94-95, 115-16

climate change, 22, 279, 294-95, 303

Clinton, Hillary, 26, 58, 209-10, 213-14, 232

CNN (Cable News Network), 16, 37-40, 163, 169, 173, 206, 209, 213, 331, 337

coduction as reasoning. *See* Wayne Booth

cognitive approach to bias, 218, 223-24. *See also* bias

Coles, Robert, 276,

Colley, Linda, 61

Commission on Freedom of the Press (Hutchins Report), 225, 309-10

Committee to Protect Journalists, 36, 196, 306

common (commons, green), 44, 166, 257

community: building, 7, 44-48, 59, 79, 91, 270, 280, 284-85, 328-30, 333-35, 338; dialogue and conversation, 69, 85-88, 255, 260, 268; journalism as ally, 15-24, 141, 165-69, 174-75, 180-83, 187, 195, 233, 268-69, 272, 281, 318-19, 333, 341, 345. *See also* Cupertino California multicultural dialogue

conflict, 5, 31, 238, 263, 278-79, 300, 308, 313, 320-23

Constitution and communication: impact of language, 61, 71, 112; presuming everyday conversation, 5, 56, 61, 237-39, 244, 254, 274-75

context in journalism, 208, 212-14, 224, 228, 247-49, 253, 267, 282, 297

Cooke, Janet, 143

Cooper, Natasha, 136

copy editor, 193, 194

corporate issues and newsrooms, 18, 32, 103-4, 160, 169, 171, 187, 217, 324, 327

Cosby, William, 49-51

cosmopolitan ethics, 260, 373. *See also* Danielle Allen; Kwame Anthony Appiah

Cotton, Tom, 171

Covid-19 pandemic: disinformation and misinformation, 29-30, 38, 189-90, 279; First Amendment, 91; impact, 16, 24, 30, 76, 133, 153, 158, 179, 191, 253, 328

Craig, David: compassion, 233; journalism ethics, 215, 368, 370

credulity/complicity and public life: complicity, 8, 211, 234, 299-304, 337; credulity, 302, 304

criterion of public interest, 73, 99, 134, 212

critical race theory, 4, 12, 70-71, 355n46

Cross, Katherine, 234

Cuomo, Mario, 287

Cupertino, California multicultural dialogue: outcomes, 289; Public Dialogue Consortium case study, 288-89; tensions and distrust, 288

custodianship of fact, 226

Daly, Christopher, 52

Dardenne, Robert W., 8

Date, S. V., 28-29

Declaration of Independence: and communication, 5, 302; history, 50, 52, 54; importance, 71, 273

deep background, 246

deep state, 210, 253, 337

"Deep Throat," 142

defamation: falsehoods, 93; First Amendment rights, 107, 151-52; Internet service providers, 101; listeners' rights, 70; privacy, 131, 137; Times v. Sullivan, 126-30, 135-36

deliberation: compared to dialogue, 254-56; importance to democracy, 7, 31, 237; in practice, 201, 250, 255-56, 285, 308, 317; and speech, 33, 69-70, 238; traditions of reason and news, 33, 166, 273, 284

Department of Journalism and Digital

Communication, University of South Florida St. Petersburg, 167-68, 329

Department of Justice, 102, 119, 298

DeSantis, Ron, 111, 150

Dewey, John: faith in democratic conversation, 240, 316; listening, 291; pragmatism, 306-7; public judgment, 240

Dialogue: clearing spaces, 234, 242-43; compared with deliberation, 255-56; conflict, 202, 251-52; conversation, 32, 133, 238, 241-42, 341; described, 254-55; "imagining the real," 300-301; in journalism, 8-9, 167, 237, 254-55, 313; in practice, 42, 75, 107, 109, 152, 201, 220, 229, 268, 279, 287, 300, 313-23, 341

Dierks, Konstantin, 47

digital news, 23, 171-72, 339

direct democracy, 237

disinformation/misinformation distinction: disinformation, 4, 37, 219, 295, 336, 343, 362, 368, 369, 371; misinformation, 22, 30, 39, 205, 211, 224, 350

dismissiveness, 8, 31, 201, 215, 220-22, 229, 234, 255, 257, 284, 287, 306, 309, 315

The Dissident, 176

Ditto, Peter, 223

Di Vece, Phil, 23

diversity: citizen disregard for, 13; civic life, 271, 281, 293, 315; in newsrooms, 162, 165, 193, 227, 320; respect for, 155; right to information, 101

documentary news, 175-76

Door County Advocate, 17-20

Douglas, Justice William O., 130

Durant, Will, 161

eavesdropping laws, 111-12

"economy of moral disagreement," 308

ecumenical journalism, 257

editor, 184, 192-94, 252
Ehrenreich, Barbara, 23
Electoral College, 12, 58, 210
Ellsberg, Daniel, 117-24
Emerson, Thomas, 69
empathy, 25, 237, 245, 252. *See also* enlarged mentality
"enemy of the people," 2, 14, 32, 36, 123, 171, 231, 232, 314
engaged citizen, 279-81
engaged orientation of journalism, 183-84
enlarged mentality, 237, 251-52, 309. *See also* empathy
equality-based First Amendment theory, 70-71
Espionage Act, 94
Essential Partners, 313. *See also* Public Conversations Project
ethics: guidelines, 197, 215-16, 221-22, 233, 260-61, 289-91; issues and definitions, 7, 102, 148-49, 151-52, 196, 366, 368, 370, 373-75
explanatory orientation of journalism, 178-79
Eyre, Eric, 15, 155-57, 174

Facebook: dangers of, 6, 26-27, 35, 41, 107, 150, 228, 292; interpersonal connection, 32, 47, 85, 102, 228; and journalism, 128, 150, 228, 292, 313-14, 327, 355
fact-checking: citizen checks, 164, 186, 303, 331; false or misleading claims, 28-31, 163, 251, 259, 297-99; in journalism, 29, 38, 92, 163, 170, 182, 197, 199, 226, 296, 309
Fairness and Accuracy in Reporting, 205
"fake news": as accusation, 2, 6, 28, 36, 38, 150, 183, 206, 258, 306; consequences, 35-36, 145, 150, 163, 192, 203, 223-24, 231, 304

false equivalence, 210, 213, 223
Faris, Rob, 219-20
Farr, William, 142
Fauci, Anthony, 13
Federalist Papers, 62, 274-75
Felt, W. Mark, 142
fighting words, 70
First Amendment: origin and importance, 7, 32, 33, 63, 66-71, 88-104; the press, 75-76; protections, 79-85; Supreme Court, 112-16
Fish, Stanley, 110
Fishkin, James: America in One Room sessions, 321-22; deliberative polling, 321; opinion polls, 320-21
Fiss, Owen M., 84
Floyd, George, 11, 19, 30, 81, 109
Ford, Matt, 13
Fourteenth Amendment, 95
Fourth Amendment, 130, 146-47
Fox News, 14, 164; and attack on Capitol, 38-39; and bias, 206; ethical norms, 206; fair and balanced claim, 38, 206; and journalism, 38; trust, 224, 331
framing, 245, 247-49, 296
Franklin, Benjamin, 54, 59, 129, 311-12
Freedman, Samuel G., 185
Freedom of Information Act, 138-39, 156, 306
free spaces (open spaces), 234, 258, 261, 315
*Front Porch Forum* (Vermont), 335

Gaber, Vanessa Maria, 269
Galella, Ron E., 131
Gallup Poll, 202, 331
Gannett Company, Inc., 17-18, 133
gaps to assist communication, 242, 313
Garfinkle, Adam, 74
gaslighting, 29
gatekeeping, 221, 266-67
*Gawker*, 151-52

general interest journalism, 37, 226, 253, 257, 258
General Motors, 176, 179
gerrymandering, 58
Gessen, Masha, 35, 232
Gilleo, Margaret, 78-80, 84, 105, 112, 123
Glynn, Carroll J., 219
Godfrey, Elaine, 22
Goebbels, Joseph, 298
Goffmann, Erving, 249
Goldwater, Barry, 199
Google, 32, 67, 101-2, 185, 186, 292, 327
Gordon-Reed, Annette, 74-75
Government in the Sunshine Act (Florida), 139
Graham, Katherine, 123-24
grand jury, 109
Grant, Tracy, 232
"Gray Lady" (*New York Times*), 170
Green, Elizabeth, 327
*Griswold v. Connecticut* (Supreme Court), 130
Gutmann, Amy, 308
Guzman, Kara Meyberg, 338-39
Gwynne, Peter, 295

Hagi, Sarah, 108
Hamilton, Alexander, 50, 58, 62, 274
Hanauer, Nick, 276, 308
hard news/soft news, 19, 24, 156, 161, 169, 172, 230, 323
Harlan, Justice John Marshall II, 97-98
Hassell, Hans, 221-22
hate speech, 5, 12, 70, 88-89, 244, 259, 315, 339
Hay, Jeremy, 320. *See also* Spaceship Media
Hemmer, Nicole, 201
Highlander Folk School, 333. *See also* Myles Horton
Holliday, Darryl, 165
Holloway, Kali, 181-82

Holmes, Justice Oliver Wendell, 94-95
Horton, Myles, 335
humane orientation of journalism, 181-82
Hutchins, Robert M., 225, 309-10. *See also* Commission on Freedom of the Press
Hutchinson, Cassidy, 4
Huxley, Aldous, 101
hyperlocal news, 174-75

Inclusive citizen, 285-89
*Independent Journal*, 275
infodemic, 30
Information Quality Act of 2001, 294
informed citizen, 77, 134, 141, 269, 278-79
Internet: attempts at regulation, 100-102; diminished journalism, 9, 34-35, 76, 250-51; election interference, 25-28; opportunities, 23-24, 164, 172, 173-74, 186, 259-61
intersection of journalism, citizenship, and political talk, 1, 5, 6, 204, 269, 310
interviewing, 187
inverted pyramid, 177
Investigative orientation of journalism, 182-83, 208, 324

Jackson, Greg, 21
Jaffe, Greg, 181
Jamieson, Kathleen Hall, 226, 247-49
January 6 insurrection, 2-4, 38-39
Jarvis, Jeff, 315
Jay, John, 62, 274
Jefferson, Thomas, 33, 47, 57, 62, 68, 78
Jenkins, Esau, 333
Jim Crow laws, 97, 125-26, 333-34
Johnson, Lyndon B., 46, 138
Johnson Amendment, 46
Jones, Alex S., 17
Jost, John T., 223-24

journalism education, 196
journalist's privilege, 141-45
judicial restraint/judicial activism
    (Supreme Court), 14-15

Kaepernick, Colin, 84-85
Kellner, Douglas, 225
Kelly, Mary Louise: National Public
    Radio interview with Secretary of
    State Mike Pompeo, 305-6
Kettering Foundation's National Issues
    Forums, 316-17
*Kialo.com*, 339
Kovach, Bill, 265-69, 279
Kristol, Irving, 72-73
Krugman, Paul, 30
Ku Klux Klan, 88

Lambeth, Edmund, 290
language, 245-46
League of Women Voters, 268, 271
leaking, 145, 147-48
lede (lead), 188-89, 191
legacy media, 18, 21, 25, 168, 199, 318
Leonnig, Carol, 3
Lepore, Jill, 59-60, 231
Levitsky, Steven, 31
Levy, Leonard W., 51
Lewis, Seth, 184
LGBTQ coverage, 324, 332
Libby, I. Lewis, 211
libel tourism, 137
liberal media bias. *See* bias
Licensing Act, 48
Lichter, S. Robert, 218
Light, Jennifer, 271
limited argument pool, 359. *See also*
    Cass Sunstein
Lin, Herb, 27
Lincoln, Abraham, 93, 117, 197
Lipinski, Ann Marie, 39
listening: for citizenship, 31, 43, 61, 87,
    201, 220, 239, 246, 253, 256, 285, 287,

301-3, 308, 314-15, 322; for journal-
    ists, 167, 193, 268, 284, 290-92, 319,
    330; to self, 200, 241; as aspect of
    speech, 70, 262-63
Liu, Eric, 276, 308
local journalism: community benefits,
    40, 159, 167-68, 183, 280; concerns, 5,
    7, 15, 16-24, 40, 177, 194-95, 206, 231,
    341; fresh initiatives, 174-75, 269,
    288-89, 311, 312-15, 316-20, 324-30,
    332-35, 338-39, 341
long form journalism, 247
Louis, J. Jeffry, 17-18
lying, political, 92-93, 211, 215, 260,
    294-302, 306-7

Macintyre, Alasdair, 240-41
MacKinnon, Catherine A., 70
MacWilliams, Matthew, 12-13
Maddow, Rachel, 284
Madison, James, 33-34, 56, 66-67, 274
mainstream media: current status, 5,
    9, 14, 20-21, 35-36, 41; news value,
    168-69, 172-73, 175; responding to
    political claims, 199, 202, 209-10,
    215, 222, 228, 232, 293, 323
*Marbury v. Madison*, 113
marginalized groups, 287, 288, 315
Markel, Michelle, 270
marketplace of ideas theory, 34-35
Marshall, Justice Thurgood, 87
Marsy's Law, 139-40
Mathews, David, 316-17
McCarthy, Joseph, 138
McChesney, Robert W., 326
McCraw, David E., 36, 150, 203, 217,
    222, 232
McDonald, Forrest, 55
McGinniss, Joe, 290
McKesson, DeRay, 111
Meadows, Mark, 4, 38
Media Research Center, 203-4
Meiklejohn, Alexander, 69, 136

Mencken, H. L., 162
Miller, Judith, 311
Milosz, Czeslaw, 241, 282
Milton, John, 34
Miranda warning, 96
misinformation. *See* disinformation/
  misinformation distinction
monitorial citizen, 276-77
Moriarty, Liam, 41
*Morning Joe*, 210
Morris, Gouverneur, 61, 64
Moss, John E., 138
Moyers, Bill, 232, 280
Moynihan, Daniel Patrick, 29
MSNBC, 37, 39, 159, 163, 210, 284, 331
muckraking, 182, 280
Mueller, Robert S. III, 26, 28
multiculturalism, 162
Muratov, Dmitry, 37
Murdoch, Rupert, 38, 206
Murray, Donald, 161, 188
Murrow, Edward R., 176
Muslim citizens, 27, 108, 186, 216, 257,
  307
muted groups, 92

National Issues Forums, 316-17
National Public Radio, 24, 305-6
National Rifle Association, 324
National Security Agency, 122
negligence standard, 130
Neighborhood News Bureau (St.
  Petersburg, Florida), 329
New Media Investment Group, 17
*Newsbusters*, 203
*New York Times: New York Times v. Sul-
  livan*, 126-29, 135-37, 332; *New York
  Times v. United States*, 119; reputa-
  tion, 169-71, 205, 208, 210, 217, 222,
  224, 305; trust and Pentagon Papers,
  118-24, 150
niche/specialty news, 173
Nichols, John, 326

Nieman Foundation for Journalism, 39,
  103, 119, 196, 318
Nixon, Richard M., 33, 38, 102, 121, 124-
  25, 141, 206, 290
nonprofit model for news, 324
Nunes, Devin, 137
Nussbaum, Martha, 288, 293

*Oaklandside*, 330
Obama, Barack, 122, 176, 190, 211
objectivity, 40-41, 201, 220, 280, 294,
  317, 352
O'Brien, David, 98
obscenity, 89-90
Office of Management and Budget,
  294-95
O'Leary, Kevin C., 73
Onassis, Jacqueline Kennedy, 131
op-ed, 38, 156, 208, 279
open meetings and records, 14, 137-41
oral arguments in Supreme Court, 79,
  119
originalism, 115
Orwell, George, 101
Overholser, Geneva, 318

Packer, George, 342
Paine, Thomas, 54
Palin, Sarah, 169
Palmer, Parker, 242-43
pamphlets, 1, 47, 48, 51, 52, 75
Parham, Angel, 259-60
Pauly, John, 165, 313
paywall, 24
Pearce, W. Barnett. *See* gaps assisting
  communication
Pearlman, Eve, 320. *See also* Spaceship
  Media
Pearson, Andrew, 122
Pelosi, Nancy, 24, 150
Pence, Michael R., 3, 4, 13, 91
Pentagon Papers, 118-25, 133, 136
Pew Research Center, 18, 20-21, 162, 219

Pirro, Jeanine, 39–40
*Planet Money*, 179
Plato, 257
"plumbers," 124
plurality decision (Supreme Court), 143
polarization: absence of conversation, 259, 335; emotional issues, 114; extreme partisanship, 31, 204, 219–20, 234, 292, 307; mistrust of news, 24, 180, 295; political accusation and falsehoods, 12, 218
political correctness, 108
political friendship. *See* Danielle Allen; Aristotle
*Politico*, 37, 172
politics of inclusion, 274, 288
Pompeo, Mike, 305–6
Postman, Neil, 101
Powell, Justice Lewis F., 92
Prados, John, 210
Preamble to Constitution, 14, 256, 283
*Press Watch*, 191
Preston, David, 312–13, 319, 339
Priest, Dana, 121
prior restraint, 66, 67, 119–21
Privacy Protection Act, 146–48
privacy rights, 107, 130–33
privatization, 140
*ProPublica*, 139–40, 324
Proud Boys, 30, 307
public (civic) journalism, 183–84, 318
Public Conversations Project, 201, 313, 367
Public Dialogue Consortium, 288–89
public judgment, 65, 240, 250, 309, 316, 321. *See also* Kettering Foundation; David Mathews; National Issues Forums
public/private distinction, 45, 59, 63, 129–32, 233, 243–44, 250, 251
public sphere, 36, 47, 66, 91, 290
"Publius" (James Madison, Alexander Hamilton, John Jay), 62, 274

Pulitzer Prize, 15, 59, 121, 122, 143, 156, 188, 233, 244, 324, 327

QAnon, 34, 83

Rauch, Jonathan, 6
Raushenbush, Stephen, 301
Rawls, John, 281–82
Ray, Laura Krugman, 120
Raymond, Linda and Mike, 140
reader advocates, 193, 197
reasonable citizen, 5, 33, 274–75, 281–85, 292, 295
Rehnquist, Chief Justice William, 134–35
*Reno v. American Civil Liberties Union* (Supreme Court), 34
Reporters Committee for Freedom of the Press, 141–42, 196
Report for America, 174, 329
republic, 59, 65, 73, 166, 237–40
Ressa, Maria, 37
Rich, Adrienne, 301
Richardson, Heather Cox, 174
right to know, 123
Riis, Jacob, 154
Ritz, Joseph P., 158–59
Roberts, Chief Justice John, 134–35
Robinson, J. Dennis, 53–54
*Roe v. Wade* (Supreme Court), 114–15, 130
*Rolling Stone*, 182–83
Romero, Anthony D., 80
Roose, Kevin, 34
Roosevelt, Eleanor, 270–72, 273, 279
Roosevelt, Franklin D., 125, 270
Rosenstein, Rod, 26
Rosenstiel, Tom, 266, 267, 279
Rousseau, Jean-Jacques, 281
Royko, Mike, 146
Rudenstein, David, 121
Rushdie, Salman, 336
Rutland, Robert Allen, 62
Ryfe, David, 256, 342

Sanders, Sam, 161
Sanford, Justice Edward T., 95
Saslow, Eli, 244
Save Journalism Project, 327
Schauer, Frederick, 69-71
Schudson, Michael, 66, 73, 217, 264, 273-74, 277
*Scientific American*, 307
*Sean Hannity Show*, 38, 224
Sedition Acts (1798, 1918), 93-94
seditious libel, 49, 51, 67, 93, 124, 127
separation of powers, 56
serious reflection and real situations as ethical criteria (Dietrich Bonhoeffer), 299-300, 303-4
service, 276
Sheehan, Neil, 118, 121-22
shield laws, 141, 144
silos of belief, 74, 250, 251, 266
Sinclair, Upton, 182
Sinclair Broadcast Group, 206
Sinitiere, Phillip Luke, 332
SLAPP lawsuits (strategic lawsuits against public participation), 107
Smith, Merriman, 189
Smith, Shepard, 250-51
Smith, Walter (Red), 187
Smolla, Rodney, 69
Snowdon, Edward, 122
Snyder, Timothy, 34
Social cognition research on bias, 222-23
Society of Professional Journalists, 195, 233
sock puppet, 27
Socrates, 258
solutions journalism, 180, 318
Sons of Liberty, 52-53
"sourcery," 144-45
Southern Christian Leadership Conference, 334
Spaceship Media, 313, 315, 319-20
Spicer, Sean, 209

spin, 158-59, 171, 205, 249, 296
*Spotlight*, 216
Stamp Act, 52-53
Standing Rock Sioux reservation protests, 110
*Stanford Daily* newsroom search, 146-47
Stecula, Dominik, 214
Steffens, Lincoln, 232, 280-81, 303
Steinem, Gloria, 97
Stevens, Justice John Paul, 34, 79-80, 134
Stewart, Justice Potter, 90, 123-24, 143-44
*St. Louis Globe-Democrat*, 180
*St. Louis Post-Dispatch*, 18
Stockman, Farah, 190
Stone, Geoffrey R., 89
*Storyful*, 172
storytelling, 177, 192, 313, 316, 320
Stout, Harry, 46
stranger, the, 242-44. *See also* Parker Palmer
Strauss, David, 253
subpoena, 4, 125, 141-44, 146, 147
subsequent punishment theory, 67
*Substack*, 173-74
Sullivan, L. B., 126-29
Sullivan, Margaret, 18
Sulzberger, A. G., 36, 170
Sulzberger, Arthur Ochs, 118, 123
sunshine laws. *See* open meetings and records
Sunstein, Cass: "limited argument pool" in online communication, 358-59; public forum doctrine of the Bill of Rights, 234
Surfside Condominium collapse, 194-95

Talley, Manuel, 97
*Tampa Bay Times*, 29, 150, 175, 324
Tannen, Deborah, 229

Taylor, Astra, 42
Taylor, Breonna, 109, 140
Thiel, Peter, 151
Thomas, Justice Clarence, 135-36
time, place, and manner standard
  (Supreme Court), 84
Tiny News Collective, 338
Town hall meetings, 45-46, 273
Trump, Donald J.: accusations, 36, 117,
  145, 149-50, 163, 168, 203; administration, 147; authoritarianism, 306-
  7; effect on civic talk, 25, 307, 323;
  elections, 58, 114; fact-checks, 28-29,
  31, 190, 217, 221; investigations of, 26,
  138; January 6 insurrection, 2-4, 31,
  38-39; supporters, 12-13, 30, 31, 34,
  38-39, 81, 206, 210, 342
Trump, Mary, 29
Tufekci, Zeynep, 12

*USA Today*, 230

venture philanthropy, 338
*Virginia v. Black* (Supreme Court), 88
Voltaire, 67, 69

Wagman, Robert, 239
Waldman, Paul, 126, 247-49
Waldman, Steve, 329
Walker, Darren, 87
*Wall Street Journal*, 16, 24, 172, 208
Ward, Stephen, 280

Wardle, Claire, 163
Warren, Chief Justice Earl, 96
Washington, George, 32, 55, 59, 64
*Washington Examiner*, 208
*Washington Post*, 3, 11, 297. *See also*
  Pentagon Papers
Watergate, 124-25, 142, 162, 182, 206,
  339
Weiss, Bari, 171
Wells, Ida B., 160
Wenzel, Andrea, 167
whistleblower, 148-49, 277
White, Adam, 73
White, Justice Byron, 147
Wicker, Tom, 198-99
Wilder, Laura Ingalls, 107-8
Wilson, William Julius, 254
Winston, David, 25
wire news, 173, 176-77
wokeness, 108-9
Wolff, Michael, 290
Wood, Gordon S., 59
Wood-Lewis, Michael and Valerie, 335
Woodward, Bob, 30, 40, 124-25, 142,
  182, 296

Yang, Jia Lynn, 193
yellow journalism, 130-31
Young, Iris Marion, 274

Zenger, John Peter, 48-51, 93
Ziblatt, Daniel, 31

# About the Authors

**G. Michael Killenberg** is emeritus professor of journalism and founding director of the Department of Journalism and Media Studies at University of South Florida St. Petersburg. He grew up hanging around and later working at the *St. Louis Globe-Democrat*, where his father was top news executive. Mike's research, publications, and books have focused on community journalism, public affairs reporting, and news-gathering rights under the First Amendment. At USF, he created and founded the Neighborhood News Bureau, a working student newsroom in the historic African-American section of St. Petersburg known as Midtown. He, his wife Penny, and three of their four adult children—along with their spouses, and six of eight grandchildren—now call Door County, Wisconsin, home. You can reach him at killenberg@gmail.com, or if you run into his neighbor Rob Anderson, he can point down the road to where Mike lives.

**Rob Anderson** is emeritus professor in the Department of Communication at Saint Louis University. An award-winning teacher, he studies dialogue in everyday interpersonal communication, public media, intellectual history, and communication ethics. His previous books include: *Dialogue: Theorizing Difference in Communication Studies, Moments of Meeting, The Martin Buber-Carl Rogers Dialogue*, and *Questions of Communication*. Long-term collaboration with Mike Killenberg has taught him a great deal about journalism and its critics—resulting in *The Conversation of Journalism* and other works. Since retirement, he continues to write and learn, while nursing along his vintage turntables, studying the varied moods of Lake Michigan, and savoring quiet dinners with Dona. Feel free to contact him by emailing robertjport@gmail.com or, maybe, by driving through Jacksonport, Wisconsin, and yelling his name out the window. It is a tiny but invigorating place.